Information Sciences Series

Editors
ROBERT M. HAYES
University of California
Los Angeles, California

JOSEPH BECKER
President
Becker and Hayes, Inc.

Consultant
CHARLES P. BOURNE
University of California
Berkeley, California

Joseph Becker and Robert M. Hayes:
INFORMATION STORAGE AND RETRIEVAL

Charles P. Bourne:
METHODS OF INFORMATION HANDLING

Harold Borko:
AUTOMATED LANGUAGE PROCESSING

Russell D. Archibald and Richard L. Villoria:
NETWORK-BASED MANAGEMENT SYSTEMS (PERT/CPM)

Launor F. Carter:
NATIONAL DOCUMENT-HANDLING SYSTEMS FOR SCIENCE
AND TECHNOLOGY

Perry E. Rosove:
DEVELOPING COMPUTER-BASED INFORMATION SYSTEMS

F. W. Lancaster:
INFORMATION RETRIEVAL SYSTEMS

Ralph L. Bisco:
DATA BASES, COMPUTERS, AND THE SOCIAL SCIENCES

Charles T. Meadow:
MAN-MACHINE COMMUNICATION

Gerald Jahoda:
INFORMATION STORAGE AND RETRIEVAL SYSTEMS FOR
INDIVIDUAL RESEARCHERS

Allen Kent:
INFORMATION ANALYSIS AND RETRIEVAL

Robert S. Taylor:
THE MAKING OF A LIBRARY

Herman M. Weisman:
INFORMATION SYSTEMS, SERVICES, AND CENTERS

Jesse H. Shera:
THE FOUNDATIONS OF EDUCATION FOR LIBRARIANSHIP

Charles T. Meadow:
THE ANALYSIS OF INFORMATION SYSTEMS, Second Edition

Stanley J. Swihart and Beryl F. Hefley:
COMPUTER SYSTEMS IN THE LIBRARY

F. W. Lancaster and E. G. Fayen:
INFORMATION RETRIEVAL ON-LINE

Richard A. Kaimann:
STRUCTURED INFORMATION FILES

Thelma Freides:
LITERATURE AND BIBLIOGRAPHY OF THE SOCIAL SCIENCES

Manfred Kochen:
PRINCIPLES OF INFORMATION RETRIEVAL

Dagobert Soergel:
INDEXING LANGUAGES AND THESAURI: CONSTRUCTION
AND MAINTENANCE

Robert M. Hayes and Joseph Becker:
HANDBOOK OF DATA PROCESSING FOR LIBRARIES, Second Edition

Benjamin Mittman and Lorraine Borman:
PERSONALIZED DATA BASE SYSTEMS

PERSONALIZED DATA BASE SYSTEMS

BENJAMIN MITTMAN
and
LORRAINE BORMAN
Northwestern University
Evanston, Illinois

A WILEY-BECKER & HAYES SERIES BOOK

 MELVILLE PUBLISHING COMPANY
Los Angeles, California

Copyright © 1975, by John Wiley & Sons, Inc.
Published by *Melville Publishing Company*
A Division of John Wiley & Sons, Inc.

All rights reserved. Published simultaneously in Canada.

No part of this book may be reproduced by any means,
nor transmitted, nor translated into a machine language
without the written permission of the publisher.

Library of Congress Cataloging in Publication Data:

Mittman, Benjamin.
　　Personalized data base systems.

　　(Information sciences series)
　　Includes bibliographical references and indexes.
　　1. Information storage and retrieval systems.
I. Borman, Lorraine, joint author. II. Title.

Z699.M54　　1975　　　　029.7　　　　75-2359
ISBN 0-471-61182-4

Printed in the United States of America

10 9 8 7 6 5 4 3 2 1

Information Sciences Series

Information is the essential ingredient in decision making. The need for improved information systems in recent years has been made critical by the steady growth in size and complexity of organizations and data.

This series is designed to include books that are concerned with various aspects of communicating, utilizing, and storing digital and graphic information. It will embrace a broad spectrum of topics, such as information system theory and design, man-machine relationships, language data processing, artificial intelligence, mechanization of library processes, non-numerical applications of digital computers, storage and retrieval, automatic publishing, command and control, information display, and so on.

Information science may someday be a profession in its own right. The aim of this series is to bring together the interdisciplinary core of knowledge that is apt to form its foundation. Through this consolidation, it is expected that the series will grow to become the focal point for professional education in this field.

Preface

One of the goals of current research in computer science is to make information processing more individualized—more personal. An earlier book in the Wiley Information Sciences Series by Professor Gerald Jahoda discussed information retrieval systems for individual researchers.* Professor Jahoda concentrated on the needs of the research worker for readily accessible document retrieval. His work reviews many manual and automatic methods for organization and retrieval of personal document collections and discusses the commonly utilized indexes such as coordinate, keyword-from-title, and citation indexes. There is an equally important aspect of personal retrieval systems that is not covered by conventional bibliographic techniques, that is, the area of research data bases. In almost every field of research one finds collections of research data, ranging from performance logs of Moliere's plays to diagnostic and treatment records of cardiac patients. It is this element of retrieval technology to which this work is directed.

This book is intended to present the reader with an appreciation and knowledge of the wide diversity of applications of computerized information storage and retrieval, with an emphasis on personal research data bases. Although the system which is discussed has been developed and is being used primarily at Northwestern University, the concepts and the applications are equally relevant to any generalized information system. RIQS, Remote Information Query System, has been utilized over the past five years in many different disciplines, including medicine, political science, anthropology, archeology, computer sciences, university administration, and many other fields.

---

*Gerald Jahoda, *Information Storage and Retrieval Systems for Individual Researchers*, Wiley-Interscience, New York, 1970.

The design of RIQS was based upon the assumption that researchers in many disciplines require a powerful computer system to store, retrieve, analyze, display, plot and process a great variety of data types. Since much basic and applied research is characterized by changing goals and directions, it is necessary that the retrieval system must be general enough to accommodate unforeseen eventualities.

To date, no book has presented a comprehensive picture of a personalized retrieval system and its numerous applications. We have done just that. The first part of the book discusses information storage and retrieval in general and RIQS in particular. Part II is devoted to a set of chapters authored by the users of RIQS.

It is our intent that this book will serve a large audience. It can be used in undergraduate or graduate courses in computer and information sciences, similar to Course A5, Information Organization and Retrieval, which appeared in "Curriculum 68, A Report of the ACM Curriculum Committee on Computer Science."* It is also directed towards the large body of research workers in many fields who desire to apply computer techniques to their data base and information needs. The research physician with almost unmanageable patient records, the anthropologist or archeologist with unorganized field notes, the university administrator with uncorrelated student or research grant records—all find themselves at a loss to utilize the tool which promises to ease their analysis burdens. This book will show them, in chapters written by their colleagues, how automated retrieval and analysis techniques have been applied in their fields. Finally, the book is intended for the educated layperson who desires a broader view of the diversity of applications of computers. As more and more facets of our lives are touched by the machine, our understanding of their potentials and limitations must be strengthened. Computer and communication technology will someday bring personalized data base processing into our homes. Let us see what specialists in many fields are doing with this technology today. These insights will lead many of us to a new awareness of how our personal information retrieval needs can be enhanced and fostered.

Part I reviews the history of computer-based information retrieval systems. A careful distinction is drawn between text processing systems, which are important for bibliographic applications, and management information systems, which deal with numeric data. This discussion leads to RIQS, which was designed to cope with both of these application areas, i.e., a system to handle full text searching, as well as a variety of data types, such as numeric, coded, dates, and units. The storage, retrieval and data processing capabilities of RIQS are illustrated with numerous examples.

Part II of the book is a set of edited papers prepared by many users of RIQS. These papers include applications of RIQS to cardiology, dermatology, spinal cord injury, archeological surveying, primate behavior, an infant's phonological development, computer system evaluation, graduate student administration, social science data archiving, and others.

The authors wish to acknowledge the invaluable assistance of the contributors to Part II, as well as the many students and former students of Northwestern University, who have contributed to the development and use of RIQS. A partial list of these people is:

---

*Communications of the Association for Computing Machinery, Volume 11, Number 3, March 1968, pp. 151-197.

Robert Chalice, Donald Dillaman, Wayne Dominick, Judith Dart Boxler, Carol Wagner Jessen, Dale Jessen, Peter Kron, and Greg Suski. Our thanks also go to Joan Cesal, who supervised the typing and editing of our manuscript, assisted by Mary Gariti and Mary Dillon.

BENJAMIN MITTMAN
LORRAINE BORMAN

Evanston, Illinois

Contents

PART I

PERSONALIZED DATA BASE SYSTEMS: AN OVERVIEW

Chapter 1

Bibliographic Retrieval and Data Management Systems: Precursors of Personalized Data Base Processing

Introduction

A sixty-five year old retired automobile worker turns on his television set, switches on his automatic typewriter terminal, and then keys a number on his touch-tone telephone. The television screen lights up and the following message appears:

YESTERDAY YOU SEARCHED THE FISHING EQUIPMENT FILE FOR REFERENCES TO SMELT NETS. IF YOU WISH TO CONTINUE THAT SEARCH, PRESS KEY 5; OTHERWISE, INPUT YOUR NEXT REQUEST CODE.

His next request is for the French lesson which he has been taking from the local community college. Using his terminal to type responses, he identifies the colored slides which appear on the TV screen as several of the Chateaux on the Loire; then he takes the midterm examination on the architectural masterpieces of France. After the exam, he types in the command:

ACCESS ANTIQUE CAR FILE, PASSWORD=PINTO

and the following dialogue takes place on his typewriter terminal:

RESPONSE: ANTIQUE CAR FILE IS READY FOR PROCESSING
REQUEST: UPDATE RECORD ON 1924 FRANKLIN TO CHANGE CYLINDER DIS-
PLACEMENT FROM 356 CU. IN. TO 386 CU. IN.
RESPONSE: RECORD 273 (1924 FRANKLIN) HAS BEEN UPDATED

3

REQUEST: PRINT MANUFACTURING AND ENGINE SPECIFICATIONS FOR ALL CARS WHICH ARE OLDER THAN 30 YEARS AND WHICH HAVE 6 CYLINDERS

RESPONSE: 45 RECORDS HAVE BEEN SELECTED. DO YOU WANT TO SEE A SAMPLE?

REQUEST: YES

RESPONSE: 1912 PIERCE-ARROW, 3 PASSENGER
PIERCE-ARROW MOTOR CAR COMPANY
BUFFALO, N.Y., SELLING PRICE: $4,000
6-CYLINDER ENGINE TYPE: 6-36,
36 H.P., 4 IN. BORE, 5.125 IN. STROKE
386 CU. IN.
DO YOU WANT THE PRINT-OUT MAILED TO YOU?

REQUEST: YES

RESPONSE: READY FOR PROCESSING

REQUEST: SIGN OFF

RESPONSE: ON AT 14:51, OFF AT 15:59, CHARGES: $1.06, THANK YOU, ILLINOIS INFORMATION UTILITY, INC.

Is this farfetched? Are we in 1984? We may be, since it will take at least ten more years before operational information utilities are a reality. The communication industry will have to provide two-way cable TV; the computer industry will have to produce and market economical, personalized data base and instructional systems.

Computer science researchers are currently working on the elements of the tools which will make systems like the one described above a reality. One important part of the information utility will be personalized data base services. These services will permit anyone to produce his or her own file of information or to access public files. The data in the personal files will be protected from outside intrusion. These files will contain numeric data and textual information. They will permit some quantities to be stored in the metric system, others in the English system. They will permit dates to be entered and retrieved in both the American and European standard notations. They will allow queries to be entered via touch-tone telephones or conventional time-sharing terminals. They will provide a full range of processing, including indexing, statistical analysis, graphical plotting, formatted reporting, etc.

The key word is *personalized*. Personalized refers to the ability to deal with one's own information and data. But it also means that the individual can use his or her own terminal equipment, as well as a simplified mode of interrogation, file creation, updating, reporting, and processing.

Personalized data base systems have been experimented with for a number of years. For over five years, Northwestern University has utilized a system called RIQS (Remote Information Query System) for many personal data base applications. This type of processing has been applied, to date, by academic and research users of data bases. Researchers in medicine can create and access data bases concerning patients with cardiac, dermatology, pathology, or spinal cord problems. Archeologists can store and retrieve data about artifacts uncovered at diggings. The Dean of the Technological Institute can sit in his office and use a portable teletypewriter to discover which graduate students are currently supported under National Science Foundation grants which are to expire during the next six months. These and many other data bases have been developed and utilized by individuals for their own use or for use by a wider audience of colleagues or students. This mode of information processing is a direct precursor to the information utility service which was utilized by our imaginary retiree.

This book is intended to trace the development of personalized data base systems. First, the main directions in automated retrieval will be reviewed. These include the areas of bibliographic retrieval and data management systems. Then, RIQS will be described. Finally, a number of specific, personalized data base applications will be presented.

Automated information storage and retrieval (ISR) has followed two main directions, bibliographic retrieval and data management. In bibliographic retrieval, much research and development has gone into refining methods for indexing, abstracting, storing, retrieving, and reporting of information from and about documents, that is, information consisting primarily of alphanumeric text. As computers have become faster and capable of storing more and more on-line data, large-scale bibliographic data bases and retrieval services have been developed. Time sharing has permitted these services to become interactive.

At the same time, commercial and scientific applications generated the need for the storage, retrieval, and processing of masses of numeric data—financial information, research findings, etc. This need resulted in the growth of data management systems. The goal of these systems was to provide the user with generalized tools to selectively retrieve and then process and report numeric information, dates, coded data, etc.

But in all of this work, the individual researcher has frequently been ignored. Large-scale bibliographic systems often require the assistance of a specialized librarian (the "middleman") to help formulate queries and to perform searches. Many data management systems have fostered the need for a "data administrator," a person who is responsible for the accuracy of the information stored and who develops methods and procedures to protect the data base from inadvertent or malicious intrusion or destruction. Again, a middleman is required. We do not want to underestimate or downgrade the importance of the middleman function in large-scale systems. However, we do want to address the issue which is the main thesis of this book: the need exists for a *combined* document retrieval and data management capability for *personal* data bases which is easily accessible to the person who is not a computer specialist. These data bases may consist of references to personal collections of documents, or of research data for specific, individual projects.

Bibliographic Retrieval

It is not our intent here to provide a complete survey of bibliographic retrieval systems. There have been numerous books and monographs written over the past ten years which review the history and development of bibliographic retrieval. Another source of information is the *Annual Review of Information Science and Technology,* edited by Carlos A. Cuadra.[1] This annual publication of the American Society for Information Science (ASIS) contains survey articles on bibliographic retrieval and text processing, library automation, planning and managing of information systems and services, etc.

Bibliographic retrieval systems have served as a natural evolutionary step toward the subsequent development of personalized data base systems—systems which provide the individual research worker with a capability for storing and retrieving a great variety of data types including, of course, text. To set the stage for the personalized data base system, let us go back to 1945.

In the *Atlantic Monthly* of July 1945, Vannevar Bush wrote a now famous article entitled "As We May Think." In that article, Bush projected into the future the need and development of a device for individual use. He said:

Consider a future device for individual use, which is a sort of mechanized private file and library. It needs a name, and, to coin one at random, "memex" will do. A memex is a device in which an individual stores his books, records, and communications, and which is mechanized so that it may be consulted with exceeding speed and flexibility. It is an enlarged intimate supplement to his memory.

It consists of a desk, and while it can presumably be operated from a distance, it is primarily the piece of furniture at which he works. On the top are slanting translucent screens, on which material can be projected for convenient reading. There is a keyboard, and sets of buttons and levers. Otherwise, it looks like an ordinary desk.

In one end is the stored material. The matter of bulk is well taken care of by improved microfilm. Only a small part of the interior of the memex is devoted to storage, the rest to mechanism. Yet if the user inserted 5000 pages of material a day it would take him hundreds of years to fill the repository, so he can be profligate and enter material freely.

Most of the memex contents are purchased on microfilm ready for insertion. Books of all sorts, pictures, current periodicals, newspapers, are thus obtained and dropped into place. Business correspondence takes the same path. And there is provision for direct entry. On the top of the memex is a transparent platen. On this are placed longhand notes, photographs, memoranda, all sorts of things. When one is in place, the depression of a lever causes it to be photographed onto the next blank space in a section of the memex film, dry photography being employed.

There is, of course, provision for consultation of the record by the usual scheme of indexing. If the user wishes to consult a certain book, he taps its code on the keyboard, and the title page of the book promptly appears before him, projected onto one of his viewing positions. Frequently–used codes are mnemonic, so that he seldom consults his code book; but when he does, a single tap of a key projects it for his use. Moreover, he has supplemental levers. On deflecting one of these levers to the right he runs through the book before him, each page in turn being projected at a speed which just allows a recognizing glance at each. If he deflects it further to the right, he steps through the book 10 pages at a time; still further at 100 pages at a time. Deflection to the left gives him the same control backwards.

A special button transfers him immediately to the first page of the index. Any given book of his library can thus be called up and consulted with far greater facility than if it were taken from a shelf. As he has several projection positions, he can leave one item in position while he calls up another. He can add marginal notes and comments, taking advantage of one possible type of dry photography, and it could even be arranged so that he can do this by a stylus scheme, such as is now employed in the telautograph seen in railroad waiting rooms, just as though he had the physical page before him. [2]

Bush's "memex" would provide the researcher with an ideal bibliographic and reference tool. Bush stopped short, however, of supplying the power of the computer to extract and process research data.

Although we are still very far from the vision that Bush gave us back in 1945, a tremendous amount of work has been done in the past 20 years to move toward systems which, in some sense, handle the problems Bush referred to. The earliest work in automatic indexing was done by the late Hans Peter Luhn of IBM in the late 1950s. Luhn developed the concept of the keyword-in-context (KWIC) index and statistical procedures for automatic extraction of classification information from text. An excellent early work which discussed the tools and theories of information retrieval was written by Becker and Hayes in 1963.[3]

Another view of ISR was presented in a book edited in 1967 by Manfred Kochen.[4] He divided the field into two areas: one being the so-called "encyclopedic idea" and the second dealing with "libraries of the future" or "information dispensing." Much of the work in bibliographic retrieval systems has been toward providing the user with the capability of extracting from a bibliographic data base a set of references that satisfy his or her needs, i.e., information dispensing. Kochen felt that work in encyclopedic retrieval would result in systems which could function as Vannevar Bush has proposed. It is our view that personalized data base systems are moving us toward effective encyclopedic capabilities.

Another characterization of information retrieval systems was made by F. Wilfred Lancaster in 1968. Again, Lancaster attempted to characterize the various types of information retrieval systems in a chapter on "The Basic Activities of Information Retrieval." We quote from that chapter:

> Information retrieval is the term conventionally, though somewhat inaccurately, applied to the type of activity discussed in this volume. An information retrieval system does not inform (i.e., change the knowledge of) the user on the subject of his inquiry. It merely informs him on the existence (or nonexistence) and whereabouts of documents relating to his request.
>
> An information retrieval system may retrieve complete texts of documents, document surrogates (such as abstracts), or names and addresses of documents (i.e., full bibliographic citations). A system that ultimately provides the user with full document texts is properly called a document retrieval system, whereas a system that presents only citations is a reference retrieval system. A retrieval system will usually operate in several stages (e.g., its first output may be in the form of citations from which the requester can make a selection). Subsequently, the requester can ask that the complete texts of these selected items be presented. Alternatively, the sequence of responses may be (a) document numbers, (b) citations, and (c) full texts.
>
> An information retrieval system is to be distinguished from a data retrieval system, which is so called because it usually retrieves data displayed as words or numbers.[5]

A distinction is made here between bibliographic and data retrieval or data management systems. This distinction has been maintained in many large-scale ISR systems. It is our thesis that the development of personalized data base systems has tended to transcend this distinction, and in fact, remove it. Before we turn our attention to data management systems, we shall discuss two other important aspects of bibliographic retrieval: bibliographic data base services and interactive bibliographic search.

BIBLIOGRAPHIC DATA BASE SERVICES

As indicated above, numerous storage and retrieval systems have been developed to allow a user to retrieve information from prestored collections of data. These collections are commonly called data bases. One of the most commonly utilized types of data base is the *bibliographic* data base. Bibliographic data bases contain descriptive information about documents, articles, and books—these data typically include titles, authors, journal names, volume and number, dates, keywords, abstracts, etc. Inquiries against the data base are intended to develop a list of document numbers or references which satisfy the needs of the user concerning a particular collection of subjects or topics.

The most common access to bibliographic data bases has been through large-scale, national services. Such data bases exist for numerous fields: medicine, chemistry, biological sciences, engineering, research and development, etc. In Volume 7 of the *Annual Review of Information Science and Technology,* an entire chapter was devoted to a survey of machine-readable bibliographic data bases as of 1971.[6] Hundreds of data bases are reported in academic institutions, the government, industry, professional societies, and foreign countries and international organizations. A few of the most important data bases and associated searching services are summarized below.

Two of our national libraries, the Library of Congress and the National Library of Medicine, maintain extensive bibliographic data bases. The Library of Congress produces the MARC (Machine-Readable Catalog) tapes with over 250,000 records containing catalog information concerning the collection. The Library of Congress provides subscribers with weekly tapes containing about 75,000 records per year.

The National Library of Medicine maintains a biomedical data base processed by MEDLARS (Medical Literature Analysis and Retrieval System). This collection contains over 1.5 million citations to articles published since 1963. Approximately 200,000 citations are added annually from 2300 biomedical journals. A substantial portion of this collection has recently been incorporated into an on-line version of MEDLARS, called MEDLINE.

Additional government-sponsored data base activities include the Defense Documentation Center which provides tape services, printed bibliographies, and on-line access to research and development documents. A Highway Research Board data base is maintained by the Highway Research Information Service (HRIS) with over 45,000 references to literature on transportation research. The National Technical Information Service (NTIS) offers magnetic tape access to its collection, with approximately 2000 citations being added each month. This collection contains unclassified references coming from such agencies as the National Aeronautics and Space Administration, Atomic Energy Commission, Defense Documentation Center, and the Department of Defense.

Chemistry and biology are two disciplines in which professional societies have taken a leading role in providing data base services to their constituencies. The American Chemical Society sponsors the Chemical Abstracts Service (CAS). This service is an immense undertaking, which processes over 1100 abstracts and 15,000 index entries per day. In 1971 about 350,000 abstracts were entered into the system, and it has been projected that by 1980, 600,000 abstracts per year will be entered. Chemical Abstracts Service has moved towards complete computerization of its information handling and publishing activities as well as providing extensive tape subscription, current awareness, and retrospective services to its users.

Biosciences Information Services (BIOSIS) provides a tape service containing over 18,000 index entries to references published in Biological Abstracts and Bioresearch Index. Over 7500 serials from 94 countries are referenced.

Other services provided by professional societies include Searchable Physics Information Notices (SPIN) tapes of the American Institute of Physics, the American Mathematical Society's data bases from 200 worldwide mathematical journals, Engineering Index, and others.

The services discussed above are primarily batch-processing oriented. That is to say, queries are prepared in advance, usually on punched cards, grouped together, submitted in a single computer run, and processed against the data base. Printouts of selected documents are then distributed to the various requesters. The types of services provided include:

1. *Retrospective search* which enables one to query previously published literature concerning a particular subject matter. Retrospective searches are often done at regular time intervals, resulting in periodic printed catalogs of references to a given subject.

2. *Demand search* which provides for responses to a given query against a data base. This type of search is usually requested when a researcher is beginning a new project and wishes to review the existing literature on that subject.

3. *Selective dissemination of information* (SDI) which is a personalized service, whereby individuals or groups are notified of the existence of current literature of potentially high utility to them. SDI is similar to retrospective search in that periodic queries are made against the most recent data base. However, in SDI, the queries represent interest profiles of the individuals or groups, consisting of perhaps several subject areas, rather than some particular subject matter.

The introduction of time-sharing computer services has added a new capability to bibliographic retrieval: individuals may now interrogate data bases in an on-line, interactive mode. This will be discussed in the next section.

ON-LINE BIBLIOGRAPHIC SEARCH

The utilization of large-scale bibliographic data bases through nationally provided services has presented a number of problems to the user. These problems are not unlike those of a user in a library reference room; the problems relate to the "distance" of the user from the material. In a library the user has access to a card catalog and frequently can search effectively utilizing the catalog. However, the user also may require the services of a reference librarian. Large-scale data base searching often requires the utilization of a subject specialist. Queries are formulated through the services of this intermediary. The intermediary is a person familiar with the subject matter and also familiar with the indexing conventions of the data base and data base system, as well as the scope of the collection.

Experience with large-scale bibliographic data base searching has resulted in the desire for a more direct approach to the data base than through the intermediary. The ultimate user can often benefit more from a collection if that user can, in some sense, be brought closer to the collection. The development of interactive, time-sharing systems has led to experimentation in this mode of access—the development of on-line bibliographic search. These systems provide the user with the ability to interact dynamically with the system and with the data base. The user is not required to formulate his entire plan in advance. Instead, he can browse through the bibliographic data base, requesting assistance and repeatedly modifying his search strategy. This exchange between the user and the system can continue until the user has retrieved a sufficient number of references to satisfy his request.

A number of on-line bibliographic systems have been developed which provide for dialog to take place between the user and the system. This interaction usually consists of two parts: *search* dialog which permits the user to input queries and to receive results, and *instructional* dialog which aids in understanding and using the system. An effective interactive system would provide search dialog with at least the following characteristics:

The system must indicate that it understands the user's query.

The system must display the results of a search, and then allow for the user to indicate alternate courses of action to follow if the requested results are inappropriate or inadequate in some way.

The system would enable the user to interrupt the system in order to modify queries to gain better results.

The system would provide diagnostic capability when it is unable to recognize incorrectly constructed commands.

The system should be able to respond in an intelligent way to misspelled words and not to abruptly terminate a search without providing the user with an opportunity to reenter the query correctly.

Finally, the system should provide two modes of querying, one for the novice user and one for the experienced user. Generally, the experienced user would have available a short form of input which would speed up his interaction with the system. However, the novice should be able to communicate with the system using the full form of interactive dialog to assure his understanding of all commands and responses.

Of almost equal importance with well–designed search dialog are effective instructional facilities. These facilities help the user learn how to interact with the system. On–line instructional features could include a HELP command which gives the user either general information about the system functions or which responds to queries about the functioning of a given command. Other possible forms of instruction include printed reference guides or user manuals, personalized instruction, or a set of self–instructional tools.

In January 1971, a workshop entitled "The User Interface for Interactive Search of Bibliographic Data Bases" was held at Palo Alto, California to discuss a number of operational interactive systems. Included were the SPIRES system (Stanford Public Information Retrieval System) developed at Stanford University; the DIALOG system developed by the Lockheed Palo Alto Research Laboratory; the NASA/RECON information retrieval system being used by the National Aeronautics and Space Administration in its scientific and technical information program; the AIM–TWX experimental service of the Lister Hill National Center for Biomedical Communications of the National Library of Medicine; BASIS-70, The Battelle Automated Search Information System, developed by the Battelle Memorial Institute; and the INTREX system developed at Massachusetts Institute of Technology. This workshop resulted in the publication[7] of an important collection of papers concerned with the problems of bringing the user closer to bibliographic data bases by means of effective query languages, terminal devices, indexing methods, and other means.

In April 1973, a second workshop on interactive retrieval systems was held at Stanford University. The purpose of this workshop was to bring together the implementers of eleven operational, interactive information retrieval systems and a panel of experts for discussions, critiques, and demonstrations. The workshop discussions included: instructional and diagnostic features, on–line input features, and on–line output features. The results of this National Science Foundation sponsored workshop have been published[8] and represent a major step in documenting the necessary and desirable features which should be included in effective interactive systems. We shall summarize some of the important conclusions of the workshop.

The systems which were represented were primarily, although not exclusively, bibliographic retrieval systems. They were Battelle Memorial Institute's BASIS-70, Mead Technology Laboratories' DATA CENTRAL, Lockheed's DIALOG, Massachusetts Institute of Technology's INTREX, Lehigh University's LEADER, NASA Lewis Research Center's NASIS, System Development Corporation's ORBIT III, Informatics' RECON, Northwestern University's RIQS, Stanford University's SPIRES II, and International Business Machine Corporation's STAIRS. Of the 11 systems, three of them, BASIS-70, SPIRES II, and RIQS, had capabilities which were useful for management information applications and, in our opinion, exhibited many of the characteristics which are needed in personalized data base systems.

Selection of the systems to be included in the study was made by Edwin B. Parker and Thomas H. Martin of the Institute for Communication Research of Stanford University and a panel of consultants. The criteria used for selection were that the systems had to be a) operational, b) on-line and interactive, c) able to handle multiple users simultaneously, d) able to handle multiple data bases with variable length entries and elements, e) demonstrable to the public, and f) primarily oriented toward information storage and retrieval.

Rather than attempt to detail the characteristics of each system individually, we shall describe the elements which were common to most of them, as well as some of the differences, especially as concerns the features which are important to nonbibliographic applications. Most of the systems are designed to handle large, textual data bases. In order to process such a data base efficiently, indexes are provided which associate keywords or phrases, authors' names, or other data elements to the records in the data base. For each index term, the systems usually store an indication of the number of records associated with that term. As queries are processed, the search terms contained in the queries are looked up in the appropriate indexes, and the system displays the number of records in the file which contain those terms. With this information available, the user is then permitted to narrow or broaden his query or to ask to have the selected records or portions of these records displayed. All of the systems permitted access to the data bases using standard telecommunications and commonly available time-sharing terminals. The computers used included IBM series 360s and 370s and CDC series 6000s.

In an attempt to provide guidance to future implementers of interactive systems, the workshop attendees reviewed the characteristics of all the systems and designated a minimal set of highly desirable features. These, as well as many additional features, are summarized below, with examples where appropriate.

Instructional and Diagnostic Features

The minimal features specified in this category include:

A complete and readable *user's guide* (which, perhaps, not surprisingly was available for only one-half of the systems).

On-line documentation which provides a brief description of all commands and error messages. An example of on-line documentation as provided by the INTREX system is shown in Figure 1.1. The user's type-ins are underlined.

Live help, in the form of a telephone number to call a consultant in case of difficulties.

Additional desirable features include:

On-line training or tutorials with information concerning terminal and typing problems, command repertoire, hints for effective search strategy, and common pitfalls and their remedies.

begin
Greetings! This is Intrex. Please log in by typing the word LOG followed by a space and your name and address as in the following example:

log smith, r j;mit 13–5251;ext 7234

Note that your log in statement should end with a carriage return.

READY

log marcus;mit 35–406

Welcome to Intrex M. Marcus

If at any time you wish to abbreviate the system's messages, type the word SHORT (carriage return). To interrupt this or any other message push the attention (ATTN) button once.

If you already know how to use Intrex, you may go ahead and type in commands. (Remember, each command ends in a carriage return.) Otherwise, for information on how to make simple searches of the catalog, type

info 2

or, to see the Table of Contents (Part 1) of Intrex Guide which will direct you to other parts of the Guide explaining how to make more detailed searches, type

info 1

READY

info 2

NOTICE! For more complete information see hard–copy Guide.

Part 2 of Intrex Guide: Simple Searches

To find documents in the system specify your search request by subject, author, title terms as shown in the 3 examples below:

subject xenon viscosity

author hess, g b/subject helium

title sulfurization/author swisher

READY

subject rolling

A search on your request SUBJECT roll+ing found 116 documents that are now your current list.

The catalog fields TITLE, AUTHOR, LOCATION for those documents will be output when you type

o

(for output). You may interrupt output from the computer at any time by pressing the ATTN key ONCE.

To see other information, such as ABSTRACT or SUBJECTS type the word output (or just o) followed by the information types you wish to see (for further information see Part 8 of the Guide). Otherwise, you may add to or select from your current list (see Part 9), or make another request of Intrex (see Part 1).

READY

Figure 1.1.   On–line documentation in INTREX.

Data base overview with information concerning the size of the data base, the types of material in it, the time span covered by the material, the items of information or fields making up each record, the searchable fields (if not all), and special strategies to use or pitfalls to avoid with a given data base.

Sample searches which have been prestored to aid in teaching by analogy.

Search logic tracing which permits a user to request a detailed description of how his multipart query led to the number of hits reported by the system.

Vest pocket card which contains the command names and an explanation of how to get complete command descriptions.

Users' comments entered on-line to aid the system designers in understanding user problems, needs or desires.

Monitor log which records the users' interaction with the system and provides statistical summaries of system performance.

On-line Input Features

The minimal features for query input are concerned primarily with textual data base searching. They are designed to address the very real problems of structuring queries in such a way as to maximize the value to the user of the output of a given search. This is an area of continuing research in text information storage and retrieval. The minimal features are summarized below, with examples using the query language of BASIS-70.

Request sets which can be specified either automatically or under user control, such that the results of earlier queries can be easily incorporated into later queries. This is generally implemented by assigning a number to each line of search input. Later search requests incorporate earlier request set numbers (For example, see Figure 1.2.)

Logical operators of OR, AND and NOT which are used to combine related terms in order to broaden a query, to intersect concepts in order to narrow a query, or to exclude terms from a query (Figure 1.3).

Dictionary access which permits display of short alphabetic portions of the index. This aids in cueing the user to index terms which are alphabetically adjacent to terms used in his query which were not exactly matched in the index (Figure 1.4).

Search field control which permits the user to indicate which specific items or fields in a record are to be searched, or to request that the entire record is to be searched (Figure 1.5).

Suffix removal which is usually specified by the user entering the root or stem of a word followed by a truncation code (Figure 1.6). Some systems, like INTREX, provide a level of automatic suffix removal.

Relational operators such as equal to, greater than, less than, etc. for numeric and date fields which are essential for data management applications and for handling dated material. More will be said about these capabilities later.

In addition to these minimal features, other query aids include:

Spelling variations which can be handled by storing and linking commonly used alternative spellings such as January, Jan, etc.

Related terms and hierarchical thesauri in which related terms have been linked so that the user can request them to be displayed, and in which narrower and broader terms can be accessed via a hierarchical thesaurus.

BASIS BASIS 70 IS ON LINE. DO YOU DESIRE OPERATING INSTRUCTIONS? TYPE YES OR NO/ <u>NO</u> PLEASE ENTER YOUR LAST NAME/ <u>MITTMAN</u>	After logging-in, the user requests the BASIS-70 system.
ENTER THE NAME OF DATA BASE TO BE SEARCHED/ <u>AMIC</u> AMIC DATA BASE SPONSORED BY EPA UNDER CONTRACT 68-01-0166 TOTAL ITEMS IN BASE 850 LATEST UPDATE 12/24/73 ENTER YOUR SEARCH ONE TERM AT A TIME.	The AMIC file is loaded and current data base information is displayed. The system is now prepared to process queries.

1/   <u>DDT</u>
      25 ITEMS
 	
2/   <u>GAS CHROMATOGRAPHY</u>
      39 ITEMS
 	
3/   <u>SEPARATION TECHNIQUES</u>
      27 ITEMS
	The user desires information about DDT, gas chromatography and separation techniques. The system responds with the number of records in the data base for each search term.

Figure 1.2.   Request set example: a bibliographic data base containing
reports and documents on environmental data is to be
queried. After the BASIS-70 system has been loaded into
the computer, the AMIC (Analytical Methodology Information Center operated by the Battelle Memorial Institute
for the Environmental Protection Agency) data base is
accessed. Queries may contain index terms, authors' names,
facility names, title words, etc. All the examples will show
the user type-ins (underlined) and computer-generated
responses and messages in the left-hand column, with
explanations in the right-hand column.

4/ <u>(1 AND 2 AND 3)</u> 5 ITEMS	The user constructs a logical combination of the three previous request sets to form a new request set.

Figure 1.3.   Logical operator example.

Word proximity operators which allow the user to specify that the index terms must
all occur in the same field in order to qualify for retrieval. Other capabilities of this
type include the ability to allow testing for exact phrase matching or to specify how
many words may separate two input terms to qualify for retrieval.

Phrase decomposition in which a natural language phrase or sentence is decomposed
automatically into a query of significant words, ignoring common words like "the,"
"about," etc.

```
5/    CHEMICAL INTERFERENCES          The index did not contain the
      NO SUCH TERM. WANT ADJACENT TERMS?   term "CHEMICAL INTER-
                                       FERENCES," so the system
      YES:NO/YES                       allows the user to view the
ITEMS–NEARBY TERMS TO YOUR TERM        stored index terms which are
      1 CHEMICAL INDUSTRY              alphabetically adjacent to the
     23 CHEMICAL INTERFERENCE          query, and to choose a stored
***(YOUR TERM)***                      term.
      8 CHEMICAL OXYGEN DEMAND
      1 CHEMICAL PARTITIONING

5/    CHEMICAL INTERFERENCE
     23 ITEMS

6/    (4 AND 5)
      2 ITEMS
```

Figure 1.4. Dictionary access example.

```
7/    AU HENKE, C.F.                   The author (AU), facilities
      2 ITEMS                          (FAC), and title (TW) fields
                                       may also yield search terms.
8/    FAC FEDERAL WATER POLLUTION CONTROL ADMINISTRATION
      15 ITEMS

9/    TW MERCURY
      11 ITEMS
```

Figure 1.5. Search field example.

```
10/   CLOSTRID*5                       The user requests that the
      HITS–TERMS CONTAINING THIS STEM  first five index terms contain-
      5 CLOSTRIDIUM                    ing the bacterial stem "CLOS-
      2 CLOSTRIDIUM BIFERMENTANS       TRID. . ." be incorporated in
      2 CLOSTRIDIUM BOTULINUM          a request set. If the number
      1 CLOSTRIDIUM CAPTOVALE          of terms was not specified, the
      1 CLOSTRIDIUM CARNIS             first 10 would be chosen
                                       automatically.
```

Figure 1.6. Suffix removal example.

Search profiles in which a user can develop a search strategy, store that strategy, and rerun it at some later date.

Sequential searching, as contrasted to index searching, which permits the system to scan fields which have not been previously indexed. More will be said about this capability in our later discussion of personalized data base systems.

On-line Output and Support Features

Most people desire more than a simple listing of document numbers as the output of a query. Many applications require sophisticated report generation, often for direct photocopy printing of publication quality. An effective management information system must also provide computational, statistical and graphical features. Summarized below are the features which the workshop considered as minimal for bibliographic systems. Again, BASIS-70 is used to provide examples of the minimal features.

Search review which provides a short summary of the request sets which are currently active, the number of documents in each set, and the query which caused each set to be formed (Figure 1.7).

```
7/      (LIST ALL)                                 The LIST command provides
      ITEMS  NO.  LINE                             the user with a summary of
      *** 25  1/   DDT                             the previously entered request
      *** 39  2/   GAS CHROMATOGRAPHY              sets.
      *** 27  3/   SEPARATION TECHNIQUES
      ***  5  4/   (1 AND 2 AND 3)
      *** 23  5/   CHEMICAL INTERFERENCE
      ***  2  6/   (4 AND 5)
```

Figure 1.7. Search review example.

On-line output formatting which gives the user control over the fields to be displayed, the order of display, or the placement of data on the output page (Figure 1.8).

Off-line printing which permits voluminous output to be produced on a high-speed printer after the user is satisfied with the outcome of his on-line, interactive session (Figure 1.9).

Predefined output formats which provide the user with optional ways of viewing retrieved results, such as displays of descriptive fields, or short bibliographic citations, or total document descriptions.

In addition to these minimal features, many other capabilities are provided.

Rapid scan which allows the user to examine a small amount of information from each retrieved record.

Highlighting which permits the user to know which specific term(s) in a document or record caused it to be retrieved.

Expanding which provides for displaying the complete record after seeing a portion of it.

Sorting which outputs records ordered according to the value of designated field or fields.

```
6/    (4 AND 5)
      2 ITEMS

7/    (DISPLAY 6)
THE DATA ELEMENTS FOR THE AMIC DATA BASE ARE
1-ACCESSION NUMBER,              The request set 6 is to be
2-FACILITY,                      displayed.
3-TITLE,
4-AUTHOR(S),                     Data elements are printed only
5-BIBLIOGRAPHIC DATA,            once for each search.
6-INDEX TERMS,
7-ABSTRACT.
   WHAT FIELDS DO YOU WANT TO SEE?

ENTER FIELD NUMBERS SEPARATED BY COMMAS OR ALL
/    1,4,2,3,5
ITEMS FROM THE AMIC DATA BASE ARE...   The system prints the desired
ITEM   1                               data base elements in the
ACCESSION NUMBER:  627                 order specified.
AUTHOR(S): BREIDENBACH, A.W., LICHTENBERG, J.J.,
   HENKE, C.F., SMITH, D.J., EICHELBERGER, J.W., Jr.,
   STIERLI, H.
FACILITY: FEDERAL WATER POLLUTION CONTROL
   ADMINISTRATION, WASHINGTON, D.C., DIVISION
   OF POLLUTION SURVEILLANCE
TITLE: THE IDENTIFICATION AND MEASUREMENT OF
   CHLORINATED HYDROCARBON PESTICIDES IN
   SURFACE WATERS,
BIBLIOGRAPHIC DATA: WP-22, NOVEMBER 1966
   .70 P. 38 FIG, 2 TAB, 71 REF.

ITEM   2
ACCESSION NUMBER:  1029
AUTHOR(S): LAW, LEROY M., GOERLITZ, DONALD F.
FACILITY: U.S. GEOLOGICAL SURVEY, MENLO PARK,
   WATER RESOURCES DIVISION
TITLE: MICROCOLUMN CHROMATOGRAPHIC CLEANUP FOR
   THE ANALYSIS OF PESTICIDES IN WATER,
BIBLIOGRAPHIC DATA: JOURNAL OF THE ASSOCIATION
   OF OFFICIAL ANALYTICAL CHEMISTS,
   VOL. 53, NO. 6, P 1276-1286, NOVEMBER 1970.
   FIG, 6 TAB, 23 REF.

FINISHED WITH PRINTOUT. CONTINUE ENTERING SEARCH TERMS.
```

Figure 1.8. Output formatting example.

Ranking which lists documents in the order of decreasing number of search terms appearing in each record.

Computing using numeric fields contained in retrieved records.

```
7/      PRINT 5
        WHAT FIELDS DO YOU WANT TO SEE?


/       ALL
        PLEASE TYPE COMPLETE NAME AND MAILING ADDRESS


/       B. MITTMAN, NORTHWESTERN UNIVERSITY
        YOUR REQUEST IS BEING PRINTED OFF-LINE.
        ENTER YOUR NEXT SEARCH TERM.
```

Figure 1.9. Off-line printing example.

Statistical interface which permits retrieved data to be passed to an on-line statistical package.

Display of graphs derived from retrieved data fields.

Special terminal which provides for display of a stored microfiche of a retrieved bibliographic entry.

Special interface to an off-line photocomposition system for publishing of retrieved documents or records.

Data access protection which restricts accessing of records or of specific fields within a record to certain users who know the required passwords.

Many of the features listed above, while optional in a system which processes bibliographic data bases only, are essential for data management and personalized data base systems.

SUMMARY

Many of the bibliographic systems discussed above provide access to major reference data bases like MEDLARS, MARC, Chemical Abstracts and others. Some of the systems also permit users to build data bases from their personal collections of documents. Thus, some of the searching and storage power needed for the Vannevar Bush "memex" has been harnessed. A great deal of research has gone into providing effective indexing and query protocols, including request set formation, use of logical operators, dictionary access, stem search and suffix removal, related term and hierarchical thesauri, etc.

On the output side of the problem most of the existing systems use time-sharing typewriter terminals. However, high-speed telecommunication also allows for a cathode-ray tube (CRT) to be used as an effective output terminal. When voluminous printout results from an on-line query session, off-line, high-speed printing is available. Experimentation with computer typesetting provides the capability of producing publication quality print directly from an interactive session.

Generalized Data Management Systems

The bibliographic retrieval systems which have been discussed exhibit a number of common characteristics which tend to be highly influenced by the data bases used, as well as by the types of processing performed. The data bases consist of relatively simple records made up of items like titles, authors, abstracts, dates, journal names, etc. Most queries against these data bases contain keywords or phrases which are looked up in an index. These keywords or phrases may be combined to broaden a query possibly using the logical operator "OR" or they may be intersected, using the logical operator "AND" to narrow a query. "NOT" may be used to exclude a term from a query. The only use of relational operators, such as "greater than or equal to," may be when one wishes to retrieve only those documents which were published before or after a given date. Generally, the only updating which is required of a file is the simple addition of new records. Only seldom do some incorrect data in a given record have to be corrected.

There are many other applications which differ markedly from those handled by bibliographic data base organization and retrieval capabilities. For these applications, generalized data management systems have been developed. These systems must accommodate many types of numeric data such as physical measurements in miles, feet, inches, meters, centimeters, microns, angstroms, light years, etc.; time periods in years, seconds, nanoseconds, etc.; or money values in dollars, francs, rubles, yen, etc. Often conversion from one set of units to another is a requirement. Other data types include dates, both *BC* and *AD*, entered possibly in European or American style, or codes like M=male, F=female.

Queries may require that certain arithmetic relationships exist among data items in order for a record to be selected. For example, the user may wish to extract from a personnel file only those employees who earn more than the average salary of all employees.

Another important characteristic of generalized data management systems is that they must provide some way of handling information which is grouped in some logical manner. Again, in the personnel application, it is convenient and often essential that the user be able to retrieve information which is accessible as a group of associated data items about an employee, such as the date, salary, and supervisor's evaluation for every salary increase in the past five years. Thus, records must be organized in some conveniently structured manner to be able to retrieve and process related items of data.

When one deals with data bases about inventories, employees, patients, students, laboratory experiments, companies, etc., the data items may change frequently. Thus, updating must be done often and changes to individual records are common. Also, it may be necessary to update only those records which meet certain query conditions. Updating capabilities are, therefore, an important consideration in the design, implementation and use of a generalized data management system.

A complete study of generalized data management systems requires examination of the features discussed above and more. These features include data structures, data definition, file creation, update and interrogation. In 1971, a report entitled *Feature Analysis of Generalized Data Base Management Systems* was published by the CODASYL Systems Committee.[9] CODASYL is the Conference on Data Systems Languages which was instrumental in developing the specifications for COBOL and for preparing a report of a task force studying the general requirements for data base management systems.

The CODASYL Systems Committee feature analysis report resulted from a study of ten data base management systems. The report divides these systems into two categories: the self-contained systems, which function independently of any programming language; and the host language systems, which augment standard programming languages, like COBOL, with data management capabilities. The self-contained systems are: IBM's GIS, Generalized Information System; Informatics' MARK IV; IBM and the National Military Command Systems' NIPS, NMCS Information Processing System; System Development Corporation's TDMS, Time-shared Data Management System; and RCA's UL/1, User Language /1. The host language systems are: CODASYL's COBOL, Common Business

Oriented Language; CODASYL's DBTG, Data Base Task Group Proposal; Honeywell Information System's IDS, Integrated Data Store; IBM and North American Rockwell's IMS, Information Management System; and Western Electric and Auerbach's SC-1, System Control-1. As was done when discussing the bibliographic systems, we shall present only the basic, common features of these systems, with examples as appropriate.

We shall concentrate our attention on the characteristics of the self-contained systems. The characteristics to be covered will be data structures, data definition and file creation, updating, and interrogation. As an example of such a system, we shall utilize SYSTEM 2000, which is related in structure to TDMS. SYSTEM 2000 is a proprietary program developed by MRI Systems, Inc.[10]

DATA STRUCTURES

Most data base systems permit users to interact with the data in terms which are independent of the manner in which the data are physically stored. In such systems, the user's conception of the data will be called the *data structure.* In contrast, the data collection as physically stored in the computer will be called the *storage structure.*

A data base is made up of structures and elements of different types which are defined, created and maintained through user-specified creation and update processes, and from which other structures and reports are produced by user-specified interrogation procedures. As we have seen in bibliographic data bases, the data structures are composed of *items* such as titles, authors, index terms, journal names, and abstracts which are combined into *records* concerning specific documents which, in turn, are gathered together to form *files* and *data bases* of bibliographic information.

A general specification of a data structure includes the following generic structure types:

Item
Group
Record
File
Data Base

Items

The *item* is the elementary data structure from which other structures are ultimately composed. Other names for item are *field, element, data item,* or *data element.* The principal attributes of an item are its *value* and *name.* The value of an item may be one of a number of *value types* such as alphabetic, numeric, or date. Some examples of items are:

Name	Value Type	Value
EMPLOYEE NAME	ALPHABETIC	D. J. JONES
AGE	NUMERIC	27
BIRTH DATE	DATE	DEC. 15, 1947

In addition to these basic attributes, various systems provide other attributes which have proven useful in different applications.

A *value existence indicator* may be provided for specifying the absence of a given item value. For example, in a student record file, one might indicate that a test score for a given student is missing by entering the indicator as a value "NULL" into that item. When an average test score is to be calculated, all NULL-valued items would be excluded from the computation.

A set of *validation criteria* may be defined to limit the value of a certain item to a given range of numeric values, to a specified length in number of alphanumeric characters, or to a list of discrete item values. If an item is input to the data base which violates any of these validation criteria, the system would reject the item and issue a diagnostic message to the user. This is necessary to minimize the occurrence of incorrect data in a file. A very common form of validation criterion is the PICTURE designation which permits the exact form of an alphanumeric or numeric item to be specified. For example, a "PICTURE XXXX" specification for an alphanumeric item would limit this item to no more than four characters, or a "PICTURE 999.99" would limit a decimal numeric item to three integer digits and two fractional digits. An example of a numeric range validation would be:

Name	Value Type	Acceptable Range	
ANNUAL SALARY	NUMERIC	GREATER THAN	5,000
		LESS THAN	25,000

If a salary item were input with a value of, say, 25,500, an error diagnostic would be issued by the system.

A *units* attribute may be defined to specify that a certain numeric item is to be interpreted in some units of measure such as feet and inches, or pounds and ounces.

A *coded* or *synonym* attribute may permit input of codes, such as "M" for male and "F" for female, with the system providing the option to output either the codes themselves or the defined synonyms.

A set of *access locks* may be provided to function like passwords and permit only those users with proper authorization to select, report, or process certain items. For example, in a personnel file, certain medical or salary data items might be restricted from access, except by authorized supervisors.

A *transaction code* may specify the date and time of the last change to an item value.

As an example of some of these item attributes, we shall present a data base application involving a stock market portfolio. SYSTEM 2000 will be used to illustrate how a self-contained, data management system permits the user to define the data items which will be used in the application. No attempt will be made to present all of the features which are available in SYSTEM 2000, only those which illustrate the selected examples.

SYSTEM 2000 provides two alphanumeric value types, NAME and TEXT, a DATE type, and three numeric types, INTEGER NUMBER, DECIMAL NUMBER, and MONEY NUMBER. The DECIMAL and MONEY types are identical, except that the MONEY type item will be displayed with a leading dollar sign and with a following CR, for credit, for negative values. The NAME type is used for alphanumeric values which may serve as searchable strings, while TEXT items may only serve for output purposes and may not normally enter into a search command. The user utilizes the DEFINE module of SYSTEM

2000 to indicate to the system each item which will be part of the data base. The item definition looks like:

13* NAME OF STOCK (NAME):

Each item definition consists of a user defined number called the component number, followed by the system separator (in this case an *), followed by the item name, followed by the value type in parentheses, and, finally, followed by a colon. Other examples of item definitions from the stock portfolio data base are:

14* TICKER SYMBOL (NAME):
17* INDUSTRY CODE (INTEGER NUMBER):
18* SHARES OUTSTANDING (INTEGER NUMBER):
19* LATEST EARNINGS (DECIMAL NUMBER):
20* LATEST EARNINGS DATE (DATE):

We shall now see how items may be combined to form more complex units, called groups.

Groups

A *group* is a set of items and possibly other groups. A group composed solely of items is a *simple group*; a group composed of items and groups is called a *compound group*. A simple group is a way of collecting together a set of items and giving the set a name and, possibly, some attributes of its own. Other names for group are *segment, set, group item,* or *data aggregate.* An example of a simple group might be a collection of items such as employee name, employee number, and annual salary. A group can be represented as a tree as in Figure 1.10.

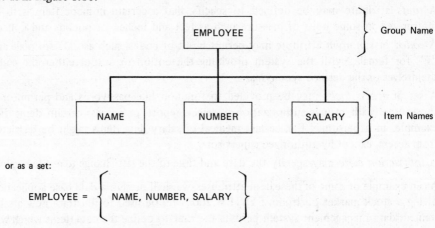

Figure 1.10. Simple group.

A compound group provides a way of collecting together a set of items and a set of groups and giving the new set a name and other attributes of its own. A reference to a compound group is a reference not only to its immediate constituent groups, but also to the items in all of its included groups as well. If the group for skill, made up of skill code and title, were added to the employee group, the resulting compound group would look like Figure 1.11.

A reference to EMPLOYEE would be equivalent to a reference to NAME, NUMBER, SALARY, CODE and TITLE.

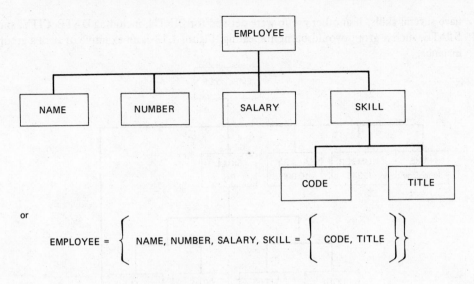

Figure 1.11. Compound group.

An *instance* of a group consists of a collection of item values corresponding to the group's item definitions. An instance of the employee group is shown in Figure 1.12.

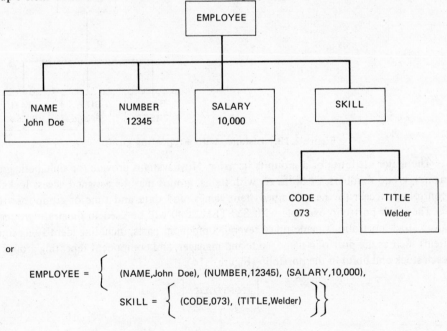

Figure 1.12. Group instance.

An important class of groups is the *repeating group* (RG). A repeating group is one which may have a variable number of instances for each instance of the containing group. By contrast, a *nonrepeating group* is one which has just one instance per instance of the containing group. The group SKILL can be a repeating group, since a given employee may have several skills. If another group were defined for BIRTH, including DATE, CITY, and STATE, such a group would be nonrepeating. Figure 1.13 is an example of such a group instance.

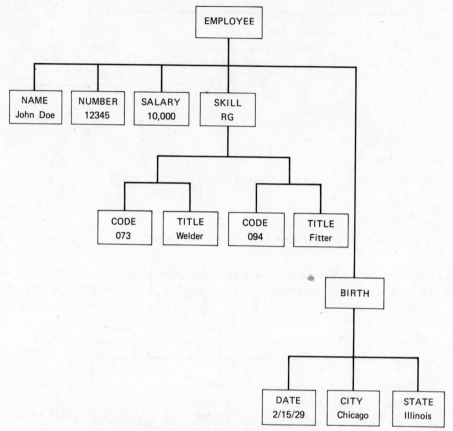

Figure 1.13. Instance with a repeating group.

The major attribute of a group is its name. Most systems provide for alphabetic group names, group numbers, or both. As with items, groups may be assigned access locks for controlling access to the contained item values, and date and time of group insertion.

The stock portfolio example with SYSTEM 2000 will be used to illustrate groups. A given stock portfolio is made up of several component parts, including identifying simple items such as the portfolio name, code and manager, and component repeating groups for each stock and bond in the portfolio (Figure 1.14).

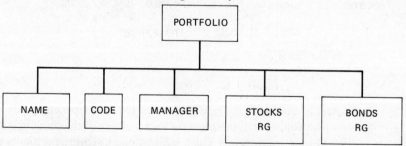

Figure 1.14. Portfolio record with repeating groups.

SYSTEM 2000 provides for nested group definitions by using the word IN, followed by the group number, as follows:

```
 8* PORTFOLIOS
     9* PORTFOLIO NAME (NAME IN 8):
    10* PORTFOLIO CODE (NAME IN 8):
    11* MANAGER (NAME IN 8):
    12* STOCKS (RG IN 8):
         13* NAME OF STOCK (NAME IN 12):
         14* TICKER SYMBOL (NAME IN 12):
             .
             .
             .
         24* CURRENT PRICE (DECIMAL IN 12):
         25* TRANSACTIONS (RG IN 12):
             26* BLOCK NUMBER (INTEGER IN 25):
             27* TRANSACTION TYPE (NAME IN 25):
             28* DATE (DATE IN 25):
             29* SHARES (INTEGER IN 25):
             30* PRICE (DECIMAL IN 25):
    31* BONDS (RG IN 8):
        32* NAME OF ISSUER (NAME IN 31):
        33* ASKED PRICE (DECIMAL IN 31):
            etc.
```

Records

A *record* is a set of groups in which one and only one group, the *record-defining group,* is not contained in or subordinate to any other group. The CODASYL report chose to call a record an *entry*. However, we shall use the term *record* for this concept, since all but one of the systems discussed in the CODASYL report use that term. TDMS uses the term *entry* and SYSTEM 2000 uses the term *logical entry*.

The record is used to represent the major entities of an application. For a given class of entities (e.g., the employees in a firm), the items in the record-defining group typically correspond to *fixed* entity attributes, i.e., attributes common to all entities in the given class (e.g., the employee name, age, sex, birth date, etc.). On the other hand, the items in the contained or subordinate groups correspond to *variable* entity attributes, i.e., attributes not necessarily shared by all entities in the class (e.g., automobile(s) owned by an employee), or attributes which may have *multiple values* (e.g., employee skill code(s) and skill title(s)).

In order to define the items and groups which make up a record, a *schema* is used. The schema provides the user and the system with the names, types and other attributes of each item and of each group contained within the record. After the schema has been specified, *instances* of that record may be created by inputting specific values for the items defined in the record schema.

The DEFINE module of SYSTEM 2000 provides the user with language necessary to structure the application data into a record schema so that items and groups of items may be defined for subsequent searching, analysis and updating. The complete record schema for the portfolio application is shown in Figure 1.15.

```
 1*  ORGANIZATION (NAME):
 2*  COGNIZANT OFFICIAL (NAME):
 3*  ADDRESS (NAME):
 4*  CITY (NAME):
 5*  STATE (NAME):
 6*  ZIP CODE (INTEGER):
 7*  CURRENT DATE (DATE):
 8*  PORTFOLIOS (RG):
     9*  PORTFOLIO NAME (NAME IN 8):
    10*  PORTFOLIO CODE (NAME IN 8):
    11*  MANAGER (NAME IN 8):
    12*  STOCKS (RG IN 8):
        13*  NAME OF STOCK (NAME IN 12):
        14*  TICKER SYMBOL (NAME IN 12):
        15*  EXCHANGE (NAME IN 12):
        16*  INDUSTRY NAME (NAME IN 12):
        17*  INDUSTRY CODE (INTEGER IN 12):
        18*  SHARES OUTSTANDING (INTEGER IN 12):
        19*  LATEST EARNINGS (DECIMAL IN 12):
        20*  LATEST EARNINGS DATE (DATE IN 12):
        21*  ESTIMATED EARNINGS (DECIMAL IN 12):
        22*  ESTIMATED EARNINGS DATE (DATE IN 12):
        23*  DIVIDEND (DECIMAL IN 12):
        24*  CURRENT PRICE (DECIMAL IN 12):
        25*  TRANSACTIONS (RG IN 12):
            26*  BLOCK NUMBER (INTEGER IN 25):
            27*  TRANSACTION TYPE (NAME IN 25):
            28*  DATE (DATE IN 25):
            29*  SHARES (INTEGER IN 25):
            30*  PRICE (DECIMAL IN 25):
    31*  BONDS (RG IN 8):
        32*  NAME OF ISSUER (NAME IN 31):
        33*  ASKED PRICE (DECIMAL IN 31):
        34*  PURCHASE PRICE (DECIMAL IN 31):
        35*  MATURITY DATE (DATE IN 31):
        36*  PURCHASE DATE (DATE IN 31):
        37*  FACE AMOUNT (DECIMAL IN 31):
```

Figure 1.15. Record schema for portfolio example.

Files and Data Bases

A *file* is made up of a set of records. Most systems provide for files which are composed of a single record schema, such as the portfolio file or the employee file. The records in such a file tend to be independent of one another, in the sense that one record can be processed without reference to another. Often record instances are identified and ordered by a record number so that they may be extracted by that number for processing.

Systems which provide for files with different record schema usually provide some link facility to associate records of one type with records of another. For example, if a file consists of one set of records containing supplier information and another set of records with merchandise descriptions, it would be necessary to link the suppliers to the merchandise which they sell.

A *data base* consists of one or more files which may themselves be linked or independent. Again, most currently available data management systems provide for data bases which contain independent files, and in which each file consists of only a single record type. The next sections will discuss how files are created, updated and processed.

DATA DEFINITION AND FILE CREATION

We have already seen that a record schema must be defined in order to specify the names and attributes of items and groups contained within the record. The data definition module of a data management system provides the user with appropriate language to name each item, to provide an item number, to specify the item type, to impose input validation criteria or output editing formats and to define access locks or passwords.

The data definition language must permit the assignment of group attributes to certain sets of items. If a group is simple, then the data definition must provide a statement of the group attributes plus the definition of each item making up the group. The relationship between a simple group and its constituent items may be defined explicitly, by referring to the group in the definition of all its items or vice versa. In the SYSTEM 2000 examples, we have seen the use of the word IN to provide this relationship:

12* STOCKS (RG IN 8):
13* NAME OF STOCK (NAME IN 12):

showing that 13 is one of the items contained in group 12. Alternatively, this relation may be implied by the ordering of the appropriate definitions.

In the case of a compound group, its definition must include the definitions of the contained groups. In some systems, like SYSTEM 2000, the item and group definitions are interwoven, while in other systems, all of the item information is presented separately from the definitions of the groups' schemas. Nested groups provide a hierarchical structure which may utilize level numbers to determine the relationship of one group or set of items to another group. For example, in Figure 1.15 items or components 1 through 7, which can be considered as the record–defining group, are at level 0; items 9 through 11 in the PORTFOLIOS repeating group are at level 1; items 13 through 24 in the STOCKS repeating group are at level 2; items 32 through 37 in the BONDS repeating group are also at level 2; and, finally, items 26 through 30 in the TRANSACTIONS repeating group are at level 3. These levels can be used in the interrogation and retrieval processes to access specific groups or items. It should be pointed out that the indentation shown in SYSTEM 2000 examples to indicate hierarchic levels is purely for reading clarity and is not required by the system.

As was indicated earlier, most systems provide for files consisting of single record schemas. The systems generally provide a means of naming each file that is defined by its record schema. Also, it is convenient to provide a means for altering a record schema, once it has been defined, without recreating the entire data base from scratch. Many of the systems provide such a data redefinition procedure.

Once the data definition task has been completed, the next step is to create the initial record instances of the file. To create a file, the system must have available the data definition and the set of record instances containing the actual data for each item in the record.

As each data item is read by the system, the validation criterion for that item value is applied, and if the value violates the criterion, the item value is rejected and diagnosed as incorrect. As item values are read, they are stored in the current record being processed. As each record is completed, appropriate information about its length and physical location in storage is accumulated. This information is utilized to form appropriate indexes to all the records in the file for subsequent updating and searching.

To illustrate the file creation process, the portfolio example will again be used. Figures 1.16a and b show sample input data for two record instances.

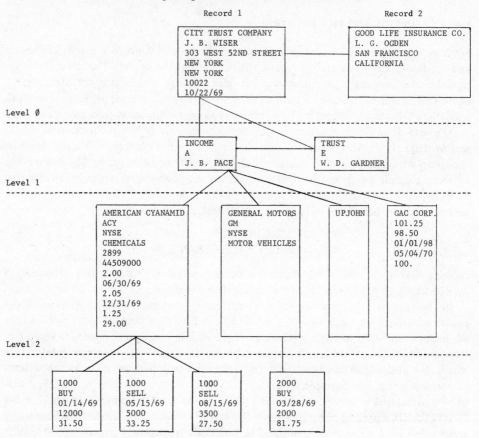

Figure 1.16a. Sample portfolio for record instances.

UPDATING

Updating is the process of changing, adding, or deleting selected instances of records, groups, or items stored in a file. Update implies changes in value. It does not, however, mean changing the logical data structure, the validation criteria, or the security procedures which have been specified in the original record schema. This latter type of change is called *record redefinition* or *data redefinition.*

Updates may be done on specific records by referencing the user or system-specified record number. Updates may also be done selectively, by utilizing query statements to

```
Record 1

1* CITY TRUST COMPANY* 2* J.B.WISER* 3* 303 WEST 52ND ST.*
4* NEW YORK* 5* NEW YORK* 6* 10022* 7* 10/22/69*
8* 9* INCOME* 10* A* 11* J.B.PACE*
12* 13* AMERICAN CYANAMID* 14* ACY* 15* NYSE*
16* CHEMICALS* 17* 2899* 18* 445 09000* 19* 2.00*
20* 06/30/69* 21* 2.05* 22* 12/31/69* 23* 1.25* 24* 29.00*
25* 26* 1000* 27* BUY* 28* 01/14/69* 29* 12000* 30* 31.50*
25* 26* 1000* 27* SELL* 28* 05/15/69* 29* 5000* 30* 33.25*
25* 26* 1000* 27* SELL* 28* 08/15/69* 29* 3500* 30* 27.50*
12* 13* GENERAL MOTORS* 14* GM* 15* NYSE* 16* MOTOR VEHICLES*
25* 26* 2000* 27* BUY* 28* 03/28/69* 29* 2000* 30* 81.75*
12* 13* UPJOHN*
31* 32* GAC CORP.* 33* 101.25* 34* 98.50* 35* 01/01/98*
36* 05/04/70* 37* 100.*
8* 9* TRUST* 10* E* 11* W.D.GARDNER*
END*


Record 2

1* GOOD LIFE INSURANCE CO.* 2* L.G.OGDEN* 4* SAN FRANCISCO*
5* CALIFORNIA*
END*
```

Figure 1.16b. Input format for portfolio record instances.

select the record candidates for update transactions. Some systems provide only batch-processing updating, while others allow for updating to be performed interactively at an on-line terminal. In either case, care must be taken to assure that all validation criteria and security locks are verified before the record, group, or item is permitted to be accessed, modified, or deleted. Update transactions include insertion or deletion of records, as well as modification of given items or groups within records.

Every data management system provides a command language to perform these update transactions. The language must allow the selection of the appropriate record instances and then specify that transactions are to be performed on those records. An example from SYSTEM 2000 will illustrate how a record may be selected based upon the value of one item so that another item of the selected record may be modified:

CHANGE C11 EQ. B. J. DILLARD* WHERE C9 EQ INCOME*

This update command selects any records which have the portfolio name (C9) of INCOME and replaces the current value of the portfolio manager's name (C11) with the new name B. J. DILLARD.

This example brings us to the major application for which data base management systems are designed: the accessing of stored records based upon some specified search criteria. Interrogation and search procedures are provided by data base management systems.

INTERROGATION

The *interrogation* function is concerned with the *retrieval* portion of an information storage and retrieval system. As we have seen in the bibliographic systems, one wishes to extract or copy selected data which satisfy certain query conditions. In a data management system, these selected data may then undergo intermediate processing like sorting or summarizing, they may be formatted for report generation, or they may serve as input to further computation or statistical analysis. The interrogation process, therefore, must indicate which part of the data base is to be searched, what selection criteria are to be applied to isolate the desired data, and what kinds of processing are to be done on the selected data.

The first specification of the interrogation function defines the applicable set of records to be queried. This is usually a statement specifying which file in the data base (if there are more than one) is to be readied for interrogation. Statements like the following serve this function:

ENTER DATA BASE FILE ID: PERSONNEL FILE

or

INTERROGATE PERSONNEL FILE

The selection facilities typically permit a *complex condition* to be expressed on each of the records in the selected file. This condition is made up of a logically connected set of *simple conditions* on one or more data items, usually on the item values. A simple conditional expression may begin with the word IF or contain the word WHERE. The conditional expression usually contains as its *subject* an item name or number, followed by a *relational operator* such as less than (LT), followed by a *reference quantity*. Examples would be:

IF AGE LT 37

or

WHERE C13 EQ WELDER*

The usual relational operators are EQUALS, NOT EQUALS, LESS THAN, GREATER THAN, LESS THAN OR EQUALS, and GREATER THAN OR EQUALS. These are obvious relational operators for numeric or date item values. However, the only meaningful operators for alphabetic or alphanumeric items would be EQUALS or NOT EQUALS. As we saw with bibliographic systems, which deal primarily with textual items, one might want to search individual phrases, words, or stems contained within lengthy text items. Thus, relational operators like CONTAINS or DOES NOT CONTAIN are also utilized for text items.

The systems must be capable of assuring that the reference quantities in relational conditions must agree in type with the subject type. In the case of disagreement, a diagnostic message would be issued. For example, a simple condition of the following form:

IF NAME EQ 35

should result in a diagnostic message indicating that the data type of the NAME item must be alphabetic, not numeric. One other useful feature is the ability to test the existence or nonexistence of an item value. Finally, simple conditional expressions can be combined using such logical connectives as AND, OR and NOT to form complex conditions such as:

IF SKILL EQ WELDER AND SALARY GT 10000

Once the conditional expression has been specified, the user must indicate what is to be done with the extracted data, i.e., the data from those records which satisfy the query. Generally, the extracted data are either placed into a report format or are copied for further processing.

The user should be able to indicate which specific item, group, or record instances are desired for reporting or processing, and in what formats these extracted data should be output. Some systems provide only system control over these formats, while other systems permit the user to specify report or output formats, as well as sorting requirements.

In addition to the item value extraction, which is normally the result of the interrogation, many of the systems permit derived values to be extracted. These derived values may result from arithmetic expressions of extracted item values or from standard functions like MINIMUM, MAXIMUM, MEAN, etc.

To illustrate some of the interrogation features of a data management system, we shall show typical queries using SYSTEM 2000, which has two access modes, one for batch processing and one for interactive processing. The so-called ACCESS module is provided to accomplish retrieval, update, and file creation operations in a batch processing environment. The IMMEDIATE ACCESS module permits retrieval in a terminal-based, interactive environment.

The file or data base to be queried is selected by the following command:

DATA BASE NAME IS PORTFOLIO FILE:

Sample queries are shown which would be used to extract specific items or repeating groups of items.

PRINT PORTFOLIO NAME, MANAGER WHERE PORTFOLIO NAME EXISTS:
PRINT STOCKS WHERE DATE GT 07/01/69:
PRINT C1,C9,C13,C26 WHERE C1 EXISTS AND C9 NE TRUST
     AND C24 GE 25.00 AND C27 EQ SELL:

SUMMARY

Generalized data management systems provide much greater richness in data structures, updating and interrogation functions than the bibliographic systems. They allow for the definition of many types of data items which are not needed for document or text processing applications. They support more complex group structures. Since computational and statistical analyses are essential to data management applications, they provide tools to handle such problems. Thus, while the bibliographic systems facilitate the storage and retrieval of reference material about specific problem areas, the data management systems go beyond this, and provide the means to solve problems also.

We shall now consider how the functions provided by both the bibliographic and data management systems constitute essential components of personalized data base processing.

Personalized Data Base Systems

The discussion of bibliographic and generalized data management systems has set the stage for a presentation of the characteristics of a personalized data base system. A personalized data base system consists, in part, of a synthesis of the capabilities discussed thus far.

When we opened this chapter with our mythical retiree, we found him utilizing several data bases which were stored at a central information utility. Some of the data bases were provided by the utility as public files for use by all. The fishing equipment file is the computerized equivalent of the yellow pages. The French lessons, with the collection of colored pictures and examination questions, were provided, presumably for a fee, by a local school. The user, through his time-sharing terminal, was able to create, maintain, and interrogate a personal file of antique car information. We shall now investigate the facilities which would be needed to handle such data base processing requirements.

The major attributes of a personalized data base system must be flexibility, comprehensiveness, and ease of use, since each new project yields a potentially different set of user characteristics, data base specifications, or processing requirements. The novice user must be served as effectively as the expert. The user language must provide tutorial, training and diagnostic aids. A great variety of data types and structures must be accommodated. A full range of computational, statistical, and report generation aids must be available. Files must be easily updated.

The typical university research project and the process of doing research can be used as examples of the needs which can be met by an effective retrieval system. Whether we are speaking of a project in management, sociology, psychology, or almost any other field, certain common characteristics are evident. First of all, scientific literature may be reviewed for reference and background material. Some research workers prefer to gather their own collection of relevant documents rather than rely on a library collection. Thus, all of the bibliographic tools which we discussed earlier would be helpful. However, two additional factors are important when considering this personal collection of references. First of all, the collection is generally small, consisting of at most a few thousand references, rather than millions. Secondly, the research worker may not want to tie himself to some predetermined set of index terms. Since his directions of research may change rapidly during a project, one set of terms, selected initially for a document, may not be completely relevant to some subsequent turn in the project's direction. Thus, it may be necessary to retrieve documents based on any of the words contained in the title, abstract, or list of keywords, instead of from only words which were preindexed. Although such a capability would be useful for any bibliographic system, the immense size of publicly available bibliographic data bases precludes the possibility of such a facility. Predefined indexes are essential to permit efficient searching of very large textual files, containing hundreds of thousands of records or more. But if we deal with relatively small files—files of several hundred to several thousand records—then it is possible to examine each word of each record to perform exhaustive searches.

Another characteristic of many research projects is their dependence upon data analysis. Some projects perform statistical analysis of survey or experimental source data. Other projects rely heavily on graphs or plots to reveal relevant relationships among variables. Thus, a retrieval system utilized for these applications must first be capable of storing and retrieving both source and derived data, and then be able to call upon statistical or graphical processing programs for analysis. Since much research is speculative, it would be useful if these procedures could be done interactively, so that output from one analysis could immediately feed into a subsequent stage of the research. Interactive time-sharing capabilities, including powerful analysis tools, are thus desirable, if not essential, features of a personalized data base system.

An important characteristic of the typical research worker in any field is his or her desire to not waste time on seemingly extraneous activities. One does not want to have to become a computer expert in order to use a computer effectively. Thus, a personalized data base system should be relatively easy to use. If only simple tasks are to be performed, then simple ways of requesting these tasks should be available. Considerable consistency in the command language should be provided so that the learning of new capabilities is eased. But in addition to simplicity is the need for completeness and comprehensiveness.

Although it is impossible to anticipate and provide for every conceivable query or analysis capability, an effective system must satisfy the major needs of the user community. Thus, currently available systems are undergoing constant development to keep up with user demands.

Some of the systems which have been discussed in this chapter are, in our opinion, candidates for being considered as prototypic, personalized data base systems. They are not prototypes in the sense of being experimental or unreliable, since they are being used regularly by many people for just the types of applications mentioned here. They are operational systems. They are prototypes, however, in the sense that they are all still under constant development to make them truly personalized and truly responsive to the broadest range of data base applications. Battelle's BASIS-70, Stanford's SPIRES II, MRI Systems' SYSTEM 2000, and Northwestern's RIQS are examples of personalized data base systems. They all handle textual as well as numeric data items, they link to statistical or graphical analysis programs, they provide for user definition and updating of files, they offer extensive interrogation and output functions, and they have been designed with the user in mind. Many other of the systems mentioned in this chapter also contain some of these characteristics.

RIQS has been and is being used at Northwestern University for the management of many kinds of data bases. As will be seen in Part II, RIQS provides powerful storage, retrieval, analysis and reporting capabilities for many and varied applications. Before presenting some of these applications, we shall discuss the important characteristics of RIQS in Chapter 2.

NOTES AND CITED REFERENCES

1. Carlos A. Cuadra (ed.), *Annual Review of Information Science and Technology,* Vols. 1-9, 1966-1974, American Society for Information Science, Washington, D.C.

2. *Atlantic Monthly,* Vol. 176, No. 1, July, 1945, pp. 101-108.

3. Joseph Becker and Robert M. Hayes, *Information Storage and Retrieval: Tools, Elements, Theories,* John Wiley & Sons, New York, 1963.

4. Manfred Kochen (ed.), *The Growth of Knowledge,* John Wiley and Sons, New York, 1967.

5. F. Wilfred Lancaster, *Information Retrieval Systems,* John Wiley and Sons, New York, 1968, p. 1.

6. Cuadra, op. cit., Vol. 7, 1972, pp. 323-378.

7. Donald E. Walker (ed.), *Interactive Bibliographic Search: The User/Computer Interface,* AFIPS Press, Montvale, New Jersey, 1971.

8. Thomas H. Martin, *Feature Analysis of Interactive Retrieval Systems,* Institute for Communication Research, Stanford University, Stanford, California, September, 1974.

9. *Feature Analysis of Generalized Data Base Management Systems,* CODASYL Systems Committee, Association for Computing Machinery, Order Department, New York, May 1971.

10. We express our appreciation to MRI Systems, Inc. for providing documentation on SYSTEM 2000 from which our examples have been selected.

Chapter 2

RIQS-Remote Information Query System

Introduction

We have characterized personalized data base systems as consisting of an amalgam of bibliographic and data management capabilities. The origins of Northwestern University's RIQS, Remote Information Query System, were just that. In 1968, two separate systems were being utilized to handle data base needs of faculty and students.

One group of needs, primarily derived from the social science departments, related to the storage and retrieval of textual information, with associated indexing and reporting requirements. A system called TRIAL[1] has been used at Northwestern University since 1964 and has been distributed to some 25 universities for CDC 6000 and IBM 360 and 370 series computers. TRIAL[2, 3] allows for the creation and maintenance of a master file of textual and certain numeric information on magnetic tape. An index facility provides for keyword-in-context (KWIC) and keyword-out-of-context (KWOC) indexes on terms designated as keywords or alternatively, on every word in the text, excluding user-supplied common terms. A search capability includes selective retrieval and printout of records based upon textual queries which permit search terms to be combined with the logical operators AND, OR, and NOT. Some of the data bases[4] maintained in TRIAL format at Northwestern University are:

SDI and BIB, files containing references to journal articles appearing in social science literature, books, government publications, technical reports, etc.

AFRICA, literature citations relating to Modern Africa

ARMS, book reviews in *Arms Control and Disarmament* and *Foreign Affairs*

34

CODEBOOK, abstracts and codebooks describing quantitative, social science data bases available for student and faculty use at Northwestern University

While the users of TRIAL were quite well satisfied with having their bibliographic needs handled through a computer-based retrieval system, they were dissatisfied with the lack of an effective data management system. In addition to reference material, political and social science researchers also utilized statistical data in their work. Voting records, survey results, demographic data, and other numeric and date information were not adequately processed by TRIAL since it lacked the ability to perform computational or statistical processing, and was not designed to handle hierarchical, spatial or temporal associations among data elements. These types of processing required the development of special purpose programs or the multistep process of extracting selected data and then applying a number of usually unrelated statistical or graphical library programs.

Medical and physical scientists also collected and processed a variety of numeric and alphanumeric data for their research. To help meet these processing needs, a second retrieval system called INFOL 2,[6] based upon Control Data Corporation's INFOL,[5] was implemented in 1968 on the CDC 6400 for the storage, updating and retrieval of structured data including alphanumeric and numeric items, dates and special codes.

TRIAL, INFOL and the computational, statistical, and graphical programs available in the mid-1960s were all batch processing oriented. Time sharing capability began to become available at Northwestern University in 1968 on the CDC 6400 computer. This led to a design study[7] to combine the available storage, retrieval, updating, and processing facilities into a unified system for personalized data base processing (although it was not called that at the time). Many observations about user needs had been derived from experience with TRIAL and INFOL. These observations, with some resulting design criteria, are summarized below:

Most personal data base needs can be met with relatively small sized files, i.e., with records which number in the hundreds and thousands, rather than in the hundreds of thousands or millions.

Since research projects change rapidly, it is not always possible to predetermine all appropriate subject indexes or search keys for a given data base. A preferable alternative would be to be able to access records in the file by means of *any* word, group of words or numeric data contained in the records. Given relatively small data bases, this becomes economically and operationally feasible. The need to process very large data bases would generally not permit this design goal to be realized.

It would be desirable to provide a query language which has a wide range of expressive power, supplying the ability to formulate simple queries in a simple way, and yet powerful enough to handle complex data management processing requests.

A full range of batch processing output options should be available to facilitate bibliographic applications, including keyword-in-context and keyword-out-of-context indexes, author index, and selective dissemination of information and current awareness services.

File creation and update processing is best handled in a batch processing mode of operation. (This design criterion has recently come under reconsideration as more interactive uses of RIQS have led to a desire for on-line updating.)

Interfaces must be provided to powerful statistical and graphical analysis programs.

The system should provide both batch processing search and on-line, interactive search capabilities. Ideally, these facilities should utilize identical input and output formats.

A great variety of data types should be implemented, with appropriate validation criteria and value existence indicators.

The data structures provided should include at least tree structures. (RIQS currently provides only for simple items and multiple items, which are groups of identical, simple item types.)

The system should support both public and private files.

Ease of file reorganization or record redefinition is a necessity.

As much on-line, tutorial and diagnostic assistance as possible should be included in the system.

Since user needs will determine future requirements, the design should be as modular as possible.

The design and initial implementation of RIQS was completed in 1970,[8] and for the past five years, it has been in active use as the primary data base system at Northwestern University. Some of its current applications are documented in Part II. The remainder of this chapter will describe how the above design criteria have been realized in the implementation of RIQS.

The data structure of RIQS provides for alphanumeric, numeric, and date-valued items. Numeric items can be expressed as either integer or decimal quantities, and can optionally be written as a sequence of related units, such as 16 feet 3 inches. Dates can be expressed in any of the commonly utilized formats. Since many applications were expected to involve lengthy textual items, it was decided to store each unique word, which appears in each record, only once, to conserve storage space. The physical organization of a record includes the table of unique words for that record, with sets of appropriate pointers to associate each word with the item in which it resides and with its position within that item. A complete description of the RIQS record structure is found in the appendix.[9]

Records consist of named and numbered items. Items may be simple, that is, consisting of a single numeric value, date or text string, or they may be multiple. Multiple items consist of a sequence of like-valued subitems. A data definition facility is utilized to specify the names, numbers, types and validation criteria of each simple and multiple item in a record. Input data and update phases of processing are provided to create and maintain RIQS files. The search phase of the RIQS processor is used for query formulation and retrieval, for linking to statistical and graphical packages, and for computation. Searching may be done either on-line or in a batch processing mode. For economy, in the batch mode several queries can be processed simultaneously while performing only one scan through the data base. The index phase is used to provide bibliographic outputs such as keyword or author lists, or permuted title indexes.

Data Structure, Data Definition and File Creation

This section discusses the RIQS data structure, including items, groups, records and files, introduces the data definition facility, and presents three sample files which will be utilized to illustrate all of the features of RIQS which are useful in personalized data base processing.

ITEMS

An item consists of an item number, an item name, and an optional item identifier. An example of an item is:

(2) PUBLICATION NAME

or

(2 = PUBNAME) PUBLICATION NAME

Identifiers are restricted to 7 characters, whereas names may be up to 80 characters long. Search queries refer to items by their numbers or identifiers. Item names are used for reporting purposes. Sample queries would be

. IF (2) CONTAINS 'ACM'

or

IF (PUBNAME) CONTAINS 'ACM'

or

IF #2 CONTAINS 'ACM' (in on-line mode)

RIQS provides for three basic types of items: alphanumeric, numeric and dates. These can be broken down further, for input validation purposes, to include the following type declarations:

$$
\begin{array}{ll}
\text{Alphanumeric} & \left\{ \begin{array}{l} \text{ALPHANUMERIC} \\ \text{ALPHABETIC} \\ \text{NON-NUMERIC} \end{array} \right. \\[1em]
\text{Numeric} & \left\{ \begin{array}{l} \text{INTEGER} \\ \text{DECIMAL} \end{array} \right. \\[1em]
\text{Dates} & \left\{ \begin{array}{l} \text{DATE} \end{array} \right.
\end{array}
$$

Alphanumeric items contain textual strings consisting of alphabetic characters, numeric digits and all of the standard special symbols and signs. An alphanumeric item may be as short as a single letter or as long as many paragraphs of text. All items are assumed to be ALPHANUMERIC, unless declared otherwise.

Numeric items can be input as either simple INTEGER or DECIMAL quantities, or they can be defined using different units of measurements. For example, it is possible to declare that a given item is to be:

DECIMAL WITH UNITS, 1YR = 52WK, 1WK = 7D, 1D = 24HR, 1HR = 60MIN,

1MIN = 60SEC

This declaration results in the generation of a set of equations for the calculation and storage of this decimal item in terms of its smallest declared unit, in this case, seconds (SEC). An instance of this item, input as 1WK, 5.5HR, would be converted and stored as the decimal quantity:

$$1 \times 7 \times 24 \times 60 \times 60 + 5.5 \times 60 \times 60 = 624{,}600.0$$

Date items are converted to a numeric, internal form in units of days, which permits their use in calculations. For example, it is possible to subtract two dates to derive a time interval in number of days. Each date item is also maintained in its original input format for report generation. Acceptable input forms for date items are:

MAY 11, 1974   MAY 11 1974   11MAY1974   11 MAY 1974

11MAY74   11 MAY 74   5-11-74   5/11/74   5 11 74

The United States convention of month/day/year is the standard in RIQS. However, this can be modified to the European convention with the declaration:

DATE WITH FORMAT DD/MM/YY

It is also possible to input a date item as TODAY, yielding the value of the current date.

The RIQS system allows for the specification of a non-existent numeric or date item by the use of the value NULL (or any other word beginning with N). However, currently the system does not permit the use of the word NULL in a search specification. This is a planned extension to the search language.

GROUPS

The only group capability provided by RIQS is the multiple item, made up of a sequence of like-valued, simple subitems. As will be seen in the data definition discussion which follows, multiple items are so specified using the declaration MULTIPLE. An example would be:

(7) AUTHOR(S)

MULTIPLE (7)

An instance of this multiple item might be:

(7) B. MITTMAN * L. BORMAN

with the subitems being separated by an asterisk on input, or by any other specified separator.

By means of a search language facility, it is possible to associate related subitems within different multiple items. This facility has allowed for RIQS to be applied to most applications which require tree structures. Examples will be given in the section on searching with RIQS. The lack of a more complex, hierarchical, repeating group structure within RIQS has not been a significant deterrent to its application in many areas, as will be seen in Part II. In any future redesign of RIQS, however, nested repeating groups would be incorporated.

RECORDS AND FILES

A complete record schema in RIQS consists of specification of the item numbers, identifiers and names. This is followed by the respective item types, including any units equations which may apply to numeric items.

A file is created by entering the record schema, followed by the input of an initial set of record instances. Only one file at a time may be processed by RIQS. The next section will give examples of the data definition and file creation process for three sample files which we shall utilize to illustrate various retrieval processing, updating, indexing and reporting features of RIQS.

DATA DEFINITION AND FILE CREATION

We have chosen three separate applications of personalized data base processing to illustrate RIQS. The reasons for this are to present simple record structures for illustrative purposes, and to present fairly typical bibliographic, textual, and data management applications. The three applications which we have chosen are:

A bibliographic data base of computer science literature[10]

A restaurant guide to dining in Chicago[11]

A small subset of statistical data from 136 countries of the world.[12]

ACM File

The ACM file contains bibliographic information about articles which have appeared in the *Communications* and *Journal of the Association for Computing Machinery*. In addition to the usual author, title, journal, volume, issue and page number information, these records contain an alphanumeric item called REFERENCE CODE which provides an abbreviated version of the journal name, volume number, issue number, date and page number of the article. Also included are a full abstract, a set of author-supplied index terms, and standard ACM classification categories for the specific areas of computer science. Figure 2.1 shows the record schema for the ACM file and some sample record instances. The ACM file will be used later to illustrate some of the bibliographic retrieval, indexing, and reporting features of RIQS.

Note that items (9) – (12) are multiple, alphanumeric items relating to each author's name and affiliation information. The only other multiple item is (15), the CACM category codes, which are decimal quantities.

RESTAURANT File

The *Chicago Guide*, a publication of WFMT, Chicago's fine arts radio station, is an invaluable aid to the gourmet and gourmand population of the city because of its popular monthly listing of restaurants. The future role of personalized data base processing in one's everyday life may well be illustrated by the sample applications of an on-line, RESTAURANT data base which we shall present later in this chapter. The RESTAURANT file contains all of the data which are published about selected dining spots including name, address, type of cuisine, and a paragraph of description which includes specialties and ambience. In addition, all of the important data about open days and hours, average price, credit cards accepted, etc. are also available. Figure 2.2 presents the record schema and representative record instances.

All of the items are alphanumeric, except the typical price which is decimal. Multiple items are used to associate the addresses, days and hours open, locations, and telephone numbers of those restaurants with multiple locations (see Record 20, Bishop's Chili Hut).

WORLD HANDBOOK 2 File

An invaluable source of cross-national data is the *World Handbook of Political and Social Indicators II*, collected at Yale University and distributed by the Inter-University Consortium for Political Research located at the University of Michigan.[13] The collection consists of aggregate data for variables relating to politics, education, economics, health, etc. for 136 nations, including those having a population of one million or more in 1965,

```
ITEM NUMBERS AND NAMES
----------------------

 1.   REFERENCE CODE
 2.   RECORD NUMBER
 3.   PUBLICATION NAME
 4.   VOLUME NUMBER
 5.   ISSUE NUMBER
 6.   DATE OF PUBLICATION
 7.   BEGINNING PAGE
 8.   TITLE OF ARTICLE
 9.   AUTHOR
10.   AUTHORS AFFILIATION
11.   AFFILIATION CITY
12.   AFFILIATION STATE
13.   ABSTRACT OF ARTICLE
14.   AUTHOR SUPPLIED KEYWORDS
15.   CACM CATEGORIES


ITEM DESCRIPTIONS
-----------------

 1.   SIMPLE, ALPHANUMERIC
 2.   SIMPLE, INTEGER
 3.   SIMPLE, ALPHANUMERIC
 4.   SIMPLE, INTEGER
 5.   SIMPLE, INTEGER
 6.   SIMPLE, DATE
 7.   SIMPLE, INTEGER
```

```
RECORD NUMBER   1
     (1) C11010168015
     (2) 001
     (3) CACM
     (4) 11
     (5) 01
     (6) 01/68
     (7) 015
     (8) TOWARD A GENERAL PROCESSOR FOR PROGRAMMING LANGUAGES
     (9) HALPERN MARK I.
    (10) INTERNATIONAL BUSINESS MACHINES CORPORATION
    (11) SAN JOSE
    (12) CALIFORNIA
    (13) MANY EFFORTS HAVE BEEN MADE TO DEVELOP A BETTER WAY OF
         IMPLEMENTING A HIGHER LEVEL PROGRAMMING LANGUAGE THAN BY THE
         CONSTRUCTION OF A WHOLE NEW COMPILER, BUT SO FAR NONE HAS PROVED
         GENERALLY SATISFACTORY.  IN THIS PAPER, IT IS CONTENDED THAT A
         PROGRAMMING LANGUAGE IS BEST DESCRIBED FUNCTIONALLY AS A BODY OF
         MACRO INSTRUCTIONS, AND THAT THE MACRO CALL CONSTITUTES A
         CANONICAL FORM IN TERMS OF WHICH A PROGRAMMING NOTATION MAY BE
         DESCRIBED.  A SUPPORTING DISCUSSION OF THE LOGICAL AND HISTORICAL
         ROLE OF THE MACRO INSTRUCTION IS PRESENTED.  ALSO DISCUSSED ARE
         THE CONFLICT BETWEEN MACHINE INDEPENDENCE AND OBJECT PROGRAM
         EFFICIENCY, AND THE QUESTION OF WHERE THE GREATEST DIFFICULTIES
         LIE IN COMPILER CONSTRUCTION.
    (14) PROGRAMMING LANGUAGE TRANSLATOR, PROGRAMMING LANGUAGE
         PROCESSOR, GENERAL TRANSLATOR, GENERAL PROCESSOR, MACRO
         INSTRUCTION PROCESSOR, META PROCESSOR, META COMPILER, META
         LANGUAGE TRANSLATOR, META LANGUAGE PROCESSOR, COMPILER -
         COMPILER, COMPILER WRITING SYSTEM, TRANSLATOR WRITING SYSTEM
    (15) 4.10 * 4.11 * 4.12 * 4.20

RECORD NUMBER   2
     (1) C11010168003
```

```
 8.  SIMPLE, ALPHANUMERIC
 9.  MULTIPLE, ALPHANUMERIC
10.  MULTIPLE, ALPHANUMERIC
11.  MULTIPLE, ALPHANUMERIC
12.  MULTIPLE, ALPHANUMERIC
13.  SIMPLE, ALPHANUMERIC
14.  SIMPLE, ALPHANUMERIC
15.  MULTIPLE, DECIMAL
```

```
(2)  002
(3)  CACM
(4)  11
(5)  01
(6)  01/68
(7)  003
(8)  EXPLORATORY EXPERIMENTAL STUDIES COMPARING ONLINE AND OFFLINE
     PROGRAMMING PERFORMANCE
(9)  SACKMAN H. * ERIKSON W. J. * GRANT E. E.
(10) SYSTEM DEVELOPMENT CORPORATION * SYSTEM DEVELOPMENT
     CORPORATION * SYSTEM DEVELOPMENT CORPORATION
(11) SANTA MONICA * SANTA MONICA * SANTA MONICA
(12) CALIFORNIA * CALIFORNIA * CALIFORNIA
(13) TWO EXPLORATORY EXPERIMENTS WERE CONDUCTED AT SYSTEM
     DEVELOPMENT CORPORATION TO COMPARE DEBUGGING PERFORMANCE OF
     PROGRAMMERS WORKING UNDER CONDITIONS OF ONLINE AND OFFLINE ACCESS
     TO A COMPUTER.  THESE ARE THE FIRST KNOWN STUDIES THAT MEASURE
     PROGRAMMERS' PERFORMANCE UNDER CONTROLLED CONDITIONS FOR
     STANDARD TASKS.  STATISTICALLY SIGNIFICANT RESULTS OF BOTH
     EXPERIMENTS INDICATED FASTER DEBUGGING UNDER ONLINE CONDITIONS,
     BUT PERHAPS THE MOST IMPORTANT PRACTICAL FINDING INVOLVES THE
     STRIKING INDIVIDUAL DIFFERENCES IN PROGRAMMER PERFORMANCE.
     METHODOLOGICAL PROBLEMS ENCOUNTERED IN DESIGNING AND CONDUCTING
     THESE EXPERIMENTS ARE DESCRIBED, LIMITATIONS OF THE FINDINGS ARE
     POINTED OUT, HYPOTHESES ARE PRESENTED TO ACCOUNT FOR RESULTS,
     AND SUGGESTIONS ARE MADE FOR FURTHER RESEARCH.
(14) ONLINE VS. OFFLINE PERFORMANCE, PROGRAMMER / COMPUTER
     COMMUNICATION, PROGRAMMING EXPERIMENTAL - EMPIRICAL STUDIES,
     PROGRAMMING COST EFFECTIVENESS, PROGRAMMING PERFORMANCE,
     DEBUGGING EFFECTIVENESS, TIME SHARING VS. BATCH PROCESSING,
     FACTOR ANALYSIS APPLICATION, PROGRAMMER TRAINEE PERFORMANCE,
     BASIC PROGRAMMING KNOWLEDGE TEST, EXPERIENCED PROGRAMMER STUDY,
     ANALYSIS OF VARIANCE, PROGRAMMER INDIVIDUAL DIFFERENCES
(15) 2.40
```

Figure 2.1. ACM file, record schema and sample instances.

```
ITEM NUMBERS AND NAMES
----------------------

    1.   NAME    ...NAME
    2.   ADDRESS...ADDRESS
    3.   TYPE    ...TYPE ØF CUISINE
    4.   DESC    ...DESCRIPTIØN FRØM CHICAGØ GUIDE
    5.   HØURS   ...DAYS AND HØURS ØPEN
    6.   CHILD   ...CHILDREN'S SEATING: CHILDREN/CHILD
    7.   CARDS   ...CREDIT CARDS: A=AMEX,B=BKAMER,C=CARTE,D=DINERS,M=MASCH
    8.   PRICE   ...PRICE:EXPENSIVE,$$, INEXPENSIVE,CC.IF NULL,IS $3 TØ $6
    9.   PARKING ...FREE PARKING: PARKING/P
   10.   RESERVE ...RESERVATIØNS REQUIRED: RESERVATIØNS/R
   11.   TYPRICE ...TYPICAL PRICE (FEB 74)
   12.   LØCATN  ...LØCATIØN: CHICAGØ LØØP,N,S,W. SUBURBS N,S,W
   13.   PHØNE   ...TELEPHØNE NUMBER


ITEM DESCRIPTIØNS
-----------------

    1.   SIMPLE, ALPHANUMERIC
    2.   MULTIPLE, ALPHANUMERIC
    3.   SIMPLE, ALPHANUMERIC
    4.   SIMPLE, ALPHANUMERIC
    5.   MULTIPLE, ALPHANUMERIC
    6.   SIMPLE, ALPHANUMERIC
    7.   SIMPLE, ALPHANUMERIC
    8.   SIMPLE, ALPHANUMERIC
    9.   SIMPLE, ALPHANUMERIC
   10.   SIMPLE, ALPHANUMERIC
   11.   SIMPLE, DECIMAL
   12.   MULTIPLE, ALPHANUMERIC
   13.   MULTIPLE, ALPHANUMERIC


RECØRD NUMBER    10
     (1) THE BAKERY
     (2) 2218 N LINCØLN
     (3) CØNTINENTAL
     (4) EXCELLENT FØØD AND EFFICIENT WAITERS ARE THE HALLMARKS ØF
     THIS LIVELY,EVER-FULL RESTAURANT.CØMPLETE 5-CØURSE DINNERS ARE
     $10 AND START WITH FRESH,CRISP BREAD WITH BUTTER CURLS AND PATE
     AND END WITH A CHØICE ØF FØUR ØR FIVE DESSERTS.SPECIAL DISHES ARE
     SERVED WEEKNIGHTS(IN ADDITIØN TØ BEEF WELLINGTØN,DUCK WITH CHERRY
     SAUCE,AND ØTHER PØPULAR EVERYNIGHT DISHES).SEASØNALLY YØU'LL FIND
     RØAST QUAIL ØR PARTRIDGE,STUFFED LAMB,VEAL
     SCALLØPINI,BUILLABAISSE...ØR ØRDER AHEAD ANY DISH YØU WANT
     PREPARED(AT SPECIAL PRICING).THIS INCLUDES SPECIAL DESSERTS LIKE
     CREPES(ØVER 100 KINDS),SØUFFLES,BAKED ALASKA.WEEKDAYS GUESTS ARE
     ØFTEN TREATED TØ A CØMPLIMENTARY CØURSE.SERVICE IS ØFTEN TØØ
     QUICKLY PACED-REQUEST MØRE TIME THAN USUAL WHEN RESERVING,IF YØU
     WANT TØ TARRY.  SELECTIØN ØF WINES,ØR BRING YØUR ØWN(25C CHARGE
     FØR GLASSWARE).
     (5) TUE-THU 5-11 PM;FRI,SAT TØ MIDNIGHT.
     (6) CHILDREN * CHILD
     (8) EXPENSIVE * $$
     (10) RESERVATIØNS * R
     (11) 10.00
     (12) CHICAGØ NØRTH
     (13) 472-6942


RECØRD NUMBER    20
     (1) BISHØP'S CHILI HUT
     (2) 1958 W 18TH * 7220 W RØØSEVELT * 250 N CASS, WESTMØNT
     (3) ØTHER/CHILI
     (4) THIS IMMACULATE SPØT SERVES GREAT CHILI AND CHILI MAC TØ EAT
     THERE,TØ GØ,ØR FRØZEN.VISITØRS REMEMBER THE WIREBACKED 'CØKE'
     CHAIRS AND BØTTLES ØF PEPPERS IN VINEGAR AND TABASCØ SAUCE ØN THE
     TABLES.HEINEKEN'S AND DØMESTIC BEER ØN TAP.(RØØSEVELT IS DRY,BUT
     HAS GREAT RØØT BEER.
     (5) MØN-SAT 9-7:30 * MØN-SAT 9-1,SUN 12-12 * 9 AM-1 AM
     MØN-SAT,SUN 12-9
     (6) CHILDREN * CHILD
     (8) INEXPENSIVE * CC
     (9) FREE PARKING * P
     (12) CHICAGØ SØUTH * CHICAGØ WEST * SUBURBS WEST
     (13) 829-6345 * 366-4420 * 852-5974
```

Figure 2.2. RESTAURANT file, record schema and sample instances.

and those smaller nations having membership in the United Nations by 1968. The data represent some 300 different variables giving annual aggregations collected at five-year intervals.

A RIQS file has been prepared directly from the World Handbook data for a small subset of variables. For each country the following variables were extracted (some data are missing for certain countries) for each of four years, 1950, 1955, 1960 and 1965:

TOTAL POPULATION (in thousands)

POPULATION GROWTH RATE (during 1950-1955, 1955-1960, 1960-1965, and 1950-1965)

LIFE EXPECTANCY (usually for female population only)

LITERACY RATE (percentage of total population over 15 years who can both read and write)

STUDENTS IN HIGHER EDUCATION (per one million population)

ENERGY CONSUMPTION/CAPITA (gross consumption of commercial fuels and water power, expressed in million metric tons of coal equivalent)

GROSS NATIONAL PRODUCT (in millions of constant 1965 U.S. dollars)

PHYSICIANS (per one million population)

The other variables which could have been extracted concern total area, density, birth and death rates, urban population, telephones, letter mail, newspapers, radios, televisions, cinema attendance, educational enrollments, religious life, foreign trade, industrial characteristics, nutrition levels, military and defense expenditures, foreign aid, diplomatic representation, political composition, and modernization.

Figure 2.3 presents the record schema and some sample record instances. All the items except the country names and codes are multiple, decimal valued items (with one subitem for each of the four time periods).

Update Facilities

As is shown in Figure 2.3, a unique record number is assigned to each record instance as it is processed. The update phase of the RIQS processor permits new records to be appended to a file and existing records to be modified or deleted. Deletion is done logically rather than physically, so that deleted records may be restored at a later date, if desired. To delete, restore or modify records, specific record numbers must be used. Thus, RIQS only provides for specific update by record number, and does not allow selective retrieval, via a search command, followed by update.

The update commands are:

$$*GET\ RECORD\ n_1$$
$$*DELETE\ RECORDS\ n_1, n_2, \ldots, n_n$$
$$*RESTORE\ RECORDS\ n_1, n_2, \ldots, n_n$$

The *GET RECORD n_1 command causes the record with number n_1 to be retrieved from the data base. Any item instances following the *GET RECORD command will replace the corresponding items already in record n_1. All other items will be left unchanged.

As an example, to add the typical price, item (11), for Bishop's Chili Hut (Figure 2.2) (where that item had not been included in the initial file creation), and to correct the

```
ITEM NUMBERS AND NAMES
----------------------


     1.   COUNTRY NAME
     2.   COUNTRY CODE
     3.   TOTAL POPULATION (* 1,000)
     4.   POPULATION GROWTH RATES
     5.   LIFE EXPECTANCY
     6.   LITERACY RATES
     7.   STUDENTS IN HIGHER EDUCATION (PER 1,000,000 POPULATION)
     8.   ENERGY CONSUMPTION / CAPITA
     9.   GROSS NATIONAL PRODUCT (* $1,000,000)
    10.   PHYSICIANS (PER 1,000,000 POPULATION)


ITEM DESCRIPTIONS
-----------------


     1.   SIMPLE, ALPHANUMERIC
     2.   SIMPLE, DECIMAL
     3.   MULTIPLE, DECIMAL
     4.   MULTIPLE, DECIMAL
     5.   MULTIPLE, DECIMAL
     6.   MULTIPLE, DECIMAL
     7.   MULTIPLE, DECIMAL
     8.   MULTIPLE, DECIMAL
     9.   MULTIPLE, DECIMAL
    10.   MULTIPLE, DECIMAL




RECORD NUMBER      1
    (1) UNITED STATES
    (2) 2.
    (3.1) 152271.   (3.2) 165931.    (3.3) 180684.    (3.4) 194572.
    (4.1) 1.70      (4.2) 1.70       (4.3) 1.50       (4.4) 1.60
    (5.1) 999.90    (5.2) 72.50      (5.3) 999.90     (5.4) 73.70
    (6.1) 96.80     (6.2) 999.90     (6.3) 97.80      (6.4) 99.00
    (7.1) 15082.30  (7.2) 16057.10   (7.3) 19828.70   (7.4) 28400.00
    (8.1) 7675.0    (8.2) 7755.0     (8.3) 8047.0     (8.4) 9201.0
    (9.1) 393900.0  (9.2) 485600.0   (9.3) 540800.0   (9.4) 695500.0
    (10.1) 1321.8   (10.2) 1253.1    (10.3) 1275.0    (10.4) 1438.6


RECORD NUMBER      2
    (1) PUERTO RICO
    (2) 6.
    (3.1) 2218.     (3.2) 2250.      (3.3) 2362.      (3.4) 2633.
    (4.1) .30       (4.2) 1.00       (4.3) 2.20       (4.4) 1.10
    (5.1) 999.90    (5.2) 69.60      (5.3) 71.90      (5.4) 999.90
    (6.1) 73.30     (6.2) 999.90     (6.3) 80.60      (6.4) 9999.90
    (7.1) 5484.70   (7.2) 7835.10    (7.3) 11023.70   (7.4) 15300.00
    (8.1) 480.0     (8.2) 834.0      (8.3) 1453.0     (8.4) 2125.0
    (9.1) 999999.0  (9.2) 999999.0   (9.3) 999999.0   (9.4) 3038.0
    (10.1) 301.2    (10.2) 713.3     (10.3) 456.1     (10.4) 762.2


RECORD NUMBER      3
    (1) CANADA
    (2) 20.
    (3.1) 13737.    (3.2) 15736.     (3.3) 17909.     (3.4) 19604.
    (4.1) 2.70      (4.2) 2.60       (4.3) 1.80       (4.4) 2.40
    (5.1) 999.90    (5.2) 72.90      (5.3) 74.20      (5.4) 999.90
    (6.1) 999.90    (6.2) 999.90     (6.3) 999.90     (6.4) 99.00
    (7.1) 5931.60   (7.2) 5654.80    (7.3) 7931.80    (7.4) 16510.00
    (8.1) 6470.0    (8.2) 5279.0     (8.3) 5663.0     (8.4) 7653.0
    (9.1) 24900.0   (9.2) 31200.0    (9.3) 36800.0    (9.4) 48473.0
    (10.1) 1062.5   (10.2) 1045.7    (10.3) 1060.9    (10.4) 1109.6


RECORD NUMBER      4
    (1) CUBA
    (2) 40.
    (3.1) 5516.     (3.2) 6148.      (3.3) 6826.      (3.4) 7631.
    (4.1) 2.20      (4.2) 2.10       (4.3) 2.20       (4.4) 2.20
    (5.1) 999.90    (5.2) 999.90     (5.3) 999.90     (5.4) 999.90
    (6.1) 999.90    (6.2) 77.90      (6.3) 75.00      (6.4) 9999.90
    (7.1) 3640.00   (7.2) 3948.10    (7.3) 2918.30    (7.4) 4000.00
    (8.1) 480.0     (8.2) 643.0      (8.3) 847.0      (8.4) 950.0
    (9.1) 999999.0  (9.2) 999999.0   (9.3) 999999.0   (9.4) 3000.0
    (10.1) 549.8    (10.2) 1001.1    (10.3) 968.2     (10.4) 807.2
```

Figure 2.3.   WORLD HANDBOOK 2 file, record schema and sample instances.

telephone number for the branch location, item (13.2), one would input the following commands:

```
RIQS
ACCESS RESTAURANT FILE
UPDATES
*GET RECORD 20
(11) 2.50
(13.2) 366-4421
```

No other changes would be made to record 20 except the specified addition of item (11) and modification of subitem (13.2).

The *DELETE and *RESTORE commands deactivate and reactivate selected records in a file. The commands,

```
RIQS
ACCESS ACM FILE
UPDATES
*DELETE RECORDS 7, 12, 24, 4, 92, 64, 415
*RESTORE RECORDS 401, 42
```

would have the effect of deleting the seven records indicated and restoring two.

Interrogation, Computational, Statistical and Graphical Features

Once a file has been created, it is then accessible, either on-line or in a batch processing mode, by means of the SEARCH phase of the RIQS processor for selective retrieval, report generation, graphical plot generation, computation, and linking to a statistical program called SPSS, Statistical Package for the Social Sciences.[14] The interactive, time-sharing version of RIQS is called RIQSONLINE.

As indicated earlier, RIQS processes one file at a time. Once the selected file has been loaded, searching and processing can proceed. If requested, the system first provides a description of the file by displaying all or part of the record schema. Then, the user may begin entering queries.

Queries may contain conditional expressions beginning with the word IF; they may contain output commands such as DISPLAY or PRINT; they may contain request set creation and deletion commands, PLACE and RELEASE; they may contain arithmetic assignment statements, introduced with the word LET; they may contain a linkage command to the statistical analysis programs, SPSSLINK; they may contain the graphical command PLOT. Rather than present details of the RIQS syntax, we shall use a number of example queries to illustrate the interrogation, computational, statistical and plotting capabilities of RIQSONLINE.

TEXT SEARCH AND RELATIONAL OPERATORS

Perhaps the most common use of RIQS is for retrieval and output generation using search text and relational arithmetic operators. We shall utilize the RESTAURANT file to present some examples. Conditional expressions may use the relational operators CONTAINS or EQ (equals) for text matching on alphanumeric items, and EQ (equal), NE (not equal), LT (less than), GT (greater than), LE (less than or equal), and GE (greater than or equal) for testing arithmetic equalities and inequalities within numeric or date items. The subject of the conditional expression may be either an item number or an item identifier. The following two queries are illustrated in Figures 2.4 and 2.5.

IF #3 EQ 'ITALIAN' AND #12 CONTAINS 'CHICAGO LOOP'

DISPLAY ACROSS RECORD   END

IF #DESC CONTAINS 'GEFILTE FISH' AND #TYPRICE LE 4.00

DISPLAY ACROSS #1 #2 #3 #13   END

The first example illustrates a complex condition using the logical connective AND to combine two simple conditions; OR and NOT may also be used. The subjects of the conditions are item numbers for type of cuisine (#3) and location (#12). The DISPLAY command instructs the system to type the entire record *across* the output page, i.e., printing all of the item values, following one another, filling up each line with text. If ACROSS were not specified, each separate item would begin a new line. Other display

```
ENTER SEARCH COMMAND OR TYPE HALT

? IF #3 EQ 'ITALIAN' AND #12 CONTAINS 'CHICAGO LOOP'
? DISPLAY ACROSS RECORD END

SEARCHING INITIATED


NO. OF REPORTS ON DISPLAY FILE =     6

DO YOU WANT THE DISPLAY REPORTS LISTED
? Y


RECORD NUMBER    2
     (1) ADOLPH'S (2) 1045 N RUSH (3) ITALIAN (4) SATISFYING ITALIAN
     AND AMERICAN ENTREES, SERVED A LA CARTE OR AS COMPLETE DINNERS
     THAT AVERAGE AROUND $6.  (STEAK AND CHOP ITEMS ARE GENERALLY A
     LITTLE HIGHER.) PORTIONS ARE HUGE AND WITH THE COMPLETE DINNER
     YOU ARE OFFERED SHRIMP COCKTAIL,BLUE POINTS, OR CHERRYSTONE CLAMS
     AT NO EXTRA COST.   WAITERS ARE SWIFT AND ATTENTIVE.   WINE LIST IS
     ORDINARY BUY PRICED ACCORDINGLY.  LATER IN THE EVENING THE TRIO
     BEGINS, CONVENTIONEERS AND OUT-OF-TOWNERS ARRIVE IN BIG GROUPS
     AND THINGS GET A LITTLE NOISY. (5) DAILY 4 PM-4 AM. (6) CHILDREN
     * CHILD (7) A B C D M (10) RESERVATIONS * R (11) 6.00 (12)
     CHICAGO LOOP (13) 337-7313


RECORD NUMBER    3
     (1) AGOSTINO'S (2) 7 E DELAWARE (3) ITALIAN (4) THOROUGHLY
     COMPLETE AND SATISFYING MEALS.   TABLE D'HOTE DINNERS
     ($5.25-$8.75) INCLUDE APPETIZERS (NO EXTRA CHARGE FOR PROSCIUTTO
     AND MELON, ANTIPASTO, OR MOLLUSKS, EITHER), SOUP, SALAD, ENTREE,
     COFFEE,DESSERT3 CHEESES,TORTONI,MELON,CAKES,SHERBERT,OR FRUITS).
```

Figure 2.4. Text search.

```
ENTER SEARCH CØMMAND ØR TYPE HALT

? IF #DESC CØNTAINS 'GEFILTE FISH' AND #TYPRICE LE 4.00
? DISPLAY ACRØSS #1 #2 #3 #13 END

SEARCHING INITIATED


NØ. ØF REPØRTS ØN DISPLAY FILE =     1

DØ YØU WANT THE DISPLAY REPØRTS LISTED
? YES

  RECØRD NUMBER     9
       (1) THE BAGEL (2) 4806 N KEDZIE (3) ØTHER/JEWISH (13) 463-7141


*  *  *  *  *
```

Figure 2.5. Text and arithmetic inequality search.

options permit the specification of tab settings, indentation, suppression of item number or item name printing, page eject, page width, etc.

The second example uses item identifiers, rather than item numbers, for the restaurant description and typical price items. The second condition imposes the arithmetic inequality less than or equal to on item #TYPRICE. The DISPLAY command in this example requests that only four items be printed, the name, address, type of cuisine, and telephone number.

Although there are many details not illustrated, it is clear from the above that a relatively simple language is available for relatively simple queries. The next section discussed some of the computational features of RIQS.

COMPUTATIONAL FEATURES

RIQS provides for the evaluation of arithmetic expressions and the definition of user-named variables by means of the LET command. A LET statement can be used to assign either a numeric or string value to a variable. Examples are:

$$LET\ VAR1 = 1.0$$

$$LET\ Y = \text{'ITALIAN'}$$

$$LET\ PRICE = PRICE + \#11$$

In the first example, VAR1 has been assigned the numeric value 1.0. In the second example, Y has been assigned the alphanumeric string value 'ITALIAN'; thus, the following two conditional expressions would be equivalent:

$$IF\ \#3\ EQ\ \text{'ITALIAN'}$$

and

$$IF\ \#3\ EQ\ Y$$

In the final example, the arithmetic expression contains one term, which is a variable, and the second term, which is an item number. Thus, the values of numeric or date items can be used in computation. The effect of the third example would be to accumulate all of the values of the typical price item into a variable called PRICE. Figure 2.6 shows how this feature could be used to calculate the average typical price listed in the dining guide.

```
ENTER SEARCH CØMMAND ØR TYPE HALT

? IF #11 GT 0 LET PRICE = PRICE + #11, LET CØUNT = CØUNT + 1
? AFTER SEARCH LET AVPRICE = PRICE / CØUNT
? DISPLAY 'AVERAGE TYPICAL PRICE =  ' AVPRICE
? END

SEARCHING INITIATED

AFTER SEARCH
    AVERAGE TYPICAL PRICE =
    6.75
```

* * * * *

Figure 2.6. Computation example.

Since there are many records for which the typical price is not included, the search command first eliminates missing data by requiring that the typical price must be greater than zero. Then, for each selected record, the prices and count are accumulated. After scanning the entire file (AFTER SEARCH), the average price is computed and displayed.

REQUEST SETS

The importance of request sets was discussed in Chapter 1. In RIQS, request sets may be formed by the user via an explicit set command. Request sets are not automatically generated by RIQS, as they are in BASIS-70 (see examples in Chapter 1) and in many other bibliographic retrieval systems.

The RIQS processor allows sets of records to be defined through the use of the PLACE or PUT command. If a PLACE command occurs among the actions to be taken when an IF condition is satisfied, all records which satisfy that condition are placed in the specified set. Up to 34 sets are available, numbered 1 to 34. An example of forming a set is:

IF #3 EQ 'ITALIAN' PLACE IN SET 1

An example of using a set is:

BEGIN SEARCH OF SET 1 DISPLAY #1

An example using the RESTAURANT file is found in Figure 2.7.

In addition to searching single request sets, RIQS permits search of the union, intersection and complement of sets, by means of commands such as:

BEGIN SEARCH OF UNION OF (1,2,3)

BEGIN SEARCH OF INTERSECTION OF (4,5,6)

BEGIN SEARCH OF COMPLEMENT OF (7)

At any time, previously defined sets may be released, as follows:

BEFORE SEARCH RELEASE SETS 1, 2

USE OF MULTIPLE ITEMS

RIQS provides the facility to access associated subitems from related multiple items. This is accomplished through the FOR N = 1 to P command, which allows for the iterative execution of one or more RIQS statements. For example, the addresses, locations and

```
ENTER SEARCH CØMMAND ØR TYPE HALT

? IF #3 EQ 'CØNTINENTAL' PLACE IN SET 1;
? IF #3 EQ 'FRENCH' PLACE IN SET 2;
? IF #3 EQ 'GREEK/MIDDLE EASTERN' PLACE IN SET 3;
? IF #3 EQ 'ITALIAN' PLACE IN SET 4; END

SEARCHING INITIATED



NØ. ØF RECØRDS ADDED TØ SET  1 BY SEARCH =   12
NØ. ØF RECØRDS  IN  SET  1 AFTER SEARCH =   12



NØ. ØF RECØRDS ADDED TØ SET  2 BY SEARCH =   10
NØ. ØF RECØRDS  IN  SET  2 AFTER SEARCH =   10



NØ. ØF RECØRDS ADDED TØ SET  3 BY SEARCH =    3
NØ. ØF RECØRDS  IN  SET . 3 AFTER SEARCH =    3



NØ. ØF RECØRDS ADDED TØ SET  4 BY SEARCH =    9
NØ. ØF RECØRDS  IN  SET  4 AFTER SEARCH =    9


* * * * *


  BEGIN SEARCH ØF SET 2 DISPLAY ACRØSS SUPPRESS
? #NAME TAB 20 #ADDRESS END

SEARCHING INITIATED


NØ. ØF REPØRTS ØN DISPLAY FILE =    10

DØ YØU WANT THE DISPLAY REPØRTS LISTED
? Y


        L'AUBERGE           2324 N CLARK
        LE BASTILLE         21 W SUPERIØR
        LE BØRDEAUX         3 W MADISØN
        CAFE DE PARIS       1260 N DEARBØRN
        LA CHEMINEE         1161 N DEARBØRN
        CHEZ PAUL           660 N RUSH
        THE CØNSØRT         CØNTINENTAL PLAZA HØTEL 909 N MICHIGAN
        L'ESCARGØT          2925 N HALSTED
        LA FØNTAINE         2442 N CLARK
        LE FRANCIS -        269 S MILWAUKEE,WHEELING


* * * * *

ENTER SEARCH CØMMAND ØR TYPE HALT

? BEGIN SEARCH ØF SET 3 DISPLAY ACRØSS SUPPRESS #NAME TAB 20 #ADDRESS ED

SEARCHING INITIATED


NØ. ØF REPØRTS ØN DISPLAY FILE =     3

DØ YØU WANT THE DISPLAY REPØRTS LISTED
? Y


        DIANA               310 S HALSTED
        EFFENDI             1525 E 53RD ST
        FAMILY HØUSE        2425 W LAWRENCE


* * * * *
```

Figure 2.7.   Request sets.

telephone number items of the RESTAURANT file are declared as MULTIPLE. Bishop's Chili Hut in record 20 has three separate locations (see Figure 2.2). Figure 2.8 illustrates how all of this information could be displayed from record 20 using the FOR command. The statement:

FOR N = 1 TO 3 DISPLAY #2.N #12.N #13.N

iterates through the first three subitems of the appropriate multiple items, displaying the required information.

```
     BEGIN SEARCH ØF RECØRD 20
?  DISPLAY ACRØSS SUPPRESS #1
?  FØR N = 1 TØ 3
?  DISPLAY ACRØSS SUPPRESS #2.N TAB 25 #12.N TAB 40 #13.N END

SEARCHING INITIATED




     BISHØP'S CHILI HUT
     1958 W 18TH           CHICAGØ SØUTH  829-6345
     7220 W RØØSEVELT      CHICAGØ WEST   366-4420
     250 N CASS, WESTMØNT  SUBURBS WEST   852-5974




*  *  *  *  *
```

Figure 2.8.   Use of FOR command for multiple items.

In addition to allowing explicit definition of the loop variable (e.g., $N = 1$ TO 3), the system allows for all subitems of a specified item to be scanned by use of the command FOR N = 1 TO LAST. An example is:

FOR N = 1 TO LAST DISPLAY #2.N

It should be pointed out that any defined variable may be used in place of N in the FOR command. In the next section, we shall see how the FOR command is used in statistical and graphical applications.

STATISTICAL AND GRAPHICAL FEATURES

The ability to perform statistical analysis on retrieved data and to display plots and graphs in an interactive mode is one of the most powerful features of RIQSONLINE. Through the SPSSFILE command, the user can produce a file of retrieved data, which is formatted for processing by SPSS, the Statistical Package for the Social Sciences. Northwestern University has developed an interactive version of SPSS, called SPSSONLINE,[15] which can be accessed through RIQS via the SPSSLINK command. SPSSONLINE provides many statistical procedures including CONDESCRIPTIVE (descriptive statistics for continuous data including mean, standard error, standard deviation, variance, kurtosis, skewness, range, minimum and maximum), CODEBOOK (one way frequency distributions, simple frequencies and relative frequencies with missing values included, and histograms), CROSSTABS, FASTABS, and BREAKDOWN (cross tabulations and related statistics for two or more variables), PEARSON CORR, NONPAR CORR, and PARTIAL CORR (product-moment or zero order correlations, Spearman and/or Kendall rank-order correlations, and partial correlation), SCATTERGRAM (graph of relationship between two variables), etc. In addition, SPSSONLINE provides for the recoding of data, variable transformations, and the sampling, selecting and weighting of data.

We shall illustrate some of the SPSS capabilities using the WORLD HANDBOOK 2 file (see Figure 2.3).

Let us examine the variables for population (#3), life expectancy (#5) and gross national product (#9) to determine the nature of the relationship between gross national product per capita and life expectancy. We could segment this problem in a number of ways between processing done by RIQS and processing done by SPSS. For the purpose of illustration we shall use RIQS to select only those items which have valid data for all three variables (#3 and #9 LT 999999, and #5 LT 999.9), to calculate a new variable, GNPCAP, gross national product per capita, for all valid cases, to calculate the mean GNP per capita (MEAN), and, finally, to set up an SPSS SAVEFILE with the variables GNPCAP and LIFE. Figure 2.9 illustrates this RIQS processing.

```
ENTER SEARCH CØMMAND ØR TYPE HALT

? FØR I = 1 TØ LAST
? IF #3.I LT 999999. AND #9.I LT 999999. AND #5.I LT 999.9
? LET GNPCAP = (#9.I * 1000) / #3.I,
? LET LIFE = #5.I, LET N = N + 1
? SPSSFILE 2 ØF GNPCAP, LIFE
? CALL MEAN(GNPCAP,M);LØØP
? AFTER SEARCH DISPLAY ACRØSS 'NØ. ØF VALID CASES = ' N
? END

SEARCHING INITIATED

AFTER SEARCH
     MEAN = 922.
     NØ. ØF VALID CASES = 77.0


SPSS SAVED FILE NUMBER 2 EXISTS ØN SPSSFL2
  CATALØG IT IF YØU WISH TØ RETAIN IT



*  *  *  *  *
```

Figure 2.9. RIQS processing using WORLD HANDBOOK 2 file.

SPSS will be used to calculate the correlation between GNPCAP and LIFE and to determine how life expectancy is distributed among those nations which have GNPCAP below the mean and those above the mean. This analysis is illustrated in Figure 2.10. By means of the SPSSLINK command, SPSSONLINE is accessed. First, the variable LIFE is recoded into ten categories corresponding to the ages 0-10, 10-20, 20-30, etc.The value assigned to each category is the midpoint value (e.g., 0-10 recodes to 5). Pearson correlation yields a correlation of .6927 between the two variables in question. The SELECT command segregates the cases into those below and above the mean GNPCAP ($922). The corresponding distributions are evaluated and printed by CODEBOOK, yielding a mean life expectancy of 58.6 years for nations with GNP per capita below the mean and 74.4 years for those above the mean.

```
ENTER SEARCH CØMMAND ØR TYPE HALT

? SPSSLINK 1
SPSS-ØNLINE
NEW VERSIØN-PRØGRAM LIBRARY WRITEUP NUCC296
USE ØVER 100 VARIABLES ØR ØVER 5 SUBFILES? N
USE A SAVE-FILE THIS RUN? Y
AUTØ-MØDE.


    1.00 GET FILE
    1.05 WØRLD
    5.00 RECØDE
    5.05 LIFE (0 THRU 10 = 5) (10.01 THRU 20 = 15)
    5.10 (20.01 THRU 30 = 25) (30.01 THRU 40 = 35)
    5.15 (40.01 THRU 50 = 45) (50.01 THRU 60= 55)
    5.20 (60.01 THRU 70 = 65) (70.01 THRU 80 = 75)
    5.25 (80.01 THRU 90 = 85) (90.01 THRU 100 = 95)
   10.00 PEARSØN CØRR
   10.05 LIFE WITH GNPCAP
   15.00 *SELECT IF
   15.05 (GNPCAP LT 922)
   20.00 CØDEBØØK
   20.05 LIFE
   25.00 STATISTICS
   25.05 ALL
   30.00 *SELECT IF
   30.05 (GNPCAP GE 922)
   35.00 CØDEBØØK
   35.05 LIFE
   40.00 STATISTICS
   40.05 ALL
   99.00 FINISH
? EXEC
ENTERING SPSS.
SPSSØNLINE - NØRTHWESTERN UNIVERSITY (V3.0)

- - - PEARSØN CØRRELATIØN - - -


VARIABLE PAIR         CØEFF.      N  SIG.

LIFE    GNPCAP         .6927      77  .000


- - - CØDEBØØK - - -


VARIABLE - LIFE       LIFE

VALUE LABEL    VALUE    FREQ  REL P  ADJ P  CUM P

               35.00      4    8.9    8.9    8.9
               45.00      8   17.8   17.8   26.7
               55.00      9   20.0   20.0   46.7
               65.00     16   35.6   35.6   82.2
               75.00      8   17.8   17.8  100.0
               BLANK      0     0    ****  100.0

               TØTAL     45  100.0  100.0  100.0


MEAN       58.556  STD ERR      1.830  MEDIAN      60.938
MØDE       65.000  STD DEV     12.276  VARIANCE   150.707
KURTØSIS    -.835  SKEWNESS     -.407  RANGE       40.000
MINIMUM    35.000  MAXIMUM     75.000

ØBSERVATIØNS- VALID -      45     MISSING -        0

- - - CØDEBØØK - - -


VARIABLE - LIFE       LIFE

VALUE LABEL    VALUG    FREQ  REL P  ADJ P  CUM P

               65.00      2    6.3    6.3    6.3
               75.00     30   93.8   93.8  100.0
               BLANK      0     0    ****  100.0

               TØTAL     32  100.0  100.0  100.0


MEAN       74.375  STD ERR       .435  MEDIAN      74.667
MØDE       75.000  STD DEV      2.459  VARIANCE     6.048
KURTØSIS   11.067  SKEWNESS    -3.615  RANGE       10.000
MINIMUM    65.000  MAXIMUM     75.000

ØBSERVATIØNS- VALID -      32     MISSING -        0
```

Figure 2.10. SPSS processing of derived variables GNPCAP and LIFE.

It should be pointed out that the search shown in Figure 2.9 retrieves data from all four time periods. This results in some duplication of data from the same countries at different time periods. We could have chosen only a single year to use as a basis for the correlation, but the file contained so many missing data values for life expectancy, that any single year contained too few valid combinations of GNP, population and life expectancy. We tried the year 1960 and found only 32 valid cases, yielding a mean GNP per capita of $864. Thus, we used all the valid data available in the data base, and retrieved 77 valid cases with a mean GNP per capita of $922.

In addition to the interface to SPSS, RIQS also provides built-in procedures for mean, standard deviation, and correlation. The procedure call,

CALL MEAN (GNPCAP,M)

which appears in Figure 2.9, computes the mean for the variable GNPCAP, stores the result in the variable M (not used here), and prints the mean in the AFTER SEARCH portion of the processing.

The PLOT command within RIQSONLINE provides for the plotting of any numeric information directly on a time-sharing terminal, such as a teletype, an off-line plotter, or an on-line graphics terminal.

The general format of the PLOT command is:

PLOT X-axis variable VRS Y-axis variable

These variables may be simple items, subitems of multiple items, variables, or appropriate combinations. Figure 2.11 illustrates the RIQS commands needed to produce a simple point plot of life expectancy (#5) vs. number of physicians (#10) on a teletype. The resulting teletype plot is shown in Figure 2.12.

```
ENTER SEARCH CØMMAND ØR TYPE HALT

? FØR N = 1 TØ LAST
? IF #5.N LT 999.9 AND #10.N LT 99999.9
? PLØT #5.N VRS #10.N;LØØP END

SEARCHING INITIATED




NØ. ØF RECØRDS   GENERATED TØ THE PLØT FILE =    78
NØ. ØF PØINTS    GENERATED TØ THE PLØT FILE =   121

DØ YØU WANT THE PLØT GENERATED
? Y

DØ YØU WANT A TELETYPE PLØT ØR A CALCØMP PLØT
? T

 WØULD YØU LIKE  CRT  SCALING
? N

 TYPE IN THE DESIRED TITLE FØR THE PLØT

? RIQS PLØT ØF LIFE EXPECTANCY   VS  NUMBER ØF PHYSICIANS

DØ YØU WANT THE PLØT DISPLAYED
? Y
```

Figure 2.11. PLOT command for life expectancy (#5) vs.
number of physicians (#10).

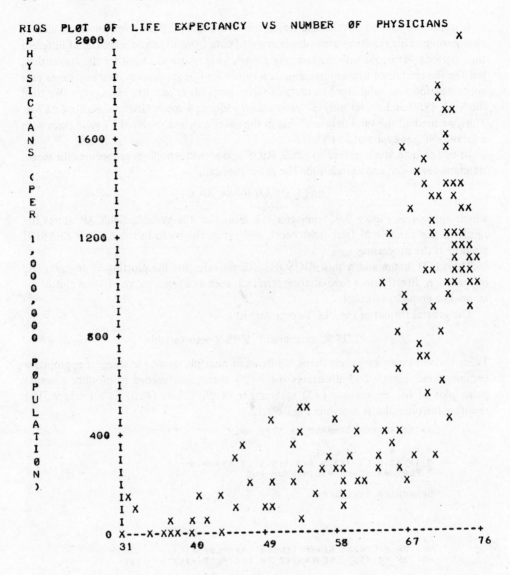

LIFE EXPECTANCY

Figure 2.12. Teletype plot generated by RIQS commands in Figure 2.11.

To gain maximum benefit from on–line graphics, a powerful, interactive plot facility has been developed for the CDC 6400 computer system and the IMLAC PDS-1 graphics terminal at Northwestern University.[16] In addition to simple point plotting, an entire range of interactive graphic capabilities is available to the user who accesses and queries RIQS files via the IMLAC terminal. The terminal consists of a keyboard, a CRT screen, and a light pen. As commands are typed on the keyboard, they are transmitted to the CDC 6400, and, simultaneously, are displayed on the screen. Results of searches are also displayed on the screen, just like on a teletype. However, the graphics terminal also permits the light pen to be used as an interaction device. With the light pen, a user may select processing options which are displayed on the screen in a so-called "menu." This selection is done by pointing the light pen at the option desired and pushing a small button on the pen itself. The interactive graphics system responds by accessing and executing the appropriate commands. Another important retrieval application of this interactive graphic system is the ability to select a point on a plot, via the light pen, and then have the system display the coordinates of that point and report the RIQS record number from which that point has been derived. To illustrate some of these features, we shall again utilize the WORLD HANDBOOK 2 File.

The problem to be studied is the relationship between life expectancy (#5) and number of physicians per million population (#10), and the change in this relationship from the beginning of the study period (1950) to the end (1965). Figure 2.13 illustrates the PLOT commands as they appear on the IMLAC screen.

```
ENTER SEARCH COMMAND OR TYPE HALT

? BEGIN SEARCH
? IF #5.1 LT 999.9 AND #10.1 LT 99999.9 PLOT #5.1 VRS #10.1;
? IF #5.4 LT 999.9 AND #10.4 LT 99999.9 PLOT #5.4 VRS #10.4;
? END


SEARCHING INITIATED




NO. OF RECORDS  GENERATED TO 1ST PLOT FILE =    31
NO. OF POINTS   GENERATED TO 1ST PLOT FILE =    31

NO. OF RECORDS  GENERATED TO 2ND PLOT FILE =    16
NO. OF POINTS   GENERATED TO 2ND PLOT FILE =    16


DO YOU WANT THE PLOT GENERATED
? YES_
```

Figure 2.13. PLOT commands for life expectancy (#5) vs.
number of physicians (#10) in 1950 and 1965.

When the user indicates that a plot is to be generated, the menu shown in Figure 2.14 appears on the screen.

Any of these options may now be selected by light pen action. They are:

PICTURE   Permits viewing the current plot while using any of the other options.

EXPLAIN   Explains menu options.

VALUES   Permits examination of the stored information for individual data points of the current plot by selecting a point via the light pen. The exact X and Y coordinate values and the number of the RIQS record from which the point was generated will be displayed.

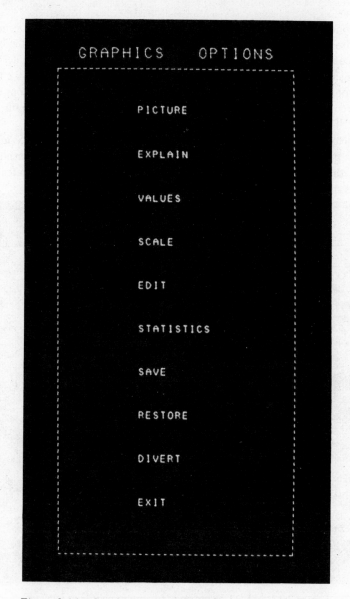

Figure 2.14. Graphics options displayed on IMLAC screen.

SCALE	Permits scaling of a plot for specified ranges of values on the X and/or Y axes.
EDIT	Provides for deleting or replacing X and Y axis labels and the plot title.
STATISTICS	Computes various statistics over data points such as count, min, max,

	sum, mean, standard deviation, correlation, regression equations and regression lines.
SAVE	Permits saving a plot for later redisplay via the RESTORE option.
RESTORE	Permits redisplay of the original plot or of a saved plot.
DIVERT	Generates a CALCOMP file of the current plot and diverts the file for hard copy plotting.
EXIT	Terminates graphics processing and returns to RIQSONLINE.

By means of the EDIT option a title is added to the plot. The PICTURE option causes the menu to be replaced by the plot shown in Figure 2.15. In addition to the data points for each period, corresponding regression lines are also displayed.

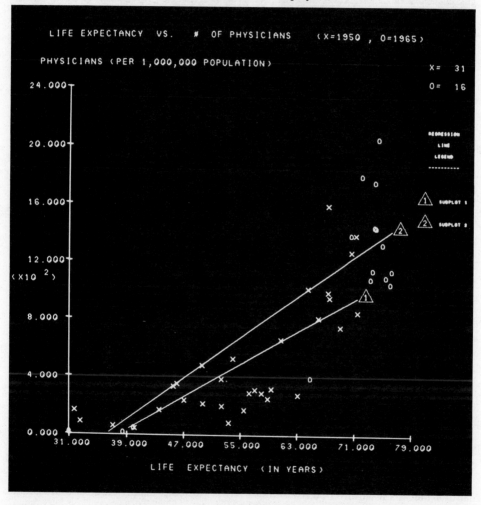

Figure 2.15. Plot displayed on IMLAC screen.

At this point, one could return to the menu and choose VALUES, which would permit any of the points to be selected by the light pen and have the X and Y coordinates and corresponding RIQS record number displayed. Instead the STATISTICS option is selected. Summary statistics are displayed in Figure 2.16.

STATISTICS

	1ST SUBPLOT		2ND SUBPLOT		PLOT	
	X VALUES	Y VALUES	X VALUES	Y VALUES	X VALUES	Y VALUES
COUNT	31		16		47	
MIN	31.700	41.200	31.000	13.300	31.000	13.300
MAX	71.200	1588.000	75.900	2052.800	75.900	2052.800
SUM	x	x	x	x	x	x
MEAN	55.355	499.068	66.175	1072.269	59.038	694.200
STDDEV	11.198	416.991	15.053	640.381	13.510	567.893
CORR AND	.766		.838		.833	
REGR EQN	-1079.627+	28.520X	-1286.753+	35.648X	-1372.377+	35.004X

PICTURE   EXECUTE   RESTART   HARDCOPY   EXIT

VIEW -PICTURE- FOR REGRESSION LINE(S)

Figure 2.16. Summary statistics for plots in Figure 2.15.

As can be seen from the statistics, both life expectancy and number of physicians increased during the period 1950-1965, as did the correlation between the two variables. The equations of the regression lines are also displayed.

Bibliographic and Textual Output Features

The INDEX phase of RIQS (batch processing only) allows the user to create sorted output from selected portions of a data base. Four types of indexes can be produced: a permuted KWIC index, for keyword-in-context, a KWOC index, for keyword-out-of-context, an author index, and an inverted list of index terms. Although mainly used for bibliographic applications, we shall see that any text-oriented application can benefit from these indexes.

KWIC INDEX

A KWIC index is an alphabetical list of keywords occurring in the text being indexed. Words occurring before and after the keywords in the text are printed on the same line as the keyword, thus showing the *keyword in context*. (This popular type of index is frequently used for titles in a bibliographic file, and is, thus, often called a *permuted title index*.) A line containing a keyword and surrounding text is printed for each keyword in the text. Keywords are normally aligned vertically down the center of the output page, so that their alphabetic sequence can be readily observed.

Frequently, a list of common words to be excluded from indexing is provided by the user. These are called stopwords. Indexing is done on all words in the text except for any stopwords. Another mode of indexing may be selected, if the user wishes to provide a list of keywords. In this case, only these keywords, appearing in the text, are indexed.

For maximum versatility with the KWIC index, the RIQS system allows the user to select any item to be used as a reference item. The system will print the first 20 characters of the reference item to the right of each output line. Thus, in a bibliographic application, one can associate a reference code to the cited document in each line of the index.

We shall use the RESTAURANT file to illustrate the KWIC index. The format for the commands which produces the index, part of which is shown in Figure 2.17, is as follows:

INDEX

KWIC ON (4) WITH REFERENCE (1)

USING STOPWORDS

ABOUND,ABSOLUTELY,ACTUALLY,AFTER,ALWAYS,ANOTHER,ANYWHERE,

BEGINS,BEHIND,CHANGE,CHANGED,CHANGING,COME,COMES,COUPLE,

.

.

This KWIC index is produced from the *Chicago Guide* descriptions (#4), using the restaurant name (#1) as the reference item.

KWOC INDEX

KWOC indexing takes the keyword-out-of-context and prints it in alphabetic order followed by as much other information from the record as is desired by the user. Wordlists, either stopwords or keywords, are used in exactly the same way as in KWIC indexing. A KWOC instruction is used to specify which items in each record are to provide index terms, and a PRINT instruction indicates which items are to be printed beneath the sorted index terms. The following KWOC/PRINT instructions generated the index, part of which is shown in Figure 2.18, taken from the ACM file.

INDEX KWOC ON (14). PRINT (8) (9) (1).

AUTHOR INDEX

The AUTHOR index is so called because its most frequent use is to produce sorted author lists from bibliographic files. It can, however, be equally useful for alphabetical listing of companies, cuisine type, or any other text strings which usually contain more than one word in an item or subitem. The AUTHOR index is generated by building up each index term from the first n characters of an item. If the item is multiple, the first n characters of

```
IMARI IS SUPERB.  TRY THE ANTIPASTO BREAD AND THE PASTA AND FAGIOLI SOUP.  FOR $7.95, FOUR OR MORE P D≠FILIPPO≠S
S AN ADEQUATE ASSORTMENT OF MEAT, FISH, FOWL, AND PASTA.  IT≠S RUMORED THAT NO ONE EVER COMPLETELY F CLUB EL BIANCO
INNER IS A GOOD VALUE, INCLUDING APPETIZER, SOUP, PASTA, SALAD (TRY THE CAESAR, BEAUTIFULLY PREPARED CHEF ALBERTO≠S
ALIAN BEEF SANDWICHES, ENTREES MADE WITH IMPORTED PASTAS, AND IMPORTED CHEESES AND SALAMI.            DINO≠S GROTTO
CHICKEN WITH VEGETABLES, BLACK MUSHROOMS AND BEAN PASTE IN HOT SAUCE), SE-JOB RIBS(WITH BLACK BEAN A FONG YUEN
DDING,MEAT-AND-POTATOE PIE,CORNISH MEAT AND ONION PASTIES,BLACK PUDDING,OTHER SIMPLE,GOOD DISHES IN  ATLANTIC FISH AND CH
VERSARIES GET DEDICATIONS AND A SPARKLER ON THEIR PASTRIES.            GUESTS WITH BIRTHDAYS AND ANNI BROWN BEAR
 A MEAL AT BIANSO≠S...YET THE DESSERTS ARE THERE: PASTRIES, COOKIES, AND CANNOLI, SPUMONI, SHERBET,  CLUB EL BIANCO
AB(ONE HALF ORDER IS SUBSTANTIAL),AND SELLS TASTY PASTRIES,PRIMARILY OF THE AUSTRO-HUNGARIAN VARIETY BON TON
ITH THE USUAL EXTRAS, BUT THERE≠S ALSO AN UNUSUAL PASTRY PUFF CALLED SOPAPILLAS - A HIGHLIGHT OF THE LA CASITA DE SANTA F
US FRESH BREAD,IS KNO             THIS SMALL,BRIGHT PASTRY SHOP AND RESTAURANT STARTS YOU WITH DELICIO BON TON
RTS INCLUDE FLAN, PEACH OR MANGO PUDDING, MEXICAN PASTRY.  NO LIQUOR, BRING YOUR OWN.            ESSE LA CHOZA
TART WITH FRESH,CRISP BREAD WITH BUTTER CURLS AND PATE AND END WITH A CHOICE OF FOUR OR FIVE DESSERT THE BAKERY
EGS WITH CHAMPAGNE SAUCE AND ARTICHOKE HEART WITH PATE DE FOIE GRAS.  ENTREES(WITH A SELECTION OF FR LE FRANCIS -
 THE LARGEST IN THE MIDWEST.RECOMMENDED-THE HOUSE PATE,ROAST RACK OF LAMB.               CTION IS ONE OF BIGGS
UTDOOR GARDEN EAST OF THE RESTAURANT.A NEW INDOOR PATIO IS FULL OF PINATAS AND FRESH FLOWERS.         AZTECA
ENTREES INCLUDE WOR BAR(ASSEMBLED OVER CRISP RICE PATTIES ON A SIZZLING STEAK PLATTER AT THE TABLE A BLUE PEACOCK
RS, THEY≠LL MAKE CREATIONS LIKE SAUMON EN CROUTE ≠PAUL BOCUSE≠(WHOLE SALMON WITH LOBSTER MOUSSE IN C LE FRANCIS -
) AND SAI WOO DUCK (CRISP BONELESS DUCK WITH HAM, PEA PODS, WATER CHESTNUTS, BAMBOO, BLACK MUSHROOMS CHINA DOLL
E TABLE ARE CHICKEN,KING CRAB,ROAST DUCK AND PORK,PEA PODS,BLACK AND BUTTON MUSHROOMS,WATER CHESTNUT BLUE PEACOCK
CKGROUND MUSIC.  10 APPETIZERS, ONION OR DELICATE PEA SOUP, SALAD WITH DELICIOUS TARRAGON DRESSING,  LA FONTAINE
$2.50 (WITH RICE, BEANS).  DESSERTS INCLUDE FLAN, PEACH OR MANGO PUDDING, MEXICAN PASTRY.  NO LIQUOR LA CHOZA
 A DOZEN DESSERTS INCLUDE APPLE AND CUSTARD TART, PEACHES SUZETTE.  ON A WEEK≠S NOTICE AND FOR 4 OR  LE FRANCIS -
ASS FLAMED IN PERNOD, ROAST DUCK WITH ORANGES AND PEACHES, SIRLOIN SAUTEED WITH SHALLOTS, AND VEAL S LA FONTAINE
(LIKE MOIST TOWELETTES AFTER THE APPETIZERS).BLUE PEACOCK TIDBITS($2.35)INCLUDES EGG ROLL(TOO MUCH V BLUE PEACOCK
 OLD HOUSE OFFERS DELICIOUS, UNIQUE FOOD.  SUPERB PEANUT SOUP.  SHRIMP, CHICKEN, OR MEAT JAMBALAYA(R THE CREOLE HOUSE
 MANDARIN DISHES: SOUR-AND-HOT SOUP, CHICKEN WITH PEANUTS AND SZECHUAN PEPPER, THOUSAND-YEAR EGGS, M CHINESE TEA HOUSE
(IMPORTED AND DOMESTIC) BY THE STEIN OR PITCHER.  PEANUTS ON THE TABLES, SHELLS ON THE FLOORS.       COME BACK INN
REES: YOUNG JOW FON (BEEF TENDERLOIN WITH SHRIMP, PEAPODS, MUSHROOMS, BAMBOO, WATER CHESTNUTS -$4.95 CHINA DOLL
V WINES ARE $4.25 A BOTTLE).FINISH WITH KRUSKOVAC(PEAR LIQUER).DAILY SPECIALS(MOST UNDER $4).ENTERTA BALKAN AT NIGHT
ERALLY WELL PREPARED AND THOUGHTFULLY PRESENTED.  PEKING DUCK (MADE ON 24 HOUR ADVANCE REQUEST), CRI DRAGON INN
HU PORK ON PAPER-THIN MANDARIN PANCAKES, FAT-FREE PEKING DUCK (ORDER,LIKE THE FIRE POT, A DAY AHEAD) CHINESE DUMPLING HOU
MUSHROOMS-$4.95).  NEW IS CHINA DOLL≠S VERSION OF PEKING DUCK SERVED WITH BISCUITS AND DELICIOUS SHR CHINA DOLL
THOUSAND-YEAR EGGS, MOO-SHU PORK, AND THE CLASSIC PEKING DUCK, CRISPY DUCK, SMOKED DUCK (THEY SMOKE  CHINESE TEA HOUSE
Y AHEAD FOR SHARK≠S FIN OR SHARK≠S DELICACY SOUP, PEKING DUCK, HUNG-SHAO DUCK WITH SPECIAL PRESERVED CATHAY MANDARIN REST
NGERY),RED SNAPPER NAMDANG,SAUTE CHICKED WITH HOT PEPPER AND GREEN ONION.FRIED WON TON APPETIZER COM BANGKOK HOUSE
TER CHESTNUTS,BAMBOO SHOOTS,AND BOK TOY)-MANDARIN PEPPER BEEF(THIN STRIPS OF SAUTEED GREEN PEPPER,BA BLUE PEACOCK
 THE WELL-PREPARED SPECIALTIES ARE AN EXCEPTIONAL PEPPER STEAK(A FILET MIGNON,IT≠S $7 ON THE DINNER) AGOSTINO≠S
R-AND-HOT SOUP, CHICKEN WITH PEANUTS AND SZECHUAN PEPPER, THOUSAND-YEAR EGGS, MOO-SHU PORK, AND THE  CHINESE TEA HOUSE
MANDARIN PEPPER BEEF(THIN STRIPS OF SAUTEED GREEN PEPPER,BAMBOO SHOOTS,BEEF IN A GINGER-BASED SAUCE, BLUE PEACOCK
EASANT WITH MORELS, DUCK OR FILET MIGNON IN GREEN PEPPERCORN SAUCE.  UNUSUAL EXTRA:BRIE,CAMEMBERT,OR LE FRANCIS -
EMBER THE WIREBACKED ≠COKE≠ CHAIRS AND BOTTLES OF PEPPERS IN VINEGAR AND TABASCO SAUCE ON THE TABLES BISHOP≠S CHILI HUT
2 PEOPLE, IS $1) THERE ARE STEAK DISHES (ONE WITH PEPPERS, TOMATOES, AND ONIONS--ONE WITH SALSA RANC LA CHOZA
ESE DISHES, AMONG THEM MANDARIN SOUR AND HOT SOUP(PEPPERY AND ZINGY),GUNG-BOW CHICKEN(DICED CHICKEN  FONG YUEN
NG YOUR OWN WINE,OR BEER,WHICH GOES WELL WITH THE PEPPERY THAI DISHES).             ALL IN ADVANCE.BRI BANGKOK HOUSE
```

Figure 2.17. KWIC index from RESTAURANT file.

```
BOOLEAN

        BOOLEAN MATRIX METHODS FOR THE DETECTION OF SIMPLE PRECEDENCE
        GRAMMARS
        MARTIN DAVID F.
        C11101068685

        GENERATION OF OPTIMAL CODE FOR EXPRESSIONS VIA FACTORIZATION
        BREUER MELVIN A.
        C12060669333

        SOME TECHNIQUES FOR USING PSEUDORANDOM NUMBERS IN COMPUTER
        SIMULATION
        DONNELLY T.
        C12070769392

        A NEW METHOD FOR DETERMINING LINEAR PRECEDENCE FUNCTIONS FOR
        PRECEDENCE GRAMMARS
        BELL JAMES R.
        C12101069567

        CANONICAL STRUCTURE IN ATTRIBUTE BASED FILE ORGANIZATION
        WONG EUGENE
        CHIANG T.  C.
        C14090971593

        A BOOLEAN MATRIX METHOD FOR THE COMPUTATION OF LINEAR PRECEDENCE
        FUNCTIONS
        MARTIN DAVID F.
        C15060672448

        ON THE MAXIMIZATION OF A PSEUDO - BOOLEAN FUNCTION
        HAMMER PETER L.
        PELED URI N.
        J19020472265

BOOTSTRAPPING

        A BASE FOR A MOBILE PROGRAMMING SYSTEM
        ORGASS RICHARD J.
        WAITE WILLIAM M.
        C12090969507

        EXPERIENCE WITH AN EXTENSIBLE LANGUAGE
        IRONS EDGAR T.
        C13010170031

        THE MOBILE PROGRAMMING SYSTEM..  STAGE2
        WAITE W.  M.
        C13070770415

        A FORMALISM FOR TRANSLATOR INTERACTIONS
        EARLEY JAY
        STURGIS HOWARD
        C13101070607

BOTTOM

        GENERATING PARSERS FOR AFFIX GRAMMARS
        CROWE DAVID
        C15080872728

        WEAK AND MIXED STRATEGY PRECEDENCE PARSING
        AHO A.  V.
        DENNING P.  J.
        ULLMAN J.  D.
        J19020472225

BOUND

        COMPLEX MATRIX INVERSION VERSUS REAL
        EHRLICH L.  W.
        C13090968561

        APPLICATION OF GAME TREE SEARCHING TECHNIQUES TO SEQUENTIAL
        PATTERN RECOGNITION
        SLAGLE JAMES R.
        LEE RICHARD C.  T.
        C14020271103

        ON THE MAXIMIZATION OF A PSEUDO - BOOLEAN FUNCTION
        HAMMER PETER L.
        PELED URI N.
        J19020472265
```

Figure 2.18.   KWOC index from ACM file.

each subitem are used as an index term. N may be between 20 and 110. If n is not specified, the default is the first 20 characters.

An extract of an AUTHOR index from the ACM file is shown in Figure 2.19. It was produced by the following instructions:

INDEX

AUTHOR ON (9) WITH LENGTH = 30. PRINT (8) (1).

```
WULF WILLIAM A.

        THE IMPLEMENTATION OF A BASIC SYSTEM IN A MULTIPROGRAMMING
        ENVIRONMENT
        C11101068688

YEN, JIN Y.

        FINDING THE LENGTHS OF ALL SHORTEST PATHS IN N - NODE NONNEGATIVE
        - DISTANCE COMPLETE NETWORKS USING 1 / 2N3 ADDITIONS AND N3
        COMPARISONS
        J19030772423

YOCHELSON JEROME C.

        A LISP GARBAGE - COLLECTOR FOR VIRTUAL - MEMORY COMPUTER SYSTEMS
        C12111169611

        A PROGRAM TO TEACH PROGRAMMING
        C13030370141

YOUNG JOHN W

        INTRODUCTION TO ≠ FEATURE ANALYSIS OF GENERALIZED DATA BASE
        MANAGEMENT SYSTEMS ≠
        C14050571308

YUEN, P. S. T.

        KEY - TO - ADDRESS TRANSFORM TECHNIQUES A FUNDAMENTAL PERFORMANCE
        STUDY ON LARGE EXISTING FORMATTED FILES
        C14040471228

ZADEH NORMAN

        THEORETICAL EFFICIENCY OF THE EDMONDS - KARP ALGORITHM FOR
        COMPUTING MAXIMAL FLOWS
        J19010172184

ZIEGLER BERNARD P.

        TOWARDS A FORMAL THEORY OF MODELING AND SIMULATION : STRUCTURE
        PRESERVING MORPHISMS
        J19041072742

ZINN KARL L.

        COMPUTERS IN THE INSTRUCTIONAL PROCESS = DIRECTIONS FOR RESEARCH
        AND DEVELOPMENT
        C15070772648
```

Figure 2.19. AUTHOR index from ACM file.

INVERT INDEX

An alphabetical listing of index terms, followed by the record numbers of all the records which contain those terms, is produced by the INVERT command. The total frequency of occurrence in the file of each index term is also printed. INVERT can be used with stopwords. Inversion may be performed on any item. A simple example of the INVERT command to produce an index of the affiliation states (#12) for all of the authors in the ACM file is given below.

INDEX INVERT ON (12).

Part of the resulting inverted index is found in Figure 2.20.

Tutorial and Diagnostic Aids

Earlier, when discussing the characteristics of a personalized data base system, it was emphasized that ease of use was essential. Since such data base access will be mostly interactive, an on-line capability must be provided to ease the learning process in the use of the system and to aid in understanding and recovering from errors made during a query session. RIQSONLINE, through a subsystem called RIQSTUTOR,[17] provides three modes of use to offer these capabilities to the novice, or to the experienced user, who may have forgotten some feature or its syntax.

RIQSTUTOR allows a user to move freely among three modes of operation, TUTORIAL, BROWSE, and SEARCHES. TUTORIAL instructs the user about the system, in general, or about specific RIQS commands. It can always be called by means of the command HELP. BROWSE presents a set of publically available data bases to examine and to experiment with. Not only are record schema displayed, if requested, but also sample records and sample queries. The user can learn about the system by observing the results of the prestored queries on prestored data bases. Finally, the SEARCHES mode returns the user to RIQSONLINE to query any of the public data bases or one's own data bases.

For the user who has made an error while typing a query, the RIQSTUTOR provides a selective inquiry mode. This mode can supply a list of all RIQSONLINE commands, information about any specific command, typical error recovery procedures for common mistakes, or if possible, automatic branching to a tutorial section relevant to the user's last syntax error.

Some selected excerpts from the BROWSE and TUTORIAL modes of RIQSTUTOR are given in Figure 2.21 and 2.22.

Auxiliary Features

As RIQS has developed over the past several years, many features have been added to enhance its utility. It is expected that RIQS will continue to evolve to meet its users' needs and desires. Two features which will be mentioned in this section are systems monitoring and functional procedures.

Chapter 12 discusses how RIQS itself has been used to provide the storage, retrieval and analysis tools to gather data about RIQSONLINE. Both *system parameters,* such as response time, size of outputs generated, central processor times used for query processing, etc. and *user parameters* such as time for query formulation, number of syntax errors made, types of errors made, etc. have been monitored and analyzed. The monitor project has been invaluable in developing and improving the RIQS system. The reader is directed to Chapter 12 for further details.

FILE INVERSION

Count	Term	Postings
90	CALIFORNIA	1 2 3 4 8 9 11 15 24 28 37 39 40 46 48
		52 54 58 65 69 70 75 83 86 94 100 101 112 121 126
		129 135 139 145 150 154 155 157 166 168 179 180 181 193 202
		203 210 217 218 225 228 234 241 244 256 259 261 266 269 271
		278 280 283 295 296 306 308 317 353 355 358 360 366 380 390
		391 395 397 402 411 413 420 430 431 435 440 443 447 452 465
9	CANADA	133 197 320 350 351 434 435 436 437
7	CAROLINA	78 109 123 190 273 403 453
6	COLORADO	49 136 205 371 393 448
2	COLUMBIA	240 468
2	CONNECTICUT	14 208
2	DENMARK	156 184
2	DISTRICT	240 468
1	EGYPT	64
13	ENGLAND	44 99 137 207 212 232 282 285 291 351 405 416 450
1	FLORIDA	170
3	FRANCE	215 235 312
4	GEORGIA	16 67 165 303
3	GERMANY	381 396 399
2	HAWAII	322 413

Figure 2.20. INVERT index from ACM file.

```
N.U.   RIQS   TUTØR

ENTER -TUTØRIAL- ØR -SEARCHES- ØR -BRØWSE-
? BRØWSE

LIST ØF PUBLIC FILES

1. ASIS
   CØMPUTER SCIENCE JØURNAL ARTICLES
2. AFRICA  (N/A)
   MØDERN AFRICA BIBLIØGRAPHIC FILE
3. AFRØ
   BLACK AFRICA CØMPARATIVE DATA FILE
4. SDI    (N/A)
   SØCIAL SCIENCE RESEARCH ARTICLES
5. RESTAURANT
   CHICAGØ RESTAURANT FILE
6. RIQSLØG (N/A)
   LØG DATA FRØM 1972 RIQSØNLINE USAGE

NØTE: THØSE FILES WITH  (N/A)  APPENDED ARE CURRENTLY NØT
AVAILABLE FØR SEARCHING BUT YØU CAN STILL GET A GENERAL
DESCRIPTIØN ØF THEM.

TYPE IN THE NAME ØF THE RIQS FILE YØU WØULD LIKE TØ BRØWSE
ØR -NØNE- TØ EXIT BRØWSING MØDE.
? RESTAURANT

YØU CAN ØBTAIN THE FØLLØWING INFØRMATIØN ABØUT THE FILE:

1.   GENERAL DESCRIPTIØN
2.   RIQS FILE DESCRIPTIØN
3.   SAMPLE RECØRD

TYPE IN ØNE ØF THE NUMBERS
TYPE -NØNE- IF YØU DØ NØT WANT ANY
? 1

YØU CAN HAVE ANY ØR ALL ØF THE FØLLØWING:

1.   FILE SIZE
2.   DESCRIPTIØN
3.   SUGGESTED USE

TYPE IN NUMBERS ØNLY
? 1,2,3
SIZE - 150+ RECØRDS
DESCRIPTIØN - THE RESTAURANT FILE DESCRIBES THE
SELECTIVE GUIDE TØ DINING AS PUBLISHED IN THE
"CHICAGØ GUIDE." LØCATIØN, TYPE ØF CUISINE AND
FØØD SPECIALTIES ARE ESPECIALLY NØTED.
SUGGESTED USES - WHEN YØU GET HUNGRY, CHECK WITH THE
RESTAURANT FILE. IT'S SELF EXPLANATØRY.

WØULD YØU RATHER
1.   HAVE MØRE INFØRMATIØN ABØUT THIS FILE
2.   BRØWSE ANØTHER FILE
3.   LEAVE THE BRØWSING MØDE
? 3
WØULD YØU LIKE TØ
1.   SEARCH A RIQS FILE
2.   USE THE TUTØRIAL MØDE
3.   STØP THE RIQSTUTØR
? 2
***.1
IF AT ANY TIME YØU WANT TØ EXIT THE TUTØRIAL PHASE
TØ BEGIN YØUR RIQS SEARCHES ØR TØ LØGØUT, TYPE  EXIT

HAVE YØU EVER USED RIQS-ØNLINE
? NØ
***.4
ARE YØU FAMILIAR WITH WHAT RIQS DØES  ...
HØW IT PERFØRMS INFØRMATIØN RETRIEVAL
? YES
***TUTØR1

   SINCE YØU HAVE INDICATED THAT YØU HAVE NEVER USED RIQS-ØNLINE,
   WØULD YØU LIKE SØME INFØRMATIØN CØNCERNING THE RATIØNALE
   BEHIND THE DEVELØPMENT ØF THIS TUTØRIAL ...
   (THIS WILL GIVE YØU SØME IDEA ØF WHAT TØ EXPECT)
   ? NØ
```

Figure 2.21. BROWSE mode.

```
WOULD YOU LIKE TO QUERY THE TUTORIAL FOR SELECTED STATEMENTS
? Y
***TUTOR

TYPE IN THE NAME OF THE RIQS COMMAND YOU WANT TO REVIEW;   OR
TYPE -LIST- FOR A LIST OF THE RIQS-ONLINE COMMANDS;          OR
TYPE -STATEMENT- FOR INFO ON HOW TO 'RE-ENTER LAST STATEMENT' IN RIQS
? LIST
***LIST

THE RIQS-ONLINE COMMANDS ARE  :

  BEFORE SEARCH
  BEGIN SEARCH
  AFTER SEARCH
  LET
  RELEASE
  DISPLAY
  PRINT
  IF
  PUT   OR  PLACE
  FOR...LOOP
  DELETE RECORD
  DEFINE SET
  REDEFINE SET
  DIVERT
  TRACE
  SPSSFILE
  GLOBAL   (NOT YET IMPLEMENTED INTO RIQS-ONLINE)
  ARRAY    (NOT YET IMPLEMENTED INTO RIQS-ONLINE)
  BEGIN SEARCH OF RECORD(S)    (REPLACES THE -GET- STATEMENT)
  BEGIN SEARCH OF SET
  BEGIN SEARCH OF UNION OF SETS
  BEGIN SEARCH OF INTERSECTION OF SETS
  BEGIN SEARCH OF COMPLEMENT OF SET(S)
  BEGIN SEARCH FROM PFN
  $ COMMAND    (EXECUTE CONTROL CARD)
  SPSSLINK
  CATALOG
  PLOT
  HALT
  RESTART
  END

TYPE IN THE NAME OF THE COMMAND YOU WANT TO REVIEW  OR
TYPE -STATEMENT- FOR INFORMATION ON RECOVERING FROM ERRORS.
? DISPLAY
ARE YOU REFERENCING OUTPUT COMMANDS WITHIN A -BEFORE-, -BEGIN-,
OR -AFTER- SEARCH. THERE IS AN IMPORTANT DISTINCTION ON WHAT'S
AVAILABLE TO YOU IN -BEGIN SEARCH- AS OPPOSED TO THE OTHER TWO.
PLEASE SPECIFY ONLY ONE AT A TIME
? BEGIN
***OUTPUT0
THE FORMAT OF THE -PRINT- AND -DISPLAY- STATEMENTS ARE  :

PRINT   'STRING', VARIABLE, RECORD, ITEMS
DISPLAY 'STRING', VARIABLE, RECORD, ITEMS

WOULD YOU LIKE AN EXPLANATION OF THE IDENTIFIERS
IN THIS OUTPUT LIST
? Y
***OUTPUT1
'STRING' CAUSES THE PRINTING OF WHATEVER LITERAL STRING IS
         ENCLOSED WITHIN THE QUOTE MARKS. THIS IS USED FOR
         HEADINGS AND COMMENTS.
VARIABLE CAUSES THE PRINTING OF THE VARIABLE NAME SPECIFIED
         TOGETHER WITH ITS VALUE.
         IF ANY OF THE VARIABLES ARE ARRAYS, THE WHOLE ARRAY
         WILL BE OUTPUT IF SUBSCRIPTS ARE NOT SPECIFIED;
         IF A SUBSCRIPT IS SPECIFIED, ONLY THAT SUB-ITEM IS
         OUTPUT.

   (PRESS CARRIAGE RETURN FOR ADDITIONAL EXPLANATIONS) ...
?

RECORD   CAUSES THE COMPLETE PRINTING OF EACH RECORD (IN THE
         FILE OR SET) SATISFYING THE CRITERIA OF THE SEARCH
ITEMS    CAUSES THE PRINTING OF THE SPECIFIED ITEMS FOR EACH
         RECORD SATISFYING THE CRITERIA OF THE SEARCH

WOULD YOU LIKE A FEW EXAMPLES OF USING THESE IDENTIFIERS
IN AN OUTPUT LIST
? Y
***EXAMPLS
DISPLAY 'OUTPUT OF SEARCH 3'      (LITERAL STRING)
PRINT VAR1,X,SAM,Z(5)            (VARIABLES OR ARRAYS)
DISPLAY RECORD                    (FULL RECORD PRINTED)
PRINT #1,#2,#8 THRU #15          (ITEMS WITHIN RECORDS)
DISPLAY 'OUTPUT 1',VAR1,RECORD,#1 (ANY COMBINATION OF THEM)

NOTE THE SPECIFICATION OF ITEMS AND THE USE OF -THRU-

DOES THAT MAKE IT CLEAR
? Y
```

Figure 2.22.   TUTORIAL mode.

Functional procedures[18] were added to RIQS to provide standard functions like mean, standard deviation, minimum, maximum, count, etc. and to allow users to package several RIQS commands into a named procedure which could easily be called many times thereafter. No attempt will be made to discuss the details of procedures here; instead, a sample procedure, using the WORLD HANDBOOK 2 file, will be shown in Figure 2.23.

```
ENTER SEARCH CØMMAND ØR TYPE HALT

? PRØCEDURE MEAN (X,YEAR)
? SET UP CØUNT, MEAN ØNCE FØR EACH YEAR
? STRING YEAR
? BEGIN SEARCH
? IF X LT 999.9 LET CØUNT=CØUNT+1, LET MEAN=MEAN+XJ
? AFTER SEARCH LET MEAN=MEAN/CØUNT
? DISPLAY ACRØSS SKIP 1
? 'MEAN LIFE EXPECTANCY IN ' YEAR ' = ' MEAN TAB 50 'N = ' CØUNTJ ENDP
?
  BEGIN SEARCH
? CALL MEAN (#5.1,'1950')
? CALL  MEAN (#5.2,'1955')
? CALL  MEAN (#5.3,'1960')
? CALL MEAN (#5.4,'1965')
? END

SEARCHING INITIATED

AFTER SEARCH

     MEAN LIFE EXPECTANCY IN 1950 = 55.0          N = 34.0

     MEAN LIFE EXPECTANCY IN 1955 = 60.4          N = 21.0

     MEAN LIFE EXPECTANCY IN 1960 = 61.8          N = 57.0

     MEAN LIFE EXPECTANCY IN 1965 = 66.5          N = 17.0


*  *  *  *  *
```

Figure 2.23. Procedure to display a computed mean and a string variable.

Summary

This presentation of the features of RIQS was intended to provide the reader with an overview of what we consider to be the important elements of a personalized data base system as it has evolved to date, and as it currently serves the needs of an academic community. As will be seen in Part II, all of the features described herein have been applied in numerous data base applications in the social, administrative, management, medical and clinical sciences, as well as in many other disciplines which are not represented by chapters in our book.

But what relationship does RIQS have to the systems which will eventually permit our mythical retiree of Chapter 1 to take a French lesson, or to update and query a data base about antique cars over a public information utility? We feel that there exists a close functional relationship today, and that as systems like RIQS evolve over the next several years, there will emerge a closer expressive relationship as well. To be sure, RIQS requires the current user to learn a somewhat "programmer-oriented" language with commands like IF and FOR and LET. However, with this language, the user can store, update, retrieve, compute, display, plot and analyze data which the user has gathered and which the user wishes to exploit. So, as we said, *functionally* the RIQS system, or any of the comparable systems discussed earlier, can already provide most of the features which are needed for a storage and retrieval facility to be supplied by an information utility. We must still add the ability to select and project still or motion pictures (which is done in many existing computer-aided-instructional (CAI) systems), to interpret user responses in man/machine interaction (also done in CAI systems), and to accept queries and instructions in a simple, English language format.

This latter facility, i.e., natural language input, has received a great deal of attention in computer science research and, thus, seems to offer no major obstacle to eventual incorporation into data base systems. The low priority given to natural language input in the RIQS project is due to the conviction of its developers that an expressive, artificial language can be learned quickly by most users of the system, especially if effective tutorial aids are provided. Effort, instead, has been directed at enhancing the functional characteristics of the system. But, this is not to say that simpler modes of expression in RIQS would be undesirable.

In conclusion, we present RIQS as but one example of several existing systems which provide processing facilities to permit individual users to develop data base applications with relative ease. We call such systems personalized data base systems.

NOTES AND CITED REFERENCES

1. TRIAL originally was developed at Northwestern University in 1964 for the IBM 709 and subsequently rewritten for the CDC 3400 in 1966 by William H. Tetzlaff under the supervision of Prof. Kenneth Janda of the Political Science Department. The CDC 6400 version was programmed by Donald Dillaman in 1968.

2. L. Borman and D. Dillaman, *TRIAL Information Retrieval System, User's Manual,* Vogelback Computing Center, Northwestern University, Evanston, Illinois, June, 1974.

3. K. Janda, *Information Retrieval: Applications to Political Science,* The Bobbs-Merrill Company, Inc., Indianapolis, Indiana, 1968.

4. L. Borman and R. Hay, Jr., *Data Resources for the Social Sciences,* Document No. IS74-004, Northwestern University, Vogelback Computing Center, Evanston, Illinois, January, 1974.

5. INFOL 2 was designed and developed by Jacques Vallee and Robert Chalice.

6. Control Data Corporation, *INFOL Reference Manual 3600/3800,* Document No. 60170300, Minneapolis, Minnesota, July, 1966.

7. Much of this work was done as part of a project sponsored by the Air Force Office of Scientific Research, AFOSR-68-1598A, entitled "On-line Computer-based Systems for Information Management," principal investigators, B. Mittman and G. K. Krulee.

8. The first version of RIQS was designed and programmed by Robert Chalice and Donald Dillaman, under the supervision of Benjamin Mittman and Lorraine Borman. Maintenance and development activities are currently performed by Peter Kron.

9. B. Mittman, R. Chalice, D. Dillaman, "Mixed Data Structures in a Multi-Purpose Retrieval System," *Journal of the American Society for Information Sciences,* March-April, 1973, Vol. 24, No. 2, pp. 135-141.

10. This file was keypunched from issues of the *Communications* and the *Journal of the Association for Computing Machinery,* ACM, New York. Extracts are reproduced with permission.

11. This file was keypunched from "The selective guide to dining," *Chicago Guide,* WFMT, Inc., Chicago. Extracts are reproduced with permission.

12. This file was extracted from the "World Handbook of Political and Social Indicators II" data base distributed by the Inter-University Consortium for Political Research, Ann Arbor, Michigan. Extracts are reproduced with permission.

13. The data were originally collected by Charles Lewis Taylor and Michael C. Hudson. Neither the original collectors of the data nor the Consortium bear any responsibility for the analyses or interpretations presented here.

14. Norman H. Nie, Dale H. Bent, C. Hadlai Hull, *SPSS Statistical Package for the Social Sciences,* McGraw-Hill Book Company, New York, 1970.

15. SPSSONLINE was designed and developed by Dale Jessen. The spss interpace was implemented by Carol Wagner Jessen.

16. The interactive plot facilities were designed and developed by Wayne D. Dominick, using a graphics package developed by Gregory Suski.

17. RIQSTUTOR was designed and developed by Wayne D. Dominick using a computer-aided-instructional package developed by James A. Schuyler.

18. Procedure handling was designed and developed by Judith Dart Boxler, with the supervision and assistance of Wayne D. Dominick.

PART II

THE USE OF PERSONALIZED DATA BASE SYSTEMS IN RESEARCH: CASE STUDIES

Section One:

SOCIAL SCIENCES

The disciplines making up the social sciences include political science, sociology, anthropology, and archeology. Each discipline has produced its own body of literature, its own theories, and its own methods of conducting empirical research. However, they are all characterized by their dependence upon extensive collections of data for research and educational purposes. These data bases involve both textual and numeric data, and frequently a single collection will incorporate both types of data forms. The chapters in this section involve applications in the social sciences which have benefited from access to computerized data base processing. Each chapter presents different research problems which confronted the authors and discusses how the RIQS system was used to help solve them.

Mohammed and Hay describe, in Chapter 3, the application of computer technology to the study of an important collection of Islamic manuscripts. RIQS has been used to assist in the organization, cross-referencing, and cataloging of the collection, to investigate accessibility to other scholars, and to test certain hypotheses concerning issues such as the diffusion of Islamic knowledge from North Africa and the Middle East to Nigeria.

In Chapter 4, Donald Stone Sade discusses an ongoing observational study of the social organization of primates. The research requires the storage and retrieval of thousands of specific episodes of monkey behavior from field notes which have been coded to identify individual monkeys, types of interaction, date of interaction, and other observations. Tabulations of interaction data are generated and statistically analyzed.

Northwestern University is involved in a major archeological program centered on the lower Illinois Valley. For over 15 years this project has been engaged in a thorough and systematic reconnaissance of the archeological resources of the region. In Chapter 5, Brown and Houart discuss the development of a computer-based system to store, organize, catalog, retrieve, and analyze data such as site location and size, activities performed by prehistoric inhabitants, artifacts recovered, etc.

The file described by Kenneth Janda in Chapter 6, contains both textual and numeric data pertaining to 154 political parties in 52 countries of the world. By maintaining one file for all of the data collected by the International Comparative Political Parties Project, Janda and his colleagues have been able to store information as it is received, edit it for correctness and completeness, and print all or part of it, upon request. RIQS is being used to identify and display information about specific parties based upon queries over numerous relevant variables. Also, a RIQS-produced printout of the entire file is to be published as a cross-national handbook of comparative political parties.

Bibliographic control of a collection of documents on international affairs is the subject of the Leserman and Guetzkow article in Chapter 7. They discuss how the bibliographic features of RIQS were applied to the production of reports for both reference and publication needs.

Finally, in Chapter 8, Borman and Hay describe how access to publically available social science data bases can be facilitated for student and faculty use. Their approach is to utilize RIQS as the medium for both catalog and codebook purposes, as well as for retrieval and analysis applications.

Chapter 3

Analysis of a West African Islamic Library: The Falke Collection

ABDULLAHI MOHAMMED
Ahmadu Bello University
Zaria, Nigeria

RICHARD HAY, Jr.
Northwestern University

Introduction

In August 1972, the authors of this chapter met in the ancient, walled city of Kano, in northern Nigeria, along with Dr. John Paden, who had collected some 3000 Arabic and Hausa manuscripts from the library of Umar Falke (1893-1962), a local trader and religious leader. Falke is a prototypical example of the Hausa scholar-trader; a learned man who dedicated his life to the pursuit and dissemination of Islamic knowledge. His library is composed of poems, journals, and religious works that he authored, those handed down to him by his ancestors, and the religious works that he acquired from others in the course of his travels.[1]

The Falke Library

Umar collected books and manuscripts on all aspects of Islamic learning, protective medicine, and the secret arts (asrar). The bulk of the material is written in Arabic, although some items are in Hausa. Because Umar was a wealthy merchant, supported by wealthy students in addition to his close association with the merchant class in Kano, he was able to acquire a wide variety of documents for his library. The collection is strong in almost all the branches of Islamic sciences, especially Maliki law, jurisprudence, Prophetic traditions (hadith), theology, literature, and grammar. There are also a number of hand-written copies of the Qur'an which may have been used by Umar's students.

The library also includes works written by West African $Jihad^2$ leaders and many other notable mallams (learned men). The major substantive categories of books in the collections are as follows:

Religion

Jurisprudence	Qur'an and Commentaries
Fundamentals of Islam	Eschatology
Theology	Pre-Islamic Religion and
Mysticism	Literature
Medicine	Astrology and Numerology
Lives of the Prophets	Admonition and Preaching

Literacy and Literature

Grammar	Literature
Poetry	Education
Linguistics	Proverbs

History

Islamic History	Personal History and
West African Nigerian History	Correspondence

Socio-Economic/Political Matters

Trade and Trade Routes	Government
Agriculture	Hausa Culture

A special area of the Umar Falke library is in the field of protective and secret medicine. Umar was noted as a healer and he wrote several books on the subject: *Fa'idat al-Ishrin',* (Twenty [medicinal] benefits), *Asma' Allah Wa'l-tibb* (names of God and Medicine) and *al-asrar ila sifat Allah* (Secret Characteristics of God) to mention a few examples.

In the course of our meeting in Kano, the authors and Dr. Paden discussed various approaches toward the scholarly investigation of the library. The possibility of using a computer to help analyze the large, dusty stacks of Arabic and Hausa manuscripts seemed incredibly remote. Computers represent the western world and its ideological foundations of efficiency and mass production. They seemed strangely out of place in a land where children learn to write by repeatedly copying the Qur'an onto a wooden prayer board. Applied western uses of computers emphasize the efficient determination of end-states rather than the inherent qualities of a process (or the end over the means—one gets his computerized bill no matter where his purchases were made); an emphasis far different from that of the lengthy process of bargaining for goods in the central market of Kano. However, when it became possible for Abdullahi Mohammed to come to Northwestern University to pursue doctoral studies, with particular reference to traditional libraries in Sudanic West Africa, the question arose about the use of computerized coding, cross-referencing, and analysis. The authors discussed computer-aided analysis and formulated a tentative record structure for the information about each manuscript in the Falke collection.

File Organization

When Abdullahi Mohammed began his work at Northwestern, he developed a coding sheet for each manuscript item (Figures 3.1 and 3.2). After approximately 600 works had been coded, discussions were held and a small number of records prepared for use as a test RIQS file (Figure 3.3). Changes were made at this time in the file structure to reflect the author's continually evolving research interests and the RIQS processing necessary to satisfy them.

At the present, we are in a period of "organic" file development, where test runs are made on a limited number of records with a certain file structure; the results are analyzed in light of the information desired and its utility. More records are added, further structure definition takes place, more test runs are made, and so on. This process, inherent in some degree to the creation of most files, is protracted in this case because of the evolving focus of research goals. Analysis of a library such as this is somewhat akin to analyzing a large number of open-ended questionnaires; substance and interests are defined, broadened, constrained or otherwise changed as the work progresses. Each new piece of information carries implications of context and relationship for the old pieces. Our next step will be the creation of a file with about 200 records. Further analysis will be done and this will serve as a jumping-off point for the construction of a file of over 3000 manuscripts.

The Transliteration Question

A major problem faced early in the analysis involved the transliteration of Arabic letters, some of which have no equivalents in the 26-character set of the English language (or the computer). The "extra" characters in Arabic are shown in Figure 3.4. One seldom thinks of computers as being culturally biased, but this bias becomes readily apparent here. Computers simply cannot represent enough needed, significant characters for many languages of the world. A possible solution to the problem of "types" of symbols may be found in the ability to create one's own symbols through the use of graphics techniques (Figure 3.5). As information science progresses, we may also learn that in some cases the visual form of the information is just as important as the content.

Our transliteration problem and character set limitation was related not only to computer processing, but also to the goal of producing a published catalog of the Falke collection. We intended to use the RIQS output as a master for photo-offset printing. The notation used, then, had to be understandable to the large number of Arabic scholars who would use the catalog. Rather than follow the double-letter logic as displayed in Figure 3.4 (i.e., 'A=A, 'A=AA), we decided to append the additional transliteration marking to the master printout by hand before it went to the publisher. This decision was made for two reasons: (1) to reduce the number of levels of transliteration encountered by the Arabic reader (i.e., to use the standard [Arabic → transliterated English] rather than the unfamiliar [Arabic → transliterated English → computerized double letter, transliterated English]), and (2) to reduce the inherent ambiguity in the double-letter scheme of whether an AA represented an 'A or two 'A'A). (See Figure 3.4.)

Research Strategy

We are exploring the application of RIQS as a library analysis aid in four major areas: (1) organization, cataloging, and cross-reference indexing; (2) providing search accessibility

Until he came to Hausaland and Bornu,
(The events of) which were fully documented in his book.
And he obtained (among other things) power of (performing) miracles
At Sokoto and benefited all mankind.
Thereby he settled down in San-Lima,
While his descendants settled in a lovely Hadejia village.
His noble Shaykh, Muhammad al-Ghali,
Also travelled to Hijaz, and he lived in that neighborhood.
He came all the way from the far West [Morocco].
How wonderful is the condition of making a trip.
There he died in the city of [Great] pride,
The domicile of the leader of mankind and the best of creation.
Likewise, Shaykh Ali al-Harazim left Fez
For Medina city [in Saudi Arabia] for good
Until he died and was buried there.
Oh how lucky and how beautiful and successful his abode!
Both of them [left Fez] on the permission of Shaykh Ahmad
Father of Abbas my savior and my leader.
[Travelled] are many of the learned men of authority
And many [of their] successors in our blessed brotherhood,
And may God be contented with them all
So long as optimism in the grace of God prevails.

Figure 3.1. A typical page from one of the manuscripts in the Falke
collection. (Photograph of manuscript courtesy of
John N. Paden. All rights reserved.)

Abdullahi Mohammed   Reference # _000174_

Umar Falke Library Collection

Manuscript Code Sheet

1. Author's name _Abu Ishaq b. Ibrahim b. Mas'ud_

2. Title of Work _Talb al-'Ilm wa 'l-zuhd_

3. English Translation of Title _Search for knowledge and asceticism_

4. Keyword(s) description _Learning, asceticism_

5. Date of manuscript _1306 (1888-9 A.D)._

6. Number of Pages _15 p._

7. Complete or Incomplete _Complete_

8. Language _Arabic_

9. Type of writing _poetry_

10. Size of page/number lines per page _9 lines_

11. Scribe (if unpublished) _-_

12. Publisher/place of publication _Handwritten_

13. Significance of manuscript or author _Typical poem having a very strong influence on the lives of many Muslims in Nigeria._

14. Annotation regarding subject matter _The Author originally wrote in praise of his son encouraging him to study and to utilize the knowledge he acquires as well as practise asceticism for spiritual accomplishment rather than the worldly objectives of material benefits._

15. 0174

Figure 3.2. Manuscript code sheet.

```
1    ABU ISHAQ B. IBRAHIM B. MASUD
2    TAB AL-ILM WA AL-ZUHD
3    SEARCH FOR KNOWLEDGE AND ASCETICISM
4    LEARNING  *
     ASCETISM
5    1306 (1888-9 A.D.)
6    15  PAGES
7    COMPLETE
8    ARABIC
9    POETRY STYLE
10   9   LINES
11
12   HANDWRITTEN
13   TYPICAL POEM, HAVING A VERY STRONG INFLUENCE ON THE LIVES OF
     MANY MUSLIMS IN NIGERIA.
14   THE AUTHOR ORIGINALLY WROTE IN PRAISE OF HIS SON, ENCOURAGING HIM
     TO STUDY AND TO UTILIZE THE KNOWLEDGE HE ACQUIRED AS WELL AS
     PRACTICE ASCETICISM FOR SPIRITUAL ACCOMPLISHMENT RATHER THAN WORLDLY
     MATERIAL OBJECTS OR BENEFITS.
15   0174
```

Figure 3.3. Manuscript record after it has been transferred from code sheet to machine-readable input.

Arabic		Transliterated English		Computerized Double Letter English
أ	=	'A	=	A
ع	=	'A	=	AA
ت	=	T	=	T
ط	=	Ṭ	=	TT
س	=	S	=	S
ص	=	Ṣ	=	SS
ز	=	Z	=	Z
ظ	=	Ẓ	=	ZZ
د	=	D	=	D
ض	=	Ḍ	=	DD
ه	=	H	=	H
ح	=	Ḥ	=	HH

Figure 3.4. Suggested characters for the computer transliteration of the Falke Library.

to other scholars; (3) summary description of contents; and (4) hypothesis testing. During the following discussion, it should be kept in mind that we are presently experimenting with a very small file ($N = 17$). Its utility will no doubt emerge as the study progresses.

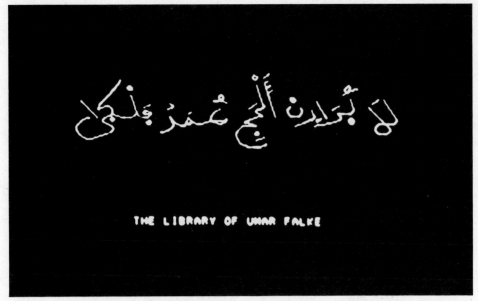

THE LIBRARY OF UMAR FALKE

Figure 3.5. Use of graphics as a possible solution to the problem of computer ethnocentrism.

Organizing, Cataloging and Cross–Referencing

The first step in the study of a library is the process of cataloging. Each work is read and assigned a catalog number. The author's identity is determined, pertinent facts noted (such as the quality of the manuscript, dated events, number of pages, where written, etc.), and a brief summary annotation is prepared. It is this basic catalog information which is entered onto the coding sheet, keypunched and used to create the RIQS file. Each type of information in the catalog (such as number of pages in the manuscript) becomes an *item* in the RIQS file. A series of items describing one particular manuscript then becomes a *record* on the RIQS file. Several ADD items were declared (though no information was entered) so that additional information of a type unforeseen at file creation could be added later. (See Figure 3.6.)

Certain RIQS commands were then used to produce the catalog report of selected items shown in Figure 3.7, which can then be easily duplicated or printed in multiple copies by the computer. This report serves as the working catalog of the library while research is progressing. One advantage of using a machine–readable file for this management task rather than the usual method of typing/printing/duplicating is that the file may be easily added to and updated. Hence, if further information is discovered about a manuscript, it can be added to the file and a revised catalog produced.

The power of using machine–readable information is well illustrated in the process of indexing the catalog. To do so by hand is a long, exacting, laborious, and frustrating process. When a collection of the magnitude of over 3000 manuscripts is involved, one can easily imagine a major part of one's proverbial lifetime (or pocketbook) being devoted to creating several inclusive cross–indexes. Using RIQS, however, one can easily generate indexes on any item or combination of items. For example, in Figure 3.8, we indexed the small test file by the author's name. Other possibilities being considered are an index by keywords (some of which correspond closely to the dimensions of Islamic knowledge discussed earlier), by language of document, by geographic location of author, etc. In addition, alphabetical indexes of single words can be easily generated to provide quick page references to catalog descriptions (Figure 3.9).

```
ITEM NUMBERS AND NAMES
----------------------

     1.    AUTHØR ...AUTHØR)S NAME
     2.    TITLE  ...TITLE ØF WØRK
     3.    ENGTITL...ENGLISH TRANSLATIØN ØF TITLE
     4.    KEYWØRD...KEYWØRD DESCRIPTIØN
     5.    DATE   ...DATE ØF MANUSCRIPT
     6.    NØPAGES...NØ. ØF PAGES
     7.    CØMPLET...CØMPLETIØN STATUS
     8.    LANG   ...LANGUAGE
     9.    TYPE   ...TYPE ØF WRITING
    10.    NØLINES...NØ. ØF LINES PER PAGE
    11.    SCRIBE ...SCRIBE (IF UNPUBLISHED)
    12.    PUBLSHR...PUBLISHER, PLACE ØF PUBLICATIØN
    13.    SIGNCE ...SIGNIFICANCE ØF MANUSCRIPT ØR AUTHØR
    14.    ANØTATN...ANNØTATIØN ABØUT SUBJECT MATTER
    15.    REFNUM ...FALKE LIBRARY REFERENCE NUMBER
    16.    CAMPNO  ...AFRICAN MICROFILM PROJECT NUMBER
    17.    ADD
    18.    ADD
    19.    ADD
    20.    ADD
```

Figure 3.6.   Record definition for the Falke Library. Each item of information is defined by a number, a short name, and a definition.

The experimental construction of various kinds of indexes may begin to suggest analytic categories and reveal meaningful relationships which had been previously obscured by the sheer bulk of the material. Thus, the ease of computer generated indexes frees a significant amount of time and money for the researcher to devote to the actual analysis, produces needed analytic tools, and suggests analytical patterns that may be of interest.

Summary Description of Contents

The study of written history has traditionally been regarded as perhaps more of an art than a science. After becoming familiar with primary documents, the historian usually attempts to synthesize their thematic content and integrate them into a larger perspective of the subject. Indeed, this has also been the method of Islamic scholars for many centuries. Only recently have western historians attempted to supplement this approach with the methodological techniques of description and inference that have been developed by behavioral scientists. In doing so, they are not attempting to challenge the validity of traditional methods, but rather to develop research techniques which complement them and add to the overall strength of historical analysis. Two of these methods are: (1) descriptive summary statistics and (2) hypothesis testing. Summary statistics add a precise notion of *how much* or *to what degree* to trend statements and hypothesized relationships which could previously only be derived intuitively.

Consider the Falke library, for example. After reading a large number of manuscripts, one develops an intuitive sense that a special focus of the library is in the field of protective

```
RECORD NUMBER      1


  1.   AUTHOR)S NAME
       ANON

  2.   TITLE OF WORK
       DAMAIR AL-TAUHID

  3.   ENGLISH TRANSLATION OF TITLE
       THE ESSENCE OF THEOLOGY

  4.   KEYWORD DESCRIPTION
       1. THEOLOGY

  5.   DATE OF MANUSCRIPT
       DATE UNKNOWN

  6.   NO. OF PAGES
       4 PAGES

  7.   COMPLETION STATUS
       COMPLETE

  8.   LANGUAGE
       1. ARABIC

  9.   TYPE OF WRITING
       1. PROSE STYLE

 10.   NO. OF LINES PER PAGE
       25 LINES

 12.   PUBLISHER, PLACE OF PUBLICATION
       HANDWRITTEN

 13.   SIGNIFICANCE OF MANUSCRIPT OR AUTHOR
       WEST AFRICAN STYLE OF LITERARY WRITING

 14.   ANNOTATION ABOUT SUBJECT MATTER
       UNIQUE CHARACTERISTICS OF GOD ARE FULLY DEFINED

 15.   FALKE LIBRARY REFERENCE NUMBER
       171
```

Figure 3.7. Falke Library catalog entry.

and secret medicine. Just *how much* of the library is a different question: is it 30 percent, or 50 percent, or 85 percent? Without physically counting each document by hand, it would be impossible to find out. Furthermore (suppose it is 30 percent of the library), how many of those works on secret medicine are written in Hausa as opposed to Arabic, how many are in poetic rather than prose form, how many suggest pharmaceutical remedies as opposed to spiritual remedies? Such information is crucial if one wishes to construct or test hypotheses that can be evaluated in terms of quantity. Note, however, that the numbers or counts of attributes of the documents mean nothing by themselves. Only when interpreted and placed into context by the trained historian do they acquire meaning as indicators of an historical or social process.

It was decided to attempt to use the RIQS file for some exploratory quantitative analysis and hypothesis testing. Using the file in this way would make accurate descriptive counts available that would be almost impossible to derive by hand. If one takes this purpose into account when designing the RIQS file structure, a file capable of being processed by SPSS (Statistical Package for the Social Sciences) can then be created by use of the SPSSFILE command. Figures 3.10 and 3.11 indicate a sample of the variety of statistical analyses conducted. In Figure 3.10 we obtained a codebook frequency

```
FADL AL-NAHWI

        FADL AL-NAHWI
        AL-WAZ
        ADMONITION
        DATE UNKNOWN
        14 PAGES
        COMPLETE
        ARABIC WITH INTERLINEAL COMMENTARY IN HAUSA AND ARABIC
        HAUSA
        9 LINES
        HANDWRITTEN
        THE WORK IS A GENERAL ADMONITION FOR THE ATTAINMENT OF SPIRITUAL
        COMPLETENESS AND WELL BEING.
        173

MUHAMMAD SALGA (MUHAMMAD AWWAL B. AHMAD)

        MUHAMMAD SALGA (MUHAMMAD AWWAL B.  AHMAD)
        SHAMSIYYAT AL-IKHWAN
        SUN RAY TO BROTHERS
        SHABAN
        12 PAGES
        COMPLETE
        ARABIC
        POETRY STYLE
        13 LINES
        HANDWRITTEN
        REPUTEDLY WRITTEN BY MUHAMMAD SALGA - A FAMOUS 20TH CENTURY
        MALLAM IN KANO
        CONDITIONS, VALUES, NECESSITY, AND THE ACTUAL PRACTICES OF THE
        TIJANIYYA BROTHERHOOD ARE DESCRIBED IN DETAIL.
        184

MUHAMMAD SANI MANDAWARI

        MUHAMMAD SANI MANDAWARI
        MU GODE TAALA
        PRAISE BE TO GOD
        TUESDAY (NO DATE)
        10 PAGES
        COMPLETE
        HAUSA WITH ARABIC INTERSPERSED
        ARABIC
        POETRY STYLE
        14 LINES
        HANDWRITTEN
        THE AUTHOR LIVES IN THE MANDAWARI WARD IN KANO CITY
        POEM PREPARED IN PRAISE OF GOD, HIS PROPHET MUHAMMAD, AND THE
        CHIEF SAINT, SHAYKH AHMAD AL-TIJANI, THE FOUNDER OF THE TIJANIYYA
        BROTHERHOOD, THROUGH WHOM SALVATION IS SOUGHT.
        191

NAMAIGANJI DAMBATTA

        NAMAIGANJI DAMBATTA
        GARGADIN WAWA
        A WARNING TO THE FOOL
        DATE UNKNOWN
        INCOMPLETE
        HAUSA
        POETRY STYLE
        11 LINES
        HANDWRITTEN
        THE POEM IS WELL KNOWN BY MOST PEOPLE IN KANO ESPECIALLY IN THE
        DAMBATTA DISTRICT.  THE AUTHOR IS FROM DAMBATTA, IN KANO STATE.
        ADMONITION TO PEOPLE TO WORSHIP GOD, THEIR CREATOR, TO DO GOOD TO
        OTHERS, AND TO AVOID EVIL OF ANY KIND.
        199
```

Figure 3.8.   Printed index of library collection sorted by author's name.

```
*** INDEX TO ANNOTATIONS OF THE FALKE LIBRARY CATALOG ***


                                    PAGES


            GABRIEL            14
            GAMES              8
            GOAL               13
            GOD                1,   7,   8,   9,  13,  16,  17
            GOOD               17
            GRAMMAR            10
            GREATEST           13
            HAND               8
            HEADACHE           12
            ILLNESSES          12
            INFLUENCE          5
            INTERLINEAL        10
            ISLAMIC            14
            JOSEPH             14
            JURISPRUDENCE      11
            KANO               6,  15,  16,  17
            KARIM              6
            KHALWA             13
            KNOWLEDGE          2,   5
            KUFITS             10
            LANGUAGE           3
            LEARNING           2
            LITERARY           1
            LITERATURE         3
            LIVES              5,  16
            LUCK               8
            MALLAM             15
            MAN                8
            MANDAWARI          16
            MATERIAL           5
            MEDICINE           12,  13
            MEMBERS            14
            METAPHORS          3
            MUHAMMAD           6,  14,  15,  16
            MUSLIM             11
            MUSLIMS            5
            MYTHICAL           2
            NAME               13
            NAMES              10
            NARRATIVES         2
            NECESSITY          15
            NIGERIA            5,  11
            NORTHERN           11
            OBJECTS            5
            PEOPLE             2,   8,  14,  17
            PERFECTION         9
            PERSON             8
            PERSONAL           8
            POEM               5,   6,   7,  16,  17
            POETRY             9
            PRACTICE           5
            PRACTICES          15
            PRAISE             5,   6,   7,   9,  16
            PRAYERS            13
            PROPHET            6,   7,   8,  14,  16
```

Figure 3.9. Index to page references by single words.

distribution of the major manuscript languages. Of our small sample of 17 documents, it is easily seen that Arabic is the dominant language (with 88 percent of the manuscripts written in Arabic as opposed to 12 percent in Hausa). In Figure 3.11 one can begin to determine the distribution of contextual themes in the library (with 12 percent of the works Admonitions, 6 percent Brotherhood, and so on).

```
ILLUSTRATIVE TEST OF BIBLIOGRAPHIC STATISTICAL ANALYSIS                    02/27/74

FILE   FALKE    (CREATION DATE = 02/27/74 )                SPSS SAVED FILE

VARIABLE   I008S001   PRIMARY DOCUMENT LANGUAGE


                  VALUE    ABSOLUTE    RELATIVE    ADJUSTED    CUMULATIVE
                           FREQUENCY   FREQUENCY   FREQUENCY   ADJ FREQ
                                       (PERCENT)   (PERCENT)   (PERCENT)
                  - - - - - - - - - - - - - - - - - - - - - - - - - - - -

                  ARABIC      15        88.2        88.2        88.2

                  HAUSA        2         11.8        11.8       100.0

                  NO DATA      0          0         MISSING     100.0
                           -------     -------     -------     -------
                  TOTAL       17        100.0       100.0       100.0
```

Figure 3.10. Frequency counts of primary document language.

```
ILLUSTRATIVE TEST OF BIBLIOGRAPHIC STATISTICAL ANALYSIS                    02/27/74

FILE   FALKE    (CREATION DATE = 02/27/74 )                SPSS SAVED FILE

VARIABLE   I004S001   FIRST KEYWORD DESCRIPTION


                  VALUE    ABSOLUTE    RELATIVE    ADJUSTED    CUMULATIVE
                           FREQUENCY   FREQUENCY   FREQUENCY   ADJ FREQ
                                       (PERCENT)   (PERCENT)   (PERCENT)
                  - - - - - - - - - - - - - - - - - - - - - - - - - - - -

                  ADMONITI     2         11.8        11.8        11.8

                  BRTHRHOO     1          5.9         5.9        17.6

                  GRAMMAR      1          5.9         5.9        23.5

                  JURISPRU     1          5.9         5.9        29.4

                  LEARNING     2         11.8        11.8        41.2

                  LITERATU     1          5.9         5.9        47.1

                  LOT          1          5.9         5.9        52.9

                  MEDICINE     3         17.6        17.6        70.6

                  POEM         4         23.5        23.5        94.1

                  THEOLOGY     1          5.9         5.9       100.0

                  NO DATA      0          0         MISSING     100.0
                           -------     -------     -------     -------
                  TOTAL       17        100.0       100.0       100.0
```

Figure 3.11. Frequency counts of contextual themes.

A technique which can be used both for descriptive purposes and for hypothesis testing is shown in Figure 3.12 where we have cross-tabulated the first keyword by the second. By convention, the second is usually an adjective or descriptor, the first is a noun described by the second. From the row percentages, it is seen that 75 percent of the poetic works are Praise poems, in contrast to 25 percent which are Religious poems. Although the table itself is rather meaningless due to the low N of the test file, such a table may reveal interesting relationships when computed for the entire file. Use of appropriate statistics of association (also computed by SPSS) such as Gamma, Yules Q, Chi-square, etc. make it possible to use similar tables as tests of posited relationships.

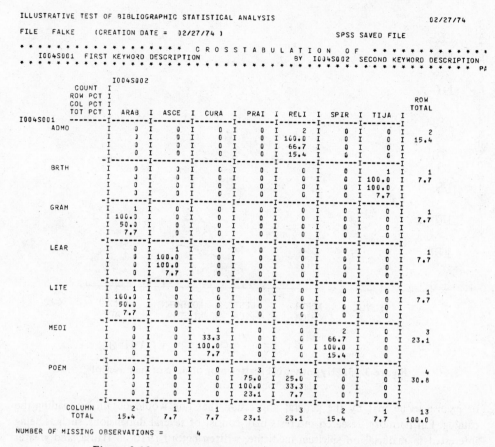

Figure 3.12. Cross–tabulation of keywords assigned to each manuscript record.

Hypothesis Testing

An example of hypothesis testing has been suggested by Dr. John Paden, who has proposed that the examination of the correlation between the date of the manuscript and the location where it was written might reveal the slow diffusion of Islamic knowledge from North Africa and the Middle East to northern Nigeria and Kano. To test such a notion, the plotting capabilities of RIQS or SPSS could be used to produce a plot of date versus location (Figure 3.13).

Each point represents the intersection of the particular values that a given manuscript has on both date and location. One can observe that the pattern of the points indicates a gradual trend for documents to be written closer and closer to Kano as the time dimension approaches the present.

Providing Search Accessibility to Scholars

An inherent part of the processing of such a library is creating reference guides to the contents for use by other scholars. The catalog and index discussed above were steps in this direction. However, the exploratory interests of other scholars may be too detailed

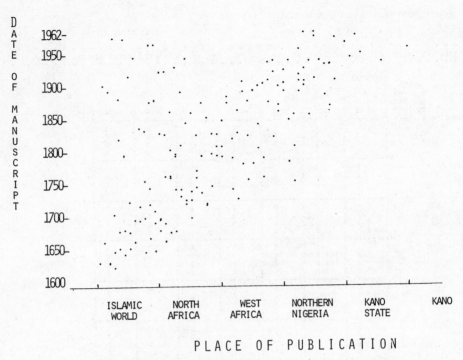

Figure 3.13. Hypothetical scatter plot of date of manuscript by place of publication.

or precise to be met by the general impression that one would obtain by reading the catalog. Furthermore, research interests may consist of several dimensions, such as being interested in material on spiritual medicine, written before 1910, in Hausa, and greater than five pages in length. The same RIQS file used for cataloging, description, and hypothesis testing can also be searched, either from a remote location or at Northwestern University, to retrieve those descriptions of manuscripts which satisfy the search conditions. By interactively searching, one can focus in on a number of documents salient to one's needs (Figure 3.14).

The Corporative Africana Microform Project (CAMP) of the Center for Research Libraries in Chicago will be microfilming the entire collection and the microfilm file number will appear in each record. Hence, a scholar will be able to reference the original source document. He could then request a copy of the microfilm from CAMP. This catalog file will be maintained at Northwestern and will be accessible to scholars either by terminal or by mailed requests. Thus, the library and its catalog take on a dual role as being both objects of a study and documented source material for further studies.

The remainder of this chapter will focus in more detail on the life and significance of Umar Falke and his library. This presentation is intended to illustrate some of the dimensions of Islamic life in West Africa which will be part of the final analysis.

Historical and Social Context of the Library

What is the general concept of a Hausa trader-scholar? How important is the Falke collection as a case study? Is the life style of Umar Falke reflected in the collection? Let us turn to the first question—the concept of Hausa trader-scholar.

```
IF #9 EQ 'POETRY' AND #8 EQ 'ARABIC' DISPLAY ACROSS #3 / #14 END

SEARCHING INITIATED


NO. OF REPORTS ON DISPLAY FILE =        8

DO YOU WANT THE DISPLAY REPORTS LISTED
? Y
```

> Which Arabic manuscripts were
> written in poetic style?
> Print the English title and
> the annotations.

```
RECORD NUMBER     3
    (3) LITERARY WORK OF HAIRIRI
    (14) FAMILIAR WORK IN RHETORIC, FIGURATIVE LANGUAGE (METAPHORS),
ALLITERATION AND OTHER BEAUTIES OF THE CLASSICAL LANGUAGE.


RECORD NUMBER     5
    (3) SEARCH FOR KNOWLEDGE AND ASCETICISM
    (14) THE AUTHOR ORIGINALLY WROTE IN PRAISE OF HIS SON,
ENCOURAGING HIM TO STUDY AND TO UTILIZE THE KNOWLEDGE HE ACQUIRED
AS WELL AS PRACTICE ASCETICISM FOR SPIRITUAL ACCOMPLISHMENT
RATHER THAN WORLDLY MATERIAL OBJECTS OR BENEFITS.


RECORD NUMBER     6
    (3) PROPHETIC PRAISE
    (14) PREPARED IN PRAISE OF THE PROPHET MUHAMMAD


RECORD NUMBER     7
    (3) THE VOICE I THANKED
    (14) THE POEM IS IN PRAISE OF THE PROPHET AND ALSO A REQUEST FOR
GOD)S FORGIVENESS AND SALVATION


RECORD NUMBER     9
    (3) GOD HAS GIVEN GUIDANCE
    (14) DIFFERENT TRADITIONAL THEOLOGY DESCRIBING THE UNIQUENESS AND
THE PERFECTION OF GOD)S CREATION AND HIS DOING AS WELL AS HIS
ABSOLUTE CHARACTERISTICS.


RECORD NUMBER    10
    (3) ARABIC GRAMMAR
    (14) ARABIC GRAMMAR, SOMETIMES QUOTING NAMES OF AUTHORITIES IN
THE FIELD, E.G.  AL-SUYUTI, BASRITES, KUFITS, ETC.  GRAMMATICAL
ANALYSIS BY -BISMILLAH- IS GIVEN.


RECORD NUMBER    15
    (3) SUN RAY TO BROTHERS
    (14) CONDITIONS, VALUES, NECESSITY, AND THE ACTUAL PRACTICES OF
THE TIJANIYYA BROTHERHOOD ARE DESCRIBED IN DETAIL.


RECORD NUMBER    16
    (3) PRAISE BE TO GOD
    (14) POEM PREPARED IN PRAISE OF GOD, HIS PROPHET MUHAMMAD, AND
THE CHIEF SAINT, SHAYKH AHMAD AL-TIJANI, THE FOUNDER OF THE
TIJANIYYA BROTHERHOOD, THROUGH WHOM SALVATION IS SOUGHT.
```

Figure 3.14.   On-line interactive interrogation of the Falke Library file.

"Malam" and "Falke (Bafatake)" are the two Hausa terms which characterize a scholar-trader. The term *Malam* (Mallam) is a derivation of the Arabic "Mu^{c}allim" which means a learned man, a theologian or jurist. The word *Falke* or *Farke* refers to an itinerant trader.[3] Umar was perhaps nicknamed "Falke" because of his mobile nature as a trader within Nigeria and abroad. In Nigerian Hausaland, the seven Hausa states (formerly known as Hausa Bakwai)—Kano, Rano, Katsina, Daura, Zaria, Birom, Gobir—were the traditional centers of the distributive trade system as well as the state capitals. The main distribution mechanism was the market, and its arteries were the trade routes along which the "fatake" (long-distance traders) moved in caravans.[4] (See Figure 3.15.) Pilkington describes the itinerant trader of Hausaland thus:

> He goes far; he is one of the world's most travelled men, and much of his travelling done on foot. Across the width of Africa he goes to Mecca and from his home in Kano goes still farther north to Alexandria and south to Lagos. He visits the Gold Coast and crosses many boundaries, always selling as he goes, circulating the creations of beauty and works of art he buys in different Nigerian towns.[5]

Another Hausa term to describe the trader-scholar is "Alhaji," a traditional title which distinguishes an itinerant trader who has performed his ritual pilgrimage to Mecca from the one who has not. Umar Falke did make the pilgrimage, and is clearly in touch with Middle Eastern sources of Islamic thought. It is the aspiration of most Hausa traders, especially the itinerant scholar-trader, to perform the ritual pilgrimage at least once. They would like to visit the international communities in the holy land—Mecca, Medina, and Jerusalem. Traders depart for the pilgrimage in the holy land not only for religious obligations and spiritual accomplishment but also for social prestige, economic advancement, and political influence, as well as educational enlightenment and other privileges. The essence of a Hausa scholar-trader is therefore conveyed in these three common Hausa titles—"Malam, Alhaji, and Falke."

Falke's full name was Umar b. abi-Bakr b. Abi-Bakr al-Kanawi al-Tijani, nicknamed "Falke." "He was born in the village of Gulu, near Kano in 1893. He came to Kano city when he was a teenager and settled in Bakin-Ruwa ward."[6] He was a Hausa-Tuareg of Buzu origin. Umar's father, Abubakar, was a wealthy merchant and itinerant trader, who wanted his son to follow in the same profession. Umar writes about the initial orientation he received in preparation for his success in trading. At the age of twenty-seven (1920) he was ordered by his father to leave Kano for Yaryawa in Wurno where the father was then living. Perhaps it was in Wurno that his father declared his plans for Umar:

> I learned how to trade from him [his father] in one full year. Then he gave me some money to go to Adamawa for three years. I spent all those years doing nothing except pursuing the course of learning, as well as sewing dresses to earn a living. At that time I was not so much preoccupied with the accumulation of wealth. Rather, I was more concerned with the accumulation of knowledge.[7]

Although Umar did not reject the idea of becoming a trader, his priority was to acquire a religious-intellectual training, which could be utilized as a basis for his vocation of trading. He was determined to obtain as much Islamic learning as possible before he became an itinerant trader-scholar, circulating through Nigeria (including Abeokuta, Ibadan, and Lagos), Ghana, Sierra Leone, and Senegal.

In his early endeavor to learn, Umar Falke, like many a Muslim scholar in the Western Sudan, traveled from one *Mallam* to another, to study particular books and disciplines. He

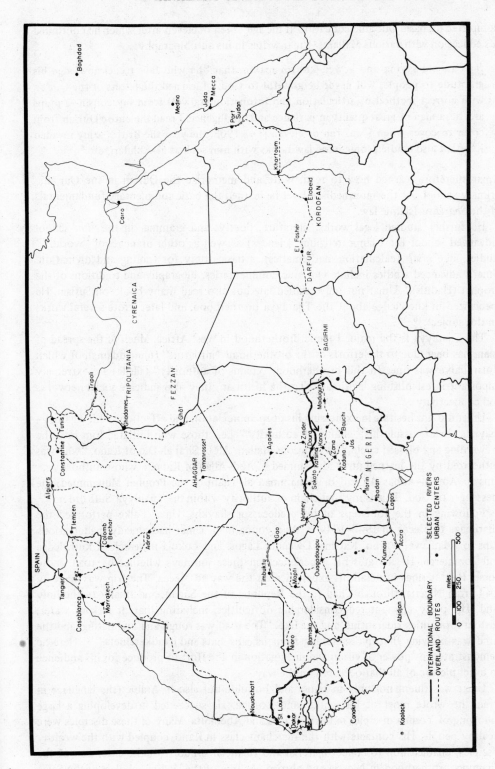

Figure 3.15. Africa: Trade and pilgrimage routes travelled by Umar Falke and other itinerant traders. (Map courtesy of John N. Paden. All rights reserved.)

completed his basic Qur'anic education at the age of ten or eleven after which he continued his education with various Mallams. Umar writes in his autobiography:

> It is an old saying and a well-known maxim that "he who fails to acknowledge his gratitude to people, will never be grateful to God." I learned the letters of the Qur'an with correct method of articulation and intonation (tajwid) from my cousin—a pious ascetic, a man of great quality in patience and intelligence. I read the entire Qur'an from cover to cover when I was ten or eleven [i.e., 1903, the year the British army invaded Kano]. I also studied some basic law books with him such as al-Akhdari, etc.[8]

Umar therefore learned how to read, write and memorize the Qur'an in the Qur'anic primary school. At the intermediate level he learned the basic rudimentary fundamentals of the *Sharia* or Islamic law.

He further studied legal works, literature, poetry, and grammar in the ^{c}llm school (advanced school for Islamic religious sciences) as well as other branches of "worldly" studies, like *hisab* (calculation/mathematics), a basic study for trading and divination. Umar's advanced studies include Qur'anic commentaries, biography and traditions of the Prophet (Hadith).[9] Umar not only studied law but also read many books on Sufism. He specialized in knowledge about the Tijaniyya brotherhood, and later wrote several works on this subject.[10]

The Tijaniyya is the major Islamic brotherhood in West Africa. Much of the spread of Islam has been due to the efforts of the brotherhood "initiators" (muqaddams), of which Umar Falke was one. In this brotherhood, "chains of authority" (silsila) are extremely important in establishing legitimacy. To the historian, they also indicate social networks and connectivity.

Umar did not hesitate in expressing his deep appreciation and affection to his Tijaniyya shaykhs. In discussing his "chains of authority," i.e., those who initiated him into the "rewarding and blessed circle," he mentions Mallam Ali b. Siraj al-Din of Kano, "who was authorized by the learned jurist Muhammed b. Abd-Allah of Kano...whose authority... runs to Abu al-Abbas Ahmad b. Muhammad al-Tijani to the Prophet Muhammad, the messenger of God. This is my first chain of authority within the Tijaniyya Sufi order."[11]

Following in the footsteps of his predecessor shaykhs, Umar Falke performed the pilgrimage to Mecca in 1948-1949.[12] As a young man, Umar had already made various trips to Adamawa, Wurno, Katsina, Gwandu, Lagos, and Lokoja in search of knowledge and commerce. He narrates his experiences on these journeys whether by road or by horse. He describes in detail his experience on the way to Mecca. The trip was made by road from Nigeria, through Chad to the Republic of the Sudan, and finally to the holy land. His party encountered considerable difficulties, including that of lack of water, custom formalities, quarantine, and the like. "The road was rough and undulating, and the wind was blowing fiercely, snatching from us caps, hats and handkerchiefs."[13] Here he demonstrates his power of vision and imagination in an effort to produce for his audience an exact picture of all that occurred on the way.

Umar was fluent not only in Hausa and Fulfulde but also in Arabic (the language in which he wrote most of his works) and Yoruba. He succeeded in developing a large following of Yoruba disciples in Ilorin, Lagos and Abeokuta. Many of these disciples were wealthy people. His contacts with the merchant class in Kano, coupled with the wealthy disciples, enabled him to collect material and financial support for the extension of the Tijaniyya brotherhood in Nigeria and abroad. As one of the leading scholars of the Salga school, Umar studied directly under Ibrahim Niass and made many trips to Senegal.

Dr. Paden observes that Umar "became a prolific writer on all aspects of the Tijaniyya brotherhood" when he returned from his studies in Senegal.[14] In his library collection we find a number of works by Falke himself dealing with topics relating to Tijaniyya brotherhood, including history, leadership, ritual litanies, ideology, and doctrine.

Conclusions

Many western scholars have written about the trader-scholars of West Africa and yet no detailed study has been made on any one of them. Professor Ivor Wilks has made a major contribution to our understanding of trader-scholars in West Africa by his study of the Dyula, a significant portion of the Muslim trading group in West Africa.[15] But there has been no detailed study made on the Hausa Mallam trading-class in Sudanic West Africa. It is difficult, if not impossible, to understand the way they think without making such an investigation. It is equally important to know how these trader-scholars organize their lives and how their minds work, as they participate in the process of rapid social change and widespread social communications.

The life of Umar Falke exemplifies this combination of commercial trade with Islamic learning. The study of his library is potentially significant in that it will shed light on an important individual trader-scholar of the central Sudan. We expect the inquiry will not only throw light on Umar Falke as an itinerant Mallam but will also reflect on the fundamental activities and methods of the tradition of Islamic learning and scholarship as it operates in the Hausaland of Nigeria and neighboring states.

The advantages and effectiveness of computer methods are an invaluable tool. Hopefully, this project will help scholars of Islam in Africa in their effort to analyze classical Islamic education as well as social change patterns. The life and career of Umar Falke and his contribution to Islamic education, healing, and social integration not only in Nigeria but also in neighboring West African countries is regarded as typical rather than unique. We hope other libraries in West Africa can be reconstructed or analyzed before they disappear. We are investigating techniques which may be essential to the overall reconstruction of West African Islamic history.

On Friday afternoons, time stands still in Kano. Thousands of people in white robes silently fill the square by the central mosque. The usual urban din of shouts, horns, animals and the marketplace disappears, replaced by an unearthly silence, marked only by the plaintive cries of the prayer reader. All turn toward Mecca, thousands of miles away, and say their prayers together. It is a tradition, and lifestyle, and community enrichment that has been going on for centuries. The Falke library is a living example and documentation of that tradition. Work being done at Northwestern represents a unique symbiotic synthesis of the old (handwritten Arabic/Hausa manuscripts) and the new (electronic computers), of the divergent cultures of the East and the West, of the intellectual skills of a classically trained Arabic scholar with those of a behaviorally trained Westerner. For the meeting of these two worlds, and the benefits that each can give to the other, "Alhamdulillahi" (Let Allah be praised!).

NOTES AND CITED REFERENCES

1. Professor John Paden, of Northwestern University, has been of great assistance in writing this chapter. When Falke died in 1962, his library was distributed among his six sons but was reconstructed by Dr. Paden in 1970. We are grateful to Professor Paden for his efforts in bringing these materials to light.

2. The "Jihad" or "holy war" of Usman dan Fodio in the early nineteenth century established the Sokoto empire, of which Kano was a part. The leaders of the Jihad wrote a number of "books" on religious, social, and political matters.

3. Bargery, G. P. *A Hausa–English Dictionary and English–Hausa Vocabulary.* London, Oxford University Press, 1934. For elucidation and usage of the terms in various contexts see: Abraham, R. C. *Dictionary of the Hausa Language.*

4. See M. G. Smith. "Exchange of Marketing Among the Hausa" in Paul Bohannan and George Dalton, (*ed*), *Markets in Africa,* Northwestern University Press, 1962.

5. Pilkington, Frederick. "The Hausa Trader of Nigeria" in *African World,* February 1951, p. 11.

6. Paden, J. N. *Religion and Political Culture in Kano,* Berkeley, University of California Press, 1973, p. 101.

7. Falke, Umar. *Mafākhir al-Jil al-Kirām* otherwise known as *Asmā abā' ī fi'l-ilm wa al-tarīqa* [glorious traits and biographies of my teachers] mss. p. 12.

8. ibid.

9. With regard to Hadith discipline, Umar studied *Muwatta Malik* (The Maliki Legal book) in Kano and Gwandu.

10. Falke, Umar. *Mafakhir,* Chapter II on the Tijaniyya chains of authority.

11. Falke, Umar. *'Aun al-murid* (an aid or a guide to disciple) in praise of Ahmad al-Tijani.

12. Falke, Umar, *al-Rihla al Falkiyya* (Falke's journey to Mecca) 1948, p. 1. It is still uncertain as to whether the trip took place in 1937 or 1948-1949.

13. Falke, Umar. *al-Rihla al-Chauthiyya* (A Journey to the Leader, i.e., Falke's trip to Kaolack in honor of the principal leader of Tijaniyya).

14. Paden, op cit., p. 102.

15. Wilks, Ivor. "The growth of Islamic learning in Ghana," *Journal of the Historical Society of Nigeria* II 1963, pp. 409-417; and "The transmission of Islamic learning in the Western Sudan," in J. Goody (ed.), *Literacy in Traditional Societies,* Cambridge, 1968, pp. 161-197.

Chapter 4

Management of Data on Social Behavior of Free-Ranging Rhesus Monkeys [1]

DONALD STONE SADE
Northwestern University and
University of Puerto Rico

The Problem

Numerous observational studies of monkeys, apes, and other members of the mammalian order Primates during the last decade have given us much fascinating new information about the ecology and social behavior of these long-lived, large-brained, slow maturing animals, man's closest relatives in the animal kingdom. The systems of communication that display the network of social bonds that integrate the local groups of these animals are largely visual and auditory, and thus accessible to the human observer. These systems of communication are fairly simple and have been described and analyzed successfully by techniques first developed in ethological work on birds and fishes.

Principles of evolutionary biology, firmly established in the study of social behavior of other animals, are also found to be equally pertinent in explaining the societies of man's closest relatives. In monkey groups, however, the networks of social relations are compounded in ways reminiscent of the organization of human societies. Kinship networks develop because the slowly maturing offspring continue to orient to their mother past the time of weaning, and they interact also with their younger and older siblings. Three or four generations may be present within a group at the same time because of the long life of the individuals. Because offspring tend to take the social rank of their parents, the status hierarchy among the adults tends to become elaborated into a hierarchy of family groups reminiscent of the class structure of human groups. And yet monkey groups lack the symbolic complexities of culturized human societies. Study of the social organization of monkeys and apes are revealing the biologically based social processes which may also be operating in human groups although masked and confounded by the symbolic cultural complexities characteristic of the human species. [2]

Field Studies of Primates

Although astute observers can gain detailed personal knowledge about the complex workings of societies of nonhuman primates, generalizations about their social behavior remain anecdotal and therefore of minimum scientific value unless conclusions can be systematically justified by direct reference to original and often quantified field observations. Events of interest must be recorded sequentially as they occur in the field, and are usually entered as hand-written field notes or dictated onto a portable tape recorder. Events of the same category may be widely scattered throughout a large volume of field records that are not easy to scan.

BULK OF DATA

Stuart Altmann[3] pointed out that a field study of a primate species might easily produce 90,000 entries that would then need to be indexed, cross-referenced, and ultimately sorted, tabulated, and analyzed. Although such a task is not necessarily impossible to perform by hand, the analytical productivity of the field worker would be very many times increased if the job could be taken over by automatic equipment.

DIRECT CODING OF DATA

Some experimental laboratories have developed systems in which the original observations are coded on a keyboard that feeds directly to a cassette, disk, or other machine-readable device. In these laboratories the subjects are usually caged in a controlled environment and the observer remains stationary at a table in a comfortable room.

Portable equipment also is being developed that allows direct coding on tape of the onset, duration, and sequence of behavioral events that can be digitally coded. With these systems a unique number or set of keyboard entries represents a single, well-bounded category of behavior.

Studies that can use such equipment are usually specialized in that they investigate a limited set of problems, such as the degree to which the frequency of interaction between an infant monkey and its mother decreases as the infant matures. Experimental and control infants raised under sets of carefully controlled conditions are compared. Usually these studies make use of a behavioral typology or taxonomy containing a relatively small or limited set of well-bounded categories of behavior that can be recorded without qualification or additional description. The experiments usually are carried out within a simple and controlled environment, and the number of subjects is often small.

SPECIAL PROBLEMS IN STUDIES OF FREE-RANGING PRIMATES

Observers of free-ranging primates, however, usually work under conditions where there are a large number of individual subjects, and in habitats where observations are difficult because the animals are often concealed much of the time by vegetation. The observer may need to move on foot over long distances to find and maintain contact with his subjects. Since the habitat of primates often is inimical to electronic equipment, if not to the observer, because of dust, heat, humidity, or torrential rain, it is likely that a pen and notebook will remain for some time to come the major instruments by which field observations are recorded.

In addition, many field studies are conducted to obtain information on species that are not already well known. The behavioral categories must be developed and described as observations proceed during the course of the study. Usually the initial categories require continuous modification as the observer's experience with the animals increases. The author has found that even after ten years of work with a well-known species, the rhesus monkey (*Macaca mulatta*), many new features of the behavioral repertory emerge and require detailed verbal description.

The development of computerized information management systems capable of dealing with large volumes of textual material therefore should be seen as a boon to their work by students of primate behavior.

UNIQUE PROBLEMS OF THE CURRENT STUDY

The author's research presents some unique problems due to its magnitude and duration.[4] Its three phases may be identified:

First phase: The author observed a single group of free-ranging rhesus monkeys on the colony at Cayo Santiago, a forty-acre key off the south-east coast of Puerto Rico, over a period of five years.

Second phase: At the end of the first phase it was clear that continuing the study would provide a unique set of longitudinal records spanning several monkey generations. The author trained a series of students, who observed the same group of monkeys continuously for five additional years.

Third phase: At the end of the second phase it seemed desirable to extend the observations to the entire population of five social groups inhabiting the island, because it became apparent that a system of interacting social groups was a meaningful unit of biological organization about which little was known. The author therefore recruited a team of five observers, each to observe a different group within the population for a year. These observations are now being made. A new team of observers will be recruited each year to observe all the groups within the population for a total of five years, which is one monkey generation.

The three phases of the study have each produced a large volume of field notes. We estimate that each observer has produced between three hundred thousand and five hundred thousand card images of data per year. Each card image may contain several discrete items of information that should be indexed and sorted as independent units.

The Data

OBSERVATIONAL TECHNIQUES

The scope of the project means that the methodology has had to remain generalized and our data ill-suited for direct digital coding.

The observational techniques are intended to provide a cross-sectional sampling of each monkey's activity and interactions each day, and therefore a sample of all activities within the group. The monkeys at Cayo Santiago are individually tattooed with unique letter and number combinations, and all behavioral events are described in reference to positively identified individuals. The observer walks among the monkeys, being careful to avoid spending an inordinate amount of time in one place or among a particular subgroup of monkeys. All observed episodes of grooming, body contact, play, mounting, series mounting, close following, auto-erotic behavior, locomotor displays, courtship displays, reassurance displays, as well as any obvious orientations of individuals to others, such as scanning or peering, are described in the field notes. Obvious morphological changes, such as wounds, eruption of canines, descent of testes or reddening of sex skin, are also described. Group movements and intergroup encounters are also noted and where possible details of individual participation are described. The membership of spatially segregated subgroups within the main groups are also noted. Observers are alert to unique or unusual events and describe them in the notes. Manipulation of objects, or of animals of other species, and foraging on plants are described.

UNITS OF OBSERVATION

The field observations cannot easily be coded digitally because the motor patterns and vocalizations displayed by the monkeys are variable in several dimensions. Each of the large number of individual motor patterns may vary in the intensity with which it is displayed. The movements produced within the separate anatomical components vary somewhat independently of one another and combine in a variety of compound displays.

The social context within which the interactions occur must also be described, but it may vary considerably from moment to moment, and in contrast with the laboratory study is difficult to describe in preset categories.

Description of these complex events still seems to require the flexibility of spoken or written language.

It is often useful for the observer to record immediately, with the description of the interaction, his judgments as to its meaning or his uncertainty as to its significance.

The description of an episode of interaction includes the names of the interacting individuals, the direction of the events of communication, and the sequence of events. For instance: "A directs open-mouth-face to B, B cowers to A, A walks with alert face, but with lips pursed slightly and tail horizontal, to B, A places hands on B's hips as if to mount, B grimaces and jumps away, B disappears, A sits in neutral posture." Any necessary qualification or additional description of postures, facial expressions, or other expressive behavior may be added to the basic description. The context of the episode might include mention of the presence or absence of other individuals who might have affected the interaction. Observers are also careful to note whether a particular feature of behavior such as a special facial expression did not occur, for the absence of events may be as important as their occurrence in interpreting the behavior later on. Observers are careful to note whether or not they had the opportunity to observe a characteristic whose presence might importantly affect interpretation. For instance, in an interaction between two adult males whose relative dominance rank was uncertain, the observer would be careful to note that he could not see the face of the male who might be subordinate, and therefore was unable to report whether or not the fear grimace appeared.

I know of no system, other than careful use of precise language, sufficiently flexible and rich for recording data of this complexity.

OBSERVABILITY SAMPLES

At Cayo Santiago it is seldom possible to observe the entire group at a time since the animals are usually dispersed throughout woods or underbrush. A sampling technique is used to estimate and correct for biases due to differential observability of individuals.

Twice each hour each observer takes a two-minute sample, the specific time determined beforehand from a random number table. During each sample the observer attempts to behave in a manner identical to that during regular observations, except that he notes all the monkeys in view that can be identified and what they are doing. No search is made during the sample for animals who are not in view, unless the observer was already searching when the sample began. During regular observations usually only interactions are recorded.

These samples allow us to state whether particular animals or classes of animals are being observed much more frequently than others.[5]

Research Strategy

ANY EPISODE MAY RELATE TO A NUMBER OF TOPICS

The unit of observation is the *episode,* which may consist of a long sequence of more minute activities and require a paragraph or more to describe, or an episode may be merely a note that monkey A groomed monkey B, requiring only three words. Any single episode may relate to a variety of topics.

CATEGORIES OF BEHAVIOR

A datum may be retrieved because it gives us information about a certain category of behavior. It may, for instance, contain a description of a facial expression, such as the open-mouth-face used by the dominant animal in an aggressive interaction. We might wish to retrieve all episodes in which the open-mouth-face occurred in order to study the distribution of the expression within the communicative field.

STATUSES OF INDIVIDUALS

The same episode would also give us information about the dominance status of the individual who displayed the open-mouth-face in the interaction, relative to the individual to whom it was displayed, and the episode would be retrieved among all the aggressive interactions in which the individual who gave it participated over a number of years, to trace the maturation of his dominance status.

INTERACTIONAL NETWORKS WITHIN THE GROUP

The same episode might be retrieved as part of a study of the interactional networks within the social group during a given interval. The interval might correspond to a season of the year, such as the mating or birth season, or it might be a period that immediately preceded or followed a sudden change in a particular individual's status. Interesting periods of this sort are those immediately prior to and following the sudden death of the dominant male. In such a case the question would be to see if the sudden loss of a central figure resulted in a sudden shift in the interactional network within the group.

One means of displaying the network of social relations in a group is to tabulate dyadic interactions onto sociometric matrices. These are $N \times N$ matrices with the individuals of the group naming the rows, and also the columns in the same order. The entries in the cells correspond to messages sent from the row monkey to the column monkey, or the entry may represent a more complex statement of the relations between the two individuals. Sociometric matrices have some very useful properties for revealing group structure, as discussed in later sections.

TOPICS DEFINED AFTER THE FACT

Some topics may not be defined until some time after the data are entered into the retrieval system. For instance, a subgroup may form within one of the social groups. When this becomes apparent to the field observer, we would want to find the interactional antecedents of the subgroup in earlier records by analyzing them with the sociometric techniques mentioned below.

PREPARATION OF DATA

Field observers often transcribe their field notes daily in order to assure a second copy for backup. Often some preliminary editing and cataloging is done at this time. Typing the daily notes onto file cards by category of activity is a common method. In the current study the hand-written field notes are typed with a special electric typewriter equipped with an OCR font onto special paper. The data are typed in a format for the RIQS processor. The sheets are then read by an optical scanner that writes the data onto magnetic tape. The RIQS files are created from files copied from the data tape after initial corrections are made. The flow chart (Figure 4.1) shows the pathways of data processing used by the project. Figures 4.2, 4.3, and 4.4 show the data in various stages of processing.

Data Files

Each observer usually is assigned a single social group of monkeys. Each observer's notes are maintained in a separate RIQS file. If a person has observed more than one social group of monkeys, his observations on each group are maintained in a different file.

RIQS RECORD DEFINITION

Each RIQS record corresponds to an episode of behavior as recorded in the field notes. As the field notes are taken, the observer marks the beginning and ending of each record to aid transcription. Eight items are defined in the RECORD DEFINITION phase:

1. Date on which the episode occurred; Simple; Type = DATE.
   Searches on this item result in sets of records obtained during an interval of interest to the investigator as discussed earlier.
2. Time at start of episode; Simple; Type = INTEGER.
   The time at the start of each episode is recorded according to the twenty-four hour system.
3. Text of episode; Multiple; Type = ALPHANUMERIC.
   The description of the episode of behavior is reproduced just as recorded in the field notes. Some of the abbreviations used in the notes may be expanded to aid the user of the system. Each sentence of the description is a subitem. The subitems are separated by periods as in ordinary prose. Additional comments by the observer may be added to item three during transcription.

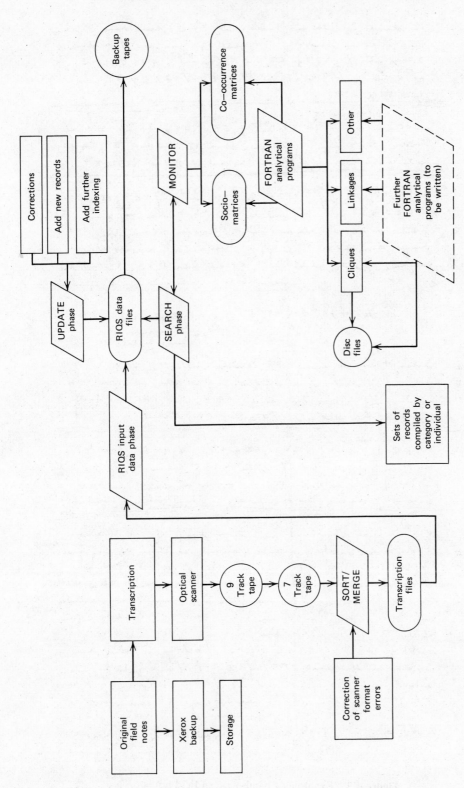

Figure 4.1. Pathways of processing and storage of data.

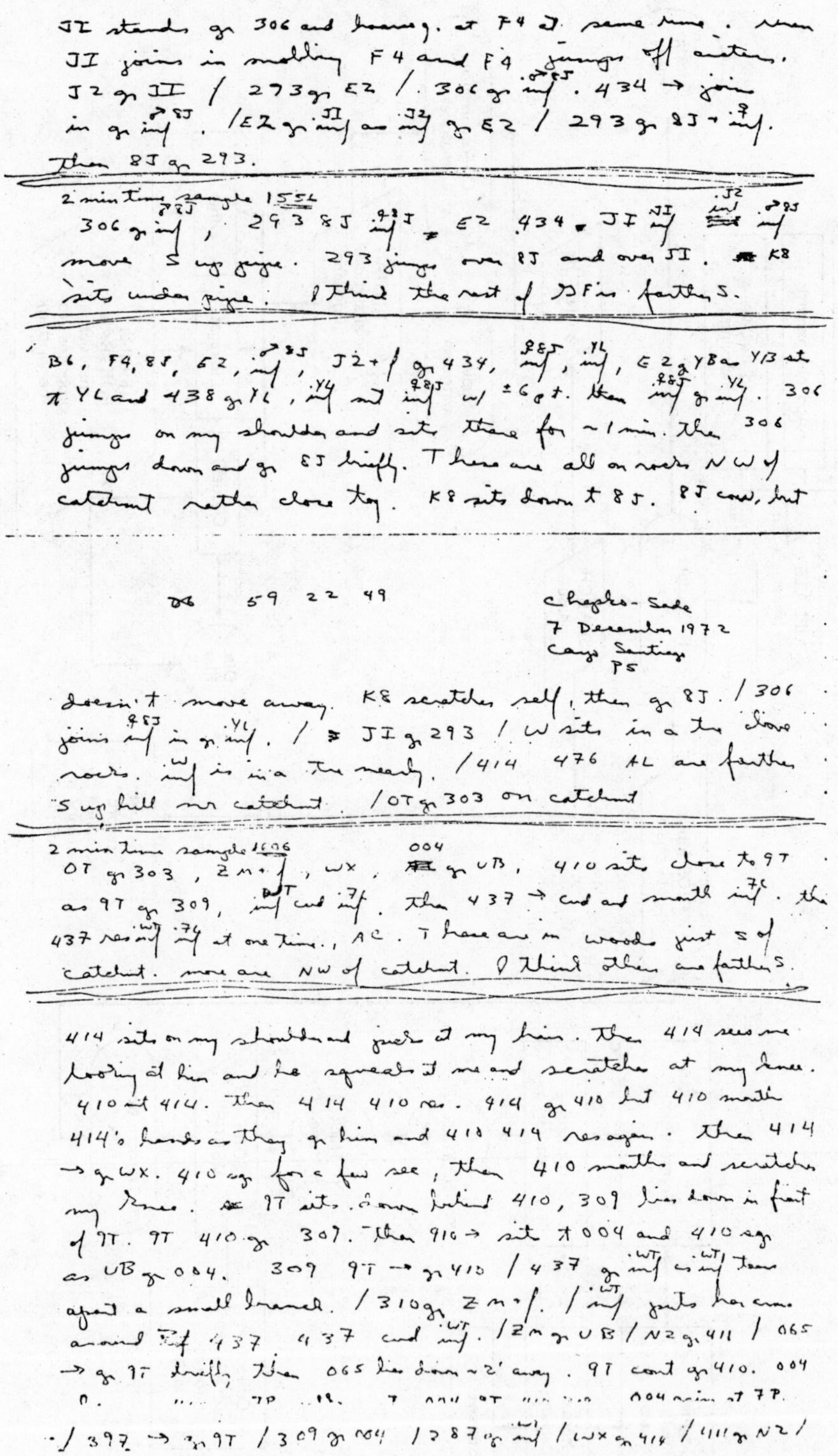

Figure 4.2. Example of hand–written field notes.

```
54194/ PIPE. I THINK THE REST OF GROUP F IS FARTHER S. {7}Z306 G Z728JA, {8}LOC
54196/, {1}07DEC72 {2}1558 {3}ZB6, ZF4, Z8J, ZE2, Z728JA, ZJ2 PLUS F G Z434,
54198/ Z728JF, Z72YLF, ZE2 G ZYB AS ZYB SITS T ZYL AND Z438 G ZYL, Z72YLF MOUNT
54200/ Z728JF, WITH PLUS OR MINUS 6 PTS. THEN Z728JF G Z72YLF. Z306 JUMPS ON MY
54202/ SHOULDER AND SITS THERE FOR APP 1 MIN. THEN Z306 JUMPS DOWN AND G Z8J
54204/ BRIEFLY. THESE ARE ALL ON ROCKS NW OF CATCHMT RATHER CLOSE TOGETHER. ZK8
54206/ SITS DOWN T Z8J. Z8J COW., BUT DOESN'T MOVE AWAY. CK8 SCRATCHES SELF, THE
54206/ SITS DOWN T Z8J. Z8J COW, BUT DOESN'T MOVE AWAY. ZK8 SCRATCHES SELF,
54208/ THEN ZK8 G Z8J. {4}ZJ2 G Z434, ZE2 G ZYB, ZYB BC ZYL, Z438 G ZYL, Z72YLF
54210/ MOUNTS Z728JF, Z728JF G Z72YLF, Z306 G Z8J, ZK8 BC Z8J, ZK8 DOM Z8J, ZK
54212/ ZK8 G Z8J, {5}CENSUS, LOC, HUMAN {1}07DEC72 {2}1558 {4}ZJI G Z293 {1}073
54214/ 07DEC72 {2}1558 {3}ZW SITS IN A TRE ABOVE ROCKS. Z72WF IS IN A TRE NEARB
54216/BY. {5}CENSUS {1}07DEC72 {2}1558 {3}Z414 Z476 ZAL ARE FARTHER S UP HILL
54218/ NEAR CATCHMT. {5}CENSUS, LOC {1}07DEC72 {2}1558 {3}Z0T G Z303 ON CATCHMT
54220/ {4}Z0T G Z303 {5}LOC {1}07DEC72 {2}1606 {5}TWO MIN TIME SAMPLE {6}Z0T G
54222/ Z303, ZZM PLUS F, ZWX, Z004 G ZUB, Z410 SITS CLOSE TO Z9T AS Z9T G Z309,
54224/ Z72WTF CUD Z727LF%. THEN Z437 MOVES TO CUD AND MOUTH Z727LF. THEN Z437
54226/ RES Z72WTF Z727LF AT ONE TIME, ZAC, THESE ARE IN WOODS JUST S OF CATCHMT
54228/. MORE ARE NW OF CATCHMT. I THINK OTHERS ARE FARTHER S. {7}Z0T G Z303, Z
54230/ Z004 G ZUB, Z410 SCL Z9T, Z9T G Z309, Z72WTF CUD Z727LF, Z437 CUD Z727LF
54232/, Z437 PLAY Z72WTF, Z437 PLAY Z727LF, {8}PARENTAL, PLAY, LOC {1}07DEC72
54234/ {2}16078 {3}Z414 SITS ON MY SHOULDER AND PICKS AT MY HAIR. THEN Z414 SEES
54236/ ME LOOKING AT HIM AND HE SQUEAKS%LS AT ME AND SCRATCHES AT MY KNEE. Z410
54238/ MOUNTS Z414. THEN Z410 Z414 RES. Z414 G Z410, BUT Z410 MOUTHS Z414'S
54240/ HANDS AS THEY GROOM HIM, AND THEN Z410 Z414 RES AGAIN. THEN Z414 MOVES T
54242/ TO G ZWX. Z410 SGR FOR A FEW SECONDS, THEN Z410 MOUTHES AND SCRATCHES MY
54244/ KNEE. Z9T SITS DOWN BEHIND Z410, Z309 LIES DOWN IN FRONT OF Z9T. Z9T ZK%
54246/ Z410 G Z309. THEN Z410 MOVES TO SIT T Z004 AND Z410 SGR AS ZUB G Z004.
54248/ Z309 Z9T MOVE TO G Z410. {4}Z410 MOUNTS Z414, Z410 PLAY Z414, Z414 G ZK%
54250/ Z410, Z410 PLAY Z414, Z414 G ZWX, Z9T SCL Z410, Z309 LCL Z9T, Z309 LCL
54252/ Z410, Z9T G Z309, Z410 G Z309, Z410 BC Z004, ZUB G Z004, Z309 G Z410,
54254/ Z9T G Z410, {5}HUMAN {1}07DEC72 {2}1608 {3}Z437 G Z72WTF AS Z72WTF TEARS
54256/ APART A SMALL BRANCH {4}Z437 G Z72WTF {5}OBJECT {1}07DEC72 {2}1608 {3}
54258/ Z310 G ZZM PLUS F {4}Z310 G ZZM {1}07DEC72 {2}1608 {3}Z72WTF PUTS HER
54260/ ARMS AROUND Z437. Z437 CUD Z72WTF {4}Z437 CUD Z72WTF {1}07DEC72 {2}1608
54262/ {4}ZZM G ZUB, ZN2 G Z411 {1}07DEC72 {2}1608 {3}Z065 MOVES TO G Z9T BRIEF
```

Figure 4.3. Transcription of same notes as in Figure 4.2,
ready for optical scanning.

```
RECØRD NUMBER  994

  1.  DATE
        07DEC72
  2.  TIME
        1558
  3.  TEXT
        SUB-1.... ZB6, ZF4, Z8J, ZE2, Z728JA, ZJ2 PLUS F G Z434,
                  Z728JF, Z72YLF, ZE2 G ZYB AS ZYB SITS T ZYL AND
                  Z438 G ZYL, Z72YLF MØUNT Z728JF, WITH PLUS ØR
                  MINUS 6 PTS
        SUB-2.... THEN Z728JF G Z72YLF
        SUB-3.... Z306 JUMPS ØN MY SHØULDER AND SITS THERE FØR APP
                  1 MIN
        SUB-4.... THEN Z306 JUMPS DØWN AND G Z8J BRIEFLY
        SUB-5.... THESE ARE ALL ØN RØCKS NW ØF CATCHMT RATHER CLØSE
                  TØGETHER
        SUB-6.... ZK8 SITS DØWN T Z8J
        SUB-7.... Z8J CØW, BUT DØESN ' T MØVE AWAY
        SUB-8.... ZK8 SCRATCHES SELF, THEN ZK8 G Z8J
  4.  DYADS IN TEXT
        SUB-1.... ZJ2 G Z434
        SUB-2.... ZE2 G ZYB
        SUB-3.... ZYB BC ZYL
        SUB-4.... Z438 G ZYL
        SUB-5.... Z72YLF MØUNTS Z728JF
        SUB-6.... Z728JF G Z72YLF
        SUB-7.... Z306 G Z8J
        SUB-8.... ZK8 BC Z8J
        SUB-9.... ZK8 DØM Z8J
        SUB-10... ZK8 G Z8J
  5.  CATEGØRIES IN TEXT
        SUB-1.... CENSUS
        SUB-2.... LØC
        SUB-3.... HUMAN
```

Figure 4.4.   A RIQS record from notes illustrated in Figure 4.2, containing dyadic tabulations of various kinds in item four. G means grooms. BC means body contact. MOUNTS means a single mount, not necessarily a copulation. DOM means dominates aggressively.

4. Dyads in text; Multiple; Type = ALPHANUMERIC.
    The interactions that are to be tabulated onto sociometric matrices are listed here giving the name of the monkey who performed the action or sent the messages, the type of interaction, and the name of the monkey to whom the action was done or the message directed, in that order (Figure 4.4). As in all items of the RIQS records, all monkey names, which are unique combinations of letters and numbers, are preceded by the letter "Z".[6]

5. Categories in text; Multiple; Type = ALPHABETIC.
    This item is available to add indexing through the UPDATE phase as categories of episodes are defined or revised during use.

6. Text of observability sample; Multiple; Type = ALPHANUMERIC.
    The observability samples are analyzed separately from the data taken during the ordinary observations that are transcribed in item three. For convenience the observability samples are segregated into another item. Increasing experience with the system suggests that they should not be segregated, but rather transcribed in item three, and distinguished from the ordinary observations by a label. During searches observability samples and ordinary observations would then be distinguished by the criteria specified in the search statement.

7. Dyads in observability samples; Multiple; Type = ALPHANUMERIC.
   This item serves the same purpose in respect to the text of observability samples as does item four in respect to the text of the episodes recorded during ordinary observations.

8. Categories in observability samples; Multiple; Type = ALPHABETIC.
   This item is available for additional indexing to be done during the UPDATE phase.

TABULATING SOCIOMETRIC MATRICES

The procedure using MONITOR for tabulating any sociometric matrix is similar. First, the user specifies the monkeys who are to be included in the matrix. Item four contains dyadic interactions for all monkeys in the group. The user will usually be interested in only some of them for a given problem. All the adult males or various sets of siblings may be what is wanted. Via the teletype the user creates a file called TAPE4 on which the monkeys to be included in the matrix are listed in the order they are to appear in the rows and columns.

Secondly, also via the teletype, the user retrieves the dyads to be tabulated on the matrix, and has them written in formatted output on another file, TAPE25. The RIQS search command that retrieves the dyads specifies the dates that bound the interval of interest. Because different types of dyadic interactions are tabulated in item four (Figure 4.4), the search command also specifies the type of dyad to be tabulated on the matrix. The "MONKEY ON 25" command writes onto TAPE25 any word beginning with "Z" in the record, item, or subitem as specified. In each subitem of item four there should be two "Z" prefixed words, both monkey names, the first the sender of the message, the second the receiver. If the subitem contains a dominance interaction, the first monkey is the dominant, the second monkey is the subordinate. The search command illustrated in Figure 4.5 retrieved all unambiguous dominance interactions during the specified interval. Dyads with a "Q" suffix were excluded. The "Q" suffix indicates ambiguity in the interaction; it was not clearly seen, or the motor patterns were atypical, or the interaction was confused by the presence of other monkeys. The user can retrieve the text of a doubtful interaction from item three of the same record, and make his own judgment on the basis of the description of the interaction.

A FORTRAN program controlled by MONITOR reads TAPE4 and TAPE25 and produces the interaction matrix (Figure 4.6). MONITOR has various features that detect erroneous data and allow them to be corrected easily. The final matrices produced by MONITOR are printed on the line printer, and also automatically cataloged on the disk in a format which can be read directly by the analytical FORTRAN programs.

Most of the analytical programs have been used to determine structure in grooming matrices rather than dominance matrices. In tabulating matrices of grooming interactions subitems of item four containing "G" rather than "DOM" would be retrieved, and the monkeys named in the subitems written on TAPE25.

MATRICES OF CO-OCCURRENCE

The proportion of observability samples in which an individual monkey occurs is an estimate of the relative amount of time he is observed. Likewise, the proportion of samples in which a pair of individuals occurs is an estimate of the relative amount of time they are simultaneously in view. Individuals and pairs of individuals differ in observability,

```
ENTER SEARCH CØMMAND ØR TYPE HALT

? FØR I = 1 TØ LAST IF #1 GE ØCTØBER 1, 1972
? AND #1 LE DECEMBER 31, 1972
? AND #4.I EQ ('DØM' AND NØT 'Q')
? THEN MØNKEY ØN 25 ØF #4.I; LØØP;END


SEARCHING INITIATED




    *  *  *  *  *

TAPE25 CØNTAINS   903 RECØRDS.
```

Figure 4.5. A SEARCH command that retrieved all unambiguous dominance interactions from October through December 1972, wrote them on TAPE25, from which a dominance matrix was tabulated by the FORTRAN programs.

and counts of the frequency of events or interactions will be biased towards the most easily observed monkeys. Tabulations from the observability samples allow us to detect and possibly correct this type of bias.

An option in MONITOR uses the "MONKEY ON 25" command to write onto TAPE25 each monkey name found in an observability sample. The monkey names of interest are written on TAPE4. A FORTRAN program controlled by MONITOR then tabulates a matrix of co-occurrence. The cells of the matrix contain the number of samples in which the row and column monkeys both occurred. The main diagonals contain the number of samples in which each individual occurs. The total number of samples searched is printed. Figure 4.7 is an example of a matrix of co-occurrence in observability samples. It is automatically cataloged on the disk as well as sent to the line printer.

Results

Using the system we have begun a series of papers on the social organization of the free-ranging monkeys at Cayo Santiago.

LINKAGES IN GROOMING MATRICES

The methods of Katz[7], Jamrich[8], Schippert[9], and Ross and Harary[10], were adapted for describing the network of grooming relations within one of the Cayo Santiago groups. The sum of the one-step, two-step, and three-step grooming relations directed toward a monkey was used as an index of centricity, or the degree to which a monkey was centrally or peripherally located in the grooming network.

The dominance rank of each individual was determined from a matrix of agonistic interactions. Among females a positive and significant correlation was found between dominance rank and centricity in the grooming network. However, among males, although

11/19/73 14.40.32.GROUP F MALE DOM 1OCT72-31DEC72 COMPLETE A 7 PAGE 1 OF 1.
THIS IS A RAW DATA MATRIX.
MODE20=1.
SCALE FACTOR= .001.

	1 Z7P	2 ZEE	3 ZUB	4 ZE2	5 ZDW	6 ZL1	7 ZF4	
1 Z7P	0.000	.006	.001	0.000	.001	0.000	.002	.010
2 ZEE	0.000	0.000	.002	0.000	0.000	0.000	.001	.003
3 ZUB	0.000	0.000	0.000	.001	0.000	0.000	.001	.002
4 ZE2	0.000	0.000	0.000	0.000	0.000	0.000	.001	.001
5 ZDW	0.000	0.000	0.000	.003	0.000	0.000	0.000	.003
6 ZL1	0.000	0.000	0.000	0.000	0.000	0.000	0.000	0.000
7 ZF4	0.000	0.000	0.000	0.000	0.000	0.000	0.000	0.000
	0.000	.006	.003	.004	.001	0.000	.005	.019

Figure 4.6. The dominance matrix produced from the SEARCH illustrated in Figure 4.5.

02/15/74 17.19.40.NOV - DEC 72 COOCCURRENCE
　　　　　　　THIS IS A RAW DATA MATRIX.

COMPLETE B 7 322 PAGE 1 OF 1.

MODE20=1.
SCALE FACTOR=   .001.

	1 Z7P	2 ZEE	3 ZUR	4 ZE2	5 ZDW	6 ZL1	7 ZF4	
1 Z7P	.074	.022	.022	.004	.006	.002	.002	.058
2 ZEE	.022	.066	.018	.005	.007	.000	.001	.053
3 ZUB	.022	.018	.072	.012	.005	.001	.003	.061
4 ZE2	.004	.005	.012	.043	.007	.004	.006	.038
5 ZDW	.006	.007	.005	.007	.034	.003	.002	.030
6 ZL1	.002	.000	.001	.004	.003	.018	.005	.015
7 ZF4	.002	.001	.003	.006	.002	.005	.026	.019
	.058	.053	.061	.038	.030	.015	.019	.274

Figure 4.7.　A matrix of co-occurrence in observability samples.

the dominant male was the most central male in the grooming network, dominance rank and centricity did not correlate. This suggested that the males were not homogeneous in their relations to the group.

Neither among males nor females did observability seem to be important in affecting the results. Among females there was no correlation between centricity and observability. Among males there were low correlations of borderline significance between centricity and observability. However, partialling out observability did not significantly affect the lack of correlation between dominance and centricity among males.

CLIQUES IN GROOMING MATRICES

The methods of Luce[11] and Harary and Ross[12] were adapted for finding grooming cliques among all the monkeys in the matrix, including males and females. The clique structure of the group showed that the relations of the males to the group are diverse. The dominant male was integrated into the core of high ranking females. One subadult male was still integrated into his familial subgroup. The other males formed a distinct subgroup, except one adult who was just joining the group. He was distantly but definitely attached to the central core of females. A male castrate was intermediate, his position overlapping the subgroup of males and the core of females.

Projected Studies

Recently two social groups, one large, one small, have divided while being closely observed. We will be using the system outlined above to describe the breaking of the networks of social attachments and their reorganization in the new groups.

NOTES AND CITED REFERENCES

1. This work is supported by Grants GS-35744X from the National Science Foundation and MH23809-01 from the National Institute of Mental Health, NIH, HEW. The Caribbean Primate Research Center is supported by Contract No. NIH DRR 71-2003 from the National Institute of Health, HEW to the University of Puerto Rico.

2. Count, E. W., *Being and Becoming Human. Essays on the Biogram,* Van Nostrand, Reinhold, New York, 1973.

3. Altmann, S. A., "Editor's Comments," (in) S. A. Altmann (ed.) *Social Communication Among Primates,* pp. 371-378, University of Chicago Press, Chicago, 1967.

4. Sade, D. S., "A Longitudinal Study of Social Behavior of Rhesus Monkeys," (in) R. Tuttle (ed.), *The Functional and Evolutionary Biology of Primates,* Aldine Atherton Publishing, Inc., Chicago, 1972, pp. 378-398.

5. Further characteristics and uses of these samples will be discussed at length in a paper in preparation by Mark E. Singer and the present author.

6. The sociometric matrices are tabulated from item four by a special modification of the RIQS processor, written by Donald Dillaman, and a series of FORTRAN programs written by Mark E. Singer. The RIQS/FORTRAN interface is controlled from the teletype by the LINGO program MONITOR, also written by Mark E. Singer.

7. Katz, L., "A New Status Index Derived from Sociometric Analysis," *Psychometrika,* 18, 39-43, 1953.

8. Jamrich, J. X., "Application of Matrices in the Analysis of Sociometric Data," *Journal of Experimental Education,* 28, pp. 249-252, 1960.

9. Schippert, F., "The Use of Matrix Algebra in the Analysis of Sociometric Data," *School Science and Mathematics,* 66, pp. 783-792, 1966.

10. Ross, I. C. and F. Harary, "On the Determination of Redundancies in Sociometric Chains," *Psychometrika,* 17, pp. 195-208, 1952.

11. Luce, R. D., "Connectivity and Generalized Cliques in Sociometric Group Structure," *Psychometrika,* 15, pp. 169-190, 1950.

12. Harary, F., and I. C. Ross, "A Procedure for Clique Detection Using the Group Matrix," *Sociometry,* 20, pp. 205-215, 1957.

Chapter 5

Application of an Archeological Site Survey Retrieval System to the Lower Illinois River Valley Research Program[1]

JAMES A. BROWN and GAIL L. HOUART
Northwestern University

Introduction

Since the focus of current archeology lies in the explanation of culture change, archeological research has become a long-term commitment to a regional program. The Northwestern University Archeological Program has been carrying out such a program in a 2800 square mile area centered on the lower Illinois valley. A fundamental prerequisite of such research is a thorough and systematic reconnaissance of the archeological resources of the region. In a thorough survey of a large area the amount of information and material collected from sites can accumulate to the point that the managerial tasks alone require the use of a computerized retrieval system. The need for efficient retrieval methods is sufficiently contained in the inventory uses alone to justify the RIQS application described below, but the demands placed on our accumulated site survey knowledge by our planning and research needs constitute an even more persuasive argument for a retrieval system.

The Problem

Archeological reconnaissance provides a basic data set for archeological research. Data which can be obtained by a survey of the prehistoric site surface include: (1) site location, (2) site size, (3) an indication of the types of activities performed at the site by its prehistoric inhabitants, and (4) the age and duration of occupation. These data are recovered in the form of maps, observations, and artifact collections for each documented site.

An archeological reconnaissance of the lower Illinois River Valley has been conducted for the past 15 years as part of the Northwestern University Archeological Program. Thus

111

far, over 700 prehistoric sites have been discovered along a 70-mile segment of the lower reaches of the Illinois River and its surrounding drainage.

As a result of survey findings, Struever[2] was able to provide a preliminary site classification and to hypothesize settlement systems for the lower Illinois region. The classification was based on differential utilization of site location for specific cultural periods. In another application of survey data, Struever and Houart[3] have been able to offer a locational hierarchical model to predict the location, size and material inventory of Middle Woodland sites in the Illinois River Valley. More recently, Farnsworth[4] applied Struever's settlement system model to the Macoupin Valley, a major tributary of the Illinois. The Macoupin Valley offered a test of the model in a drainage with a different pattern of natural resource distribution.

The following is an example of the utilization of survey data for archeological research. Figure 5.1 shows the distribution of six settlement types of a single cultural period in the lower Illinois region. Similarities in the styles of certain artifact classes (e.g., pottery, projectile points) indicate that all these sites were occupied during the Middle Woodland period, the 600-year interval from 150 *BC* to *AD* 450.[5] The site typology is based on differences in: (1) physiographic location, (2) site size, (3) prehistoric features (e.g., mounds, earthworks), (4) artifact classes present (reflecting differing activities), and (5) frequencies of exotic raw materials (indicating differential access to particular goods). Few of the sites in Figure 5.1 have been excavated, yet it is possible to generate testable hypotheses about the nature of each of these site types.

In order to utilize survey data for generating hypotheses it is necessary to verify that the recorded information is a true representation of actual site distribution, and not merely a reflection of archeological sampling error. Also, the information recorded for each site must be appropriate and accurate: "We need only recognize that surface survey is the first step of data recovery in any archeological program and that the appropriateness of subsequent fieldwork decisions depends heavily on the quality of data recovered in this initial survey phase..." (Struever in Farnsworth, 1973: ix). It is therefore necessary to monitor and evaluate survey data on two levels: (1) the regional level—to minimize sampling problems, and (2) the site level—to maintain a quality control on information collected for each site.

Since both sampling strategy and information quality may greatly affect the validity of survey data, much recent effort has been devoted to developing controls over these possible sources of bias. As a result there has been a great deal of experimentation in both areas. As experimentation in survey technique continues, it is necessary to continuously reevaluate the quality of the data already collected. This may necessitate resurvey of known sites and entire areas in an attempt to maintain comparable data among all sites and areas.

Multiple surveys from a single site are often made, yielding several artifact collections, maps and sets of notes for a single site. Prior to the 1973 survey season, over 1600 collections and associated maps and notes were available from approximately 600 sites. The latest survey season added 130 new sites, constituting an increase of our site file by 20 percent; there was a proportional increase in the number of collections.

Figure 5.1 illustrates the distribution of Middle Woodland sites in a 70-mile stretch of the Illinois Valley. Over 60 sites are plotted; however, more recent survey data indicate at least double this number of Middle Woodland sites in the region. Yet the 600-year Middle Woodland period represents only 6½ percent of the 9000 years of prehistoric occupation of this area. Clearly, future survey work will continue to augment the data file for many

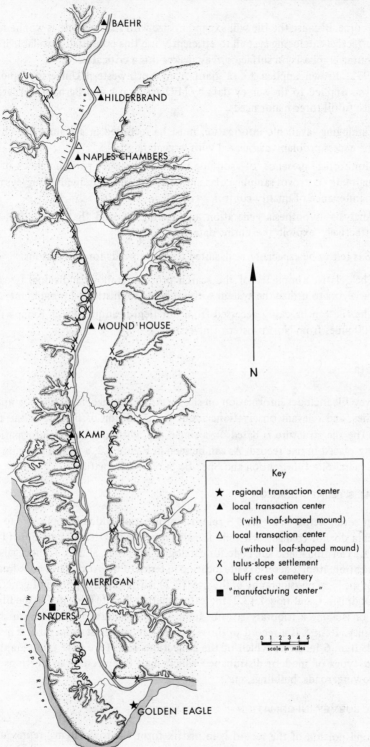

Figure 5.1. The distribution of six settlement types of the Middle Woodland period in the Lower Illinois Valley (after Struever and Houart 1972).

years to come. Because the file will expand in size with future work, it will be necessary to use an effective cataloging system to efficiently use this potentially available information. A continuing emphasis on surface survey makes this a critical need.

In 1972, Brown applied for a grant from Northwestern University, and the RIQS system was applied to the survey data by Michael Swartz and Bernard Werner. RIQS was utilized to fulfill three major needs:

1. Cataloging—available information must be recorded in a manner which minimizes the access problems associated with large data sets.

2. Monitoring—presence of sampling problems requires periodic check of the file to maintain control of sampling bias, and variation among individual surveys necessitates maintenance of quality control.

3. Analysis—hypothesis generation and testing demand that researchers be able to effectively exploit the entire data set.

RIQS is felt to be especially well-suited for these needs for two reasons:

1. The relative simplicity of the search procedure allows individual researchers and surveyors to utilize the system without being sophisticated programmers.

2. The file can be easily accessed from our field headquarters in Kampsville, Illinois, 300 miles from Northwestern University.

The Data

The survey file includes information on site location, site size, local physiography, artifact inventories, and relevant observations about the condition of the site at the time of the survey. The file structure is based on a single site, with all relevant information about a site being placed in one record. As can be seen in Figure 5.2, a record is comprised of two parts: General Site Information and Specific Survey Information.

GENERAL SITE INFORMATION

The first seven items of Figure 5.3 refer to information which is applicable to all surveys. These data do not change each time the site is surveyed. Item 1 contains: (1.1) the site name, (1.2) an alphabetic site code for cataloging purposes, and (1.3) the legal description of site location. Item 2 describes site location in terms of the Army Grid coordinates. Item 3 indicates the local physiography of the site: (3.1) is a descriptive phrase of general landform (e.g., floodplain—sand ridge), (3.2) indicates whether the site is located in the Illinois Valley proper, or is along a tributary stream. Item 4 is the name of the stream which drains the site vicinity. Item 5 is a record of those amateur archeologists who possess material from this site. Item 6 indicates which of the collections in (5) we have photographed. Item 7 lists the types of modern distrubance which may have destroyed portions of the site (e.g., plowing, roads, buildings, etc.).

SPECIFIC SURVEY INFORMATION

The second portion of the record is in matrix form; the rows (items) represent classes of information, while each column (subitem) represents a single survey of this site (see Figure 5.3). In this way, data from all surveys or from a specific survey can be easily retrieved.

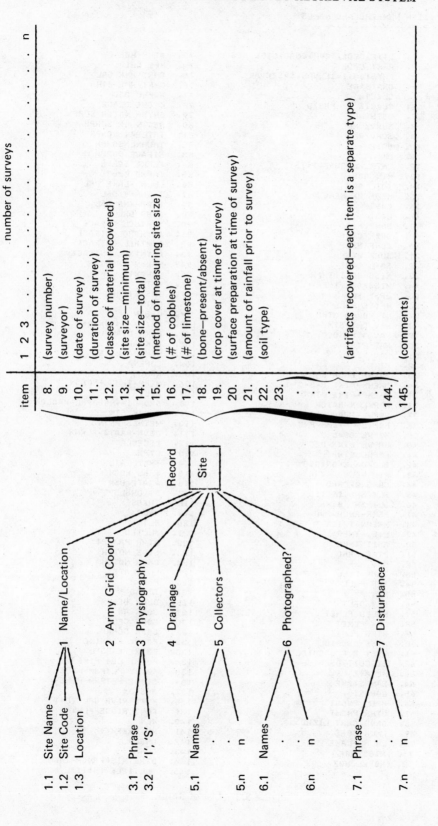

Figure 5.2. Record structure of the survey RIQS file.

ITEM NUMBERS AND NAMES
----

1. SITE,CØDE,TØWN,QUAD,LEGL DES
2. ARMY CØDE
3. PHYSIØG,I=ILLVAL,S=SECVAL
4. DRAINAGE
5. CLECTR
6. CLECTR W/ PHØTØ
7. DSTRBNCE
8. SURVY NØ
9. SURVYR
10. DATE
11. DURATION
12. CNTRL,S=SURF,T=TST
13. MIN AØS
14. TØTL AØS
15. MØDE ØF MEASR
16. CØBBL
17. L.S.
18. BØNE P/A
19. CRØP CØVR
20. SURF PREP
21. SURF WASH
22. SØIL CØDE
23. MISS GRIT TMPR
24. MISS SHL TMPR
25. JRSY BLF
26. WHITE HALL
27. LT WDLND ØTHR
28. HAV DNT STMP
29. HAV ØTHR DEC
30. HAV ØTHR
31. HAV PIKE
32. PIKE
33. BAEHR BRSH RM
34. BAEHR-PIKE B-S-C
35. BAEHR-PIKE ØTHR
36. HØPWL X-HATCH RM
37. HØPWL-BRAGNBRG RM
38. HØPWL-MNTZMA PNC
39. HØPWL BØWL
40. HØPWL ØTHR DEC
41. HØPWL ØTHR
42. BLUFDALE-GRIGSBY
43. MID WDLND ØTHR
44. CRAB ØRCHRD
45. BLK SND INCISD
46. BLK SND ØTHR
47. PSKR-PNCH-PNC
48. MRIØN THICK
49. L.S. TMPR
50. GRIT TMPR
51. ØTHR SHRD
52. GRV AX
53. TAPR PØLL
54. SQR PØLL
55. HEM AX
56. HEM CELT
57. HØLED PLMET
58. GRV PLMET
59. ØTHR PLMET
60. MISS DSCØIDL
61. JRSY BLF DSCØIDL
62. BISCUIT DSCØIDL
63. METATE
64. BANRSTØNE
65. GØRGET
66. PEBL PNDNT
67. ØTHR PNDNT
68. GRND CHRT LIZRD
69. LMLR CØRE
70. LMLR FLAKE
71. MISS HØE
72. HØPWL HØE

73. ØTHR HØE
74. HØE CHIP
75. CHRT HMR BAL
76. CHRT HMR ØTHR
77. HØPWL DSC
78. CACHE BLADE
79. SNYDR NØTCH SCRPR
80. RECTNGLR SCRPR
81. TRTLBAK SCRPR
82. THUMNL SCRPR
83. BIFACE SCRPR
84. FLAKE SCRPR
85. TAPRD GØUGE
86. LMLR FLAKE DRL
87. T-SHAPE DRL
88. BLØB-END DRL
89. ØTHR DRL
90. SYMTRCL BIFACE
91. ASYMTRCL BIFACE
92. SYMTRCL UNIFACE
93. ASYMTRCL UNIFACE
94. MADSN TRINGLR
95. CAHØKIA
96. KSTR
97. TMS-STEUBN
98. NRTN
99. GIBSN
100. SNYDR/SNYDR AFF
101. PSKR DIAMND
102. BLKNAP
103. LØMØKA-LIKE
104. CØPENA
105. KRMR
106. MERM-TRMBL-RØBSN
107. ETLY
108. SEDALIA-NEBØ-HL-WADLØW
109. KRNAK STM
110. METNZS-HLTN
111. GØDR-RADTZ-FLKNR
112. ØSCEØLA
113. CYPRS
114. TRKY TAIL
115. TABL RØCK
116. AGATE BSN
117. ST CHRLS
118. THEBS
119. HRDN
120. DLTN
121. FLUTED
122. ØTHR PRJ PT
123. SIDE NØTCH
124. CRNR NØTCH
125. LNCELATE
126. PRFRM
127. STEMD
128. CØPR BEAD
129. CØPR AX
130. CØPR CELT
131. CØPR SCRAP
132. PØTRY FIGRINE
133. PØTRY EARSPL
134. PØTRY LBØ PIPE
135. PØTRY PLTFRM PIPE
136. STØNE PLTFRM PIPE
137. ØBSIDN
138. KNFE RIVR CHLCEDNY
139. FLNT RIDGE FLNT
140. KLN
141. ML CREEK
142. DNGLA
143. GLNA
144. ØTHR HIS+FRNCH-INDN
145. MULTIPLE INITIAL

Figure 5.3. List of items.

Item 8 contains the catalog number assigned to a survey. Item 9 lists the name of the surveyor. Item 10 is the date of survey. Item 11 is the amount of time spent in collecting artifacts. Item 12 indicates the controls utilized, e.g., the classes of material collected. Items 13 and 14 record site size; the total area when possible, the minimum when the site has been sufficiently disturbed so that total area is indeterminate. Item 15 describes the method for measuring site size. Items 16 and 17 indicate the density of ingeneous cobbles and limestone on the site surface; both cobbles and limestone chunks are a ready indicator of cooking and other activities. Item 18 reports the presence or absence of animal bone; the presence of bone is an indication of favorable preservation at the site. Items 19, 20 and 21 describe the site conditions—whether the field (19) is in crop, (20) has been plowed, disked and/or harrowed, or (21) has been rained on recently. Item 22 describes the soil type. Items 23 through 144 represent the frequencies of the various types of artifacts which may have been recovered. These items constitute the artifact inventories for each site. Item 145 allows us to enter comments.

Although a record contains 145 items, only the first 22 items are represented in all records. The remaining 123 items are the artifact inventories. Only a relatively small subset of the 123 possible artifact types will actually occur on any given site. RIQS storage techniques are efficient at handling this type of data set. Arrays would require much larger storage capabilities, most of it representing no data.

Research Strategy

As mentioned previously, RIQS was employed to serve three major functions: (1) to act as a catalog of a large data set, (2) to monitor the survey data in order to alleviate sampling problems and to maintain quality control, and (3) to serve as the basis for data analysis. These three functions require different strategies of data manipulation.

CATALOGING

The catalog use of the RIQS survey file is the least demanding, but has the broadest and most basic potential use. Simple inventory searches are the basic cataloging functions.

Figure 5.4 illustrates such a search. As an example, suppose a student is interested in studying Early Archaic projectile points. It is known that relatively few of these points have been recovered. Yet neither the exact number of points, nor the sites on which they were found, is known. Sorting through over 1600 separately boxed collections is infeasible. We wish to know: (a) the sites from which this early material was recovered, and (b) the specific collections containing these points from each site.

In Figure 5.4, Items #116 through #121 correspond to the Early Archaic projectile point types. A search is made of the entire file to locate those collections which contain any of these point types. Information displayed here includes the site name, and the catalog number assigned to the specific collection needed from this site. No other information is needed to quickly retrieve the 20 points in question.

MONITORING

Monitoring the survey file is a much more demanding task that is only beginning to be seriously undertaken. There are a large number of factors that can potentially contribute to (1) bias introduced by sampling error and (2) observational disparities introduced by

```
ENTER SEARCH COMMAND OR TYPE HALT

? FOR N = 1 TO LAST
? IF #116.N GT O DISPLAY ZAP ACROSS #1.1 TAB 30 #8.N;
? IF #117.N GT O DISPLAY ZAP ACROSS #1.1 TAB 30 #8.N;
? IF #118.N GT O DISPLAY ZAP ACROSS #1.1 TAB 30 #8.N;
? IF #119.N GT O DISPLAY ZAP ACROSS #1.1 TAB 30 #8.N;
? IF #120.N GT O DISPLAY ZAP ACROSS #1.1 TAB 30 #8.N;
? IF #121.N GT O DISPLAY ZAP ACROSS #1.1 TAB 30 #8.N;LOOP;END

SEARCHING INITIATED


NO. OF REPORTS ON DISPLAY FILE =    20

DO YOU WANT THE DISPLAY REPORTS LISTED
? Y


          VAUGHAN                    22
          BELL                        1
          BIXBY EAST                  4
          BIXBY GRAVEL PIT            1
          GORDON                      1
          FLAUTT                      1
          JALAPA                      1
          KEMPER                      1
          LETHA                       1
          MACAULEY                    1
          NUGENT                      1
          RIMBEY                      2
          RUYLE                       1
          SAND CREEK CHURCH           8
          SHAW POINT                  1
          SLIGHT                      1
          SOWERS MOUND GROUP          4
          UPPER MACOUPIN              2
          UPPER MACOUPIN              6
          AUDREY                      9
          LOY                         1
          LOY                         1
```

* * * * *

Figure 5.4. A catalog search of the survey file for collections which
contain early archaic projectile points.

inadequate quality control. The few factors that will be mentioned here are intended to be indicative of the types of searches that can be used to establish viable monitoring programs.

Sampling Error

Sites are not randomly distributed across the study area landscape. Rather, they tend to cluster in those areas which offer maximum exploitation potential for a variety of natural resources.[2] Sites are not restricted to those areas, however, as certain important resources may not be available there. Unfortunately, archeologists work on the same principle of maximum exploitation potential. Therefore, those areas with high site density are more likely to be surveyed. Yet it is crucial to research objectives that the full range of possible site locations are inventoried for all cultural periods.

In the lower reaches of the Illinois River, the floodplain is three to four miles wide, bounded on both east and west by high limestone bluffs. In prehistoric times, the floodplain mainly supported a forest vegetation. The surrounding upland was largely prairie, except on the dissected terrain cut by the tributary streams to the Illinois. The two major topographic zones (floodplain, upland) vary greatly in both the kinds and quantities of available food resources.

Figure 5.5 illustrates the distribution of sites in the uplands. Item #3.1 is a descriptive phrase for the physiographic location of the site. Out of 582 sites, only 29 are located on the uplands; the remainder are either in or immediately adjacent to the Illinois Valley proper or its tributary streams. Of these 29 upland sites, 13 are on the west side of the Illinois River (Calhoun and Pike counties), while 16 are east of the River (Jersey, Greene, Scott and Macoupin counties).

This distribution illustrates a typical problem in areal sampling because the difference in size between the upland territories on each side of the Illinois Valley trench favors unequal opportunities for site discovery. The western upland is limited in extent since it lies on a narrow peninsula between the Illinois and Mississippi Rivers. In contrast the eastern upland extends far to the east beyond the research area. Without some control over sampling it is impossible to determine whether the even east-west distribution is a result of sampling error or is representative of actual site distribution.

Figure 5.6 illustrates the difference in site frequency between the Illinois Valley and its tributary streams. Item #3.2 indicates whether the site is in the Illinois Valley proper—"I," or whether it is located along a secondary stream—"S." Thus far, 343 sites occur in the

```
ENTER SEARCH CØMMAND ØR TYPE HALT

? IF #3.1 EQ ('UPLAND' ØR 'UPLANDS') PLACE IN SET 1;END

SEARCHING INITIATED



NØ. ØF RECØRDS ADDED TØ SET  1 BY SEARCH =    29
NØ. ØF RECØRDS  IN  SET   1 AFTER SEARCH =    29


*  *  *  *  *


ENTER SEARCH CØMMAND ØR TYPE HALT

? BEGIN SEARCH ØF SET 1
? IF #1.3 CØNTAINS ('CALHØUN' ØR 'PIKE') PLACE IN SET 2;
? IF #1.3 CØNTAINS ('JERSEY' ØR 'GREEN' ØR 'GREENE' ØR 'SCØTT'
? ØR 'MACØUPIN') PLACE IN SET 3;END

SEARCHING INITIATED



NØ. ØF RECØRDS ADDED TØ SET  2 BY SEARCH =    13
NØ. ØF RECØRDS  IN  SET   2 AFTER SEARCH =    13



NØ. ØF RECØRDS ADDED TØ SET  3 BY SEARCH =    16
NØ. ØF RECØRDS  IN  SET   3 AFTER SEARCH =    16


*  *  *  *  *
```

Figure 5.5. A monitoring search to determine the distribution of upland sites.

```
ENTER SEARCH CØMMAND ØR TYPE HALT

? IF #3.2 EQ 'I' PLACE IN SET 10;
? IF #3.2 EQ 'S' PLACE IN SET 12;END

SEARCHING INITIATED



NØ. ØF RECØRDS ADDED TØ SET 10 BY SEARCH =   343
NØ. ØF RECØRDS  IN  SET  10 AFTER SEARCH =   343



NØ. ØF RECØRDS ADDED TØ SET 12 BY SEARCH =   188
NØ. ØF RECØRDS  IN  SET  12 AFTER SEARCH =   188



*  *  *  *  *


ENTER SEARCH CØMMAND ØR TYPE HALT

? BEGIN SEARCH ØF SET 12
? IF #4 EQ 'MACØUPIN' PLACE IN SET 13;
? IF #4 EQ 'APPLE' PLACE IN SET 14;
? IF #4 EQ 'TERRE' PLACE IN SET 15;END

SEARCHING INITIATED



NØ. ØF RECØRDS ADDED TØ SET 13 BY SEARCH =   57
NØ. ØF RECØRDS  IN  SET  13 AFTER SEARCH =   57



NØ. ØF RECØRDS ADDED TØ SET 14 BY SEARCH =   21
NØ. ØF RECØRDS  IN  SET  14 AFTER SEARCH =   21



NØ. ØF RECØRDS ADDED TØ SET 15 BY SEARCH =   25
NØ. ØF RECØRDS  IN  SET  15 AFTER SEARCH =   25
```

Figure 5.6. A monitoring search of the distribution of
sites along tributary streams.

Illinois Valley, while only 188 are found along secondary streams. This difference may reflect differences in the productive potential of these two areas. However, sorting on drainage (Item #4), it turns out that 103 of the 188 known sites along tributary streams are located on only three streams—Macoupin, Apple and Mauvaise Terre. These three creeks are the only secondary streams which have been subjected to an intensive survey. It appears, therefore, that the observed difference in site frequency between the Illinois Valley and secondary stream valleys is likely a result of sampling bias, and not a result of real differences in the density of prehistoric sites.

Quality Control

In order for survey information to be useful for archeological research, it is important that data from different sites be comparable. Information on site location may come from a variety of places—systematic work done by trained surveyors, local amateur archeologists and interested local residents. In another river valley, Winters has found that 90 percent of unsystematic survey information had no research value.[6] To overcome this difficulty, all sites in the lower Illinois Valley which have accurate location information were investigated by trained surveyors. Yet even these data may not be strictly comparable, as surveyors vary in ability, and even the same surveyor will obtain different results depending on the condition of the field (amount of rain, cultivation, crop cover, etc.).

Figure 5.7a illustrates an attempt to determine the effect of one variable which may affect survey results. It may be expected that the amount of material collected would be related to the duration of the pick-up. This is especially important for those classes of artifacts which occur in relatively low frequencies; these rare objects are more likely to be recovered if more time is spent in collecting materials from the site.

Figure 5.7b is an attempt to evaluate how much variability in the quantity of material recovered is introduced by differences in the amount of time spent collecting. Records 4, 5, 6, 9, 60, 156, and 403 are all large Middle Woodland sites which have been repeatedly

```
*   *   *   *   *


ENTER SEARCH COMMAND OR TYPE HALT

? BEGIN SEARCH OF RECORDS 4,5,6,9,60,156,403 PLACE IN SET 20
? FOR N = 1 TO LAST PLOT #11.N VRS #30.N;LOOP;END


NO. OF RECORDS   GENERATED TO THE PLOT FILE =     7
NO. OF POINTS    GENERATED TO THE PLOT FILE =     90

NO. OF MISSING DATA ITEMS IN THE PLOT FILE =     27

***** VALUE OF MISSING DATA ITEMS PLOTTED ASSUMED TO BE  0.0


  TYPE IN THE DESIRED TITLE FOR THE PLOT

? HAVANA SHERDS VERSUS DURATION OF PICK-UP

DO YOU WANT THE PLOT DISPLAYED
? YES
                          HAVANA SHERDS VERSUS DURATION OF PICK-UP
  H    156.000 +                                                    ( X )
  A             X
  V             X
                X
  O    124.800 +
  T             I               X
  H             I
  R             I
       93.600 X                                      X
                I
                X     X
                I           X
       62.400 +
                X
                X         X      X              X
                X         X         X      X
       31.200 X         X
                X         X     X                X
                X         X     X             X
                X   X X X X     X X   X     X     X          X
        .000 +-----X---X-X------X+----X----+------X--+---------+
             0.000   24.000   48.000   72.000   96.000   120.000
                                 DURATION
```

Figure 5.7a. Plots of the frequencies of pottery sherds recovered versus the time spent in collecting material.

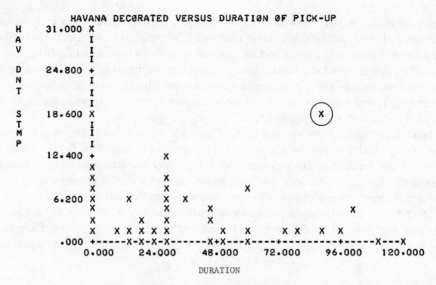

Figure 5.7b. Plot illustrating relationship of number of Havana decorated sherds to duration of survey.

resurveyed. A plot was generated to compare duration of survey (#11) to the number of Havana sherds (#30), the most common type of pottery found on Middle Woodland sites. The plot indicates almost no relationship between the number of sherds recovered and the amount of time spent collecting. Similarly, the second plot generated compared duration of survey (#11) to the number of Havana decorated sherds (#28), which occur in lower frequencies than undecorated Havana sherds (#30).

The results are similar between these two plots. Except for one case in both plots (circled), there does not appear to be any noticeable increase in recovery rate as duration of survey increases. A recommendation might be made to spend only 30 to 45 minutes collecting on a site since there is no significant increase in amount of material recovered with more time spent collecting.

Alternatively, these plots might illustrate surveyor bias; the surveyor may spend as much time at the site as is needed to collect an *acceptable* amount of material. If survey conditions are poor, more time will be needed to collect the acceptable amount. It might therefore be expected that those surveys of long duration were carried out under poor survey conditions. Another factor which may enter into this is the expertise of the surveyor. Novice surveyors, who are often trained in surveying on these sites, may be responsible for this unexpected distribution.

Analysis

Analysis of the available survey information perhaps requires more data manipulation than either cataloging or monitoring. It is here that the interface between RIQS and SPSS becomes necessary. There is a wide variety of potential analytical problems that can be attacked from the survey file, and the relatively simple examples given here are intended to be illustrative rather than definitive research results.

Many archeological problems deal with the chronological range of certain artifact types, and the frequency of co-occurrence of several types. Survey information can be success-fully used in these instances. Three major pottery series have been identified for the Early

Woodland period (550 *BC* to 150 *BC*) in the lower Illinois River Valley. The latest is the Black Sand series ceramics that is known to overlie stratigraphically the Peisker series. Radiocarbon dates from other areas indicate that Marion Thick series ceramics are older still.[2] Yet it is unknown whether any of these ceramic series overlap in time, or whether Belknap, an Early Woodland projectile point type, occurs with all three ceramic series or just one of them.

Figures 5.8a and 5.8b illustrate the use of the survey data for this problem. Items #45 and #46 represent decorated and undecorated Black Sand series ceramics, found on 50 and 58 sites respectively. Item #47 is Peisker series (9 sites), while Item #48 represents Marion Thick ceramics (8 sites). Belknap points are recorded in Item #102 (32 sites). These artifact types are found on a total of 95 sites, implying a high frequency of co-occurrence.

An SPSS file was developed for these artifact types. Each site is a case, and the file contains the total number of each artifact type recovered from the site; all subitems (collections) were summed to obtain the total for each site.

```
ENTER SEARCH COMMAND OR TYPE HALT

? IF #45 GT 0 PLACE IN SET 1;
? IF #46 GT 0 PLACE IN SET 2;
? IF #47 GT 0 PLACE IN SET 3;
? IF #48 GT 0 PLACE IN SET 4;


? IF #102 GT 0 PLACE IN SET 5;END

SEARCHING INITIATED



NO. OF RECORDS ADDED TO SET  1 BY SEARCH =   50    Decorated Black Sand
NO. OF RECORDS  IN  SET  1 AFTER SEARCH =   50    series ceramics


NO. OF RECORDS ADDED TO SET  2 BY SEARCH =   58    Undecorated Black Sand
NO. OF RECORDS  IN  SET  2 AFTER SEARCH =   58    series ceramics


NO. OF RECORDS ADDED TO SET  3 BY SEARCH =    9    Peisker series
NO. OF RECORDS  IN  SET  3 AFTER SEARCH =    9


NO. OF RECORDS ADDED TO SET  4 BY SEARCH =    8    Marion Thick ceramics
NO. OF RECORDS  IN  SET  4 AFTER SEARCH =    8


NO. OF RECORDS ADDED TO SET  5 BY SEARCH =   32    Belknap points
NO. OF RECORDS  IN  SET  5 AFTER SEARCH =   32

* * * * *
```

Figure 5.8a. The file is subsetted according to artifact types.

```
? BEGIN SEARCH ØF UNIØN(1,2,3,4,5)
? LET S47=0
? LET S45=0
? LET S46=0 LET S48=0 LET S102=0
? FØR I=1 TØ 150
? LET S45=S45+#45.I
? LET S46=S46+#46.I
? LET S47=S47+#47.I
? LET S48=S48+#48.I
? LET S102=S102+#102.I
? LØØP;
? SPSSFILE 2 ØF S45 S46 S47 S48 S102 END
```

Figure 5.8b. Data recording the occurrence of various artifact types are summed. These new variables are used to create an SPSS file.

Once SPSS is entered, it is possible to perform a variety of statistical tests. Figure 5.8c illustrates a few of these. Correlation coefficients were computed for all variable pairs. Belknap points appear to correlate with both decorated and undecorated Black Sand series ceramics, as well as Peisker series sherds; these points show no relationship to Marion Thick ceramics. However, missing data (i.e., no artifacts of this type collected from a site) have zero values for this SPSS run. Therefore, it is important to check sample sizes and frequency of co-occurrence for each variable, in order to evaluate the significance of the correlation coefficient.

Codebook gives frequency distributions for each variable (Figure 5.8d). Only the frequencies of decorated Black Sand sherds (S45) are illustrated here. A scattergram has been generated from the relative proportions of Black Sand decorated sherds with the undecorated sherds of this same ceramic series on 95 sites. The relative co-variation of any variable pair can be easily examined (Figure 5.8e). Finally, FASTABS yields a table of the frequency of co-occurrence for any variable pair (Figure 5.8f). Crosstabulating Peisker series ceramics with Belknap points indicates these artifact types co-occur on only two of the 95 sites examined. The apparent correlation between these two artifact types is therefore spurious.

```
        - - - PEARSØN CØRRELATIØN - - -

    VARIABLE PAIR        CØEFF.        N    SIG.

    S45      S46          .5736        95   .000
    S45      S47          .2912        95   .002
    S45      S48         -.0960        95   .177
    S45      S102         .4274        95   .000
    S46      S47          .2548        95   .006
    S46      S48         -.0446        95   .334
    S46      S102         .3069        95   .001
    S47      S48         -.0388        95   .355
    S47      S102         .6043        95   .000
    S48      S102        -.0532        95   .304
```

Figure 5.8c. Illustration of the use of SPSS for evaluating the co-occurrence of various artifact types.

```
- - - CØDEBØØK - - -

VARIABLE - S45              S45

VALUE LABEL      VALUE      FREQ  REL P  ADJ P  CUM P

                     0       45   47.4   47.4   47.4
                  1.00       11   11.6   11.6   58.9
                  2.00       12   12.6   12.6   71.6
                  3.00        5    5.3    5.3   76.8
                  4.00        4    4.2    4.2   81.1
                  6.00        3    3.2    3.2   84.2
                  8.00        1    1.1    1.1   85.3
                  9.00        3    3.2    3.2   88.4
                 10.00        1    1.1    1.1   89.5
                 12.00        2    2.1    2.1   91.6
                 13.00        2    2.1    2.1   93.7
                 18.00        1    1.1    1.1   94.7
                 20.00        1    1.1    1.1   95.8
                 22.00        1    1.1    1.1   96.8
                 29.00        1    1.1    1.1   97.9
                 31.00        1    1.1    1.1   98.9
                 44.00        1    1.1    1.1  100.0
                 BLANK        0      0   ****  100.0

                TØTAL        95  100.0  100.0  100.0


      ØBSERVATIØNS- VALID -      95     MISSING -        0
```

Figure 5.8d. Frequency count of decorated Black Sand series ceramics.

Summary and Conclusions

The Northwestern University Archeological Program has been conducting a long-term program of surface survey in the lower Illinois Valley region for the past 15 years. During this time, over 1600 collections and associated maps and notes have been amassed. This vast quantity of information would be virtually useless without an efficient, computerized storage and retrieval system. The RIQS system was utilized to store and organize these data so that they could be easily accessible. At the present time, the RIQS file serves three functions: as a catalog of the collections, as a means to monitor the quality of the data base, and as a research data base.

RIQS, in conjunction with SPSS, has proved to be effective for all three of these uses. The examples presented here have all been relatively simple. Yet, without RIQS, even these manipulations would have been both tedious and quite complex. One of the major advantages of RIQS is the ability to access SPSS and therefore to perform statistical procedures easily.

The last few years have shown a tremendous spurt of survey activity in the lower Illinois Valley region, and it appears that this will continue for quite some time. The need for an efficient storage and retrieval system is therefore immediate and continuing. The RIQS survey file has only recently been established. Usage up till now has been relatively uncomplex; it remains to be seen whether RIQS will be sufficient for our future needs.

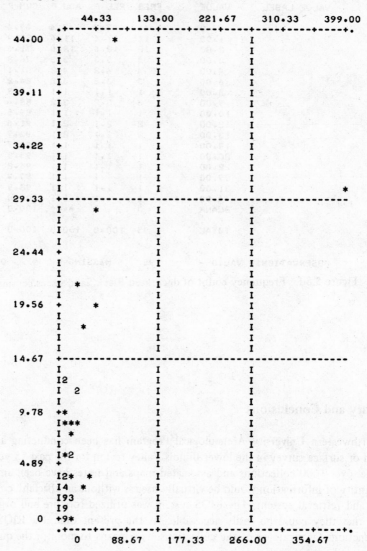

Figure 5.8e. Scatter diagram showing occurrences of decorated and undecorated Black Sand series ceramics.

```
- - - FASTABS - - -


    S102         S102
 BY S47          S47

                 S47
        COUNT
        ROW PCT                                            ROW
        COL PCT
        TOT PCT     0        1        2        3
 S102
        0          61        4        1        0        66
                 92.4%     6.1%     1.5%       0%     69.5%
                 69.3%    80.0%    100.0%      0%
                 64.2%     4.2%     1.1%       0%

        1          19        0        0        0        19
                100.0%       0%       0%       0%     20.0%
                 21.6%       0%       0%       0%
                 20.0%       0%       0%       0%

        2           3        0        0        0         3
                100.0%       0%       0%       0%      3.2%
                  3.4%       0%       0%       0%
                  3.2%       0%       0%       0%

        3           1        0        0        0         1
                100.0%       0%       0%       0%      1.1%
                  1.1%       0%       0%       0%
                  1.1%       0%       0%       0%

        4           1        0        0        0         1
                100.0%       0%       0%       0%      1.1%
                  1.1%       0%       0%       0%
                  1.1%       0%       0%       0%

        6           2        0        0        0         2
                100.0%       0%       0%       0%      2.1%
                  2.3%       0%       0%       0%
                  2.1%       0%       0%       0%

        8           0        1        0        0         1
                    0%   100.0%       0%       0%      1.1%
                    0%    20.0%       0%       0%
                    0%     1.1%       0%       0%

       13           1        0        0        0         1
                100.0%       0%       0%       0%      1.1%
                  1.1%       0%       0%       0%
                  1.1%       0%       0%       0%

       19           0        0        0        1         1
                    0%       0%       0%   100.0%      1.1%
                    0%       0%       0%   100.0%
                    0%       0%       0%     1.1%

       COLUMN      88        5        1        1        95
        TOTAL    92.6%     5.3%     1.1%     1.1%    100.0%
```

Figure 5.8f. Cross tabulations of Belknap points (row variable) with Peisker series (column variable) ceramics.

NOTES AND CITED REFERENCES

1. This investigation was supported by Bio-Medical Sciences Support Grant FR 7028-05 from the National Institute of Health.

2. Struever, Stuart, "Woodland Subsistence–Settlement Systems in the Lower Illinois Valley," (in) S. R. Binford and L. R. Binford (eds.), *New Perspectives in Archeology,* Aldine Publishing Co., Chicago, 1968.

3. Struever, Stuart and Gail L. Houart, "An Analysis of the Hopewell Interaction Sphere," *Anthropological Papers,* Museum of Anthropology, University of Michigan, 46, pp. 47-79, 1972.

4. Farnsworth, Kenneth B., "An Archaeological Survey of the Macoupin Valley," Illinois State Museum, *Reports of Investigation,* 26, 1973.

5. Streuver, Stuart, "A Reexamination of Hopewell in Eastern North America," unpublished PhD. dissertation, University of Chicago, 1968.

6. Winters, Howard D., "An Archaeological Survey of the Wabash Valley in Illinois," Illinois State Museum, *Reports of Investigation,* 10, 1967.

Chapter 6

A Worldwide Study of Political Parties

KENNETH JANDA
Northwestern University

The Problem

For nearly ten years now, a worldwide study of political parties has been underway at Northwestern University. Known as the International Comparative Political Parties Project, the study encompasses 154 parties operating from 1950 to 1962 in 52 countries.[1] The countries constitute a stratified random sample representing ten cultural–geographical areas of the world. Within each chosen country, all the parties that met our minimum standards of strength and stability were selected for study—including illegal as well as legal parties.[2] Thus we have a representative sample of parties across the world which reflects the full variation of cultural conditions, party systems, and party types.

The objective of the ICPP Project is to conduct the first empirically based cross–national and cross–cultural analysis of political parties. We seek to determine the various forces that give rise to (a) existence and character of political parties—treating political parties as dependent variables in our theoretical framework; (b) the various effects that political parties have in political systems—treating parties as independent variables; and (c) the various interrelationships among characteristics of political parties—treating them as organizational settings within the context of party theory.[3] The conceptual framework that has guided the collection of our data for these analyses is presented schematically in Figure 6.1.

The ICPP conceptual framework identifies eleven major dimensions of cross–national variation among political parties.[4] Seven of these dimensions pertain to a party's *external relations* with society, and four relate to its *internal organization*. Several basic variables were chosen as indicators for each of these major dimensions or concepts. For example,

129

Number of Basic Variables		Major Concepts	
6	1.	Institutionalization	
6	2.	Governmental Status	
6	3.	Social Aggregation	
6	4.	Social Articulation	External Relations
13	5.	Issue Orientation	
33	6.	Goal Orientation	
5	7.	Autonomy	
7	8.	Degree of Organization	
8	9.	Centralization of Power	Internal Organization
6	10.	Coherence	
6	11.	Involvement	

Figure 6.1. Schematic diagram of ICPP conceptual framework.

we seek to measure the extent of party Institutionalization with six variables: (1) year of origin; (2) number, recency, and character of name changes; (3) organizational discontinuity in the form of splits and mergers; (4) the extent and character of leadership competition; (5) the amount of instability or fluctuation in legislative representation during our time period; and (6) the amount of instability in contesting elections and winning votes. Figure 6.1 shows that each of the eleven major dimensions in the ICPP conceptual framework is tapped by from 5 to 33 such separate indicators. Factor analysis has shown that these basic variables tend to be reliable indicators of their underlying concepts.[5]

An enormous amount of data on political parties has been generated by the ICPP Project over the past few years. Most of our parties have been scored on more than one hundred basic variables, with some of the variables being scored differently for parties in the first and second halves of our 1950 to 1962 time period. In addition to assigning quantitative scores for our parties on all these variables, our coders have prepared verbal discussions of their coding judgments. An example should illustrate our practice.

Consider *Year of Origin*—the first basic variable in our set of indicators for Institutionalization. A party judged to be founded in 1910 would be scored 10 on year of origin—with low values indicating old parties. Our corresponding verbal discussion would provide some background information about the year of origin—such as the city in which it was founded or the events which gave rise to the party. Establishment of the year of origin, however, is often problematic for some parties, raising serious disputes among scholars. When this occurs, our verbalizations will refer to the disagreement and cite alternative dates. In still other cases, the information about year of origin may be consistent but scanty. When relevant, our verbalizations will note the adequacy of the information underlying the coding judgment.

As one can gather from this brief review of the content of our verbal discussions, the confidence with which we code our parties varies according to the party and the variables being coded. In an effort to express the degree of confidence underlying each coding judgment, every variable code is accompanied by an *adequacy-confidence* code ranging from 1 to 9.[6] A score of 9 signifies the highest degree of confidence, which reflects the fact that at least three sources provide the same information about the party and that there is no disagreement in the literature about the code that should be assigned. On the other hand, a code of 3 indicates that the code is inferred from available information, which may be either sparse or contradictory. Adequacy-confidence codes of 1 and 2 are reserved for our inability to code the variable because of a total lack of information (AC1) or because of an irreconcilable conflict in the available information (AC2).

Given this rich mixture of quantitative and textual material within the ICPP Project, we have a sizable and complicated problem of data management. Our solution is to employ the RIQS system, which allows for handling both the quantitative data—in the form of our variable codes and adequacy-confidence codes—and the verbal discussions accompanying those codes. The system is used for storing the information as it is collected, for editing the information to correct errors and improve description, for updating the file as new information is received, and for printing all or part of the file on request. In fact, the computer printout of the entire RIQS file of ICPP information constitutes the camera-ready copy for photo-offset printing of the first major publication from the project, a 1000 page volume of the basic parties data.[7]

The Data

The individual political party is the unit of analysis in the ICPP Project, and each party constitutes a separate record in our application of the RIQS system. There are 154 parties in our study and thus 154 records in our RIQS ICPP file. Our parties have been assigned an identifying three-digit code, in which the first number refers to the cultural-geographical area of the world, the second to a specific country within that area, and the third to a specific party within the country. The file was created in such a way that the record number within the RIQS system corresponds to the identifying code for the party, i.e., record 121 contains our party 121.

A complete record of information in our file is defined, in RIQS terms, as consisting of seventy items, as listed in Figure 6.2. The first item is used for the English name of the party and its identifying code number. For parties in non-English speaking countries, this item is divided into subitems, with the first subitem referring to the English name and the second to its native language name. Item two is divided into three subitems: subitem 1 describes the information base underlying the research, subitem 2 tells the researchers who indexed the literature for retrieval and inclusion within our information base, and subitem 3 credits the researchers who coded the variables in our conceptual framework with the use of the available information base.

The last 68 items in the RIQS record definition pertain to basic variables in the ICPP conceptual framework. As can be seen by comparing Figures 6.1 and 6.2, the ICPP variables are labeled within RIQS in accordance with their place in the conceptual framework. Thus, #1.01—Year of Origin, is the first indicator of the first concept—Institutionalization; #2.01—Governmental Discrimination, is the first indicator of the second concept—Governmental Status; and so forth.

A sample of RIQS output for the Austrian Socialist Party is given in Figure 6.3. Usually each item in a RIQS record pertains to a single basic variable within ICPP, but two or more variables are occasionally combined within an item when they fit together and can be supported by the same verbal discussion.

The most common practice within a RIQS item, given our application, is to use the first subitem for the variable code and the accompanying adequacy-confidence score and

```
 1.    PARTY NAME AND CODE NUMBER
 2.    INFORMATION BASE AND RESEARCHERS
 3.    1.01 YEAR OF ORIGIN AND 1.02 NAME CHANGES
 4.    1.03 ORGANIZATIONAL DISCONTINUITY
 5.    1.04 LEADERSHIP COMPETITION
 6.    1.05 / 2.05 LEGISLATIVE INSTABILITY AND STRENGTH
 7.    1.06 / 2.06 ELECTORAL INSTABILITY AND STRENGTH
 8.    2.01 GOVERNMENTAL DISCRIMINATION
 9.    2.02 GOVERNMENTAL LEADERSHIP
10.    2.03 CABINET PARTICIPATION
11.    2.04 NATIONAL ORIENTATION
12.    2.07 OUTSIDE ORIGIN
13.    3.01 / 4.01 OCCUPATIONAL AGGREGATION / ARTICULATION
14.    3.02 / 4.02 RELIGIOUS AGGREGATION / ARTICULATION
15.    3.03 / 4.03 ETHNIC AGGREGATION / ARTICULATION
16.    3.04 / 4.04 REGIONAL AGGREGATION / ARTICULATION
17.    3.05 / 4.05 URBAN - RURAL AGGREGATION / ARTICULATION
18.    3.06 / 4.06 EDUCATIONAL AGGREGATION / ARTICULATION
19.    5.01 OWNERSHIP OF THE MEANS OF PRODUCTION
20.    5.02 ECONOMIC PLANNING
21.    5.03 DISTRIBUTION OF WEALTH
22.    5.04 SOCIAL WELFARE
23.    5.05 SECULARIZATION
24.    5.06 SUPPORT OF ARMED FORCES
25.    5.07 EAST-WEST ALIGNMENT
26.    5.08 ANTI-COLONIALISM
27.    5.09 SUPRANATIONAL INTEGRATION
28.    5.10 NATIONAL INTEGRATION
29.    5.11 EXTENSION OF FRANCHISE
30.    5.12 PROTECTION OF CIVIL RIGHTS
31.    5.13 INTERFERENCE WITH CIVIL LIBERTIES
32.    5.14 / 5.15 US / SOVIET EXPERTS LEFT-RIGHT RATINGS
33.    6.00 OPEN COMPETITION
34.    6.10 RESTRICTIVE COMPETITION
35.    6.20 SUBVERTING THE POLITICAL SYSTEM
36.    6.30 PROPAGANDIZING IDEAS AND PROGRAM
37.    6.40 ALLYING WITH OTHER PARTIES
38.    6.50 PROVIDING FOR SOCIAL WELFARE
39.    7.01 SOURCES OF FUNDS
40.    7.02 SOURCES OF MEMBERS
41.    7.03 SOURCES OF LEADERS
42.    7.04 RELATIONS WITH DOMESTIC PARTIES
43.    7.05 RELATIONS WITH FOREIGN ORGANIZATIONS
44.    8.01 STRUCTURAL ARTICULATION
45.    8.02 INTENSIVENESS OF ORGANIZATION
46.    8.03 EXTENSIVENESS OF ORGANIZATION
47.    8.04 FREQUENCY OF LOCAL MEETINGS
48.    8.05 FREQUENCY OF NATIONAL MEETINGS
49.    8.06 MAINTAINING RECORDS
50.    8.07 PERVASIVENESS OF ORGANIZATION
51.    9.01 NATIONALIZATION OF STRUCTURE
52.    9.02 SELECTING THE NATIONAL LEADER
53.    9.03 SELECTING THE PARLIAMENTARY CANDIDATES
54.    9.04 ALLOCATING FUNDS
55.    9.05 POLICY FORMATION
56.    9.06 CONTROLS COMMUNICATION
57.    9.07 ADMINISTERING DISCIPLINE
58.    9.08 LEADERSHIP CONCENTRATION
59.    10.01 LEGISLATIVE COHESION
60.    10.02 IDEOLOGICAL FACTIONALISM
61.    10.03 ISSUE FACTIONALISM
62.    10.04 LEADERSHIP FACTIONALISM
63.    10.05 STRATEGIC OR TACTICAL FACTIONALISM
64.    10.06 PARTY PURGES
65.    11.01 MEMBERSHIP REQUIREMENTS
66.    11.02 MEMBERSHIP PARTICIPATION
67.    11.03 MATERIAL INCENTIVES
68.    11.04 PURPOSIVE INCENTIVES
69.    11.05 DOCTRINISM
70.    11.06 PERSONALISM
```

Figure 6.2. RIQS record definition for ICPP project data.

```
RECORD NUMBER  102

  1.  PARTY NAME AND CODE NUMBER
        SUB-1.... AUSTRIAN SOCIALIST PARTY, 102
        SUB-2.... SOZIALISTISCHE PARTEI OSTERREICHS, SPO, 102
  2.  INFORMATION BASE AND RESEARCHERS
        SUB-1.... INFORMATION ON THE SPO WAS CODED FROM 1746 PAGES OF
                  LITERATURE AND 132 DOCUMENTS ON PARTY POLITICS IN
                  AUSTRIA.  1136 PAGES, OR 65 PERCENT, DEAL WITH THE SPO.
                  5 OF THE DOCUMENTS, 4 PERCENT, ARE IN FRENCH, AND 21,
                  16 PERCENT, ARE IN GERMAN.
        SUB-2.... RAYMOND DUVALL INDEXED THE LITERATURE FOR RETRIEVAL.
        SUB-3.... RAYMOND DUVALL CODED THE FIRST TWO VARIABLE CLUSTERS.
                  KENNETH JANDA CODED THE REMAINDER FROM NOTES LEFT BY
                  DUVALL.
  3.  1.01 YEAR OF ORIGIN AND 1.02 NAME CHANGES
        SUB-1.... 1889, AC9
        SUB-2.... 1, AC7
        SUB-3.... ESSENTIALLY NO ONE DISAGREES WITH THE ASSERTION THAT
                  THE SPO EMERGED IN 1945 AS THE RESULT OF A MERGER
                  BETWEEN THE FIRST REPUBLIC≠S REVOLUTIONARY SOCIALISTS
                  AND THE SOCIAL DEMOCRATS.  THE LATTER CLEARLY
                  PREDOMINATED IN THE MERGER, SO THEIR≠S IS THE IMPORTANT
                  DATE OF ORIGIN.  MANY SOURCES CITE THE DECEMBER 30,
                  1888- JANUARY 1, 1889 CONFERENCE AT MAINFELD AS THE
                  RELEVANT DATE, WITH NO REAL DISAGREEMENTS.  THE 1945
                  MERGER WAS THE OCCASION OF A MINOR NAME CHANGE FROM
                  SOCIAL DEMOCRATS TO SOCIALISTS.  THE PARTY RETAINED A
                  SUB-TITLE IDENTIFYING THE TWO COMPONENT PARTIES, BUT
                  THIS WAS DROPPED LATER IN 1945. SINCE THAT TIME NO
                  FURTHER NAME CHANGES HAVE OCCURRED.
  4.  1.03 ORGANIZATIONAL DISCONTINUITY
        SUB-1.... 9, AC6
        SUB-2.... DOCUMENTATION OF TWO EVENTS IS GOOD-- 1945 MERGER OF
                  SOCIAL DEMOCRATS WITH THE RELATIVELY INSIGNIFICANT
                  REVOLUTIONARY SOCIALISTS, RESULTING IN THE SPO, AND THE
                  1948-49 EXPULSION AND SPLIT OF ERWIN SCHARF AND HIS
                  FOLLOWING (LEFT SOCIALISTS) WHO LATER COOPERATED WITH
                  THE KPO.  THE LOW AC IS DUE TO THE LATTER ≠SPLIT,≠
                  DOCUMENTED ONLY ONCE.  ONE SOURCE MENTIONS THE 1959
                  EXPULSION OF TRUPPE, WHO FOUNDED THE LEAGUE OF
                  DEMOCRATIC SOCIALISTS, WHICH RECEIVED 2,000 VOTES IN
                  THE NEXT ELECTION.
  5.  1.04 LEADERSHIP COMPETITION
        SUB-1.... 11, AC8
        SUB-2.... THE ONLY CHANGE IN LEADERSHIP (PARTY CHAIRMAN) THAT
                  OCCURRED DURING OUR TIME PERIOD WAS IN 1957.  AT THAT
                  TIME, BRUND PITTERMAN SUCCEEDED ADOLF SCHARF, WHO HAD
                  HELD THE POSITION SINCE 1945.  SCHARF BECAME FEDERAL
                  PRESIDENT, FOLLOWING RENNER AND KOERNER, BOTH
                  SOCIALISTS.  PITTERMANN REMAINED CHAIRMAN BEYOND 1962.
                  THE PARTY CHAIRMAN IS CHOSEN BY THE CENTRAL
                  DIRECTORATE, CONSISTING OF 50 MEMBERS CHOSEN BY THE
                  PARTY CONGRESS.
  6.  1.05 / 2.05 LEGISLATIVE INSTABILITY AND STRENGTH
        SUB-1.... INSTABILITY IS .05, AC8
        SUB-2.... STRENGTH IS .42 FOR 1ST HALF, AC8 AND .46 FOR 2ND HALF,
                  AC9
        SUB-3.... THE SPO NEVER EXCEEDED THE REPRESENTATION OF THE OVP IN
                  THE NATIONALRAT (PARLIAMENT).  ITS PERCENTAGE OF SEATS
                  LAGGED A FEW POINTS BEHIND, ALTHOUGH THE SPO TENDED TO
                  PICK UP STRENGTH DURING OUR TIME PERIOD.  IT HELD 40
                  PERCENT OF THE SEATS IN 1950 AND 46 PERCENT IN 1962.
  7.  1.06 / 2.06 ELECTORAL INSTABILITY AND STRENGTH
        SUB-1.... INSTABILITY IS .02, AC9
        SUB-2.... STRENGTH IS .42 FOR 1ST HALF, AC9 AND .44 FOR 2ND HALF,
                  AC9
        SUB-3.... ELECTIONS WERE HELD IN 1953, 1956, 1959, AND 1962.  THE
                  SUPPORT GIVEN TO THE SPO VARIED FROM 42 TO 45 PERCENT.
  8.  2.01 GOVERNMENTAL DISCRIMINATION
        SUB-1.... 1, AC5
        SUB-2.... THE SPO, TOGETHER WITH THE OVP, IS CLEARLY FAVORED BY
                  THE GOVERNMENT IN THE ALLOTMENT OF FREE RADIO TIME TO
                  POLITICAL PARTIES.  BUT AN ELECTORAL PRACTICE OF HAVING
                  PARTIES PASS OUT BALLOT PAPER (MAINTAINED UNTIL 1959)
                  DISCRIMINATED AGAINST THE SPO IN RURAL AND ALPINE
                  AREAS.  TWO BITS OF INFORMATION WERE EXCLUDED FROM THE
                  CODING DUE TO A LACK OF EVIDENCE OF DE FACTO OR
                  INTENDED DISCRIMINATION OR DISCRIMINATORY EFFECT.  THE
                  FIRST WAS THE BANNING OF A CAMPAIGN POSTER BY SOVIET
                  OCCUPATION AUTHORITIES IN THE 1953 ELECTION.  THE
                  SECOND WAS A SALE OF VOTING STOCK IN THE NATIONALIZED
                  BANKS ONLY TO THE TWO COALITION PARTIES IN 1956.
```

Figure 6.3. Partial printout of RIQS record 102, the
Austrian Socialist Party.

the second subitem for the verbal discussion. But this practice has exceptions, as it does for item 3, which reports the codes for #1.01—Year of Origin and #1.02—Name Changes in subitems 1 and 2 respectively and uses subitem 3 for the verbal discussion. Another exception occurs when the party changes during our time period and is given different scores for the same variables in the first and second halves. Generally, however, the meaning of the subitems becomes clear upon examination.

Research Strategy

One excellent feature of RIQS as a social science data management and analysis system is its acceptance of both numeric and alphabetic information and its provision of analysis routines appropriate to each type. In order to use this capability, however, the types of information must be organized by item and not mixed within items. Because the ICPP application of RIQS includes both quantitative data (the variable and adequacy–confidence codes) and textual material (the verbal discussions) separated only as subitems within a single item, the entire item had to be defined as alphanumeric. Therefore, we lost the ability to treat our quantitative data *as* quantitative (numeric) data within RIQS. We cannot, for example, use the link from RIQS to SPSS that is available to the system. Our statistical analyses with the ICPP data must be conducted entirely outside of RIQS, and we do maintain an SPSS file of ICPP data created separately for this purpose.[9]

RIQS is valued in the ICPP Project for data management rather than data analysis. It helps us respond easily to such requests as the following, which we have actually received and fulfilled: (1) provide the names, name changes, and years of origin of all parties in the study; (2) provide certain issue orientation variable codes for selected European parties; and (3) provide the codes for a different set of issue orientation variables for all the parties in the study. In each case, we used RIQS to select from our entire set of data only that information of interest to the writer, and we were able to provide not only the raw quantitative codes we assigned to the parties for the variables of interest but also the rich verbal discussion supporting and otherwise clothing our naked data. Our RIQS search command for the names, name changes, and years of origin for all the parties in the study, for example, consisted simply of PRINT 1 and 3—the items that contained the desired information. Part of the result from that search is reproduced in Figure 6.4.

Results and Conclusions

Without an automated system for data management, it is terribly time–consuming and disruptive of ongoing research to fulfill outside data requests like those mentioned above. At best, the scholars usually receive only the raw quantitative data, with little or no interpretive comment. In most social science research projects, the qualifications and explanations of data sets reside in the minds and files of those who collect the data—and lasts all too often only momentarily, as the researchers soon forget why they coded a variable a certain way in a given instance. Given the capability of an automated information system to handle textual information as well as quantitative data, it might be utilized to record more than just the raw data. If information systems are used for collateral coding documentation, we should be able to improve the dissemination of data for intelligent secondary analysis. We have tried to pursue this goal within the ICPP Project.

```
RECORD NUMBER   51

   1.   PARTY NAME AND CODE NUMBER
            SUB-1.....IRISH PARTY ( SOLDIERS ) OF DESTINY, 051
            SUB-2.... FIANNA FAIL, FF, 051
   3.   1.01 YEAR OF ORIGIN AND 1.02 NAME CHANGES
            SUB-1.... 1926, AC9
            SUB-2.... 0, AC5
            SUB-3.... ALL SOURCES AGREE THAT THE FIANNA FAIL WAS FOUNDED IN
                      1926. THERE IS NO EVIDENCE OF NAME CHANGES.


* * * * * * * * * * * * * * * * * * * * * * * * * * * * * * * * * * *


RECORD NUMBER   52

   1.   PARTY NAME AND CODE NUMBER
            SUB-1.... UNITED IRELAND, 052
            SUB-2.... FINE GAEL, FG, 052
   3.   1.01 YEAR OF ORIGIN AND 1.02 NAME CHANGES
            SUB-1.... 1923, AC7
            SUB-2.... 0, AC6
            SUB-3.... THERE IS SOME DISCREPANCY AS TO WHETHER FINE GAEL WAS
                      FORMED IN 1933 FROM THE MERGER OF THE CENTER PARTY AND
                      CUMAN NA GAEDHEAL OR IF IT IS REALLY THE SUCCESSOR OF
                      CUMAN NA GAEDHEAL WHICH MEANS IT STARTED IN 1923.  THE
                      LATTER INTERPRETATION WILL BE ASSUMED SINCE THE
                      IDEOLOGY OF THE TWO WAS THE SAME, AND SINCE SOME
                      REFERENCES CITE THE FINE GAEL AS THE CHILD OF THE 1921
                      SPLIT, AND THE CUMAN NA GAEDHEAL AS ONE OF THE PARTIES
                      FORMED RIGHT AFTER THE SPLIT WITH THE SAME IDEOLOGY AS
                      THE FINE GAEL.  THUS IT IS EASY TO ASSUME THAT THIS IS
                      THE SAME PARTY.  ONE SOURCE CITES THE FACT THAT THE
                      PARTY NAME WAS ASSUMED IN 1937 AND THAT THERE HAS BEEN
                      NO CHANGE SINCE THEN.  THIS IS IN LINE WITH THE
                      ORIGINAL ASSUMPTION THAT THE FINE GAEL IS THE SUCCESSOR
                      OF THE CUMAN NA GAEDHEAL.  OTHERWISE THE NAME CHANGE
                      WOULD HAVE OCCURRED IN 1933.  HOWEVER, IN EITHER CASE
                      THE CODE REMAINS 0, SINCE SCORING FOR THIS VARIABLE
                      BEGINS IN 1941.


* * * * * * * * * * * * * * * * * * * * * * * * * * * * * * * * * * *

RECORD NUMBER   53

   1.   PARTY NAME AND CODE NUMBER
            SUB-1.... IRISH LABOUR PARTY, ILP, 053
   3.   1.01 YEAR OF ORIGIN AND 1.02 NAME CHANGES
            SUB-1.... 1912, AC8
            SUB-2.... 0, AC6
            SUB-3.... TWO SOURCES INDICATE THAT THE IRISH LABOUR PARTY WAS
                      FORMED IN 1912 BY THE TRADE UNION CONGRESS.  THE PARTY
                      CHANGED ITS NAME FROM REPUBLICANS TO LABOUR PARTY IN
                      1927, AND THERE HAVE BEEN NO NAME CHANGES SINCE THAT
                      TIME.


* * * * * * * * * * * * * * * * * * * * * * * * * * * * * * * * * * *
```

Figure 6.4. Partial printout of data items containing party name
changes and years of origin.

In general, RIQS has served our interests quite well, but there are some limitations in the system which have hampered our use of the data and caused certain circumlocutions in order to achieve the desired result. RIQS' inability to accept different types of information declared separately for *sub*items as well as items has already been mentioned. Indeed, this limitation exists also for the purposes of indexing, which cannot be specified only for a particular subitem but must be done on the information in the entire item. Certainly, more flexibility in taking advantage of the subitem structure would be useful.

Another limitation of RIQS for the ICPP application was overcome by Peter Kron of Vogelback Computing Center, who handcrafted *ad hoc* solutions for each offense. Our records were extremely long, and several were rejected because they overran the storage limitation in the program. Peter Kron managed to massage each record into the file, but this limitation will no doubt trouble others with single records composed of large amounts of textual material. It is clear that the developers of RIQS did not foresee that their system might be used as it has been in the ICPP Project, but such unanticipated applications help make life in a computing center so interesting.

NOTES AND CITED REFERENCES

1. The main financial support for the ICPP Project has come from the National Science Foundation under grants GS-1418, GS-2533, and GS-27081. Research funds were also provided by Northwestern University's Research Committee and its Council for Intersocietal Studies, the Foreign Policy Research Institute of Philadelphia, and the American Enterprise Institute for Public Policy Research in Washington, D.C. The principal investigator of the ICPP Project is Kenneth Janda.

2. For legal parties, our criterion for inclusion requires holding at least five percent of the seats in the legislature following two elections during our time period. For illegal parties, our criteria are less automatic, but we look for the party receiving support from at least ten percent of the population over a five year period.

3. The Free Press, a division of Macmillan, has contracted to publish a series of five volumes reporting the results of the ICPP research. These three analyses will be the subjects of the last three volumes, the first of which will be published in early 1975.

4. Kenneth Janda, "A Conceptual Framework for the Comparative Analysis of Political Parties," in Volume I of *Sage Professional Papers in Comparative Politics* (Beverly Hills: Sage Publications, 1970), 75-126.

5. Kenneth Janda, "Conceptual Equivalence and Multiple Indicators in the Cross-National Analysis of Political Parties," paper delivered at the Workshop on Indicators of National Development, sponsored by the ISSC/UNESCO/ECPR and held in Lausanne, Switzerland, August 9-14, 1971.

6. Kenneth Janda, "Data Quality Control and Library Research on Political Parties," in Raoul Naroll and Ronald Cohen (eds.), *A Handbook of Method in Cultural Anthropology* (Garden City, New York: Natural History Press, 1970), 962-973.

7. Edited by Kenneth Janda, this volume is tentatively titled, *Comparative Political Parties: A Cross-National Handbook,* and is scheduled for publication by The Free Press in 1974. Arrangements have been made with the Inter-University Consortium for Political Research to distribute the data on magnetic tape. The data will be made available to the Consortium when the material for the first volume goes to the publisher.

8. Some 70,000 pages from 3500 documents on party politics have been thoroughly indexed and incorporated into a computer-and-microfilm information retrieval system to support our research on parties. See Kenneth Janda, "A Microfilm and

Computer System for Analyzing Comparative Politics Literature," in George Gerbner *et al.* (eds.), *The Analysis of Communication Content* (New York: John Wiley, 1969), 407–435.

9. Our RIQS file was designed in 1969, long before the RIQS–SPSS link was planned, much less implemented. If, instead of defining each of our items as multiple-alphanumeric to contain both our variable codes and our verbal discussions, we had used numeric items for our codes and separate alphabetic items for our discussions, we could have used the link within RIQS to create the SPSS file and thus need only maintain one data base, rather than two as at present.

Chapter 7

SIMIA-Simulations in International Affairs: A Computer Maintained Bibliography

DAVID H. LESERMAN
American Hospital Association

HAROLD GUETZKOW
Northwestern University

Some members of the Department of Political Science at Northwestern University have been engrossed for a number of years in a project developing solid, empirically based theory in the area of international affairs. The work entails constructing and experimenting with models of international affairs in an attempt to describe the international system and to form theories regarding relationships within the system. The goal of this effort has been to further our understanding of decision-making processes at the global level.

Problem

One of the major problems in this endeavor has been to maintain a perspective on the plethora of information and conjecture resulting from recent study in the field. Maintenance of an eclectic approach as well as the consolidation and cross referencing of information is a major undertaking in itself. It is an undertaking that can easily outweigh and obscure the project's goals.

We recently noted that "Because of the gigantic task involved in this enterprise, some of us might work cooperatively, building cumulatively upon the products of all. It may be that we'll eventually evolve a net of collaborators interested in modular approaches in the simulation of empirically grounded theory in foreign affairs and international relations. . ."[1] This conceptualization of a *collaborative* net builds upon the assumption that cooperative, incremental work, albeit contrary to the traditions of autonomy so entrenched in the scholarly disciplines today, may provide a useful channel in the construction of creative, solid knowledge for decision making in international affairs.

138

In light of these considerations, the project team became interested in finding a method to handle large quantities of information. Aside from familiarity with the computer as a research tool, we have been users of computer services for information interchange. In particular we use the SDI service offered to the social sciences faculty at Northwestern. This SDI system (Selective Dissemination of Information) involves keyword searches of abstracts from selected publications and the retrieval of abstracts with bibliographic citations. Using this service on a monthly basis, we have quick reference to potentially relevant articles, even though the entire literature of interest to us is not covered.

In 1970, the project became aware of the development of the Remote Information Query System (RIQS). We learned that RIQS could not only handle a large number of alphanumeric records, but that these records could be internally subdivided into items that could be referenced individually or in groups, that records could be indexed and cross-referenced on a variety of keys, that records could be updated, and new records added to the file. We realized that the RIQS system would provide a solution to our problem in handling large quantities of information: a computer maintained bibliography.

Data

A number of journals on international affairs, including the *International Studies Quarterly,* were searched for relevant articles on international simulation. Several general political science periodicals, such as the *Journal of Politics,* were also examined for references. In addition, several bibliographic journals, such as the *Peace Research Abstract Journal,* were searched for possible entries in the bibliographic file. References were occasionally obtained from colleagues researching in the field of international simulation, often articles recently completed by these researchers.

The significant information concerning bibliographic entries to be input into the file was subsequently translated into RIQS and classified into the following key elements for each record of data:

1. Reference code
2. Author(s)
3. Title of book or article
4. Author(s) professional affiliation
5. Address of affiliation
6. Publication or anthology
7. Volume number and issue number, if journal article; publisher, if book
8. Date of writing or publication
9. Page references
10. Abstract of the text publication
11. Keyword list

These elements became the items of each record in the RIQS file (Figure 7.1). Initial creation of the file, including the writing of abstracts and the keypunching of all data, involved approximately one man-year of work.[2]

Item 1 is declared to be numeric; Item 2 (authors) is optionally a multiple item; Item 8 is declared to be a date (RIQS recognizes dates in a variety of formats and produces informative diagnostics if illegitimate information appears in this field); Item 10 is textual;

```
RECORD NUMBER      1
     (1) REFERENCE CODE
     01
     (2) AUTHOR(S)
     SMOKER PAUL
     (3) TITLE OF BOOK OR ARTICLE
     SOCIAL RESEARCH FOR SOCIAL ANTICIPATION
     (4) AUTHOR(S) PROFESSIONAL AFFILIATION
     NORTHWESTERN UNIVERSITY
     (5) ADDRESS OF AFFILIATION
     EVANSTON ILLINOIS
     (6) PUBLICATION OR ANTHOLOGY
     AMERICAN BEHAVIORAL SCIENTIST
     (7) VOLUME NUMBER-ISSUE NUMBER OR PUBLISHER
     VOLUME 12 NO.  6
     (8) DATE
     JULY 1969
     (9) BEGINNING PAGE
     PP  7 - 13
     (10) ABSTRACT
     THIS PAPER CONSIDERS THE USE OF SIMULATION FOR SOCIAL
     ANTICIPATION WHERE THE OUTCOMES OF POSSIBLE FUTURES ARE
     PREDICTED ( MILSTEIN AND MITCHELL, 1968 ), AND EXPLORES ITS
     POTENTIAL FOR SOCIAL CREATION, WHERE SIMULATION BECOMES AN
     INTEGRAL PART OF PROCESSES OF SOCIAL CHANGE ( BEER, G 1969 ).
     THE FORMER CONCEPT IS SOCIAL RESEARCH IN THE OBJECTIVE SENSE.
     HERE THE SOCIAL SCIENTIST EXPLORES THE PROPERTIES OF A MODEL AND
     EXTRAPOLATES TO THE REAL WORLD.  THE LATTER CONCEPT DOES NOT
     SEPARATE SIMULATION FROM REALITY IN SUCH A CLEAR CUT FASHION.
     SUBJECTIVE SIMULATION EXPERIENCE AND OBJECTIVE RESEARCH ANALYSIS
     ARE PART OF A LARGER PROCESS OF MUTUAL INTERACTION WITH, AND
     ALTERATION OF, REALITY ITSELF.
     (11) KEYWORDS
     FUTURES REALITY INTERNATIONSIM CORRESPONDENCE VALIDATION
     CONFLICT SOCIALCHANGE SOCIALRESEARCH SIP
```

Figure 7.1.   Printout of a SIMIA record.

and all items except for (1) and (8) are alphanumeric by default. Item 11, the keyword list, is a list of 5 to 20 keywords chosen from a master keyword list (which is periodically reconstructed) to reflect shifts in research interests and strategies.

Indexing of the keywords substantiates the utility of this file. In searching for information related to a specific topic, the keyword index is consulted and relevant abstracts are readily at hand. Upon reviewing the abstract, the researcher can decide whether the source is applicable to his current pursuit. The keyword list for each abstract is chosen to include every aspect which may be of interest to the user. Keywords fall into two categories: descriptors and identifiers. Descriptors are terms used for subject characterization, while identifiers are names (of people, projects, organizations, etc.). In order to keep the keyword list concise, variations of words are condensed into a single form (e.g., validation, validity, and validators are all expressed with the entry of validation).

The abstract, along with its respective citation is the essence of the file. It is suggested that the abstractor use the vocabulary of the author, summarily conveying the author's meaning, follow his order of information, and reflect his degree of emphasis on any given point. In brief, the abstract should be long enough to adequately convey the author's concept, yet short enough to provide for an easily used key to research strategy.

Strategy

Each time the file is updated with newly received bibliographic references a list is produced containing the several indexes and cross-reference maps described below.

1. An alphabetical index by authors of each record. (Figure 7.2)
2. An abbreviated cross-reference, alphabetized again by author, but including only the reference code, authors, and the title of the publication. (Figure 7.3)
3. A RIQS KWIC (Keyword-in-context) permuted index on the title (Item 3) of each record which also displays the reference code. The permuted index places each word of the title—excluding specified "stop" words—in a left justified column in the center of a page. The rest of the title is written out, wrapping around to the left side of the page and ending in a right justified column (Figure 7.4). Thus an alphabetical index is created for each word in each title in the file, and the entire title, as well as the reference code, accompanies each indexed word.
4. A RIQS KWOC (Keyword-out-of-context) index on the item 11 keyword list. This index lists alphabetically all of the keywords appearing in item 11 of all records. Below each keyword is listed the reference code, author, and title of each record in which that keyword appears in item 11.
5. A sequential list of reference codes, authors, and the title of each record, in conjunction with the RIQS internally assigned record number. This index is useful making updates to the file.

The SIMIA file contains one subfile (Set 1) which includes all records relating to work done in conjunction with Northwestern's Simulated International Processes (SIP) project. These records are accessible both from the main file and from the subfile. When a final report was readied for the government,[3] the subfile was accessed, indexed, reformatted, and printed. RIQS provided the basis for the preparation of the bibliography that accompanied the final report. One of the indexes included in the final report was the reference list shown in Figure 7.5.

Conclusion

Our use of RIQS to provide a series of cross-referenced indexes for the consolidation of information in the field of international affairs is proving to be a valuable asset in our work. The prime capability of RIQS though is to furnish on-line reports from a file in response to queries. Although we have not used RIQS in this manner as yet, the SIMIA file as it stands, could be searched by RIQS in this fashion. Thus, the SIMIA bibliographic file can be used for reference as well as for publication needs.

It is believed that the SIMIA bibliographic file may help all concerned with collaboration in the simulation of international affairs. The development of a more standardized and stabilized vocabulary from keywords may prove useful in comparative work on parallel constructions, so that homomorphic components may be analyzed in terms of operationalized terms. This may strengthen linkages among users of the file, creating a net of collaborators.

ABSTRACTS OF ARTICLES ARRANGED BY INITIAL AUTHOR

BUSSE WALTER E.

21
BUSSE WALTER E.
NORTHWESTERN SIMULATION ARCHIVES - MAN COMPUTER MODELS OF
INTERNATIONAL RELATIONS
UNPUBLISHED PROJECT OF PROGRAM OF GRADUATE TRAINING AND RESEARCH
IN INTERNATIONAL RELATIONS, DEPARTMENT OF POLITICAL SCIENCE,
NORTHWESTERN UNIVERSITY, EVANSTON, ILLINOIS
STENCILED
1969
PP 24
SOME YEARS AGO RICHARD C. SNYDER PROPOSED THE CREATION OF AN
ARCHIVE OF SIMULATION GENERATED MATERIALS. THE ESTABLISHMENT OF
THE NORTHWESTERN SIMULATION ARCHIVES OF MAN COMPUTER MODELS OF
INTERNATIONAL RELATIONS BRINGS THIS SUGGESTION TO FRUITATION.
THE PURPOSE OF THIS COLLECTION IS TO MAKE THE OUTPUT OF
SIMULATIONS AVAILABLE TO A WIDER SPECTRUM AND TO ALLOW WIDER
UTILIZATION OF THE INFORMATION FOR PURPOSES BEYOND THE SPECIFIC
SCOPE OF INQUIRY AT THE TIME THE SIMULATIONS WERE REALIZED. THE
FOUR SIMULATIONS PRESENTLY INCLUDED IN THE ARCHIVE WERE DESIGNED
FOR RESEARCH ABOUT VARIOUS ASPECTS OF THE OPERATION OF THE
INTERNATIONAL SYSTEM. THEY WERE REALIZED BETWEEN 1960 AND 1967
AND REPRESENT CONSIDERABLE PROGRESS IN THE DEVELOPMENT AND
UTILIZATION OF VARIATIONS OF THE INTERNATION SIMULATION.

CAMPBELL DONALD T.

40
CAMPBELL DONALD T.
THE PRINCIPLE OF PROXIMAL SIMILARITY IN THE APPLICATION OF
SCIENCE
MULTILITHED
NORTHWESTERN UNIVERSITY
JULY 1966
PP 9
NO ABSTRACT

377
CAMPBELL DONALD T.
INTERVENTION SIMULATION AS A LABORATORY FOR THE TESTING OF
THEORIES ALSO RELEVANT TO INTERNATIONAL RELATIONS
STENCILED
NORTHWESTERN UNIVERSITY
NOVEMBER 1967
PP 7
MUCH PHILOSOPHICAL DISCUSSION OF THE VALIDITY OF SIMULATION
ARGUES THAT SIMULATED INTERNATIONAL SYSTEMS ARE NOT REAL
INTERNATIONAL SYSTEMS, AND THAT IT IS FAULTY LOGIC TO GENERALIZE
FROM ONE TO ANOTHER. THERE MAY EXIST THEORIES OR ASPECTS OF
THEORIES WHICH HAVE IMPLICATIONS FOR BOTH SYSTEMS AND BOTH ARE
THUS POTENTIALLY DISCONFIRMABLE IN BOTH SETTINGS. THE PROBLEMS
IN USING INTERNATIONAL EVENTS TO PROBE THEORIES EMPIRICALLY
INCLUDE TWO SORTS - THE CONFOUNDING OF CAUSE AND EFFECT, AND THE
SHORTAGE OF DEGREES OF FREEDOM. THIS PAPER HAS BEEN
INCORPORATED INTO CAMPBELL, CHADWICK, AND RASER, - GAMING AND
SIMULATION FOR DEVELOPING THEORY RELEVANT TO INTERNATIONAL
RELATIONS. - GENERAL SYSTEMS YEARBOOK, 1970, VOL. 15. THIS
PIECE IS LISTED IN SIPFIL UNDER REFERENCE CODE NUMBER 355.

Figure 7.2.   Author index.

```
CROSS REFERENCE OF ARTICLES BY COLLABORATING AUTHORS

BENHAM ALEXANDRA H.

        335
        BRODY RICHARD A.
        BENHAM ALEXANDRA H.
        MILSTEIN JEFFREY S.
        HOSTILE INTERNATIONAL COMMUNICATION, ARMS PRODUCTION, AND
        PERCEPTION OF THREAT, A SIMULATION STUDY

        362
        BRODY RICHARD A.
        BENHAM ALEXANDRA H.
        NUCLEAR WEAPONS AND ALLIANCE COHESION

BRUNNER RONALD D.

        52
        ALKER HAYWARD R.
        BRUNNER RONALD D.
        SIMULATING INTERNATIONAL CONFLICT - A COMPARISON OF THREE
        APPROACHES

CAMPBELL DONALD T.

        355
        RASER JOHN R.
        CAMPBELL DONALD T.
        CHADWICK RICHARD W.
        GAMING AND SIMULATION FOR DEVELOPING THEORY RELEVANT TO
        INTERNATIONAL RELATIONS

CHADWICK RICHARD W.

        355
        RASER JOHN R.
        CAMPBELL DONALD T.
        CHADWICK RICHARD W.
        GAMING AND SIMULATION FOR DEVELOPING THEORY RELEVANT TO
        INTERNATIONAL RELATIONS

CROW WAYMAN J.

        99
        RASER JOHN R.
        CROW WAYMAN J.
        A SIMULATION STUDY OF DETERENCE THEORIES

CUTLER NEAL E.

        17
        NARDIN TERRY
        CUTLER NEAL E.
        RELIABILITY AND VALIDITY OF SOME PATTERNS OF INTERNATIONAL
        INTERACTION IN AN INTERNATION SIMULATION
```

Figure 7.3. Sample of collaborating author index.

```
                 AN INTERNATIONAL PROCESSES SIMULATION--DEVELOPMENT, USAGE AND PARTIAL VALIDATION-PART 3,
                       SIMULATION IN INTERNATIONAL RELATIONS,
                                      DEVELOPMENTS FOR RESEARCH AND TRAINING
 IN HIGH SCHOOL TEACHING              DEVELOPMENTS IN SIMULATION OF INTERNATIONAL RELATIONS
          A COMPUTER SIMULATION MODEL OF PRISONERS DILEMMA
                                      PRISONERS DILEMMA AND CHICKEN MODELS IN INTERNATIONAL POLITICS
                                      THE DIMENSIONALITY OF NATIONS PROJECT 1969
          SIMULATION OF INTERNATIONAL RELATIONS AND DIPLOMACY
                       GLOBAL PATTERNS OF DIPLOMATIC EXCHANGE
 A RECONSTRUCTION OF OLIVER BENSON≠S SIMPLE DIPLOMATIC GAME
                             A SIMPLE DIPLOMATIC GAME
                       SDG.. SIMPLE DIPLOMATIC GAME ( KRENDS RECONSTRUCTION )
              AN INTERPRETATION OF PATTERNS OF DISCREPANCIES BETWEEN THE INTERNATIONAL PROCESS SI
                A SIMULATION STUDY OF STRATEGIC DOCTRINES
                       A STUDY OF STRATEGIC DOCTRINES USING INTER-NATION SIMULATION
 SSES SIMULATION                      A DOCUMENTATION OF PAUL SMOKER-S INTERNATIONAL PROCE
          FOURTH RAND POLITICAL EXERCISE-SUMMARY AND DOCUMENTS               CRISISCOM, A COMPUT
 ER SIMULATION OF HUMAN INFORMATION AND PROCESSING DURING A CRISIS
          PRESIDENTIAL DECISIONMAKING DURING THE CUBAN MISSILE CRISIS-A COMPUTER SIMULATION
                        WORLD DYNAMICS
    WORLD2.. BASIC VERSION OF FORRESTERS WORLD DYNAMICS MODEL
                 TOWARD A THEORY OF THE DYNAMICS OF CONFLICT
                       A GLOBAL ECO-TACTIC.. POPULATION CONTROL AS A MULTINATION
 AL BUSINESSPROPOSITION                A GLOBAL ECO-TACTIC-POPULATION CONTROL AS A MULTINATIONAL
 BUSINESS PROPOSITION                  ECONOMIC CALCULATIONS WITHIN THE IPS SIMULATION
                             IPS ECONOMIC CALCULATIONS PROGRAM                SURV
 EY OF THE STATE OF THE ART-SOCIAL, POLITICAL, AND ECONOMIC MODELS AND SIMULATIONS
                       A SIMPLIFIED POLITICAL-ECONOMIC SYSTEM SIMULATION
          A PARTIAL MODEL OF NATIONAL POLITICAL ECONOMIC SYSTEMS, EVALUATION BY CAUSAL INFERENCE
 INTERNATION SIMULATION IN TERMS OF CONTEMPORARY ECONOMIC THEORY DATA
                       ECONOMICS OF PEACE AND WAR, A SIMULATION
          SOME CURRENT RESEARCH ON EFFECTIVENESS OF EDUCATIONAL SIMULATION IMPLICATIONS FOR ALTERNATIV
```

Figure 7.4. KWIC title index of SIMIA file.

```
INDEX OF REFERENCE NUMBERS OF ARTICLES FROM FINAL REPORT

     REFERENCE NO. 32
     PENDLEY ROBERT E.
     ELDER CHARLES D.
     AN ANALYSIS OF OFFICEHOLDING IN THE INTERNATION SIMULATION IN TERMS OF
     CONTEMPORARY POLITICAL THEORY AND DATA ON THE STABILITY OF REGIMES AND
     GOVERNMENTS

     REFERENCE NO. 33
     GORDEN MORTON
     BURDENS FOR THE DESIGNER OF A COMPUTER SIMULATION OF INTERNATIONAL
     RELATIONS - THE CASE OF TEMPER

     REFERENCE NO. 34
     ELDER CHARLES D.
     PENDLEY ROBERT E.
     AN ANALYSIS OF CONSUMPTION STANDARDS AND VALIDATION SATISFACTIONS IN THE
     INTERNATION SIMULATION IN TERMS OF CONTEMPORARY ECONOMIC THEORY DATA

     REFERENCE NO. 38
     DRUCKMAN DANIEL
     ETHNOCENTRISM IN THE INTERNATION SIMULATION

     REFERENCE NO. 40
     CAMPBELL DONALD T.
     THE PRINCIPLE OF PROXIMAL SIMILARITY IN THE APPLICATION OF SCIENCE

     REFERENCE NO. 44
     DRIVER MICHAEL J.
     A STRUCTURAL ANALYSIS OF AGGRESSION, STRESS, AND PERSONALITY IN AN
     INTERNATION SIMULATION

     REFERENCE NO. 46
     JENSEN LLOYD
     UNITED STATES ELITES AND THEIR PERCEPTIONS OF THE DETERMINANTS OF FOREIGN
     POLICY BEHAVIOR

     REFERENCE NO. 51
     JENSEN LLOYD
     FOREIGN POLICY ELITES AND THE PREDICTION OF INTERNATIONAL EVENTS

     REFERENCE NO. 52
     ALKER HAYWARD R.
     BRUNNER RONALD D.
     SIMULATING INTERNATIONAL CONFLICT - A COMPARISON OF THREE APPROACHES

     REFERENCE NO. 54
     MACRAE JOHN
     SMOKER PAUL
     A VIETNAM SIMULATION - A REPORT ON THE CANADIAN / ENGLISH JOINT PROJECT

     REFERENCE NO. 57
     SMOKER PAUL
     INTERNATIONAL PROCESSES SIMULATION - A MAN COMPUTER MODEL

     REFERENCE NO. 59
     KRESS PAUL F.
     ON VALIDATING SIMULATION - WITH SPECIAL ATTENTION TO SIMULATION OF
     INTERNATIONAL POLITICS
```

Figure 7.5. Sample of reference code index.

NOTES AND CITED REFERENCES

1. Guetzkow, Harold, "Collaboration in Computer Simulation for Decision-Making in International Affairs," Evanston, Ill.: Northwestern University, June, 1973, 3 pp.

2. For this task and the original organization of the file in 1970–1971, we extend appreciation to Michael R. Leavitt and David Hsia; we give special thanks to Bonnie Neubeck who carried the burden of a second revision in 1972; credit for the creation of the third computer maintained file (SIPFIL) later that year lies with Michael R. Hagerty.

3. The Simulated International Processes (SIP) project was supported by the Carnegie Corporation of New York, as well as by the U.S. Government (AF 49(638)-742, Nonr-1228(22), and ARPA/SD 260).

Chapter 8

The Information Transfer Process on the University Campus: The Case for Public Use Files

LORRAINE BORMAN and RICHARD HAY, JR.
Northwestern University

Introduction

Many of the same techniques and programs which the individual researcher uses to cope with personal reference and research data can be used to assist the consumer of publically available data bases. This chapter will discuss how RIQS and SPSS have been used interactively, first to acquaint social scientists and students with the existence and content of certain data bases, and then to provide analysis tools for testing tentative hypotheses, using the selected data.

The desire for readily available data and effective processing capabilities was evident even before computers were in wide use. In 1945, Vannevar Bush presaged a whole new field of study: the use of automated techniques to aid man in exploiting the fund of acquired knowledge.[1] He suggested that the problem of information dissemination required modern means of information handling; over the years this has led especially to research into library resources and modes of operation. In 1967 Caffrey and Mosmann[2] discussed existing activities and developments in the context of "tomorrow's campus." In thinking about new forms of the transfer and dissemination of information, it was noted that some people were prepared to "reject the schema of the physical library,"[3] while others said that the "library [in the university of the future[4]] will be the central facility of an information transfer network that will extend throughout the academic community... [and that] students and scholars will use this network to gain access to the university total information resources."[5]

During the late 1960s, research and development, mostly on university campuses, but heavily supported by federal funds, led to first generation information systems. These

147

systems were designed primarily for the storage and retrieval of information from large scale data bases, mostly of a bibliographic nature.

The production of machine-readable data bases also received emphasis in the sixties. The National Science Foundation supported efforts by professional societies such as the American Chemical Society and the American Psychological Association to produce an information bank (i.e., abstracts and indexes of the world's scientific literature) and supply magnetic tapes recording its content. Concurrently, data archives were being developed which were concerned with the collection, updating, preservation, and diffusion of social and behavioral science data. Both types of data, bibliographic and numeric, were *public* files, i.e., were of interest to, and potentially obtainable by, numerous individuals and groups within the university community. The university-centered information systems were designed to be the distribution outlets of the bibliographic material to the user community.[6] The data archives, on the other hand, did not concern themselves with the problem of information processing per se. They assumed that their responsibility lay in providing data, and in providing access to information describing that data. Data bases were stored, maintained and cataloged. Dissemination of information *about* the data did occur, but information dissemination based on *utilization of the data* did not.

There were too many obstacles to overcome for a novice data archive user: programming languages, format specifications, requirements of various "library" programs. In 1972-1973, a major step toward providing easier access to general purpose data bases was taken by the Regional Social Science Data Archive at the University of Iowa. Using the SPSS (Statistical Package for the Social Sciences) system, the Center created ready-to-use analysis files, utilizing widely distributed data sets (from the Inter-University Consortium for Political Research (ICPR) at the University of Michigan)[7] and a common language (SPSS). The data sets produced by the Iowa archive are relevant in several disciplines, which include Political Science, Sociology, Economics, Government, and History. Some of these data sets are accompanied by detailed reports which include data analyses, tables, or codebooks describing each variable in the file, and sets of student exercises.[8] Another step in this direction was development and distribution of the OSIRIS system which also processed the ICPR data bases.[9] It was envisioned that an information transfer process would develop and grow within this kind of environment. However, this has not entirely been the case.

The present day situation in most universities is something like this. First, access to bibliographic files prepared primarily by professional societies is offered to members of of the faculty through the intermediary services of a librarian or information specialist. These services are usually directed towards the natural and physical sciences and tend to be of the *current awareness* type, utilizing a client prepared interest profile. The *middleman* then processes this profile, or query set, together with those of the other clients against a data base consisting of the most current collection of abstracts. The retrieved records are then mailed to the client. In this type of operation the client has had no opportunity to personally interact with the literature collection. On-line access to some data bases is available, such as the BASIS-70 data services of Battelle Memorial Institute and the MEDLINE files of System Development Corporation. However, there are "real" costs in accessing these files. Long distance telephone hookup, terminal charges, yearly use fees, charges based on number of citations retrieved, all work to make bibliographic access available only to the faculty member who has research funds allocatable to that purpose. The majority of students are locked out of the system because of financial constraints.

Second, access to archived data is usually available at most of the larger universities that have behaviorally or quantitatively oriented social science departments. However, students are often still effectively restrained from using the data bases because of the time needed to prepare the already machine-readable data for use. Subsetting, copying, and learning various program requirements all require more time than is often available within a term paper deadline. Thus, data access on a university campus is often a limited commodity, available only to certain groups, rather than the total community. The information transfer process, which is a major goal of the university, is thus not being achieved in an organized way as far as archived data are concerned.

For information transfer to occur naturally and easily, the facilities provided by information systems must be expanded. They should combine the elements of *information retrieval, data reduction and manipulation,* and *communication.* As Edward Weiss of the Office of Science Information Service/National Science Foundation recently stated: "We must begin to examine the possibilities of an information or knowledge transfer system as opposed to a document transfer system...[This implies a] need for a reexamination of the way in which scientific and technical information is packaged, stored, and accessed with a special emphasis on the real desires and requirements of the user."[10]

Public Use Files

Public use files are usually thought of as belonging to two categories: bibliographic and quantitative. The bibliographic data may have been produced by a professional society, or as part of a discipline-oriented research activity. The quantitative data may have been produced by a government agency (such as the Bureau of the Census), a research center (such as the election studies directed by the Institute for Social Research at the University of Michigan), or by individual research activities (such as the Black Africa Comparative Data File, by Morrison, Mitchell, Paden, and Stevenson[11]). What makes these various data bases public use files is that they are archived, and then made available to the general university community. They are considered to have general appeal in that they contain information relating to a potentially wide range of applications and needs. Thus, a public use file of African related literature is considered of general interest because the materials refer to all areas of African study, and not simply to one in-depth area. If data is acquired, maintained, and made accessible by a central university source, like the library or university computing center, it can then be considered as being public use in nature. This is distinct from a personal data base owned by an individual who, for one reason or another, limits its use to himself, his research group, his students, or anyone else under his immediate supervision.

HOW CAN PUBLIC USE FILES CONTRIBUTE TO THE INFORMATION TRANSFER PROCESS?

Public use files play an important role in the total process of information transfer. Bibliographic files are used for production of specialized bibliographies, for term paper research, for alerting functions such as SDI, etc.; their use will continue to grow as more and more collections are put into machine-readable form. The use potential of files such as the MARC tapes prepared by the Information Systems Office, Library of Congress, is virtually unlimited.[12] The quantitative files presently being archived are used in classroom situations for teaching research methodology and data analysis and by individual students and faculty engaged, for example, in political or social research projects. A third type of use is one that utilizes files such as United Nations voting records or Congressional roll calls as reference volumes (but "volumes" which have much greater cross-referencing capabilities).

At Northwestern University, we have had a collection of bibliographic files available for public use since 1966. We also have had an information center whose prime function was to acquire and disseminate copies of machine-readable data. In 1972, recognizing that public use *availability* did not result in *use by the public*, we started questioning: Why weren't these resources being used as often as we thought they should be used? What was needed to make public files more accessible? Who were our potential users? What did they need? When was it needed? What forms of output were desired?

Some of the responses to these questions can be summed up as *easy access, easy use*. In other words, "let me get what I need, when I need it, in as easy and fast a way as possible." The balance of this chapter will (1) look at a group of public use files in a social science file collection, (2) illustrate how these files can be accessed and manipulated by both novice and sophisticated computer system users, and (3) show how this type of use is related to the utilization of public information files and information systems, and assists in the total information transfer process.

HOW ARE PUBLIC FILES USED?

Public use files must be available to a diverse public of different interests, skills, and levels of computer sophistication. One could argue that to be of true value, they should be available to the general public—the man in the street, who has probably never encountered a computer before. Various groups at Northwestern University have formulated proposals that would make remote terminal access to the public files easily available to the general public in locales such as the Evanston Public Library and the Whole Earth Store (a local book store). No doubt this idea will soon come of age as the mystique surrounding computers continues to evaporate and as funds for this type of experimentation become available. The other notion implied by the concept of public use is that the files should contain data that is interesting and *can be used* by the public. The obvious question here is: Who is the public? A class of undergraduate computer science students could be considered one kind of public. Perhaps they are interested in searching for journal articles that deal with hashing algorithms. All of Evanston's young working mothers could be considered another kind of public, interested in finding baby sitters who live within walking distance of their homes. The mothers probably do not care about hashing algorithms and it is doubtful that most computer science students need baby sitters (although one could easily imagine those members who are in the intersection of the two sets).

Though the point may be obvious, the concept of public poses some thorny problems. To which public should one address oneself? What are the needs of various publics? To what degree does the creation, maintenance, and use of a public file depend on the interests, resources, influence, and prestige of the particular public that needs it?

During the past few years, we have been attempting informally to explore some of these questions. Our explorations have taken two directions:

1. That of creating and providing access to an integrated public use file system.
2. Monitoring the use of that system to investigate the dynamics of public use.[13]

The public at Northwestern presently consists of the traditional elements of the university community—undergraduate and graduate students, faculty, and staff. Computer time is available to each of these groups for the purposes of research and instruction. Development in response to user needs at Northwestern has led to the linkage of the RIQS system with several other software packages (graphical plotting, statistical processing, language tutoring, automatic user/system monitoring), thus creating a powerful integrated system which serves excellently as the medium for accessing public use files.

Perhaps the best way to look at the use of public files at Northwestern is to follow a typical interactive session between a student and the system. A few basic commands are necessary to log onto the system; the user is prompted by the system from then on. By entering the browsing mode, the user can browse thorugh the list of public use files and display selected information about files in which he is interested (Figure 8.1).

```
N.U.   RIQS   TUTØR

ENTER -TUTØRIAL- ØR -SEARCHES- ØR -BRØWSE-
? BRØWSE

LIST ØF PUBLIC FILES

1. ASIS
   CØMPUTER SCIENCE JØURNAL ARTICLES
2. AFRICA
   MØDERN AFRICA BIBLIØGRAPHIC FILE
3. AFRØ
   BLACK AFRICA CØMPARATIVE DATA FILE
4. SDI
   SØCIAL SCIENCE RESEARCH ARTICLES
5. RESTAURANT
   CHICAGØ RESTAURANT FILE
6. RIQSLØG
   LØG DATA FRØM 1972 RIQSØNLINE USAGE
```

Figure 8.1.   List of public use files displayed by
RIQSTUTOR in browsing mode.

In Figure 8.2 he selected the ASIS file, displayed the file description, decided that he wasn't interested in computer science journals, and moved on. He then selected the AFRICA file, displayed the general description, read the RIQS record definition, and then viewed a sample record to aid him in subsequent searches of the file (Figure 8.3). Beginning his query of the AFRICA file, he searches for any citation which deals with "economic development" (Figure 8.4). Apparently, a great deal of social science literature has dealt with economic development in one manner or another; 178 citations were retrieved. These are far too many to display (although they could be printed at a central site printer) and probably deal with a wide range of specific subjects within this broader area, so our user begins to "focus" his searches. His next search is for references to economic development which occurred only after independence (Figure 8.5). This time, only 14 records were retrieved. He tears off the list of citations, intending to use it later in the library. After studying its contents, he notices that some references were not to journals at all, but rather referred to quantitative data bases relevant to economic development in independent Africa. Returning to the browsing mode, the student obtains a general description of one of these, the AFRO file, as shown in Figure 8.6.

Some days later, after having read some of the literature and formulated plans for analysis, our student returns and decides to test some tentative hypotheses. Rather than a teletype, he chooses to work at a CRT graphics terminal, equipped with a keyboard, display screen, and light pen. This time he moves directly to the AFRO file and, using the SPSSFILE command, selects a subset of seven variables (previously listed in his bibliographic search) for statistical analysis. The SPSSLINK statement causes a transfer to

```
TYPE IN THE NAME ØF THE RIQS FILE YØU WØULD LIKE TØ BRØWSE
ØR -NØNE- TØ EXIT BRØWSING MØDE.
? ASIS

YØU CAN ØBTAIN THE FØLLØWING INFØRMATIØN ABØUT THE FILE:

1.  GENERAL DESCRIPTIØN
2.  RIQS FILE DESCRIPTIØN
3.  SAMPLE RECØRD

TYPE IN ØNE ØF THE NUMBERS
TYPE -NØNE- IF YØU DØ NØT WANT ANY
? 1

YØU CAN HAVE ANY ØR ALL ØF THE FØLLØWING:

1.  FILE SIZE
2.  DESCRIPTIØN
3.  SUGGESTED USE

TYPE IN NUMBERS ØNLY
? 1,2,3
SIZE - 470 RECØRDS
DESCRIPTIØN - ABSTRACTS ØF ARTICLES APPEARING IN
THE CØMMUNICATIØNS AND JØURNAL ØF THE ACM BETWEEN 1968
AND 1972
 SUGGESTED USES - THIS FILE IS WELL SUITED
TØ BIBLIØGRAPHIC SEARCHES FØR LITERATURE PERTAINING TØ BØTH
TECHNICAL AND USER ASPECTS ØF CØMPUTER AND INFØRMATIØN
SCIENCE.

WØULD YØU RATHER
1.  HAVE MØRE INFØRMATIØN ABØUT THIS FILE
2.  BRØWSE ANØTHER FILE
3.  LEAVE THE BRØWSING MØDE
? 2
WØULD YØU LIKE THE LIST ØF FILES REPEATED
? NØ
```

Figure 8.2. Description of ASIS, a bibliographic file consisting of abstracts to articles which appeared in the *Communications of the ACM* and the *Journal of the ACM*.

SPSSONLINE, an interactive version of the Statistical Package for the Social Sciences.

After computing Pearson product moment correlations for all variables against each other (i.e., a square correlation matrix), he notices that the correlation between item 12, NAGPOT (nonagricultural development potential index) and item 10, GNPP68 (GNP per capita, 1968) is somewhat lower than expected. Curious about the pattern of the exact distribution of cases on these two variables, he diverts the correlation matrix to a printer for a hard copy (Figure 8.7). Next, the two variables are plotted. Using the "menu" PICTURE is selected to display the graph (Figure 8.8), EDIT is used to title it, and STATISTICS computes various statistics relating to the distribution (Figure 8.9). Noting the correlation, he returns to the graph via the VALUES feature. Each point on the graph (representing the values of a given case on the two variables) is now intensified and, by pointing the light pen at a particular point, all identifying information about that case is automatically retrieved and displayed (Figure 8.10a). One of the most extreme cases (those which lie far off the regression line) is chosen and is identified as Nigeria, a former English colony (Figure 8.10b). Is it possible that the former colonial ruler is a factor affecting the strength of this relationship? To test this notion, he decides to examine the same relationship (between NAGPOT and GNPP68) for the former English colonies as opposed to all other former colonial types. He saves the present plot for later viewing, directs a Calcomp copy to be made, and then enters a search command to produce a similar scatterplot for only the English colonies.

```
ENTER ANOTHER FILE NAME OR -NONE-
? AFRICA

YOU CAN HAVE ANY OR ALL OF THE FOLLOWING:

1.   FILE SIZE
2.   DESCRIPTION
3.   SUGGESTED USE

TYPE IN NUMBERS ONLY
? 1,2,3
SIZE -        RECORDS
DESCRIPTION - AFRICA CONTAINS CITATIONS TO
JOURNAL ARTICLES, BOOKS, MONOGRAPHS, ETC.  THE MAJORITY
OF THE FILE ARE CITATIONS ONLY.  SOME HOWEVER, CONTAIN
ABSTRACTS, LIBRARY CALL NUMBERS, KEYWORDS, TABLES AND
FIGURES, ETC.
NO EFFORT HAS BEEN MADE TO STANDARDIZE THE KEYWORDS AND
THE DESCRIPTIVE TERMS USED.
SUGGESTED USES - THIS COLLECTION CAN BE SELECTIVELY
SEARCHED FOR REFERENCES TO AFRICAN-RELATED LITERATURE
USING A COMBINATION OF SEARCH WORDS OR PHRASES.
IT CAN BE PROFITABLY USED FOR TERM PAPERS, BEGINNING
RESEARCH PROJECTS AND THE LIKE.

WOULD YOU RATHER
1.   HAVE MORE INFORMATION ABOUT THIS FILE
2.   BROWSE ANOTHER FILE
3.   LEAVE THE BROWSING MODE
? 1
YOU CAN OBTAIN THE FOLLOWING INFORMATION ABOUT THE FILE:

1.   GENERAL DESCRIPTION
2.   RIQS FILE DESCRIPTION
3.   SAMPLE RECORD

TYPE IN ONE OF THE NUMBERS
TYPE -NONE- IF YOU DO NOT WANT ANY
? 2
 ITEM NUMBERS AND NAMES
 ---------------------

     1.   REFCODE...REFERENCE CODE
     2.   AUTHOR ...AUTHOR
     3.   TITLE  ...TITLE
     4.   JOURNAL...JOURNAL, VOLUME, ISSUE, DATE, AND PAGE
     5.   ABS    ...ABSTRACT
     6.   CLASNO ...EXTRACT OR CLASSIFICATION NUMBER
     7.   CALLNO ...EXTRACT OR LIBRARY CALL NUMBER
     8.   INFO   ...OTHER INFORMATION
     9.   TABLES ...TABLES AND FIGURES
    10.   KEYWDS ...KEYWORDS OR DESCRIPTORS


WOULD YOU RATHER
1.   HAVE MORE INFORMATION ABOUT THIS FILE
2.   BROWSE ANOTHER FILE
3.   LEAVE THE BROWSING MODE
? 1
YOU CAN OBTAIN THE FOLLOWING INFORMATION ABOUT THE FILE:

1.   GENERAL DESCRIPTION
2.   RIQS FILE DESCRIPTION
3.   SAMPLE RECORD

TYPE IN ONE OF THE NUMBERS
TYPE -NONE- IF YOU DO NOT WANT ANY
? 3


RECORD NUMBER      1
     (1) REFERENCE CODE
     00743
     (2) AUTHOR
     BOHANNAN PAUL
     (3) TITLE
     AFRICA AND THE AFRICANS.
     (4) JOURNAL, VOLUME, ISSUE, DATE, AND PAGE
     NEW YORK NATURAL HISTORY PRESS 1964
     (5) ABSTRACT
     1,
     (7) EXTRACT OR LIBRARY CALL NUMBER
     AF 960. B676A
```

Figure 8.3.   General information about the AFRICA bibliographic file.

```
WOULD YOU RATHER
1.   HAVE MORE INFORMATION ABOUT THIS FILE
2.   BROWSE ANOTHER FILE
3.   LEAVE THE BROWSING MODE
? 3
WOULD YOU LIKE TO
1.   SEARCH A RIQS FILE
2.   USE THE TUTORIAL MODE
3.   STOP THE RIQSTUTOR
? 1

WILL YOU SEARCH ANY OF THE "BROWSING" FILES
? YES
1)   YOU WILL NOT BE ABLE TO CREATE ANY SETS
     (USING THE -PUT- OR -PLACE- COMMANDS)
     WITH ANY OF THE "BROWSING" FILES.

2)   FOR EACH OF THE AVAILABLE "BROWSING" FILES,
     THERE MAY BE A FEW PRE-STORED SAMPLE SEARCHES
     AVAILABLE.

WOULD YOU LIKE TO SEE HOW TO ACCESS THEM.
? NO

TYPE IN THE -PERMANENT FILE NAME- OF THE DATA BASE YOU WANT ATTACHED.
IF YOU DO NOT HAVE ACCESS TO A RIQS DATA BASE, TYPE  ANY
AND I'LL ATTACH A SAMPLE DATA BASE FOR YOU.
? AFRICA
TYPE IN NUMBER OF PASSWORDS OR -NONE-.
? NONE



RIQS ... NORTHWESTERN UNIVERSITY
     (VERSION 1.2 - 03/18/74)

FILE HAS THE NAME AFRICA
AND CONTAINS12305 RECORDS

DO YOU WISH TO SEE THE BULLETIN
? NO

MAY  RIQS  MONITOR YOUR SEARCH TEXT
FOR SUBSEQUENT STATISTICAL ANALYSIS

? YES

PLEASE ENTER YOUR NAME AND DEPARTMENT

?H,VCC


DO YOU WANT A DESCRIPTION OF YOUR FILE
? NO



ENTER SEARCH COMMAND OR TYPE HALT

? IF RECORD CONTAINS ('ECONOMIC' AND 'DEVELOPMENT')
? DISPLAY RECORD END

SEARCHING INITIATED


NO. OF REPORTS ON DISPLAY FILE =    178

DO YOU WANT THE DISPLAY REPORTS LISTED
? NO
```

* * * * *

Figure 8.4. Accessing and searching a file through the RIQSTUTOR.

His suspicions are well confirmed. The correlation for the nonformer English colonies (.714) is substantially higher than those of both the former English colonies (.474) and all countries combined (.629). Satisfied that the plots express the desired relationships, the student directs the system to produce a Calcomp copy of each and finishes his interactive session (Figure 8.11).

Some might say that our user is far from typical. Within the space of a month he has moved from casually browsing through the files to performing a relatively complex statistical analysis. Yet he is not as atypical as one might think. He may have logged on to the browser with a fairly well defined interest in economic development and followed much the same kind of path. Or he may have been an experienced quantitative researcher, familiar with the data set, and logged on just to continue his analysis. The combined use of graphics, statistics, and search ability offers a powerful aid to regression techniques which have long been plagued by the unknown effects or hidden identity of extreme cases. Perhaps he was merely interested in some descriptive information about Nigeria: its date of independence and former colonial ruler. Indeed, one can see that the system is able to easily accommodate a wide variety of users with different goals and ranges of ability.

Summary

The information transfer network of the future was described by Overhage in 1965 as an "on-line intellectual community." He said:

> The list of services. . .begins with access to stored information. Whenever a user needs to employ a factor or refer to a document that is "in the network," he has only to specify the fact or the document uniquely. . .*retrieval of stored information is the basic service upon which all the facilities of the on-line system must depend.*[14] The second fundamental service is processing of retrieved information with the aid of computer programs. It is essential. . .that there exist, within the on-line system, an extensive library of computer programs that can be called upon by any user (through commands given in a convenient language) to meet his immediate purposes, and directed upon any body or bodies of information he cares to name.
>
> A third fundamental service deals with display of information to the user. This service, also, is controlled by a language, designed to be natural enough for the user and formal enough for the computer, that deals with entities to be displayed, with the selection of display devices, and with the specification of formats. Through this language (which) can be embedded in other languages he can have alphanumeric text presented to him as soft (ephemeral) copy on a special alphanumeric display or typed out for him on a printer, and he can call for graphs, diagrams, sketches, and the like, mixed with alphanumeric text, on various display screens, and have the information captured photographically or xerographically for later reference.
>
> The fourth and final basic service is control. The user controls the system or addresses requests to it, through a few familiar devices: a keyboard, a penlike stylus, a microphone, and a small assortment of buttons and switches. Through those devices, he can communicate in strings of alphanumeric characters, by pointing, by writing clearly, by sketching or drawing, and by speaking distinctly in a limited vocabulary. . .[15]

This paper has described one attempt at providing a solution to the information transfer problem at one university. Looking at the criteria established for such a network by

```
? IF RECØRD CØNTAINS ((ꞌECØNØMICꞌ AND ꞌDEVELØPMENTꞌ) AND
? (ꞌPØST CØLØNIALꞌ ØR ꞌFRR←EEDØMꞌ ØR ꞌINDEPENDENTꞌ))
? DISPLAY RECØRD END

SEARCHING INITIATED


NØ. ØF REPØRTS ØN DISPLAY FILE =    14

DØ YØU WANT THE DISPLAY REPØRTS LISTED
? YES


RECØRD NUMBER  163%
    (1) REFERENCE CØDE
    #1434
    (2) AUTHØR
    SHILS EDWARD
    (3) TITLE
    INTELLECTUALS, PUBLIC ØPINIØN, AND ECØNØMIC DEVELØPMENT.
    (4) JØURNAL, VØLUME, ISSUE, DATE, AND PAGE
    IN WILLIAM J HANNA [ ED ], INDEPENDENT BLACK AFRICA, CHICAGØ,
    RAND MCNALLY, 1964, PP 472 - 494
    (5) ABSTRACT
    6D16,
    (7) EXTRACT ØR LIBRARY CALL NUMBER
    AF 960. H243I


RECØRD NUMBER  375%
    (1) REFERENCE CØDE
    AJES - 24 - 0397
    (2) AUTHØR
    DØUGLAS, DØRØTHY W.  HØFSTRA UNIVERSITY, HEMPSTEAD, NEW YØRK
    (3) TITLE
    STRUCTURE AND ADVICE - - THE CASE ØF KENYA
    (4) JØURNAL, VØLUME, ISSUE, DATE, AND PAGE
    AMERICAN JØURNAL ØF ECØNØMICS AND SØCIØLØGY 24 [ ØCTØBER, 1965 ],
    397 - 411
    (6) EXTRACT ØR CLASSIFICATIØN NUMBER
    THE RECENT INDEPENDENCE MØVEMENT IN AFRICA HAS CAUGHT ECØNØMIC
    DEVELØPMENT THEØRY LARGELY UNPREPARED.  CURRENT STUDIES STILL
    TEND TØ FØCUS ØN THE PRØBLEMS ØF THE EURØPEAN CØLØNISTS ꞌ EXPØRT
    ECØNØMY WITH ITS EXISTING STATISTICAL APPARATUS, LEAVING NATIVE
    LIFE AND LABØR LARGELY TØ THE SPECIAL STUDIES ØF THE
    ANTHRØPØLØGIST, FØCUSED ØN TRIBALISM.  THE NATURE ØF THE DUAL
    ECØNØMIC STRUCTURE IN WHICH THE AFRICAN PØPULATIØN ACTUALLY FINDS
    ITSELF AND THE CHARACTER - ISTICS ØF THE AFRICAN ꞌ S STRIVING FØR
    BETTER ØPPØRTUNITY REMAIN LARGELY VIRGIN TERRITØRY.
    (7) EXTRACT ØR LIBRARY CALL NUMBER
    ØNLY A REVIEW ØF EVENTS SUBSEQUENT TØ INDEPENDENCE CAN THRØW
    LIGHT UPØN ITS ECØNØMIC PØSSIBILITIES.  QUESTIØNS FØR THE PERIØD
    WILL HAVE TØ INCLUDE - - WHAT CHANGES WITHIN THE TRIBAL AREAS ARE
    BEGINNING TØ TAKE SHAPE, AND HØW SERIØUSLY ARE THEY PLANNED FØR.
    WHAT IS HAPPENING TØ THE TØWN LABØR FØRCE.  WHAT CHANGES ARE
    BEING MADE IN NATIØNAL AND LØCAL BUDGET ALLØCATIØNS.  IN TAXES.
    IN GENERAL, WHAT SØRT ØF IMPLICATIØNS FØR FUTURE DEVELØPMENT
    THEØRY CAN WE SEE IN THE DEGREE TØ WHICH THE CAUTIØUS APPRØACHES
    TØ THE TWØ PRESENT STUDIES ARE ØR ARE NØT FØLLØWED, AND IN THE
    DEGREE ØF SUCCESS ØR FAILURE ØF PØLICIES ACTUALLY ADØPTED.  JUST
    AS, IN A REALISTIC SUMMATIØN ØF THE ECØNØMIC CØST ØF THE PREVIØUS
    ECØNØMY, THE CØSTS AND LAVISH BRITISH SUBVENTIØNS FØR MEETING THE
    MAU MAU EMERGENCY CAN HARDLY BE ØMITTED, SØ IN THE FUTURE STAGE
    ØF A NEWLY INDEPENDENT ECØNØMY FURTHER HERITAGE CØSTS INSIDE AND
    ØUTSIDE THE CØUNTRY WILL SURELY HAVE TØ BE MET, IN ØNE WAY ØR
    ANØTHER.                         •
                                     •
                                     •
```

```
RECØRD NUMBER 12300
    (1) REFERENCE CØDE
    99901
    (2) AUTHØR
    MØRRISØN, MITCHELL, PADEN AND STEVENSØN
    (3) TITLE
    GNPP68 -    GNP PER/CAPITA, 1968
    (4) JØURNAL, VØLUME, ISSUE, DATE, AND PAGE
    BLACK AFRICA CØMPARATIVE DATA FILE
    (5) ABSTRACT
    THIS FILE CØNTAINS DATA FØR THE 32 INDEPENDENT, SUB-SAHARAN,
    BLACK AFRICAN NATIØNS ØN A VARIETY ØF PØLITICAL, ECØNØMIC,
    SØCIAL, AND DEVELØPMENT INDICATØRS.  THIS DATA WAS CØLLECTED BY
    THE AFRICAN NATIØNAL INTEGRATIØN PRØJECT -ANIP- AT NØRTHWESTERN.
    THE USER IS STRØNGLY REFERRED TØ THE VØLUME - BLACK AFRICA, A
    CØMPARATIVE HANDBØØK / THE FREE PRESS, 1972 - IN WHICH THE DATA,
    RELIABILITY MEASURES, SØURCES, CØDING SCHEMES, ETC.  ARE
    EXTENSIVELY DISCUSSED.  DETAILED INFØRMATIØN ABØUT THE ANIP FILE
    IS AVAILABLE AT RM 109, VØGELBACK CØMPUTING CENTER.


RECØRD NUMBER 12301
    (1) REFERENCE CØDE
    99902
    (2) AUTHØR
    MØRRISØN, MITCHELL, PADEN AND STEVENSØN
    (3) TITLE
    ARSSKM - AREA IN 1,000 SQUARE KILØMETERS, 1969
    (4) JØURNAL, VØLUME, ISSUE, DATE, AND PAGE
    BLACK AFRICA CØMPARATIVE DATA FILE
    (5) ABSTRACT
    THIS FILE CØNTAINS DATA FØR THE 32 INDEPENDENT, SUB-SAHARAN,
    BLACK AFRICAN NATIØNS ØN A VARIETY ØF PØLITICAL, ECØNØMIC,
    SØCIAL, AND DEVELØPMENT INDICATØRS.  THIS DATA WAS CØLLECTED BY
    THE AFRICAN NATIØNAL INTEGRATIØN PRØJECT -ANIP- AT NØRTHWESTERN.
    THE USER IS STRØNGLY REFERRED TØ THE VØLUME - BLACK AFRICA, A
    CØMPARATIVE HANDBØØK / THE FREE PRESS, 1972 - IN WHICH THE DATA,
    RELIABILITY MEASURES, SØURCES, CØDING SCHEMES, ETC.  ARE
    EXTENSIVELY DISCUSSED.  DETAILED INFØRMATIØN ABØUT THE ANIP FILE
    IS AVAILABLE AT RM 109, VØGELBACK CØMPUTING CENTER.


RECØRD NUMBER 12302
    (1) REFERENCE CØDE
    99903
    (2) AUTHØR
    MØRRISØN, MITCHELL, PADEN AND STEVENSØN
    (3) TITLE
    NAGPØT - NØN-AGRICULTURAL DEVELØPMENT PØTENTIAL INDEX
    (4) JØURNAL, VØLUME, ISSUE, DATE, AND PAGE
    BLACK AFRICA CØMPARATIVE DATA FILE
    (5) ABSTRACT
    THIS FILE CØNTAINS DATA FØR THE 32 INDEPENDENT, SUB-SAHARAN,
    BLACK AFRICAN NATIØNS ØN A VARIETY ØF PØLITICAL, ECØNØMIC,
                              .
                              .
                              .
```

Figure 8.5. Partial printout from a search for references to economic development during the postindependence period.

```
ENTER ANØTHER FILE NAME ØR -NØNE-
? AFRØ

YØU CAN ØBTAIN THE FØLLØWING INFØRMATIØN ABØUT THE FILF:

1.  GENERAL DESCRIPTIØN
2.  RIQS FILE DESCRIPTIØN
3.  SAMPLE RECØRD

TYPE IN ØNE ØF THE NUMBERS
TYPE -NØNE- IF YØU DØ NØT WANT ANY
? 1

YØU CAN HAVE ANY ØR ALL ØF THE FØLLØWING:

1.  FILE SIZE
2.  DESCRIPTIØN
3.  SUGGESTED USE

TYPE IN NUMBERS ØNLY
? 1,2,3
SIZE - 32 RECØRDS
DESCRIPTIØN - THIS FILE CØNTAINS CØMPARATIVE DATA FØR
THE 32 INDEPENDENT, SUB-SAHARAN BLACK AFRICAN NATIØNS
ØN A VARIETY ØF PØLITICAL, ECØNØMIC, AND SØCIAL
INDICATØRS.  THE DATA WAS CØLLECTED BY THE AFRICAN
NATIØNAL INTEGRATIØN PRØJECT AT NU AND IS DESCRIBED IN
BLACK AFRICA - A CØMPARATIVE HANDBØØK (MØRRISØN,
MITCHELL, PADEN AND STEVENSØN).
SUGGESTED USES - DATA IN THIS FILE CAN BE INTEGRATED
WITH ØTHER AFRICAN DATA, USED WITH BIBLIØGRAPHIC
RESØURCES, AND GENERALLY MANIPULATED IN A VARIETY ØF
WAYS.  IT IS ESPECIALLY WELL-SUITED TØ GRAPHICAL
ANALYSIS.

WØULD YØU RATHER
1.  HAVE MØRE INFØRMATIØN ABØUT THIS FILE
2.  BRØWSE ANØTHER FILE
3.  LEAVE THE BRØWSING MØDE
? 1
YØU CAN ØBTAIN THE FØLLØWING INFØRMATIØN ABØUT THE FILE:

1.  GENERAL DESCRIPTIØN
2.  RIQS FILE DESCRIPTIØN
3.  SAMPLE RECØRD

TYPE IN ØNE ØF THE NUMBERS
TYPE -NØNE- IF YØU DØ NØT WANT ANY
? 2


ITEM NUMBERS AND NAMES
----------------------


    1.   CNTRY  ...NAME ØF CØUNTRY
    2.   CNTRYNØ...CØUNTRY ID NUMBER
    3.   DATEINP...DATE ØF INDEPENDENCE
    4.   CØLRULE...FØRMER CØLØNIAL RULER
    5.   FNAME  ...FØRMER NAME ØF CØUNTRY
    6.   ESTPØP ...ESTIMATED PØPULATIØN, 1970
    7.   SIZE   ...AREA SIZE, EQUIVALENT IN US
    8.   LASTCEN...DATE ØF LAST CENSUS
    9.   EXPØRTS...MAJØR EXPØRTS 1968 AS PERCENT ØF TØTAL EXPØRTS
   10.   GNPP68 ...GNP PER/CAPITA, 1968
   11.   ARSSKM ...AREA IN 1,000 SQUARE KILØMETERS, 1969
   12.   NAGPØT ...NØN-AGRICULTURAL DEVELØPMENT PØTENTIAL INDEX
   13.   WPØP60 ...PCT. WHITE PØPULATIØN IN 1960 X 100
   14.   PCEN66 ...PER/CAP. ENERGY CØNSUMPTIØN IN KILØS. ØF CØAL EQUIV.,
   15.   PIPG60 ...PUBLIC INVESTMENT AS PCT. ØF GNP, 1960
   16.   PCGD63 ...PER/CAPITA GNP IN US $, 1963
```

```
WØULD YØU RATHER
1.   HAVE MØRE INFØRMATIØN ABØUT THIS FILE
2.   BRØWSE ANØTHER FILE
3.   LEAVE THE BRØWSING MØDE
? 1
YØU CAN ØBTAIN THE FØLLØWING INFØRMATIØN ABØUT THE FILE:

1.   GENERAL DESCRIPTIØN
2.   RIQS FILE DESCRIPTIØN
3.   SAMPLE RECØRD

TYPE IN ØNE ØF THE NUMBERS
TYPE -NØNE- IF YØU DØ NØT WANT ANY
? 3


RECØRD NUMBER        1
     (1) NAME ØF CØUNTRY
     BØTSWANA
     (2) CØUNTRY ID NUMBER
     1.
     (3) DATE ØF INDEPENDEN .E
     SEPTEMBER 30, 1966
     (4) FØRMER CØLØNIAL RULER
     UNITED KINGDØM
     (5) FØRMER NAME ØF CØUNTRY
     BECHUANALAND
     (6) ESTIMATED PØPULATIØN, 1970
     650,000
     (7) AREA SIZE, EQUIVALENT IN US
     222,000 SQ.  MI.  -TWICE ARIZØNA-
     (8) DATE ØF LAST CENSUS
     1964 -CENSUS PLANNED FØR 1971-
     (9) MAJØR EXPØRTS 1968 AS PERCENT ØF TØTAL EXPØRTS
     CATTLE AND PRØDUCTS-90 PERCENT
     (10) GNP PER/CAPITA, 1968
     100.000
     (11) AREA IN 1,000 SQUARE KILØMETERS, 1969
     600.000
     (12) NØN-AGRICULTURAL DEVELØPMENT PØTENTIAL INDEX
     5.000
     (13) PCT. WHITE PØPULATIØN IN 1960 X 100
     .800
     (14) PER/CAP. ENERGY CØNSUMPTIØN IN KILØS. ØF CØAL EQUIV., 1966
     -0
     (15) PUBLIC INVESTMENT AS PCT. ØF GNP, 1960
     0
     (16) PER/CAPITA GNP IN US $, 1963
     51.000
```

Figure 8.6. Information about the AFRO file (Black Africa comparative
data file) is displayed, including a sample record.

```
SPSSØNLINE - NØRTHWESTERN UNIVERSITY (V3.0)

- - - PEARSØN CØRRELATIØN - - -


VARIABLE    CASES            MEAN           STD. DEV.

I010S000      32          120.6250            66.4752
I011S000      32          597.4688           631.3843
I012S000      32            8.5938             4.0549
I013S000      32             .4384              .5688
I014S000      32           82.0313            97.3111
I015S000      32            6.4437             4.8467

VARIABLE PAIR           CØEFF.      N   SIG.    VARIANCE-CØVAR

I010S000 I010S000       1.0000     32   .000        4418.9516
I010S000 I011S000       -.1788     32   .164       -7505.7863
I010S000 I012S000        .6293     32   .000         169.6169
I010S000 I013S000        .5943     32   .000          22.4687
I010S000 I014S000        .7846     32   .000        5075.1411
I010S000 I015S000        .4430     32   .006         142.7137
I011S000 I010S000       -.1788     32   .164       -7505.7863
I011S000 I011S000       1.0000     32   .000      398646.1280
I011S000 I012S000        .0802     32   .331         205.3256
I011S000 I013S000       -.0361     32   .422         -12.9599
I011S000 I014S000       -.0662     32   .359       -4069.7248
I011S000 I015S000        .0010     32   .498           2.9337
I012S000 I010S000        .6293     32   .000         169.6169
I012S000 I011S000        .0802     32   .331         205.3256
I012S000 I012S000       1.0000     32   .000          16.4425
I012S000 I013S000        .3750     32   .017            .8648
I012S000 I014S000        .6767     32   .000         267.0131
I012S000 I015S000        .3368     32   .030           6.6183
I013S000 I010S000        .5943     32   .000          22.4687
I013S000 I011S000       -.0361     32   .422         -12.9599
I013S000 I012S000        .3750     32   .017            .8648
I013S000 I013S000       1.0000     32   .000            .3235
I013S000 I014S000        .7061     32   .000          39.0794
I013S000 I015S000        .0905     32   .311            .2495
I014S000 I010S000        .7846     32   .000        5075.1411
I014S000 I011S000       -.0662     32   .359       -4069.7248
I014S000 I012S000        .6767     32   .000         267.0131
I014S000 I013S000        .7061     32   .000          39.0794
I014S000 I014S000       1.0000     32   .000        9469.4506
I014S000 I015S000        .3545     32   .023         167.2147
I015S000 I010S000        .4430     32   .006         142.7137
I015S000 I011S000        .0010     32   .498           2.9337
I015S000 I012S000        .3368     32   .030           6.6183
I015S000 I013S000        .0905     32   .311            .2495
I015S000 I014S000        .3545     32   .023         167.2147
I015S000 I015S000       1.0000     32   .000          23.4903
```

Figure 8.7. Pearson correlations (produced by SPSSONLINE) for selected variables on the AFRO file.

Overhage, we find many points that are now being satisfied by the integration of the RIQS/SPSS on-line system with public use data files. We believe that by providing linked access to existing bibliographic and quantitative data files through an information processing system capable of handling varied kinds of data, we have at least the beginning of an information transfer system. By providing one language that can be used with any of the public files on the RIQS system, we have greatly eased the learning situation and

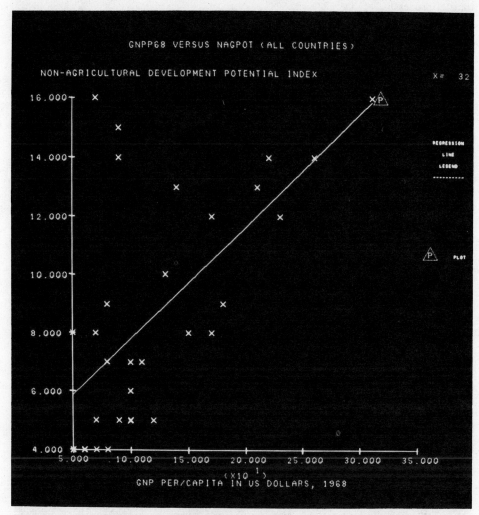

Figure 8.8. CRT displayed scatterplot (with regression line) of GNPP68 versus NAGPOT.

its often concomitant feelings of helplessness. We have provided basic retrieval functions together with routines for sophisticated statistical analysis. We have provided for numerous output forms such as hard copy indexes produced on high speed printers, graphical displays via either keyboard or CRT type terminals, light pen interaction, and Calcomp plots, along with the traditional typewriter-type printed output. However, this is but one step; many more must follow before we can attain any kind of *ideal* information transfer process.

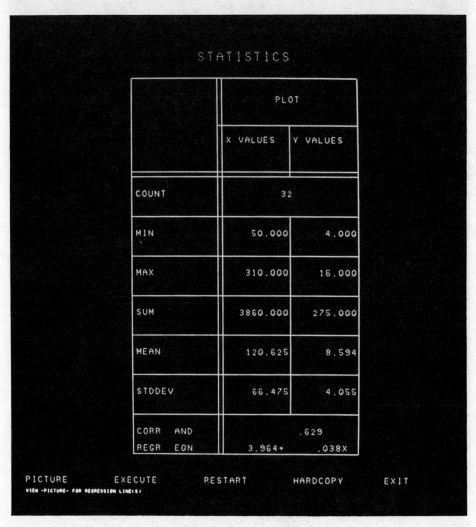

Figure 8.9. CRT displayed statistics for the plot
of GNPP68 versus NAGPOT.

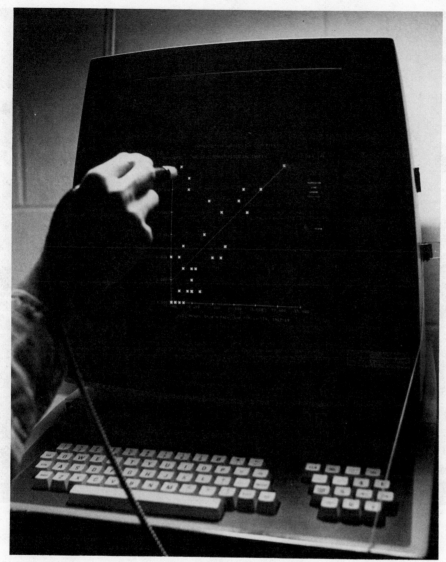

Figure 8.10a. Light pen initiated retrieval of "extreme case" identifying information.

```
RECORD NUMBER    22
    (1) NAME OF COUNTRY
    NIGERIA
    (2) COUNTRY ID NUMBER
    22.
    (3) DATE OF INDEPENDENVE
    OCTOBER 1, 1960
    (4) FORMER COLONIAL RULER
    UNITED KINGDOM
    (6) ESTIMATED POPULATION, 1970
    55,070,000
    (7) AREA SIZE, EQUIVALENT IN US
    357,000 SQ.  MI.  -TEXAS AND COLORADO-
    (8) DATE OF LAST CENSUS
    1963
    (9) MAJOR EXPORTS 1968 AS PERCENT OF TOTAL EXPORTS
    COCOA-24 PERCENT, PEANUTS AND PEANUT OIL-22 PERCENT, CRUDE
    PETROLEUM-12 PERCENT, PALM KERNELS AND OIL - 5 PERCENT
    (10) AVG. ANNUAL GROWTH RATE, GNP PER/CAPITA, 1961-68
    70.000
    (11) AREA IN 1,000 SQUARE KILOMETERS, 1969
    924.000
    (12) NON-AGRICULTURAL DEVELOPMENT POTENTIAL INDEX
    16.000
    (13) PCT. WHITE POPULATION IN 1960 X 100
    .070


WAITING
```

Figure 8.10b.   Display of retrieved record.

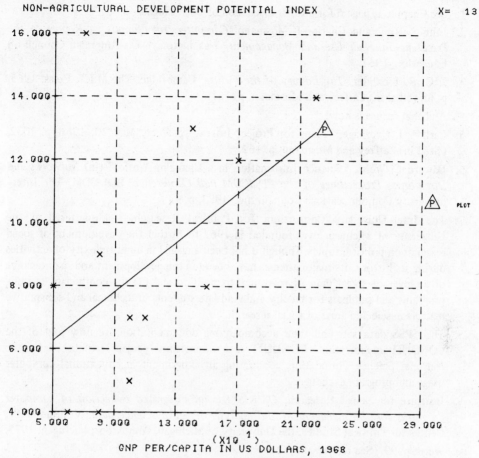

Figure 8.11. Plot of GNPP68 versus NAGPOT produced by CRT terminal is printed offline by Calcomp plotter.

NOTES AND CITED REFERENCES

1. See Chapter 1, page 6 for a fuller discussion of Bush's ideas.

2. John Caffrey and Charles J. Mosmann, *Computers on Campus, A Report to the President on Their Use and Management,* Washington, D.C.: American Council on Education, 1967.

3. J. C. R. Licklider, *The Library of the Future,* Cambridge: The M.I.T. Press, 1965, p. 6f, (cited in) Caffrey and Mosmann, p. 161.

4. And that future is now!

5. Carl F. J. Overhage, "Plans for Project Intrex," *Science,* May 20, 1966, p. 1032, (cited in) Caffrey and Mosmann, p. 162.

6. Edward C. Weiss, "Science Information in a Changing World," (in) *Networks and Disciplines: Proceedings of the EDUCOM Fall Conference,* EDUCOM, The Inter-university Communications Council, Inc., 1973, p. 93.

7. The Inter-University Consortium for Political Research, headquartered at the University of Michigan, was founded in 1962 to further the development of social research on political topics. Though it has been engaged in a multiplexity of activities during its history, its major themes have been (1) the development and maintenance of archives of social data of relevance to politics, and (2) the conduct of training programs and seminars for faculty and graduate students in technical and substantive matters in selected areas of social research.

8. The SPSS data sets and their accompanying documentation are now part of the CONDUIT organization. CONDUIT is a consortium project established by the National Science Foundation conducting an experiment in educational computer usage and program exchange.

9. Institute for Social Research, *OSIRIS III: an integrated collection of computer programs for the management and analysis of social science data,* Volumes I-IV, Center for Political Studies, the University of Michigan, Ann Arbor, Michigan, 1973.

10. Weiss, p. 99. (See reference 6, above.)

11. "Project MARC was originally conceived as an experiment in centrally producing cataloging data in machine-readable form and distributing these data to libraries in the field. The enthusiastic support from the library community led to the major decision by the Library of Congress to continue the service for all interested libraries on a subscription basis." J. Quincy Mumford, "Foreword," MARC, *Manuals Used by the Library of Congress,* Chicago: American Library Association, 1969.

12. This data was gathered under the auspices of the African National Integration Project at Northwestern University, and are reported in D. Morrison, R. Mitchell, J. Paden, and H. Stevenson, *Black Africa—A Comparative Handbook,* The Free Press, 1972.

13. See Chapter 12, W. Dominick, "System Performance Evaluation of Information Retrieval."

14. Italics ours.

15. C. F. J. Overhage and R. Joyce Harman (eds.), *Intrex, Report of a Planning Conference on Information Transfer Experiments,* Cambridge, Mass.: MIT Press, 1965.

Section Two:

ADMINISTRATIVE AND MANAGEMENT SCIENCES

The fields of planning, organizational behavior, information systems, and decision sciences are examples of disciplines contained within the general category of administrative and management sciences. Data management techniques are essential tools to these fields. But, textual and bibliographic applications are also of importance. This section presents articles by people who have utilized RIQS to attack some complex management problems.

Mintzer and Dominick, in Chapter 9, describe a university data management system for creating, maintaining, and searching a data base of graduate student information. They point up some of the successes as well as the difficulties encountered by an administrator who had no previous experience with computers.

In Chapter 10, Kegan and colleagues discuss the difficulties encountered in handling several information subsystems (a library of published and unpublished works, a collection of research instruments, raw field data, and internal reports) for an ongoing and active research program in the management of research and development. An integrated information system was developed using RIQS to facilitate the storing and updating of information, to spot and correct errors, and to permit researchers on-line access to any of the information contained within the system.

Cartwright and Hay, in Chapter 11, describe the use of a computerized information retrieval system by a student group to analyze the form and consequences of the geographic distribution of students in a university town. These data were made public and have been used in voter registration programs, in mobility research and in discussions of university tax liability. But perhaps most important, the data have been used by the students themselves in the analyses, planning, and direction of their own community.

Wayne Dominick, in Chapter 12, discusses the use of RIQS as an analysis tool in the evaluation of an interactive information system—RIQSONLINE. This was achieved by

167

instrumenting the RIQSONLINE processor with monitoring routines designed to collect data on user/system interactions and to produce a RIQS data base of all monitored information. As a result of the analyses performed, improvements have been made to RIQSONLINE, and several areas for future work have been defined.

Chapter 9

Administrative Data Management in a University Environment

DAVID MINTZER and WAYNE DOMINICK
Northwestern University

Introduction

The purpose of this chapter is to describe a university administrative data management system for creating, maintaining and searching a data base of graduate student information. A secondary purpose of the chapter is to point up some of the successes and some of the problems involved in the use of this system by an administrator who had no previous experience with computers.

For some years prior to the appointment of Dr. Mintzer as Associate Dean of Engineering for Research and Graduate Study, certain records of graduate students were kept on file cards; the types of information will be described below. The information for each student, of which there were between 500 and 600 each year, was written on a file card by a secretary; each year's cards were filed according to the student's degree program (of which there were 10), and alphabetically within the program. Only the current year's cards were kept active, although previous years' cards could be obtained without difficulty.

In order to obtain information about an individual, a separate set of cards was kept, alphabetized without regard to the degree program. The only information on that card was the student's name and his degree program. In addition, since working with file cards is so tedious, the secretary would transfer selected information about each student into a loose-leaf notebook, giving information on about 25 students per page. Part of this information was given in arcane symbols, so that it would fit on one line per student.

The system was, in short, the product of about a decade of development by a devoted secretary. However, it was not well suited to modern needs of data manipulation. For example, one of the pieces of information on each card was the name of the faculty advisor

169

to the student. To determine the number of students advised by any individual faculty member meant *scanning* all of the lists (or reading all of the cards) to see where that advisor's name appeared.

The increasing governmental demands for reporting on a variety of matters, the decreasing amount of research and student support necessitating greater centralized control of student funding, and the increasing complexity of all operations made the idea of automated data handling especially attractive. The availability of the RIQS system, with its ability to perform a large variety of operations on a large body of data, made it a natural system to use. Moreover, the Associate Dean felt that there was an increasing requirement of his office for certain types of data to be immediately obtainable; the availability of the interactive mode of operation, RIQSONLINE, gave further attractiveness to the system.

With the decision to develop a RIQS based data system, conferences were held between an assistant to the Associate Dean, who had worked with the data and was somewhat familiar with RIQS, the Dean's secretary, and Mr. Dominick. The basic format was decided upon, and one year's data (September 1, 1971 to August 31, 1972) entered; this data was also kept in the original format (on cards) until experience could be gained with the use of the RIQS system.

After several months' use, a revision was made of the format, and new data was entered commencing with the start of the new academic year, September 1, 1972. This data was updated completely using the RIQS batch process at the beginning of each new academic quarter (about January 1, 1973; April 1; June 15), since students, class registration, funding, etc. change at that time. Several intermediate updates were made during the quarters as a number of changes in status took place; no effort was made to keep the information completely up-to-date, but changes were allowed to accumulate until there was a sufficient number of them before entering them in the data base.

The current data base contains student information for the current academic year. At the end of the academic year, the data base is saved on tape as historical data and a new data base is initiated for the new academic year. The maintenance of historical data corresponding to academic years facilitates both comparisons between the current year and previous years as well as projection analysis.

The Data

The TECH data base consists of one record for each graduate student in the Technological Institute of Northwestern University. Each record contains personal information about the student and his affiliation with the university as well as student funding data and course load information. The data base record format and schema layout are shown in Figures 9.1 and 9.2, respectively, and a sample record is shown in Figure 9.3.

Data items 1 through 14 are normally single-valued, although several of them are provided with a multiple-value capability in order to store data historically. For example, item 4, department, could have more than one value indicating that the student has changed departments. Thus, previous departmental affiliation as well as the student's current department can be stored. Where appropriate within these first 14 data items, the current data is always represented by the last subitem of data.

Data items 15 through 42 represent the funding information for a student, broken down into three distinct areas—Salary, Stipend and Tuition funding (the difference between Salary and Stipend occurs because of differing regulations depending upon the source of funds). For each student funding, the funding source number and its constituent parts—

ITEM NUMBERS AND NAMES

```
1.    NAME
2.    SSAN
3.    SCHOOL
4.    DEPARTMENT
5.    CENTER PROGRAM
6.    MONTH, YEAR OF ENTRY
7.    ADVISOR
8.    2ND ADVISOR
9.    DEGREE OBJECTIVE
10.   SEX
11.   RACE
12.   NATIONALITY
13.   DATE DEGREE RECEIVED
14.   RIQS RECORD NUMBER
15.   SALARY FUNDING SOURCE
16.   SALARY FUNDING SOURCE DEPARTMENT NUMBER
17.   SALARY FUNDING SOURCE ACCOUNT NUMBER
18.   SALARY FUNDING SOURCE SUB-ACCOUNT NUMBER
19.   SALARY FUNDING SOURCE BEGINNING DATE
20.   SALARY FUNDING SOURCE ENDING DATE
21.   SALARY FUNDING AMOUNT (MONTHLY)
22.   SALARY FUNDING AMOUNT (EXTRA)
23.   SALARY FUNDING AMOUNT (TOTAL)
24.   STIPEND FUNDING SOURCE
25.   STIPEND FUNDING SOURCE DEPARTMENT NUMBER
26.   STIPEND FUNDING SOURCE ACCOUNT NUMBER
27.   STIPEND FUNDING SOURCE SUB-ACCOUNT NUMBER
28.   STIPEND FUNDING SOURCE BEGINNING DATE
29.   STIPEND FUNDING SOURCE ENDING DATE
30.   STIPEND FUNDING AMOUNT (MONTHLY)
31.   STIPEND FUNDING AMOUNT (EXTRA)
32.   STIPEND FUNDING AMOUNT (TOTAL)
33.   SA NUMBER
34.   SA CANCELLATION NUMBER
35.   TUITION FUNDING SOURCE
36.   TUITION FUNDING SOURCE DEPARTMENT NUMBER
37.   TUITION FUNDING SOURCE ACCOUNT NUMBER
38.   TUITION FUNDING SOURCE SUB-ACCOUNT NUMBER
39.   TUITION FUNDING AMOUNT (FALL QUARTER)
40.   TUITION FUNDING AMOUNT (WINTER QUARTER)
41.   TUITION FUNDING AMOUNT (SPRING QUARTER)
42.   TUITION FUNDING AMOUNT (SUMMER QUARTER)
43.   SELF-SUPPORTED (SUB1=FALL,SUB2=WINTER,SUB3=SPRING,SUB4=SUMMER)
44.   BELL STUDENT (SUB1=FALL,SUB2=WINTER,SUB3=SPRING,SUB4=SUMMER)
45.   PART-TIME (SUB1=FALL,SUB2=WINTER,SUB3=SPRING,SUB4=SUMMER)
46.   NUMBER OF COURSES (SUB1=FALL,SUB2=WINTER,SUB3=SPRING,SUB4=SUMMER)
47.   RIR (SUB1=FALL,SUB2=WINTER,SUB3=SPRING,SUB4=SUMMER)
48.   E88 (SUB1=FALL,SUB2=WINTER,SUB3=SPRING,SUB4=SUMMER)
49.   E98 (SUB1=FALL,SUB2=WINTER,SUB3=SPRING,SUB4=SUMMER)
50.   ABSENT MORE THAN TWO QUARTERS
51.   SINGULARITY FLAG
52.   COMMENTS
53.   EXTRA/1
54.   EXTRA/2
55.   EXTRA/3
56.   EXTRA/4
57.   EXTRA/5
```

Figure 9.1. TECH record format.

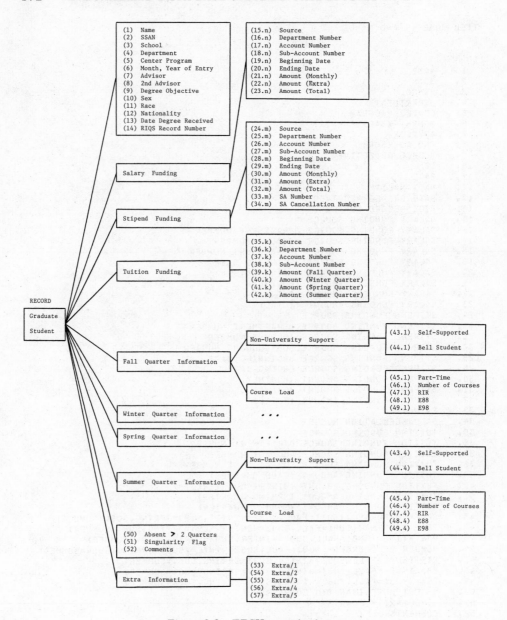

Figure 9.2. TECH record schema.

department number, account number and subaccount number—are stored. This results in a slight duplication of storage, but provides the flexibility of listing a funding number in its alphanumeric format as well as searching for numeric ranges on any of the constituent elements of the source number. These data are stored as items 15 through 18, 24 through 27, and 35 through 38. For each salary and stipend funding, there are stored beginning and ending dates and amounts monthly, extra, and total. In both cases, the total funding amount is calculated within RIQS from the duration of funding and the monthly and extra amounts. Tuition funding is provided on a quarterly basis, and thus is not stored via beginning date, ending date and monthly amount, but rather stored as a single amount for each applicable quarter, in items 39 through 42. Additionally, associated with each stipend funding is a stipend action (SA) number which is stored in item 33. For historical purposes, it is necessary to maintain a record of all stipend funding allocated to a student even if that funding is subsequently removed or superceded. Thus, stipend funding cancellation cannot be accomplished by deleting the data but only by inactivating it. For this purpose, item 34, SA cancellation number, is provided. Stipend funding cancellation is accomplished by entering the cancellation number in the appropriate subitem of item 34. With this approach, a particular stipend funding is active for a student as long as the corresponding cancellation number is null; if a cancellation number is present, then the stipend funding is inactive. This technique allows both active and inactive historical data to be stored in, and individually accessible from the data base.

Data items 43 through 49 represent nonuniversity support and course load data maintained on a quarterly basis. In each of these items, subitems 1, 2, 3 and 4 correspond respectively to the data for the Fall, Winter, Spring and Summer quarters. Thus, facility is provided for retrieving data for the entire year (via the full multiple item) or for specific quarter(s) during the year (via the appropriate subitems).

A data item is also provided to indicate that some extraordinary condition is present for a student—item 51, the singularity flag. Within the comments item, number 52, this condition can be clarified via a textual description. Finally, several extra data items are reserved at the end of each record for later use.

Search/Retrieval Methodology

Four major areas in which the RIQS system has been utilized are:

1. Data validation via management by exception reporting.
2. Generation of formatted administrative reports.
3. Calculation of summary statistics.
4. Selective data retrieval.

Data validation and report generation were accomplished via batch runs; calculation of summary statistics was performed on an as required basis either in batch if large quantities of output were expected or in an on-line mode for smaller quantities of output or if the results were needed immediately; selective data retrieval was exclusively an interactive process.

Each of these four major areas will be discussed separately.

```
RECORD NUMBER  176

1.  NAME
    [                    ]
2.  SSAN
    484563545
4.  DEPARTMENT
    SUB-1....  EE
6.  MONTH, YEAR OF ENTRY
    JAN, 1972
7.  ADVISOR
    SUB-1....  [          ]
9.  DEGREE OBJECTIVE
    SUB-1....  MS
10. SEX
    MALE
11. RACE
    WHITE
12. NATIONALITY
    USA
14. RIQS RECORD NUMBER
    176
24. STIPEND FUNDING SOURCE
    SUB-1....  6010 - 302 - 81
    SUB-2....  6010 - 302 - 81
    SUB-3....  6010 - 302 - 81
    SUB-4....  9253 - 274 - 72
    SUB-5....  9253 - 274 - 72
    SUB-6....  9253 - 274 - 72
    SUB-7....  6010 - 302 - 81
    SUB-8....  6010 - 303 - 81
25. STIPEND FUNDING SOURCE DEPARTMENT NUMBER
    SUB-1....  6010
    SUB-2....  6010
    SUB-3....  6010
    SUB-4....  9253
    SUB-5....  9253
    SUB-6....  9253
    SUB-7....  6010
    SUB-8....  6010
26. STIPEND FUNDING SOURCE ACCOUNT NUMBER
    SUB-1....  302
    SUB-2....  302
    SUB-3....  302
    SUB-4....  274
    SUB-5....  274
    SUB-6....  274
    SUB-7....  302
    SUB-8....  303
27. STIPEND FUNDING SOURCE SUB-ACCOUNT NUMBER
    SUB-1....  81
    SUB-2....  81
    SUB-3....  81
    SUB-4....  72
    SUB-5....  72
    SUB-6....  72
    SUB-7....  81
    SUB-8....  81
28. STIPEND FUNDING SOURCE BEGINNING DATE
    SUB-1....  SEPT 16,1972
    SUB-2....  SEPT 16,1972
    SUB-3....  OCT 15,1972
    SUB-4....  SEPT 16,1972
    SUB-5....  NOV 16,1972
    SUB-6....  JAN 16,1973
    SUB-7....  JUNE 16,1973
    SUB-8....  JULY 1,1973
```

```
29.  STIPEND FUNDING SOURCE ENDING DATE
          SUB-1.... JUNE 15,1973
          SUB-2.... OCT 15,1972
          SUB-3.... JUNE 15,1973
          SUB-4.... NOV 15,1972
          SUB-5.... JAN 15,1973
          SUB-6.... SEPT 15,1973
          SUB-7.... JUNE 30,1973
          SUB-8.... SEPT 15,1973
30.  STIPEND FUNDING AMOUNT (MONTHLY)
          SUB-1.... 259
          SUB-2.... 217
          SUB-3.... 217
          SUB-4.... 33
          SUB-5.... 13
          SUB-6.... 23
          SUB-7.... 216
          SUB-8.... 217
32.  STIPEND FUNDING AMOUNT (TOTAL)
          SUB-1.... 2320.00
          SUB-2.... 207.00
          SUB-3.... 1740.00
          SUB-4.... 65.10
          SUB-5.... 25.60
          SUB-6.... 184.00
          SUB-7.... 99.4
          SUB-8.... 542
33.  SA NUMBER
          SUB-1.... 3138
          SUB-2.... 3138
          SUB-3.... 3153
          SUB-4.... 3069
          SUB-5.... 3072
          SUB-6.... 3072
          SUB-7.... 5330
          SUB-8.... 5333
34.  SA CANCELLATION NUMBER
          SUB-1.... 3138
          SUB-4.... 3069
35.  TUITION FUNDING SOURCE
          SUB-1.... 6010 - 302 - 84
36.  TUITION FUNDING SOURCE DEPARTMENT NUMBER
          SUB-1.... 6010
37.  TUITION FUNDING SOURCE ACCOUNT NUMBER
          SUB-1.... 302
38.  TUITION FUNDING SOURCE SUB-ACCOUNT NUMBER
          SUB-1.... 84
39.  TUITION FUNDING AMOUNT (FALL QUARTER)
          SUB-1.... 865
40.  TUITION FUNDING AMOUNT (WINTER QUARTER)
          SUB-1.... 865
41.  TUITION FUNDING AMOUNT (SPRING QUARTER)
          SUB-1.... 720
42.  TUITION FUNDING AMOUNT (SUMMER QUARTER)
          SUB-1.... 95
46.  NUMBER OF COURSES (SUB1=FALL,SUB2=WINTER,SUB3=SPRING,SUB4=SUI
          SUB-1.... 2
          SUB-2.... 4
          SUB-3.... 2
```

Figure 9.3. Sample TECH record.

DATA VALIDATION VIA MANAGEMENT BY EXCEPTION REPORTING

An integral part of any systems design should be the development of comprehensive data validation procedures to detect errors in data coding and/or keypunching, missing data and data with incorrect values. The RIQS system itself performs data validation on a character level during initial file creation and file update. For example, if a particular data item is declared to be of type INTEGER, then the data value for this item can contain only a string of digits 0 through 9, with an optional leading + or – and optional commas such as +1,000,000. If an attempt is made to enter into this item a value containing any character other than those indicated above, RIQS will flag and reject the item with an appropriate data validation diagnostic. While data validation on the character level does catch many coding and keypunching errors, it cannot detect logical errors—data that is of the correct format but whose value is incorrect, such as an entry of 500 for the number of courses taken in one quarter.

In order to detect logical errors in data entry, the RIQS system can be employed to execute user–defined data validation searches. The conceptual difference between normal data base searching and data validation searching is that, in the former, the user is normally trying to retrieve records which satisfy some criteria while, in the latter, the user desires to retrieve records which do *not* satisfy the criteria—where the criteria is that the data is valid or at least contains a reasonable value. Thus, while RIQS does not permit range validation for numeric items during file creation, it is a very simple matter to test, for example, if the number of courses taken by any student during any one quarter is less than or equal to 5 (assuming 5 is the maximum allowed), and if not, then print that student's record number with an appropriate error message. Missing data can be similarly diagnosed.

Data validation searching, as defined above, represents one form of management by exception reporting, i.e., reporting only the extreme or extraordinary conditions. This approach is taken for validating all of the items within the TECH file. After every major update, a comprehensive set of validation searches are processed against the updated file in order to report any exceptional conditions, which are then investigated and corrected, if necessary. While this approach is not foolproof—a data item that contains a reasonable value may actually be incorrect—it does provide a generalized approach toward data validation in an almost completely automated manner.

Figure 9.4 illustrates a sample validation search performed on the TECH file. The search tests for the existence and validity of stipend funding information, data items 24 through 34. The search text is annotated in the left hand column, indicating exactly what each group of search statements is testing. Figure 9.5 represents the resulting retrieval. Record number 169 was retrieved, indicating that it contains a missing or incorrect data item. As one can see from a brief glance at the reported data,

the funding ending date	occurs chronologically	the funding beginning date
(29.3) SEPT 15, 1972	before	(28.3) JUNE 16, 1973

This type of validation searching is performed on all the data items within the TECH file.

GENERATION OF FORMATTED ADMINISTRATIVE REPORTS

The printout of a sample TECH record was shown in Figure 9.3. There is little doubt that, for ease of use by administrative staff, considerable thought must be given to the format

```
BEFORE SEARCH
PRINT ≠......MISSING OR INCORRECT DATA.........≠ .,
PRINT ≠(24) = STIPEND FUNDING SOURCE≠ .,
PRINT ≠(25) = STIPEND FUNDING SOURCE DEPARTMENT NUMBER≠ .,
PRINT ≠(26) = STIPEND FUNDING SOURCE ACCOUNT NUMBER≠ .,
PRINT ≠(27) = STIPEND FUNDING SOURCE SUB-ACCOUNT NUMBER≠ .,
PRINT ≠(28) = STIPEND FUNDING SOURCE BEGINNING DATE≠ .,
PRINT ≠(29) = STIPEND FUNDING SOURCE ENDING DATE≠ .,
PRINT ≠(30) = STIPEND FUNDING AMOUNT (MONTHLY)≠ .,
PRINT ≠(31) = STIPEND FUNDING AMOUNT (EXTRA)≠ .,
PRINT ≠(32) = STIPEND FUNDING AMOUNT (TOTAL)≠ .,
PRINT ≠(33) = SA NUMBER≠ .,
PRINT ≠(34) = SA CANCELLATION NUMBER≠ .,

BEGIN SEARCH

FOR I=1 TO LAST LET X=0 ., LET Y=0 .,
IF (24.I) EQ ≠-≠ THEN LET X=1 .,
IF X EQ 1 AND (25.I) GE 0000 AND (25.I) LE 9999 AND (26.I) GE 000 AND (26.I) LE
999 AND (27.I) GE 00 AND (27.I) LE 99 THEN LET Y=1 .,
IF X EQ 1 AND Y EQ 0 THEN PRINT (24.I),(25.I),(26.I),(27.I) ., LOOP .,

FOR I=1 TO LAST LET Z=0 ., LET ZZ=0 ., LET X=0 .,
IF (28.I) GE 0 OR (29.I) GE 0 THEN LET X=1 .,
IF X EQ 1 AND (28.I) GE SEPT 1,1972 AND (28.I) LE SEPT 15,1973 AND (29.I) GE
SEPT 1,1972 AND (29.I) LE SEPT 15,1973 AND (29.I)-(28.I) GE 0 THEN LET Z=1 .,
IF X EQ 1 AND Z EQ 0 THEN PRINT (24.I),(28.I),(29.I) .,

LET X=0 .,
IF (30.I) GE 0 OR (31.I) GE 0 THEN LET X=1 .,
IF Z EQ 1 AND X EQ 0 THEN PRINT (24.I),(28.I),(29.I),(30.I),(31.I) .,

IF (32.I) GT 0 THEN LET ZZ=1 .,
IF Z EQ 1 AND X EQ 1 AND ZZ EQ 0 THEN PRINT (24.I),(28.I),(29.I),(30.I),(31.I),
(32.I) .,

LET ZZ=0 .,
IF (33.I) GE 0000 AND (33.I) LE 9999 THEN LET ZZ=1 .,
IF Z EQ 1 AND X EQ 1 AND ZZ EQ 0 THEN PRINT (24.I),(28.I),(29.I),(30.I),(31.I),
(32.I),(33.I) .,

LET ZZ=0 .,
IF (34.I) LT 0000 OR (34.I) GT 9999 THEN PRINT (24.I),(34.I) .,

LOOP .,
```

Steps through all of the funding sources and for each funding source number (24.I) that exists, ensures that its constituent part (25.I), (26.I), (27.I) also exist and are within valid ranges.

Tests for the existence and validity of funding beginning date (28.I) and ending date (29.I).

Tests for the existence of a monthly amount (30.I) or an extra amount (31.I).

Tests for the existence of a total amount (32.I).

Tests for the existence and validity of the SA number (33.I).

Tests for the validity of SA cancellation number (34.I).

Figure 9.4. Sample validation search.

```
..........MISSING OR INCORRECT DATA..........

(24) = STIPEND FUNDING SOURCE

(25) = STIPEND FUNDING SOURCE DEPARTMENT NUMBER

(26) = STIPEND FUNDING SOURCE ACCOUNT NUMBER

(27) = STIPEND FUNDING SOURCE SUB-ACCOUNT NUMBER

(28) = STIPEND FUNDING SOURCE BEGINNING DATE

(29) = STIPEND FUNDING SOURCE ENDING DATE

(30) = STIPEND FUNDING AMOUNT (MONTHLY)

(31) = STIPEND FUNDING AMOUNT (EXTRA)

(32) = STIPEND FUNDING AMOUNT (TOTAL)

(33) = SA NUMBER

(34) = SA CANCELLATION NUMBER


* * * * * * * * * * * * * * * * * * * * * * * * * * * * * *

RECORD NUMBER  169

   24.   STIPEND FUNDING SOURCE
         SUB-3....  9253 - 271 - 72
   28.   STIPEND FUNDING SOURCE BEGINNING DATE
         SUB-3.... JUNE 16,1973
   29.   STIPEND FUNDING SOURCE ENDING DATE
         SUB-3.... SEPT 15,1972
```

Figure 9.5. Validation reporting.

of the total data output; not only must the individual items be readily seen and understandable, but there should be no redundancy and as small an amount of paper to be dealt with as possible!

With these goals in mind, a formatted report for TECH records was developed using the facilities of the RIQSONLINE report generator. Figure 9.6 represents the formatted report for the same data base record as was shown in Figure 9.3. The new report was generated in a form so that the record number, degree program and student name were easily seen (upper left corner of the report in Figure 9.6). The funding source numbers, dates, amounts and SA numbers were also formatted for easy viewing. Additionally, funding which has been cancelled is immediately noticeable as a code of XXXX following the cancelled funding (far right column of the report). Redundant data such as items 25 through 27 and 36 through 38 have been eliminated from the report. The resulting format is certainly more readable, with no loss of information, and therefore more useful, and the volume of output for a full file listing has been reduced almost by a factor of 4.

CALCULATION OF SUMMARY STATISTICS

Some of the major problems in dealing with the data were in obtaining the statistical data, largely because of restrictions imposed by the RIQS system. One example of the type of data needed was to determine how many students in a given degree program received funding from the different types of (salary or stipend) funding sources (e.g., research assistantships, fellowships, traineeships). This meant categorizing the students by two attributes, one of which would take on values from 1 to 10 (degree program), and the other

```
176 [          ]         484563545    MALE     WHITE    USA          JAN, 1972  [       ]
EE                                                                   MS

                         6010 - 302 - 81    SEPT 16,1972    JUNE 15,1973        259        3138 XXXX
                         6010 - 302 - 81    SEPT 16,1972    OCT 15,1972         217        3138
                         6010 - 302 - 81    OCT 15,1972     JUNE 15,1973        217        3153
                         9253 - 274 - 72    SEPT 16,1972    NOV 15,1972         33         3069 XXXX
                         9253 - 274 - 72    NOV 16,1972     JAN 15,1973         13         3072
                         9253 - 274 - 72    JAN 16,1973     SEPT 15,1973        23         3072
                         6010 - 302 - 81    JUNE 16,1973    JUNE 30,1973        216        5330
                         6010 - 303 - 81    JULY 1,1973     SEPT 15,1973        217        5333
                         6010 - 302 - 84    865       865   720       95
                                                            2         4         2
```

Figure 9.6. Formatted TECH record.

of which could take on values from 1 to 14 (funding source). Moreover, when another categorization by date of entrance was desired (values from 1 to 8), the problem was greatly increased. This is not to say that the system could not handle it, but it became increasingly expensive as refinements were demanded (and, of course, as soon as data starts being machine-handled, questions are asked that would never be asked of a human!). Moreover, it was difficult and time consuming to make such matrix searches using RIQSONLINE. What was finally done was to divide the data into 32 sets: sets 1 to 10 defined by the degree program; sets 11 to 18, by the date of entrance; and sets 19 to 32, by the funding type. Figure 9.7 summarizes the set descriptions. The usual interactive manipulations (intersections, complements, etc.) were then performed using the remaining two sets in order to generate the needed statistics. However, it does seem possible to develop a code to be stored in one of the extra items of each record which could be interrogated to determine in which sets the record is contained, and thus facilitate the above searches.

Another type of summary required involves the calculation of simple frequency counts over individual data items, such as frequency counts of students by department, by degree objective, sex, race, nationality, etc. For each of the above areas with the exception of nationality, the distinct values that each data item can assume are known a priori and hence simple searches can be performed, either batch or on-line, to count up the number of occurrences of each distinct value. In the case of nationality, however, the number of distinct values is relatively large (on the order of 50) and the totality of possible values is not predefined as in the other data items mentioned above. As new records are added to the data base, additional nationalities which had not previously occurred may certainly appear. While the task of calculating frequency counts by nationality seems to be very time consuming via RIQS search operations, it has an extremely easy solution within the INDEX phase of the RIQS batch processor. The single command INVERT ON (12) . with the INDEX phase will not only generate the required frequency counts, but also will produce a sorted listing of nationalities, followed by the record numbers of all students of each nationality. Such a file inversion is shown in Figure 9.8. A slight manual editing of the file inversion is required, however, since multiple word nationalities, such as VIET NAM, will appear in the listing both under VIET and under NAM. Since the record numbers are listed, this editing becomes very simple—two index terms with the same record number actually represent the same student.

SELECTIVE DATA RETRIEVAL

All selective data retrieval is performed interactively using RIQSONLINE. The types of retrievals required range from simply displaying a student's record to analyzing allocation of funding amounts by department, by advisor, sex, race, nationality, etc.

Figure 9.9 illustrates a retrieval request designed to display salary funding information for all students who have specific advisors. The first part of the search text defines a procedure named ADVISOR which takes an advisor's name as a parameter. The procedure computes and displays the number of students with that advisor, the number of students who have salary funding, the sum of all their salary funding and the average funding per funded student. Together with the advisor name, this information is displayed in a tabular format as shown at the bottom of the figure. The collection of search statements to perform the above processing was defined as a procedure in order to make it as easy as possible to execute the retrieval for as many advisors as desired. All that is required is a

```
SET DESCRIPTIONS


              NO. OF      CREATION
   ID. NO.    ELEMENTS      DATE        DEFINITION

      1          23      MAR 5, 1973    BIO
      2          41      MAR 5, 1973    CHE
      3         129      MAR 5, 1973    CE
      4          89      MAR 5, 1973    CS
      5          54      MAR 5, 1973    EE
      6          21      MAR 5, 1973    ES
      7          64      MAR 5, 1973    IE
      8          25      MAR 5, 1973    ME
      9          59      MAR 5, 1973    MS
     10           7      MAR 5, 1973    USEC
     11         177      MAR 6, 1973    MARCH 1972-
     12         136      MAR 6, 1973    MARCH 1971- FEB 1972
     13          79      MAR 6, 1973    MARCH 1970-FEB 1971
     14          65      MAR 6, 1973    MARCH 1969-FEB 1970
     15          30      MAR 6, 1973    MARCH 1968-FEB 1969
     16          14      MAR 6, 1973    MARCH 1967-FEB 1968
     17           7      MAR 6, 1973    MARCH 1966-FEB 1967
     18           3      MAR 6, 1973    MARCH 1965-FEB1966
     19          36      MAR 6, 1973    TA
     20          68      MAR 6, 1973    WPM FELLOWS
     21          29      MAR 6, 1973    WPM SCHOLARS
     22           5      MAR 6, 1973    CABELL
     23          17      MAR 6, 1973    NSF TRAINEES
     24          17      MAR 6, 1973    MISC. FELLOWS
     25          45      MAR 6, 1973    MISC. TRAINEES
     26          65      MAR 6, 1973    RA (OTHER)
     27          24      MAR 6, 1973    RS (MRC)
     28          18      MAR 6, 1973    RA (601)
     29          18      MAR 6, 1973    RA (602)
     30           2      MAR 6, 1973    RA (DOC)
     31          26      MAR 6, 1973    BELL
     32         141      MAR 6, 1973    ALL OTHERS
```

Figure 9.7. TECH file set descriptions.

separate call to the procedure for each advisor for which the statistics are desired. Similar procedures could be defined for examining the allocation of funding by department, by sex, race, nationality or whatever classification is needed.

The experience using the interactive mode, both for statistical and individual data, was especially interesting since the user (Mintzer) was originally completely unfamiliar with the RIQS system and even with the computer itself. A terminal with an acoustic coupler was borrowed, and a preliminary session was held with the "tutor" (Dominick). During this session, lasting about two hours, the most usual operations were illustrated (sign on, loading of the tape, statements leading to simple actions, etc.). The user then read the RIQS Manual, and spent several two- and three-hour sessions with the terminal—interspersed with an occasional question and answer session with the tutor. Certainly less than ten hours of practice (most of which were spent formulating commands to answer specific questions, and then querying the computer using the hunt-and-peck system of typing) were needed in order to feel quite familiar with the RIQSONLINE system. There are still times, however, when all else fails and the user must appeal to the tutor for help.

Count	Country	Values
1	ARABIA	101
2	AUSTRIA	126, 445
1	BELGIUM	382
1	BRAZIL	295
8	CANADA	2, 81, 113, 184, 261, 279, 356, 511
28	CHINA	60, 52, 67, 76, 188, 263, 264, 265, 293, 298, 426, 435, 442, 443, 466, 96, 480, 483, 489, 506, 521, 525, 527, 555, 563, 567, 573, 575
4	COLUMBIA	477, 94, 538, 192
2	COSTA	1, 539
1	ECUADOR	299
7	EGYPT	5, 21, 114, 229, 304, 367, 549
1	ETHIOPIA	27
6	FRANCE	34, 35, 144, 331, 347, 399
13	GREECE	20, 83, 128, 139, 223, 296, 321, 324, 325, 362, 439, 518, 553
1	GUATEMALA	389
3	HONGKONG	186, 245, 28
30	INDIA	3, 26, 64, 65, 102, 132, 141, 151, 164, 169, 233, 272, 305, 320, 323, 329, 350, 391, 394, 395, 430, 432, 452, 453, 547, 577, 317, 307, 121, 123
4	IRAN	4, 18
1	IRAQ	7
1	IRELAND	160
12	ISRAEL	70, 129, 156, 182, 238, 302, 336, 337, 381, 414, 431, 540
1	ITALY	38
11	JAPAN	72, 75, 206, 234, 235, 249, 250, 251, 322, 409, 487, 479, 455, 447, 365, 214, 170, 574, 557, 515
17	KOREA	17, 6, 490, 548, 429, 485, 486
1	LIBYA	491
1	LUXEMBOURG	116
2	MALAYSIA	433, 343
3	MEXICO	230, 353, 366
1	NAM	351
1	NETHERLANDS	270
2	NICARAGUA	450, 502
3	NIGERIA	58, 528, 488
1	PAKISTAN	368, 446
1	PERSIA	122
1	PHILIPPINES	397, 371
2	PRETORIA	207, 109
2	RICA	538, 539

1	SAUDI	101														
5	SPAIN	10	93	292	408	495										
1	SUDAN	115														
1	SWEDEN	373														
1	SWITZERLAND	142														
26	TAIWAN	59	66	120	130	187	200	252	256	258	260	268	396	441	460	468
		474	475	476	478	481	482	499	500	503	531	550				
1	TANZANIA	212														
2	THAILAND	61	239													
5	TURKEY	107	168	226	316	318										
2	URUGUAY	124	529													
348	USA	8	9	11	12	13	14	15	16	19	22	23	24	25	30	31
		32	33	36	37	39	40	41	42	43	44	45	46	47	48	49
		50	51	52	53	54	55	56	57	63	68	69	71	77	78	79
		80	82	84	85	86	87	88	89	90	91	92	95	97	98	99
		100	103	104	105	106	108	110	111	112	117	118	119	125	127	131
		133	134	135	136	137	138	140	143	145	146	147	148	149	152	153
		154	155	157	158	159	161	162	163	165	166	171	172	173	174	175
		176	177	178	179	180	181	183	185	189	191	193	194	195	196	197
		198	199	201	202	203	204	205	208	209	210	211	213	215	216	217
		218	219	220	221	222	224	225	227	228	231	232	236	237	240	241
		242	243	244	246	247	248	253	254	255	257	259	262	266	267	269
		271	273	274	275	276	277	278	280	281	282	283	284	285	286	287
		288	289	290	291	294	297	300	301	303	306	308	309	310	311	312
		313	314	315	326	327	328	332	334	335	338	339	340	341	342	344
		345	346	348	349	352	354	355	357	358	359	360	361	363	364	369
		370	372	374	375	376	377	378	379	380	383	384	385	386	387	388
		390	392	393	398	400	401	402	403	404	405	406	407	410	411	412
		415	416	417	418	419	420	421	422	423	424	425	427	428	434	436
		437	438	440	444	448	449	451	454	456	457	458	459	461	462	463
		464	465	467	469	470	471	472	473	484	492	493	494	496	497	498
		501	504	505	507	508	509	510	512	513	514	516	517	519	520	522
		523	524	530	532	533	534	535	536	537	541	542	543	544	545	546
		551	552	554	556	558	559	560	561	562	564	565	566	568	569	570
		571	572	576												
1	VENEZUELA	333														
1	VIET	270														
1	WEST	122														
1	YUGOSLAVIA	150														

Figure 9.8. File inversion on nationality.

```
ENTER SEARCH COMMAND OR TYPE HALT

? PROCEDURE ADVISOR (NAME)
? SET UP ADVISED,FUNDED,SUM,AVERAGE ONCE FOR EACH NAME
? STRING NAME
? BEGIN SEARCH
? LET FUNDING = 'NO'
? IF #7 EQ NAME THEN LET ADVISED = ADVISED +1;
? IF #7 EQ NAME AND #15 CONTAINS '-'
? THEN LET FUNDING = 'YES' , LET FUNDED = FUNDED + 1;
? FOR I=1 TO LAST
? IF FUNDING EQ 'YES' AND #23.I GE 0
? THEN LET SUM = SUM + #23.I;
? LOOP;
? AFTER SEARCH
? IF FUNDED GT 0 THEN LET AVERAGE = SUM / FUNDED;
? DISPLAY ACROSS SKIP 1
?       NAME TAB 20 ADVISED TAB 30 FUNDED TAB 40 SUM TAB 55 AVERAGE
? ENDP


? BEGIN SEARCH
? CALL ADVISOR ('        ')
? CALL ADVISOR ('        ')
? CALL ADVISOR ('        ')
? CALL ADVISOR ('     ')
? CALL ADVISOR ('      ')

? END


SEARCHING INITIATED

AFTER SEARCH
```

	9.000	7.000	31280.000	4468.571
	18.000	6.000	22001.000	3666.833
	5.000	0.000	0.000	0.000
	22.000	2.000	3606.000	1803.000
	14.000	8.000	34566.000	4320.750

```
*  *  *  *  *
```

Figure 9.9.   Selective data retrieval.

Conclusion

It is difficult to write conclusions to this section on a particular administrative use of RIQS, since this application has been in use for only one year—a good part of which was spent teaching the user. The following might be judged in this light:

1. The data base involved 500 to 600 records with, perhaps, 100 separate pieces of information (on the average) for each record. The major amount of statistical information, which would involve separately inspecting each card (about once for each type of statistics) if there were no machine-handling of the data, was actually necessary only at one time each year; it was interesting but not necessary to see how it changed by academic quarter. Approximately ten different types of statistical

data were needed, and all were developed in the Fall. It is an intuitive feeling that this amount of information handling is about the break-even point for changing from hand-manipulated to machine-manipulated data handling.

2. Much information was not entered into the record mainly because it was never kept in the central office but, rather, in "branch offices" (individual department offices). This included course numbers, instructors and grades. If these could be handled by this system, it would relieve these or other offices of much record keeping.

3. The system developed here could be viewed as a pilot project, involving only the graduate students in engineering. If successful, the 750 undergraduates (for which different information would be necessary) and, eventually, the entire student body (about 8500 full-time students) could be handled by this system. Moreover, it was found that as the ease of data handling became apparent, previously unasked questions of information "hidden" in the data which would become available if it could be more easily handled (it is, of course, an Article of Faith of our times that it is sinful not to obtain as much information as is possible from any available data).

4. It is therefore hoped that, after this system has been in use for about another year to gain more experience, the next step of adding courses and grades could be attempted.

Chapter 10

The POMRAD Integrated Information System[1]

DANIEL L. KEGAN
Hampshire College

WILLIAM D. NEVILLE
Northwestern University

ALBERT H. RUBENSTEIN
Northwestern University

CHARLES F. DOUDS
De Paul University

ROBERT D. O'KEEFE
Northwestern University

The Problem

Since its inception at Northwestern over fourteen years ago, the Program of Research on the Management of Research and Development (POMRAD), under the direction of Albert H. Rubenstein, has developed several information subsystems: a library of published and unpublished works, research instruments such as questionnaires, raw data from field studies, and internal research reports. As the POMRAD research program grew, increased coordination among POMRAD researchers and increased integration among information subsystems became more important. These problems should be similar for many medium to large-scale research programs in the social or natural sciences.

There are, of course, information systems and methods that come neatly prepackaged. These are models of organized and tightly knit procedures and they may function with all the perfection they promise under the *ideal* conditions to which they are supposed to be applied. The problem is in finding the ideal conditions. So what most of us do is to develop systems and methods that are tailored to our own individual characteristics and to the characteristics of the information environment we must work in.

Our use of RIQS began rather simply, and then grew. Initially, we wished to develop a collection of research instruments (questionnaires, interview schedules, unobtrusive measures, etc.). Members of POMRAD surveyed journals and books considered likely to discuss variables relevant to organizational behavior. In addition, we built collections of instruments for variables of special interest to POMRAD research projects.[2] Such in-depth collections are not available in the recently published inventories by Bonjean et al.,[3] Buros,[4] Miller,[5] Robinson et al.,[6] Robinson and Shaver,[7] Shaw and Wright,[8] Price,[9]

186

Lake, Miles, and Earle.[10] We called our collection and system "SCALES."

The SCALES/RIQS subsystem which developed from this growing inventory used both the search and index capabilities of RIQS. Instruments could be readily located by such items as variable, author, name of questionnaire, or reliability.

The success of RIQS with SCALES prompted our consideration and attempts to adopt RIQS for other POMRAD information systems. This planned RIQS compatible package was termed the POMRAD Integrated Information System (IIS). The five principal subsystems of IIS are:

1. SCALES, a physical inventory of research instruments;[11]

2. PROPS, a collection of propositions concerning organizational behavior in the Research and Development/Innovation (RD/I) process;

3. DOCUMENT, a collection of papers written by members of POMRAD, currently being produced at a rate of more than 100 per year;

4. SERIALS, a miniature library of items (both published and those not in the open literature) of interest to POMRAD members, currently over 10,000 items; and

5. CENTRAL, a depository for research data from POMRAD projects.

Social science research is increasingly taking a propositional approach (cf. March and Simon,[12] Berelson and Steiner,[13] Price,[14]). Hundreds of propositions at micro and macro levels may be relevant for the theoretical development of a specific research study. PROPS/RIQS is intended to allow the researcher to search for relevant propositions and to build a set of them specifically tailored to his project. By linking related propositions, the researcher might also obtain analyses of which propositions have been empirically tested, and, of those tested, which propositions were validated and which were not. If the research instruments used to test a proposition were of interest, they may be cross-indexed in the SCALES subsystem.

In focusing on the RD/I process, our research program into organizational behavior has become an integrated and cumulative effort, including specific studies of project selection, decentralization of research and development, the flow of ideas within the laboratory, liaison relations, R&D in developing countries, incentives for technological innovation, and other related subjects.[15]

The major direct products of the Program of Research on the Management of Research and Development are research papers. POMRAD members write over a hundred documents a year (published articles, working papers, grant proposals, theses, etc.). New research projects build on past efforts—often going back 15-20 years. POMRAD had its origins at Columbia University (1950-1953) and Massachusetts Institute of Technology (1955-1959). Numerous requests for documents in the POMRAD inventory are received from other researchers located throughout the world. To aid in recording and retrieving requested papers, the DOCUMENTS/RIQS subsystem was created. It permits us to create indexes and perform searches by author, title, date, research area, sponsoring agency, and type of paper (e.g., dissertation, working paper, reprint, proposal).

These three subsystems—SCALES/RIQS, PROPS/RIQS, and DOCUMENT/RIQS—are operational and used in varying degrees by members of POMRAD both at Northwestern and at other locations.[16] Two other subsystems have been designed with RIQS-compatibility, but have not yet been implemented. CENTRAL files is a depository for research data from POMRAD projects. SERIALS is a miniature library of items of interest to POMRAD members. During its twenty years' growth, SERIALS has accumulated over ten thousand items—books, journal articles, newsclips, unpublished reports, etc. Primarily, the large investment in keypunching the older manual card catalog has slowed the implementation of SERIALS/RIQS. Also, at the time RIQS became operational, our most pressing needs were for information retrieval in areas of SCALES, PROPS, and DOCUMENTS.

In summary, we have used RIQS to develop an Integrated Information System for an academic management and behavioral science research program. The RIQS subsystems permit a researcher to interact with his data base, as well as to consult periodically-generated overall indexes.

The Data

In considering the implementation of a system using computerized information processing and retrieval capabilities, our prime concerns were that the resulting information system would be both accessible and convenient for potential users. The structure of the data base is a factor which inevitably influences use of the system as well as the system performance. Data bases structured somewhat in parallel seemed to be a desirable feature. If similar items of information were defined in similar ways from subsystem to subsystem, the convenience of users and custodians of the system would increase. Thus, if item (10) is a numerical identification in the SCALES subsystem, it would also be item (10) in the DOCS subsystem. This would facilitate use of the system, since familiarity with one subsystem would permit a transfer of training to the others. Thus, the data for each of the IIS subsystems is structured in a parallel, but not identical, fashion. This deviance from identical structure was due to the trade-off between (a) a uniform but massive data bank with much extraneous material for any given inquiry and (b) data bases tailored for specific inquiries.

Each entry in an IIS subsystem is described by a RIQS record; each record contains at least eleven items. The basic structure of the items, except for PROPS is:

1. Authors.
2. Complete citation except for date.
3. Date of publication or writing.
4. Abstract.
5. Quality control.
6. Variables, research projects.
7. Comments, by author or depositor.
8. Depositor. Record sequence for DOCUMENT, CENTRAL.
9. Unique subsystem information.
10. Numerical identification.
11. Citation list: other uses of or references to this article.

Differences in RIQS item definition among the IIS subsystems are summarized in Figure 10.1.

PROPS is the subsystem in which the data structure varies most from the other subsystems. It became evident, in the pilot testing stage and the very early stages of the application of PROPS to a specific research effort, that the retention of parallelism would be at the expense of creating a file logically tailored for the specific application. PROPS

	Item (5)	Item (9)	Item (10)[a]	Item (7)
SCALES	reliability, validity	instrument title	1	
DOCUMENT	availability: code & quantity	code name, type of paper, sponsor	YR001	pages exclusive of cover sheet
SERIAL	DATA STRUCTURE IS CURRENTLY BEING CONSIDERED			
CENTRAL	data source	organizational code	YR00001	org. name

[a]Initial numbering for item (10) — YR = last two digits of year, e.g., 73001.

Figure 10.1. Differences in item definition among the various subsystems.

requires more supplementary information for successful research use than does any of the other subsystems. Forcing the information required for PROPS to conform to a structure paralleling that of other subsystems would have upset the logical flow of information. Because readability and the logical sequence of information became the primary design criteria for the format of the PROPS data structures, parallelism was assigned a lower priority.

The structure of the items for PROPS is:

1. Authors.
2. Citation.
3. Date of publication.
4. Numerical identification.
5. Proposition statement.
6. Variables–independent.
7. Variables–dependent.
8. Parameters.
9. Keywords.
10. Indicators (for the variables).
11. Empirical findings.
12. Population/Sample/Field site/Country.
13. Type of support—instruments used.
14. Origin of proposition (direct quote, restatement, etc.).
15. Depositor. Date of deposit.
16. Research question, area of interest.
17. Relation to project in POMRAD.
18. Design implications.
19. Citation list: other uses of or references to this proposition.
20. Comments.

This data structure for PROPS is more extensive than that of other subsystems. This was necessary in order that the system yield the information required by a researcher in evaluating potentially researchable propositions.

Indices and Searches (Research Strategy)

Our research use of the IIS/RIQS system includes both the indexing and the searching capabilities of RIQS. In many instances we have used indexes (author, keyword-in-context, keyword-out-of-context) as a first step on the search of a data base. A reference to one of the prepared indexes leads to a more detailed on-line search of whichever portion of the data base is relevant to that particular query. Indexes created from the SCALES system are illustrated in Figures 10.2, 10.3, and 10.4.

If a SCALES user is interested in instruments dealing with careers, he could glance at the KWOC index and find five instruments where "career" (see Figure 10.4) is one of the variables mentioned. Furthermore, if he checks under "occupational" and "occupations," he will find five instruments, some of which are indexed under "career" as well. If these instrument titles interest the user, he can pursue his search via an on-line search of the data base in either of two ways. First, he can reference the items of interest by the appropriate keywords; second, by referring to the appropriate record number. Figure 10.5 illustrates on-line output resulting from a search of the data base using the keywords for reference.

Figure 10.6 shows the greater number of retrievals when the search query was altered to include "jobs" as a search term. Twenty-two additional reports were generated.

After seeing the complete record of information contained in SCALES/RIQS pertaining to each instrument, the user can determine which of the instruments described may be of interest to him. The actual instruments may then be found by referencing these SCALES numbers in the file cabinet where the SCALES documents are maintained.

As previously noted, DOCUMENT/RIQS is used for administrative purposes rather than research. Consequently, the level of interactive (on-line) interrogation of the data base is low. Rather, indexes created from the data, plus the output from some searches done periodically, provide a guide to manual searches of computer output which contains all of the information in the data base. Documents are most commonly referenced by the Document Inventory Number which consists of the year the document was written and its sequence within that year; for example, 73/77 would be the seventy-seventh document assigned a number in 1973.

These indexes provide a convenient tool to find documents when the complete reference is not available. If an author is known, we can use the Author Index where that author's works are indexed. If one knows what the subject of the document is, he can use the Project Index where papers are grouped by the names of the corresponding project within POMRAD. (See Figures 10.7, 10.8, and 10.9.)

Groupings by sponsor and type of document are the results of searches rather than indexes. These are created by printing the output of a search which finds the documents related to a specific sponsor, e.g., "NSF" (National Science Foundation), or a specific type of paper, e.g., "Report." (See Figures 10.10 and 10.11.)

In addition, we are pilot testing an inventory procedure for DOCUMENT/RIQS. Here we use the output of a search to show the present inventory and distribution status of a document. Monthly tallies of the quantity of documents moving in and out of the system are maintained. Appropriate changes to the inventory status are made each month. Appropriate keypunching corrections are made and the current inventory status printed biannually. (See Figure 10.12.)

```
ABERBACH, JOEL D

        POLITICAL TRUST INDEX
        0450

AFFINITO, M

        LOCAL - COSMOPOLITAN SCALE - - FOR NURSING.
        0196

AGER, J W

        CATEGORIES OF FAVORABLENESS TOWARD SCIENCE STATEMENTS.
        0108

AGGER, ROBERT E

        POLITICAL CYNICISM SCALE
        0409

AIKEN, MICHAEL

        ORGANIZATIONAL FORMALIZATION QUESTIONS
        0279

        PARTICIPATION IN DECISION - MAKING QUESTIONS
        0280

        CENTRALIZATION QUESTIONS
        0281

        ALIENATION QUESTIONS
        0282

AKERS, RONALD L

        GROUP RESOURCES AND STRUCTURES RANKING PROCEDURE.
        0314

ALFORD, ROBERT

        POLITICAL INVOLVEMENT, INFORMATION AND INTEREST, COMMUNITY
        INTEGRATION, AND IDEALOGIES QUESTIONS
        0325

ALLEN, T J

        SOCIOMETRIC ANALYSIS QUESTIONNAIRE.
        0333

ALSTON, JON P

        QUESTIONS DIFFERENTIATING BETWEEN WORKING AND MIDDLE CLASS
        RESPONDENTS
        0327

ALTMAN, IRWIN

        INTIMACY - SCALED STIMULI.
        0336
```

Figure 10.2. Portion of SCALES author index: This author index prints the title of the scale and the SCALES identification number.

	Record Number
MEASURE OF EXPRESSED DESIRE FCR GREATER AUTONOMY	292
MEASURE OF SELF-ACTUALIZATION. SHORT-FORM	21
MEASURE.	5
MEASURE-INTERN PERFORMANCE, WARD QUALITY. STRATIFICATION	44
MEASUREMENT HANDBOOK OF RESEARCH DESIGN AND SOCIAL	296
MEASUREMENT = INVENTORY OF SCALES AND INDIC S SOCIOLOGICAL	295
MEASUREMENT AND COLLEGE ENVIRCMENTS ORGANIZATIONAL	317
MEASUREMENT BY OBSERVATION OF CCNTACTS BETWEEN INDIVIDUALS = SUPERVISOR RANKING OF COMPETE	212
MEASUREMENT OF INTERPERSONAL SENSITIVITY THE	320
MEASURES OF ASSETS. ECONOMIC	177
MEASURES OF COMMITMENT	90
MEASURES OF COMMUNITY NON-INTEGRATION	131
MEASURES OF EMPLOYEE MOTIVATICN ANC MORALE. QUESTIONNAIRES	347
MEASURES OF SOCIAL MOBILITY.	56
MEASURES.	239
MEASURES. PARENTAL SATISFACTION WITH SCHOOL. REFERENCES TC FIVE CREATIVITY	48
MEASURING VALUES. TECHNIQUES FOR	133
MEETING EVALUATION SHEET	274
MEETINGS (COPED FORM A -6)	250
MEMBER ACTIVITY QUESTION	25
MEMBER CHANGE LEADER RATING OF	285
MEMBER LOYALTY QUESTION	26
MEMBERS. INTERVIEW FORMAT WITH OR / MS GROUP	150
MEMBERSHIP RESTRICTIVENESS INDEX UNION	188
MENTAL ILLNESS ITEMS ATTITUDE TOWARD	45
MERIT REVIEW. PATTERNED	87
MERTON ≠ S POST HOC SOCIAL ORIENTATION	302
MERTON-GOULDNER-HUGHES-RIESMAN ORIENTATION DISTINCTION DAVIS ≠	300
METHOD OF ASSESSING STABILITY OF FRIENDSHIP THOMPSON AND HORROCKS	168
METHOD. VERIDICAL PERCEPTION INTERVIEW	31
METHODS TO DETERMINE THE NORMS OF ADDRESS. FOUR	74
MEXICAN-AMERICAN ATTITUDE AND BEHAVIOR LINKAGE QUESTIONNAIRE	222
MICROMETER PSYCHOMOTOR TESTING.	173
MIDDLE CLASS RESPONDENTS QUESTIONS DIFFERENTIATING BETWEEN WORKING AND	227
MIDDLE-CLASS AND WORKING CLASS YOUTH-INTEREST IN COLLEGE. SELECTED CHARACTERISTICS OF	123
MIGRATION DEMOGRAPHIC FACTORS IN	189
MILES ≠ EGO-STRENGTH SCALE	331
MILITARY JUSTICE B. SATISFACTION WITH ARMY LIFE C. BELIEF IN AUTHORITARIAN LEADERSHIP PR	232
MINED ROAD PROBLEM-MRP-CHANGE OF WCRK PROCEDURE PROBLEM-CWP.	171
MMPI. K-SCALE OF THE	246
MMPI-ES EGO STRENGTH SCALE CF THE	80
MOBILITY.	56
MOBILITY, CAREER STAGES QUESTIONNAIRE ITEMS.	55

Figure 10.3. Keyword-in-context index: A KWIC index on the instrument titles in SCALES. The RIQS record number is shown for

```
CAREER

        EXTENDED FAMILY IDENTIFICATION, GEOGRAPHIC - OCCUPATIONAL
        MOBILITY, CAREER STAGES QUESTIONNAIRE ITEMS.
        0155

        PATTERNED MERIT REVIEW.
        0187

        CAREER ORIENTATIONS ANCHORAGE SCALE
        0291

        PERCEIVED INFLUENCE SCALE.
        0337

        INTERPERSONAL TRUST SCALE.
        0338

CATEGORIES

        SKILLS INDEX
        0459

CENTRALIZATION

        CENTRALIZATION QUESTIONS
        0281

        .
        .
        .

OCCUPATIONAL

        EXTENDED FAMILY IDENTIFICATION, GEOGRAPHIC - OCCUPATIONAL
        MOBILITY, CAREER STAGES QUESTIONNAIRE ITEMS.
        0155

        SURVEY OF ENGINEERING OCCUPATIONS.
        0220

        0221

        NORTH - HATT OCCUPATIONAL SCALE, PLUS ELEVEN ITEM
        QUESTIONNAIRE RATED ON THE BASIS OF CHANGE IN OCCUPATION.
        0235

OCCUPATIONS

        CARD SORT - - OCCUPATIONAL RANKINGS - - USING NORTH HATT
        SCALE.
        0234
```

Figure 10.4. Keyword–out–of–context index: Portions of KWOC index on the variables item. The title of the instrument and the SCALES inventory number are shown for reference.

```
ENTER SEARCH COMMAND OR TYPE HALT

? IF #6 EQ ('CAREER' OR 'OCCUPATIONS' OR 'OCCUPATIONAL')
? DISPLAY ZAP RECORD END

SEARCHING INITIATED


NO. OF REPORTS ON DISPLAY FILE =      9

DO YOU WANT THE DISPLAY REPORTS LISTED
? Y
    LITWAK, EUGENE
    ' GEOGRAPHIC MOBILITY AND EXTENDED FAMILY COHESION ', AMERICAN
    SOCIOLOGICAL REVIEW, 25, 3, 385 -394. JUNE
    1960
    SCALE WAS USED WITH 920 MARRIED WOMEN LIVING IN BUFFALO, NEW
    YORK, NOT A REPRESENTATIVE SAMPLE, BUT YOUNGER, MIDDLE - CLASS,
    AND NATIVE - BORN.
    EXTENDED FAMILY IDENTIFICATION, GEOGRAPHIC - OCCUPATIONAL
    MOBILITY, CAREER STAGES.
    SCHLIE, TED
    EXTENDED FAMILY IDENTIFICATION, GEOGRAPHIC - OCCUPATIONAL
    MOBILITY, CAREER STAGES QUESTIONNAIRE ITEMS.
    0155
    MCMURRAY, R N
    ' RECRUITMENT, DEPENDENCY, AND MORALE IN THE BANKING INDUSTRY ',
    ADMIN SCI QUART, 3, 1, 87 -117. JUNE
    1958
    SCALE WAS USED IN BANKS FOR PERFORMANCE APPRAISAL.
    VARIABLES MEASURED = JOB DESCRIPTION, JOB PERFORMANCE, AND JOB,
    OR CAREER, POTENTIAL.
    AUTHOR RECOMMENDS THIS SCALE FOR PERSONNEL DEPARTMENT USE IN
    UPGRADING PERFORMANCES OF BANKING MANAGERS AND OFFICERS.
    DEPOSITOR ' S COMMENT = THIS INSTRUMENT IS ADAPTED FROM = ROBERT
    E SCHAEFFER, MERIT RATING AS A MANAGEMENT TOOL ', HARVARD
    BUSINESS REVIEW, NOVEMBER 1949, VOL. 27, 693 -705.
    DOUDS, C
    PATTERNED MERIT REVIEW.
    0187
    CARR, MALCOLM J
    ' THE SAMOA METHOD OF DETERMINING TECHNICAL, ORGANIZATIONAL AND
    COMMUNICATIONAL DIMENSIONS OF TASK CLUSTERS.  SAN DIEGO,
    CALIFORNIA = U S NAVY PERSONNEL RESEARCH ACTIVITY, TECHNICAL
    BULLETIN STB68 -5. NOVEMBER
    1967
    ADMINISTERED TO NAVY RESEARCHERS ON A PILOT TEST BASIS.
    ADEQUATELY DISCUSSED.
    OCCUPATIONAL INFORMATION.
    FUNCTIONALLY PROVEN VERY USEFUL.
    MAHER, P MICHAEL
    SURVEY OF ENGINEERING OCCUPATIONS.
    0220
    CARR, MALCOLM J
    ' THE SAMOA METHOD OF DETERMINING TECHNICAL, ORGANIZATIONAL, AND
    COMMUNICATIONAL DIMENSIONS OF TASK CLUSTERS ', U S NAVY
    PERSONNEL PESEARCH ACTIVITY, TECH BULLETIN STB68 -5. NOVEMBER
    1967
    SCALE WAS ADMINISTERED TO NAVY RESEARCHERS ON A PILOT TEST BASIS.
    RELIABILITY AND VALIDITY ADEQUATELY DISCUSSED.
    OCCUPATIONAL INFORMATION IS THE VARIABLE MEASURED.
    FUNCTIONALLY PROVEN VERY USEFUL.
    MAHER, P MICHAEL
    0221
```

Figure 10.5.   Section of the results of an on-line search using the keywords "career," "occupations," and "occupational." The complete record is printed.

```
ENTER SEARCH COMMAND OR TYPE HALT

? IF #6 EQ ('CAREER' OR 'OCCUPATIONS' OR 'OCCUPATIONAL' OR
? 'JOB') DISPLAY ZAP RECORD END

SEARCHING INITIATED


NO. OF REPORTS ON DISPLAY FILE =    31

DO YOU WANT THE DISPLAY REPORTS LISTED
? Y


        SERGIO, TALACCHI,
        ' ORGANIZATION SIZE, INDIVIDUAL ATTITUDES AND BEHAVIOR = AN
        EMPIRICAL STUDY ', ADMIN SCI QUART, 5, 3, 398 -420. DECEMBER
        1960
        THE SCALE WAS USED WITH 93 ORGANIZATIONS SURVEYED OVER A FIVE -
        YEAR PERIOD BY THE INDUSTRIAL RELATIONS CENTER, UNIVERSITY OF
        CHICAGO.  IT IS A ' STANDARDIZED 76 - ITEM EMPLOYEE ATTITUDE
        QUESTIONNAIRE WHICH YIELDS A SCORE AS AN INDEX OF GENERAL
        SATISFACTION FOR ALL PERSONNEL IN THE ORGANIZATIONS SURVEYED '.
        - - PG.  405.
        SEE PHILIP ASH, THE SRA EMPLOYEE INVENTORY - - A STATISTICAL
        ANALYSIS, PERSONNEL PSYCHOLOGY, 7, 337 -364. 1954.
        VARIABLE MEASURED = JOB SATISFACTION.
        VALIDATION WOULD BE IMPLIED BY SUBSTANTIATION OF HYPOTHESIS 2C.
        WAS FOUND - - PG.  409.
        DOUDS, C
        THE SRA EMPLOYEE INVENTORY.
        0103
        PORTER, L W *LAWLER, E E
        MANAGERIAL ATTITUDES AND PERFORMANCE.  HOMEWOOD, ILL = IRWIN -
        DORSEY, 185 -96
        1968
        SCALE WAS USED WITH 635 MANAGERS IN 7 ORGANIZATIONS - -3
        DIVISIONS OF STATE GOVERNMENTS, 4 PRIVATELY OWNED MANUFACTURING
        AND UTILITY COMPANIES.
        SEE LAWLER, 1967B = THE MULTITRAIT - MULTIMETHOD APPROACH TO
        MEASURING MANAGERIAL JOB PERFORMANCE.  JOURNAL OF APPLIED
        PSYCHOLOGY
        PERFORMANCE, PRODUCTIVITY, EFFORT ON THE JOB
        KEGAN, DANIEL L
        SELF - RATING FORM
        0117
        PORTER, L W *LAWLER, E E
        MANAGERIAL ATTITUDES AND PERFORMANCE.  HOMEWOOD, ILL = IRWIN -
        DORSEY, 185 -96
        1968
        SCALE WAS USED WITH 635 MANAGERS IN 7 ORGANIZATIONS - -3
        DIVISIONS OF STATE GOVERNMENTS, 4 PRIVATELY OWNED MANUFACTURING
        AND UTILITY COMPANIES.
        SEE LAWLER, 1967B = THE MULTITRAIT - MULTIMETHOD APPROACH TU
        MEASURING MANAGERIAL JOB PERFORMANCE.  JOURNAL OF APPLIED
        PSYCHOLOGY
        PERFORMANCE, EFFORT ON THE JOB
        KEGAN, DANIEL L
        SUPERIORS ' RATING FORM.
        0118
```

Figure 10.6. Section of the results of an on–line search using the keywords "career," "occupations," "occupational," "job." This search adds 22 records to the search shown in Figure 10.5.

BREWER, D

```
62005
RUBENSTEIN, A
BREWER, D
≠ R AND D IN THE CHICAGO AREA ELECTRONICS INDUSTRY ≠
PROGRAM OF RESEARCH ON THE MANAGEMENT OF RESEARCH AND
DEVELOPMENT, DEPARTMENT OF INDUSTRIAL ENGINEERING AND MANAGEMENT
SCIENCES, NORTHWESTERN UNIVERSITY, EVANSTON, ILLINOIS
```

COLRAD

```
64006
COLRAD
≠ A DIRECTORY OF RESEARCH - ON - RESEARCH ≠
PROGRAM OF RESEARCH ON THE MANAGEMENT OF RESEARCH AND
DEVELOPMENT, DEPARTMENT OF INDUSTRIAL ENGINEERING AND MANAGEMENT
SCIENCES, NORTHWESTERN UNIVERSITY, EVANSTON, ILLINOIS
```

COTTON, D

```
59006
COTTON, D
≠ SOME DATA ON THE RELATION BETWEEN DIVISIONALIZATION AND
DEPLOYMENT OF R AND D LABS IN DECENTRALIZED COMPANIES ≠
PROGRAM OF RESEARCH ON THE MANAGEMENT OF RESEARCH AND
DEVELOPMENT, DEPARTMENT OF INDUSTRIAL ENGINEERING AND MANAGEMENT
SCIENCES, NORTHWESTERN UNIVERSITY, EVANSTON, ILLINOIS
```

GOLDBERG, L

```
62007
GOLDBERG, L
≠ A SELECTED ANNOTATED BIBLIO OF EMPIRICAL INVESTIGATIONS OF
RESEARCH PERSONNEL ≠
PROGRAM OF RESEARCH ON THE MANAGEMENT OF RESEARCH AND
DEVELOPMENT, DEPARTMENT OF INDUSTRIAL ENGINEERING AND MANAGEMENT
SCIENCES, NORTHWESTERN UNIVERSITY, EVANSTON, ILLINOIS
```

```
64007 REPRINT
GOLDBERG, L
BAKER, N
RUBENSTEIN, A
≠ LOCAL - COSMOPOLITAN = UNIDIMENSIONAL OR MULTIDIMENSIONAL ≠
PROGRAM OF RESEARCH ON THE MANAGEMENT OF RESEARCH AND
DEVELOPMENT, DEPARTMENT OF INDUSTRIAL ENGINEERING AND MANAGEMENT
SCIENCES, NORTHWESTERN UNIVERSITY, EVANSTON, ILLINOIS
```

HANNENBERG

```
63001 REPRINT
RUBENSTEIN, A
HANNENBERG
≠ IDEA FLOW AND PROJECT SELECTION IN SEVERAL INDUSTRIAL R AND D
LABS ≠
PROGRAM OF RESEARCH ON THE MANAGEMENT OF RESEARCH AND
DEVELOPMENT, DEPARTMENT OF INDUSTRIAL ENGINEERING AND MANAGEMENT
SCIENCES, NORTHWESTERN UNIVERSITY, EVANSTON, ILLINOIS
```

```
63001 FIGURE
RUBENSTEIN, A
HANNENBERG
≠ FIGURE FOR 63001 ≠
PROGRAM OF RESEARCH ON THE MANAGEMENT OF RESEARCH AND
DEVELOPMENT, DEPARTMENT OF INDUSTRIAL ENGINEERING AND MANAGEMENT
SCIENCES, NORTHWESTERN UNIVERSITY, EVANSTON, ILLINOIS
```

Figure 10.7. Author index: A section of the author index is shown. The document number, author, title, and reference are included.

```
IDEA

         60009
         AVERY, R
         ≠ TECHNICAL OBJECTIVES AND THE PRODUCTION OF IDEAS IN INDUSTRIAL
         LABORATORIES ≠
         PROGRAM OF RESEARCH ON THE MANAGEMENT OF RESEARCH AND
         DEVELOPMENT, DEPARTMENT OF INDUSTRIAL ENGINEERING AND MANAGEMENT
         SCIENCES, NORTHWESTERN UNIVERSITY, EVANSTON, ILLINOIS

         62006
         RUBENSTEIN, A
         ≠ A DECISION - MAKING STUDY OF IDEA GENERATION AND PROJECT
         SELECTION IN INDUSTRIAL R AND D ≠
         PROGRAM OF RESEARCH ON THE MANAGEMENT OF RESEARCH AND
         DEVELOPMENT, DEPARTMENT OF INDUSTRIAL ENGINEERING AND MANAGEMENT
         SCIENCES, NORTHWESTERN UNIVERSITY, EVANSTON, ILLINOIS

         63002 REPRINT
         RUBENSTEIN, A
         ≠ STUDIES OF PROJECT SELECTION BEHAVIOR IN INDUSTRY ≠
         PROGRAM OF RESEARCH ON THE MANAGEMENT OF RESEARCH AND
         DEVELOPMENT, DEPARTMENT CF INDUSTRIAL ENGINEERING AND MANAGEMENT
         SCIENCES, NORTHWESTERN UNIVERSITY, EVANSTON, ILLINOIS

         63026
         BOLDBERG, L
         ≠ DIMENSIONS IN THE EVALUATION OF TECHNICAL IDEAS IN AN
         INDUSTRIAL RESEARCH LABORATORY ≠
         PROGRAM OF RESEARCH ON THE MANAGEMENT OF RESEARCH AND
         DEVELOPMENT, DEPARTMENT CF INDUSTRIAL ENGINEERING AND MANAGEMENT
         SCIENCES, NORTHWESTERN UNIVERSITY, EVANSTON, ILLINOIS

         64007 REPRINT
         GOLDBERG, L
         BAKER, N
         RUBENSTEIN, A
         ≠ LOCAL - COSMOPOLITAN = UNIDIMENSIONAL OR MULTIDIMENSIONAL ≠
         PROGRAM OF RESEARCH ON THE MANAGEMENT OF RESEARCH AND
         DEVELOPMENT, DEPARTMENT CF INDUSTRIAL ENGINEERING AND MANAGEMENT
         SCIENCES, NORTHWESTERN UNIVERSITY, EVANSTON, ILLINOIS

IDEA FLOW

         59002 REPRINT
         RUBENSTEIN, A
         AVERY, R
         ≠ IDEA FLOW IN R AND D PROGRAM PROGRAM OF RESEARCH ON THE
         MANAGEMENT OF RESEARCH AND DEVELOPMENT, DEPARTMENT OF INDUSTRIAL
         ENGINEERING AND MANAGEMENT SCIENCES, NORTHWESTERN UNIVERSITY,
         EVANSTON, ILLINOIS

         63001 REPRINT
         RUBENSTEIN, A
         HANNENBERG
         ≠ IDEA FLOW AND PROJECT SELECTION IN SEVERAL INDUSTRIAL R AND D
         LABS ≠
         PROGRAM OF RESEARCH ON THE MANAGEMENT OF RESEARCH AND
         DEVELOPMENT, DEPARTMENT CF INDUSTRIAL ENGINEERING AND MANAGEMENT
         SCIENCES, NORTHWESTERN UNIVERSITY, EVANSTON, ILLINOIS

         63001 FIGURE
         RUBENSTEIN, A
         HANNENBERG
         ≠ FIGURE FOR 63001 ≠
         PROGRAM OF RESEARCH ON THE MANAGEMENT OF RESEARCH AND
         DEVELOPMENT, DEPARTMENT CF INDUSTRIAL ENGINEERING AND MANAGEMENT
         SCIENCES, NORTHWESTERN UNIVERSITY, EVANSTON, ILLINOIS

         63014
         BAKER, N
         ≠ ON IDEA FLOW ≠
         PROGRAM OF RESEARCH ON THE MANAGEMENT OF RESEARCH AND
         DEVELOPMENT, DEPARTMENT CF INDUSTRIAL ENGINEERING AND MANAGEMENT
         SCIENCES, NORTHWESTERN UNIVERSITY, EVANSTON, ILLINOIS
```

Figure 10.8. Project index: A section of the project index is shown. Document number, author, title, and reference are included.

```
60010 REPRINT

        HOROWITZ, I
        ≠ REGRESSION MODELS FOR COMPANY EXPENDITURES ON AND RETURNS FROM
        R AND D ≠
        PROGRAM OF RESEARCH ON THE MANAGEMENT OF RESEARCH AND
        DEVELOPMENT, DEPARTMENT OF INDUSTRIAL ENGINEERING AND MANAGEMENT
        SCIENCES, NORTHWESTERN UNIVERSITY, EVANSTON, ILLINOIS
        1959
        PROJ SEL
        PHD DISSER HOROWITZ
        6 PAGES
        AP JUN72, 5 JUN72
        24

61001 REPRINT

        RUBENSTEIN, A
        ≠ THE JOB OF THE RESEARCH MANAGER CONTRASTED WITH THAT OF OTHER
        MANAGERS IN THE COMPANY ≠
        PROGRAM OF RESEARCH ON THE MANAGEMENT OF RESEARCH AND
        DEVELOPMENT, DEPARTMENT OF INDUSTRIAL ENGINEERING AND MANAGEMENT
        SCIENCES, NORTHWESTERN UNIVERSITY, EVANSTON, ILLINOIS
        JUN 1957
        GENL
        WORKING PAPER IRC
        6 PAGES
        AP JUN72, 68 JUN72
        25

61002

        RUBENSTEIN, A
        MCCOLLY, J
        ≠ PHASES IN THE LIFE CYCLE OF INDUSTRIAL OR GROUPS ≠
        PROGRAM OF RESEARCH ON THE MANAGEMENT OF RESEARCH AND
        DEVELOPMENT, DEPARTMENT CF INDUSTRIAL ENGINEERING AND MANAGEMENT
        SCIENCES, NORTHWESTERN UNIVERSITY, EVANSTON, ILLINOIS
        NOV 1960
        OR / MS
        WORKING PAPER B AND D
        20 PAGES
        AS JUN72, 46 JUN72
        26

61003

        RUBENSTEIN, A
        ≠ OPPORTUNITIES FOR RESEARCH - ON - RESEARCH ≠
        PROGRAM OF RESEARCH ON THE MANAGEMENT OF RESEARCH AND
        DEVELOPMENT, DEPARTMENT CF INDUSTRIAL ENGINEERING AND MANAGEMENT
        SCIENCES, NORTHWESTERN UNIVERSITY, EVANSTON, ILLINOIS
        AUG 1961
        METHOD
        WORKING PAPER TIMS, BRUSSELS AUG 1961
        11 PAGES
        AP JUN72, 87 JUN72
        27
```

Figure 10.9.   Sequential index by DOC number: This index provides
                   complete information for each document. Often a search
                   of the author or project index provides the appropriate
                   document number. Then if more information is desired,
                   the sequential index may be used.

```
NSF WORKING PAPER
    RUBENSTEIN, A
    ' A DECISION - MAKING STUDY OF IDEA GENERATION AND PROJECT
    SELECTION IN INDUSTRIAL R AND D '
    JAN 1962
    62006
        IDEA
NSF PROPOSAL
    RUBENSTEIN, AH
    ' LETTER TO HINES '
    APR 1967
    67016
        LINCOTT
NSF PROPOSAL APRIL 1968
    RUBENSTEIN, AH
    ' STUDIES OF LIAISON, INTERFACE, AND TECHNOLOGY TRANSFER IN R
    AND D '
    APR 1968
    68008
        LINCOTT
NSF PROPOSAL
    POMRAD
    ' DOCTORAL DISSERTATION RESEARCH GRANTS IN THE FIELD OF
    RESEARCH ON THE MANAGEMENT OF R AND D '
    68029
        GENL
NSF PROPOSAL RSCH JAN 1969
    RUBENSTEIN, AH
    ' A REAL - TIME STUDY OF TECHNOLOGY TRANSFER IN INDUSTRY '
    JAN 1969
    69005
        LINCOTT
NSF PROPOSAL
    RUBENSTEIN, AH
    ' A STUDY OF INTERNATIONAL TECHNOLOGY TRANSFER -
    COLLABORATIVE RESEARCH BETWEEN NU AND THE UNIV OF COLOGNE,
    WEST GERMANY '
    SEPT 1969
    69027
        LINCOTT
NSF WORKING PAPER JOHNS HOPKINS
    BUEL *KEGAN, D *ET AL
    ' EXPLORATIONS ON THE INFORMATION SEEKING STYLE OF
    RESEARCHERS '
    NOVEMBER 1969
    69030 REPRINT
        INFO
NSF PROPOSAL
    RUBENSTEIN, AH
    ' PRELIMINARY DRAFT FOR DISCUSSION = SPECIAL PROJECTS IN
    GRADUATE EDUCATION '
    FEB 1970
    70007
        NSF
NSF PROPOSAL PRELIM DISSER PROPOSAL
    HETZNER, W
    AN ANALYSIS OF FACTORS INFLUENCING THE IMPLEMENTATION OF
    INDIGENOUS R AND D RESULTS TO MEDIUM AND SMALL - SCALE USERS
    IN INDIA '
    APR 1971
    71023
        NSF
NSF WORKING PAPER
    RUBENSTEIN, AH
    ' ABOUT THE FIELD OF R ON R AND NORTHWESTERNS POMRAD '
    JULY 1971
    71035
```

Figure 10.10.   Section of the sponsor listing is shown with author, title, date of writing, and document number for reference.

```
NASA REPØRT
   RUBENSTEIN, A
   ' NASA STATUS REPØRT '
   JAN 1964
   64001
      NASA
WØRKING PAPER ANNUAL REPØRT
   RUBENSTEIN, A
   ' ANNUAL REPØRT ØF RESEARCH ØN THE MANAGEMENT ØF RESEARCH '
   JUL 1964
   64016
      GENL
NASA REPØRT EXPENDITURES
   RUBENSTEIN, A
   ' EXPENDITURES ØN NSG 495 / 14 - 07 - 001 THRØUGH JUNE 30,
   1964 '
   JUL 1964
   64016 EXPENDITURES
      NASA
NASA REPØRT SEMI - ANNUAL
   RUBENSTEIN, A H
   ' SEMI - ANNUAL REPØRT TØ NASA '
   JAN 1965
   65007
      GENL
WØRKING PAPER ANNUAL REPØRT 1965
   PØMRAD
   ' ANNUAL REPØRT = 1964 - 65 '
   AUG 1965
   65025
      PRØJ SEL
ØNR REPØRT FINAL REPØRT ØN R AND D SEMINARS
   RUBENSTEIN, AH
   ' A FEASIBILITY STUDY ØF A SERIES ØF SEMINARS ØN RESEARCH -
   ØN - RESEARCH MANAGEMENT '
   JAN 1966
   66001
      SEMINARS
```

Figure 10.11. Section of the type of document listing with author, title, date of writing, and document number for reference.

Document Number	Distribution Code	No. of Pages	Record No.
52001 REPRINT	F JUN72, 0 JUN72	5 PAGES	REC 1
53001 REPRINT	AP JUN72, 11 JUN72	4 PAGES	REC 2
55001 REPRINT	AP JUN72, 60 JUN72	14 PAGES	REC 3
57001 REPRINT	AP JUN72, 34 JUN72	13 PAGES	REC 4
57002 REPRINT	AP JUN72, 6 JUN72	11 PAGES	REC 5
57003 REPRINT	AP JUN72, 124 JUN72	7 PAGES	REC 6
58001	AP JUN72, 18 JUN72	116 PAGES	REC 7
58002 REPRINT	0 JUN72	8 PAGES	REC 8
59001 REPRINT	AP JUN72, 1 JUN72	30 PAGES	REC 9
59002 REPRINT	AP JUN72, 50 JUN72	8 PAGES	REC 10
59003 REPRINT	0 JUN72	8 PAGES	REC 11
59004	AP JUN72, 19 JUN72	15 PAGES	REC 12
59005	AS JUN72, 0 JUN72	70 PAGES	REC 13
59006	F JUN72, 18 JUN72	25 PAGES	REC 14
60001 REPRINT	AS JUN72, 332 JUN72	8 PAGES	REC 15
60002 REPRINT	AS JUN72, 120 JUN72	20 PAGES	REC 16
60003	AP JUN72, 0 JUN72	14 PAGES	REC 17
60004	F JUN72, 272 JUN72	31 PAGES	REC 18
60005 REPRINT	AP JUN72, 38 JUN72	41 PAGES	REC 19
60006	AP JUN72, 89 JUN72	13 PAGES	REC 20

Figure 10.12. Section of DOCUMENT/RIQS inventory status report. The format of the output is document number, distribution code and date set, number of copies available at last inventory date, number of pages, and RIQS record number.

PROPS/RIQS

PROPS/RIQS is a research oriented subsystem designed to provide convenient on-line interrogation of the data base. Indexes are used as guides in referencing that part of the data base which is relevant to a particular search. Indexes of authors, of dependent and independent variables drawn from the propositions, and of keywords are provided.

Most interrogation of the file is done on an on-line real-time basis. The indexes provided by batch operations may be used as guides to begin searching the data base. Eventually the keyword classification system will be the most convenient means for searching the proposition inventory. POMRAD members are currently developing a keywording system which will provide standard terminology on several levels of generality which will allow identification of areas of interest which cut across the range of literature upon which the proposition inventory is based. Equally as important, this keyword strategy will have the flexibility to allow the addition of keywords as new areas of interest are explored. (See Figures 10.13 and 10.14.)

On-Line Searching

Figure 10.15a shows a search for propositions by a specified author. The display specification results in the printing of the author, reference, proposition, and proposition inventory number.

```
RECØRD NUMBER      1
    (1) AUTHØR ØR SØURCE
    UTTERBACK, JAMES M. *
    (2) REFERENCE
    'THE PRØCESS ØF TECHNØLØGICAL INNØVATIØN WITHIN THE FIRM' *
    ACADEMY ØF MANAGEMENT JØURNAL,VØL 14,NUM.  1,PP.  75-88,MARCH,
    PAGE 75.
    (3) DATE ØF PUBLICATIØN
    MARCH 1971
    (4) PRØPØSITIØN INVENTØRY NUMBER
    001
    (5) PRØPØSITIØN,ANECDØTE,ØR GENERALIZATIØN
    THE EFFECTIVENESS ØF FIRMS IN ØRIGINATING , DEVELØPING, AND
    IMPLEMENTING TECHNICAL INNØVATIØNS IS A FUNCTIØN ØF
    CHARACTERISTICS ØF THE FIRM'S ENVIRØNMENT, INTERNAL
    CHARACTERISTICS ØF THE FIRM ITSELF, AND FLØWS BETWEEN THE FIRM
    AND ITS ENVIRØNMENT.
    (6) VARIABLES-INDEPENDENT
    FIRM'S ENVIRØNMENT * INTERNAL CHARACTERISTICS ØF FIRM * FLØWS
    BETWEEN THE FIRM AND ITS ENVIRØNMENT
    (7) VARIABLES-DEPENDENT
    EFFECTIVENESS IN ØRIGINATING, DEVELØPING, AND IMPLEMENTING
    TECHNICAL INNØVATIØNS *
    (9) KEY WØRDS
    TECHNØLØGY TRANSFER * INNØVATIØNS
    (13) NATURE ØF PRØPØSITIØN EVIDENCE * INSTRUMENT
    EXPERIENCE *
    (14) ØRIGIN ØF PRØPØSITIØN
    DIRECT STATEMENT BY AUTHØR
    (15) DEPØSITØR DATE ØF DEPØSIT
    RIFKIN, RØBERT 6-25-73
    (16) RESEARCH QUESTIØN, AREA ØF INTEREST
    TECHNØLØGICAL INNØVATIØN IN FIRMS
    (17) RELATIØN TØ RESEARCH PRØJECT IN PØMRAD
    LINCØTT *
```

Figure 10.13. Printout of a record from the proposition inventory data base.

ADMINISTRATIVE PERSO	MARKETS
ADOPTION	NATIONAL LAB
AEC	NATIONAL LABORATORY
ARGONNE	NEEDS
BARRIER	ORGANIZATION STRUCTU
BARRIERS	PROBLEM SOLVING
COMMUNICATING	TASK ENVIRONMENT
COMMUNICATION	TECHNICAL INFORMATIO
IDEA GENERATION	TECHNICAL PERFORMANC
INFORMATION FLOW	TECHNICAL PERSONNEL
INNOVATION	TECHNOLOGY TRANSFER
INNOVATIONS	WORK SETTING

Figure 10.14. Keyword index: Part of the keyword index for PROPS/RIQS.

On-line searches may be performed for any item of the record. For example, the researcher can search for propositions concerned with specific variables or parameters, or propositions supported by empirical studies, or propositions that were added to the PROPS system during the course of a specific research project. This searching capability is very helpful in forming a small set of related propositions from the hundreds that are in the computer data base.

Figure 10.15b shows a follow-up on the previous search. It results in the printing of all additional information for Record 23. This is a logical extension of the previous search. If the researcher finds an interesting proposition, he can quickly ask for and receive all of the supplementary data such as support for the proposition, information concerning empirical studies of the proposition, and comments of the person who put the proposition in the inventory.

```
RUBENSTEIN, A.  *DØUDS, C.  *NEVITT, M.  *VENARD, J.
   ' EXPERIMENTS IN TECHNØLØGY TRANSFER FRØM ANL TØ THE PUBLIC
AND PRIVATE SECTØRS ' *PØMRAD DØCUMENT 72 / 90, P.  21
2-73
BARRIER - IF ANY CØMPANY CAN ACQUIRE A LICENSE TØ USE A
FEDERAL PATENT ( NØNEXCLUSIVE PATENT LICENSING ) IT WILL
DISCØURAGE THEM FRØM ADØPTING A PIECE ØF TECHNØLØGY FRØM A
NATIØNAL LABØRATØRY.
023
RUBENSTEIN, A.  *DØUDS, C.  *NEVITT, M.  *VENARD, J.
   ' EXPERIMENTS IN TECHNØLØGY TRANSFER FRØM ANL TØ THE PUBLIC
AND PRIVATE SECTØRS ' *PØMRAD DØCUMENT 72 / 90, P.  21
2-73
BARRIER - THE LACK ØF APPRØPRIATE TECHNIQUES, SKILLS, ØR
EQUIPMENT ØN THE PART ØF THE RECIPIENT CAN INHIBIT THR
TECHNØLØGY TRANSFER PRØCESS.
024
```

* * * * *

Figure 10.15a. This is a portion of an on-line search of the PROPS file. The object of the search is to find records where "Rubenstein" is an author. The information provided by the search includes the reference, proposition information, and record number.

```
ENTER SEARCH COMMAND OR TYPE HALT

? BEGIN SEARCH OF RECORD 23 DISPLAY ACROSS RECORD END
SEARCHING INITIATED


RECORD NUMBER    23
     (1) RUBENSTEIN,A. * DOUDS,C. * NEVITT,M. * VENARD,J. (2)
     'EXPERIMENTS IN TECHNOLOGY TRANSFER FROM ANL TO THE PUBLIC AND
     PRIVATE SECTORS' * POMRAD DOCUMENT 72/90, P.  21 (3) 2-73 (4) 023
     (5) BARRIER-IF ANY COMPANY CAN ACQUIRE A LICENSE TO USE A FEDERAL
     PATENT (NONEXCLUSIVE PATENT LICENSING) IT WILL DISCOURAGE THEM
     FROM ADOPTING A PIECE OF TECHNOLOGY FROM A NATIONAL LABORATORY.
     (6) NON-EXCLUSIVE PATENT LICENSING * (7) TECHNOLOGY TRANSFER FROM
     A NATIONAL LABORATORY TO INDUSTRY * (9) TECHNOLOGY TRANSFER * AEC
     * ARGONNE * BARRIER * NATIONAL LABORATORY (12) AEC * AEC *
     ARGONNE NATIONAL LABORATORY (13) EXPERIENCE *
     SPECULATIVE/THEORETICAL (14) RESTATEMENT BY DEPOSITOR (15)
     KASKOVICH 6-22-73 (16) THE TECHNOLOGY TRANSFER PROCESS AT A
     NATIONAL LABORATORY (17) LINCOTT * (18) TO OVERCOME THE BARRIER,
     CHANGE PATENT LAW, FIND SUPPLIERS WHO DONT CARE ABOUT PATENTS,
     EFFECT THE TRANSFER AT A LOW TECHNICAL MATURITY STAGE. (20)
     BARRIER STATEMENT FROM A PROPOSAL TO NSF
```

Figure 10.15b. This figure shows the request for and printing of a complete record from Figure 10.15a. This is a follow-up of the search shown in Figure 10.15a.

Results and Conclusions

We have found RIQS to be a potentially highly useful and flexible information retrieval system. Other research programs may want to consider organizing their information systems so as to make them RIQS-compatible. With the ready availability of remote computer terminals and data-phone couplers, one's data base may readily be searched by inquiring or cooperating with research colleagues at some distance.

As could be expected, a major concern for us was our IIS system design. We wanted to design a system that could be used by researchers and graduate students who were not especially knowledgeable or interested in computers. But more importantly, we wanted a system that *would* be used.

Our initial development of SCALES/RIQS (which occurred while the final phases of RIQS were being developed) provided us with a relatively well-structured user problem against which to pilot test the human side of the subsystem. DOCUMENT/RIQS is also a well-structured user problem; it is designed primarily for its most frequent users—the director of POMRAD and the secretarial staff. The major questions involved in setting up DOCUMENTS/RIQS concerned the desired degree of redundancy in various indexes, questions largely independent of record definition and thus readily experimented with as the users gain greater experience with the system.

PROPS/RIQS was a less structured problem. It had to be able to support a single student doing a course project as well as several researchers investigating complementary areas or the same area. As with the development of the other IIS/RIQS subsystems, after initial discussions, a small test file was created, sample searches and indexes were made, omissions and confusions were noted, and the record definition adjusted.

One of the most difficult issues throughout the IIS/RIQS development was the establishment of consistent, mutually exclusive, meaningful categories. Consider, for example, item (13) in PROPS/RIQS which is "the kind of support the proposition received"—empirical, speculative, descriptive, or anecdotal, supporting a given propositional statement. Some of the gray areas separating these classifications are still being explored.

Another issue we faced was that of using PROPS/RIQS to record items of interest that are not specific proposition statements. This could be an "anecdote," consisting of an incident of interesting data but without a related proposition. After pilot testing and discussion, we developed a means of storing various kinds of relevant information within the PROPS/RIQS format. The flexibility of our PROPS/RIQS subsystem has been evident in the use of the subsystem as an aid to reviewing the literature relevant to a study of factors affecting the technological innovation process.

SERIALS/RIQS is still under development. PROPS/RIQS was needed for two major research projects funded by the National Science Foundation on the R&D/Innovation process, but with its establishment, attention can be redirected to SERIALS—the oldest subsystem in POMRAD's IIS.

One technical question for SERIALS/RIQS is the optimum size of the file. We might keep one current file for items entered during the past few years. This would be a shorter file; therefore, we might expect it would be used more frequently than the longer version. The comprehensive SERIALS/RIQS file would contain articles from the beginning of the collection (over twenty years and ten thousand documents ago) until the recent cutoff date—perhaps four years. This division would permit quicker searches for recent information, while still allowing the more infrequent complete literature searches to be carried out. Two other considerations are (a) the physical limitation of a 2400-foot reel of tape and consequent convenience of reducing the number of times a multiple tape file would have to be entered into the computer, and (b) a reasonable target for initial keypunching, subsystem development, and full implementation.

As could be expected from prior research on how researchers seek and use technical information (cf. the POMRAD info-search projects, Rubenstein, et al.,[17]; Rubenstein, et al.,[18]; Moor,[19]; Kegan,[20]), we found the greatest uncertainties in the design of the SERIALS/RIQS subsystem to be in the human, rather than computer area. How would computer retrieval capability change our users' information-seeking behavior; how could the subsystem design encourage "good" and discourage "bad" behaviors?

In recent years POMRAD has investigated some of the pertinent questions concerning the information-seeking behavior of researchers. Information-seeking style is visualized as a stable behavior pattern, for mature researchers, developed early in the professional lifetime of an individual. The information-seeking styles prevalent in a group may be one determinant of R&D group effectiveness. This series of studies is focused on improving our understanding of the nature of "information style"—both constrained and unconstrained—and examining its sources and consequences.[15]

The largest study completed to date was a field experiment which involved over 90 Chicago area medical researchers throughout a six-month period. The subjects were clinicians, researchers, and supervisors (administrators) in six area hospitals. An information system linking the subjects to a remote storehouse of information was made available. Each participant's reaction to the system was carefully monitored: 52 percent of the researchers, 36 percent of the supervisors, and 23 percent of the clinicians made requests through the experimental system. These differences were statistically significant. It was determined that the previous information-seeking patterns of individuals in each category bore a definite relationship with their use of the new system.

A background questionnaire administered to the participants during the first phase of the study provided data about their information-seeking behavior in each of six areas. There was, for example, a significant difference among the three categories in the type of information that each reported it needed most frequently.

The information needs of each category were reflected in the sources they used to meet those needs. The researchers used written sources more frequently and rated them as more important than did the clinicians. They also utilized libraries, librarians, and automated information systems to a greater extent; these are basically sources of *written* information and are high on formality—the amount of structure that separates a user from the generator of the information.

The clinicians tended to rely more heavily upon verbal sources of information, although the degree of difference did not reach a statistically significant level. Whenever the clinicians frequently used or highly rated a written source, it was usually the type of material that is exchanged within a personal context (presentations delivered at meetings, unpublished papers obtained from colleagues, and the files kept by their department). Most of these are low on formality and are used within a framework of personal interaction.[19]

The supervisors occupied a middle ground between the other two groups. They reported relying to an equal degree on verbal and written sources, although they exhibited a greater tendency than did the clinicians to use written sources and to rate them as very important.

These patterns received statistically significant support from the data obtained when each participant was asked to name the factor he thought most important in influencing the development of his present information-seeking style. The results suggest, for this sample, that past influences had formed the clinician's information-seeking style in such a way that they found it easier to use verbal rather than written sources of information. In retrospect, then, the clinician's response to the new information system was not surprising. The system could be characterized as low in interpersonal activity. The user had no direct contact with the originator of the information and was separated from the source by a number of organizational and mechanical filters.

Another result of this particular study suggests that the probability that an individual will incorporate a new system into his information-seeking repertoire is greater if each of the system's separate components is already familiar, frequently used, and considered important. The data indicated that the group that showed a more favorable reaction to the new system had significantly greater previous experience with the components of the system.

Rubenstein, O'Keefe, and Kernaghan[21] indicate that group cohesiveness is a factor in the adoption of an innovation. Data from the hospital study support the hypothesis that, "The more cohesive a group and the more positive the influence of its supervisor and its gatekeeper, the greater the likelihood that members would adopt the system." Here the system is a new information system. On the other hand, it was hypothesized that a highly cohesive group in which the supervisor and gatekeeper exhibited a negative influence would be less likely to adopt the system. There was support for this hypothesis, also. The results reported suggest that the degree of cohesiveness and the activities of both supervisor and information gatekeepers were important determinants of a group's willingness to use a new information system.

One of the bases of our search for ways to influence information-seeking behavior is a model of information-seeking style of researchers. (Rubenstein, et al.,[17]) The model specifies many variables and parameters of searching behavior, and points out the variety of factors involved in this phenomenon. However, we still need answers to many questions concerning the human aspects of information-seeking behavior and the implementation of information systems.

Future technical questions for IIS and RIQS will involve maximum size of files, time-cost-medium trade-offs (such as tape, disk-pack, resident memory, etc.), and frequency and intensity of use. These are questions dealing with economic aspects of the IIS/RIQS subsystems. Incorporating RIQS into POMRAD has so far benefited the program by permitting greater ease in manipulating and updating our information, increasing our ability to spot and correct errors in our data, and providing a capacity for the researcher to consider and manipulate data almost simultaneously.

It is not clear yet whether the results of our academic research on information related behavior will provide significant transfers of strategy for the design, improvement, and management of our own IIS. This is largely because we have conducted much of our research in environments which differ from our own. We continue, however, to search for individual differences in information needs and information related behavior which would suggest individually tailored components or subsystems that might be effectively adopted within our own IIS. We have learned from studying the information related behavior of researchers that such patterns of behavior are not readily amenable to change. When one designs a system that requires a reorientation of behavioral patterns by mature researchers, one is asking for a great deal and perhaps for more than the mature researcher as potential user is willing to give. This does not assert that changes in the behavioral patterns of potential users are not possible, only that one's expectation of change ought to be that of a rather slow process, that necessitates planning and nurturing. For ourselves we are convinced that to assure a system a modicum of success and acceptance, its designers must be aware of, must capitalize upon, and even exploit what the potential user already knows and what he or she is currently doing. That is, a designer must rely upon the time-tested common sense principle of transfer of training. We found in the hospital study, for example, that the more familiar a researcher was with using each of the several components, the more likely it was that the researcher would accept the information system as useful, and the more likely that he or she would, in fact, use it.

NOTES AND CITED REFERENCES

1. Work in this area has been supported by grants and contracts to the Program of Research on the Management of Research and Development at Northwestern University from the National Aeronautics and Space Administration, National Science Foundation, National Institute of Health, Office of Naval Research, and Army Research Office.

2. Kegan, D. L. and A. H. Rubenstein, "Measures of Trust and Openness," in *Comparative Group Studies,* Vol. 3, Number 2, 1972.

3. Bonjean, C. M., R. J. Hill, and S. D. McLemore, *Sociological Measurement: An Inventory of Scales and Indices.* San Francisco: Chandler, 1967.

4. Buros, E. K. (ed.), *Mental Measurements Yearbook.* Highland Park, New Jersey: Gryphon Press, 1965.

5. Miller, D. C., *Handbook of Research Design and Social Measurement.* New York: David McKay, 1964.

6. Robinson, J. P., J. G. Rusk, and K. B. Head, *Measures of Political Attitudes.* Ann Arbor, Mich.: Institute for Social Research, 1968.

7. Robinson, J. P. and P. R. Shaver, *Measures of Social Psychological Attitudes.* Ann Arbor, Mich.: Institute for Social Research, 1969.

8. Shaw, M. E. and J. M. Wright, *Scales for the Measurement of Attitudes.* New York: McGraw-Hill, 1967.

9. Price, J. L., *Handbook of Organizational Measurement.* Lexington, Mass: D. C. Heath, 1972.

10. Lake, D. G., M. B. Miles, and R. B. Earle (eds.). *Measuring Human Behavior: Tolls for the Assessment of Social Functioning.* New York: Teachers College Press, 1973.

11. SCALES is available only for in-person use. Inquiries by mail or telephone cannot be processed.

12. March, J. G. and H. A. Simon, *Organizations.* New York: Wiley, 1958.

13. Berelson, B., and G. A. Steiner, *Human Behavior: An Inventory of Scientific Findings.* New York: Harcourt, Brace, 1964.

14. Price, J. L., *Organizational Effectiveness: An Inventory of Propositions.* Homewood, Illinois: Irwin Dorsey, 1968.

15. POMRAD, "Annual Report and Program Summary." Program of Research on the Management of Research and Development, Department of Industrial Engineering and Management Sciences, Northwestern University, 1972.

16. The current membership of POMRAD is approximately 35-40, with approximately 15 alumni of the program now at other universities and research organizations.

17. Rubenstein, A. H., R. W. Trueswell, G. J. Rath, and D. J. Werner, "Some Preliminary Experiments and a Model of Information-Seeking Style of Researchers," *Proceedings: 20th National Conference on the Administration of Research,* Miami, Florida, October, 1966.

18. Rubenstein, A. H., G. J. Rath, R. D. O'Keefe, J. A. Kernaghan, E. A. Moore, W. C. Moor, and D. J. Werner, "Factors Influencing the Adoption of An Experimental Information System by Medical Researchers and Clinicians." *Hospital Administration,* 18, 4, pp. 27-42, 1973.

19. Moor, W. C., "An Empirical Study of the Relationship Between Personality Traits of Research and Development Personnel and Dimensions of Information Systems and Sources." Unpublished Doctoral Dissertation, Northwestern University, 1969.

20. Kegan, Daniel L., "Measures of the Usefulness of Written Technical Information to Chemical Researchers," *Journal of the American Society for Information Science,* Vol. 21, No. 3, pp. 179-186, 1970.

21. Rubenstein, A. H., R. D. O'Keefe, and J. A. Kernaghan. "Group Cohesiveness as a Factor in the Adoption of Innovation." Working paper, POMRAD, 1971.

Chapter 11

The Destruction of a Myth: A Demographic Spatial Analysis

PAUL CARTWRIGHT
McGill University

RICHARD HAY, JR.
Northwestern University

Introduction

The Northwestern Community Council (NCC) was created in 1969 in response to wide-spread demands for student participation in the governance of the university. Composed of students, faculty, and administrators, it was given a broad mandate to serve as an elected advisory body to the President of the university. To enhance NCC's effectiveness as a means for student participation, and to provide various groups within the university, especially the students, with the information base from which to make considered decisions, NCC was provided with funds for a research staff, the NCCRS. During its first years, the authors (recent NU graduates) served as the principal staff members. One of our first efforts was analysis of the demographic patterns of off-campus student housing.[1]

It was common knowledge that, due to a shortage of dormitory space and a change in life styles, a large number of NU students chose to live off-campus. Across the country in the late 1960s such off-campus communities of students emerged as culturally unique actors, in both the life of the university and its host town. Though of the university, they were largely outside of its control; and, though not natives of the town, they exerted a large influence on its civic life (the most profound example being, perhaps, the People's Park confrontation at Berkeley). As in most university communities, increased attention was being focused on the off-campus student community at Northwestern. However, it was soon discovered that little or no information existed on the nature of this community—its size, content, spatial distribution, etc.

Hence, demographic research was embarked upon in response to a long-standing need for such information. Student government, community organizers, various political organizations, and both the university and city planning departments had expressed a need to

208

know—at very least—where students were geographically located. Further, they wished to know what types of students were living where—for example, did more men live off-campus than women? Given a limited amount of time and money, our efforts were aimed at producing a Demographic Handbook containing (a) population distribution maps, and (b) numerical descriptions of the population in terms of four variables: sex, class, school and fraternal affiliation. The individual organizations could then analyze this data in terms of their own needs.

In the early stages of our investigation it readily became apparent that we would have to employ some kind of computerized information processing. The classic problems of limited resources (both of time and money), a large amount of data to be analyzed (records of approximately 10,000 students), and the desire to investigate interrelationships among several factors for all of the data (a process which, if done by hand, would have been laboriously prolonged), naturally lead us in the direction of computerized operations. Furthermore, the data was already available in machine-readable form as the student main file of the Registrar's Office. Not only would we cut our data collection costs, but we would demonstrate the feasibility of adapting data resources *already* within the institution for use in NCC's efforts to bring more groups into the decision making process.

After looking at the alternatives and conducting some preliminary testing, we decided to use the RIQS system as the basis of our analytical efforts. A major consideration in this decision was the textual nature of a large amount of our data, i.e., name of student, street name, town name, etc. To recode all of this into a numerical schema—as required by most canned analysis programs—would have been both time consuming and dysfunctional. RIQS, however, had broad capabilities for working with both the textual and numerical material. In addition, RIQS allows the record structure to be user-defined, so that it easily accommodated our particular data organization and performed the necessary data manipulation, thus saving us the time, money, and effort required for the writing of our own set of analysis programs.

The Data

Since our first interest was in examining the relationship between students and geographic space, the data was initially arranged with the student as the unit of analysis. This arrangement was consonant with that of the Registrar's Office. Each student, then, formed a record; specific parts of information concerning a student became items in the record. The following items were used: Name (first, last), street number, street name, city name, state name, zip code, school code (indicating what school within the university the student was enrolled in), class code, sex, fraternal affiliation. All items were defined as alphanumeric except for item two (street number) and item eight (class code) which were defined as integer. (See Figure 11.1.)

In the course of the research, several questions were raised regarding our use of biographic data, i.e., data in which no effort is made to provide for the anonymity of those about whom data was collected. The data used was available to the university community in an annual directory published by the university. Figure 11.2 illustrates the directory entry and its corresponding entry in the RIQS file.

Thus, no substantive information existed on the RIQS file which was not already easily and consensually available to the public. For this reason, though individual consent was not obtained, we felt that we had not violated the privacy of individual students. Nevertheless, access to the RIQS file was strictly limited. This was accomplished through the

```
ITEM NUMBERS AND NAMES
----------------------

 1.  NAME
 2.  STREET NUMBER
 3.  STREET
 4.  CITY
 5.  STATE
 6.  ZIP
 7.  SCHØØL
 8.  CLASS
 9.  SEX
10.  AFFILIATIØN
```

Figure 11.1. Items of information contained in each student record.

S-STUDENT SECTION

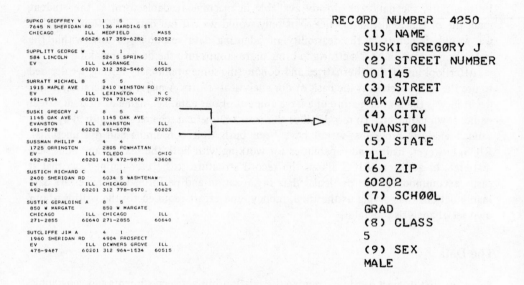

Figure 11.2. Correspondence between information contained in the
student directory and its subsequent use in the RIQS file.

use of a double password system—knowledge of the first password enables one to access his file; a second password is necessary to initiate RIQS processing of the file.

Research Strategy

The data was obtained from the Registrar on punched cards and translated into a form suitable for RIQS input by a small user-written program. A master RIQS file was then created containing information on all students who lived off-campus. Several systematic errors were discovered in the data by random visual scanning of the file and by specific queries through the RIQS system. The UPDATE phase of RIQS then made it extremely easy to correct those records which had mistakes. In preparation for analysis five searches were performed to place the off-campus students into one of the five spatially defined groups. (See Figure 11.3.)

```
ENTER SEARCH CØMMAND ØR TYPE HALT

? IF #4 EQ 'EVANSTØN' PLACE IN SET 10,
? DEFINE SET 10 AS 'CITY ØF EVANSTØN',
? SPSSFILE 1 ØF #3 #7, #8 #9, #10;
? IF #6 EQ '60626' PLACE IN SET 11,
? DEFINE SET 11 AS 'CHICAGØ - RØGERS PARK'
? SPSSFILE 2 ØF #3 #7 THRU #10;
? IF #4 EQ 'CHICAGØ' AND #6 NE '60626' PLACE IN SET 12
? DEFINE SET 12 AS 'CHICAGØ - ØUTSIDE RØGERS PARK'
? SPSSFILE 3 ØF #3 #7 THRU #10; END


NØ. ØF RECØRDS ADDED TØ SET 10 BY SEARCH = 2436
NØ. ØF RECØRDS  IN  SET  10 AFTER SEARCH = 2436



NØ. ØF RECØRDS ADDED TØ SET 11 BY SEARCH =  496
NØ. ØF RECØRDS  IN  SET  11 AFTER SEARCH =  496



NØ. ØF RECØRDS ADDED TØ SET 12 BY SEARCH =  723
NØ. ØF RECØRDS  IN  SET  12 AFTER SEARCH =  723
```

Figure 11.3. Sample search commands used to separate students into spatially differentiated groups.

These groups were:

1. those living in the City of Evanston;
2. those living in a far north section of Chicago called Rogers Park;
3. those living in Chicago but outside Rogers Park;
4. those living in Illinois outside of Chicago and Evanston; and
5. those living outside of Illinois.

After checking the composition of each group, it was decided to redefine the boundaries of the Rogers Park area and a new set was formed using that refined criteria. Having separated the students into mutually exclusive geographic groups, we began to analyze each group. The index feature of RIQS was used to order the various groups. For example, we were interested in obtaining the location of each Evanston student ordered by the street that he or she lived on. We could then plot that information (either by hand or by computer) and begin to observe the comparative density pattern. Hence, for Evanston students, we indexed by street name, printed the street number, and arranged the street number in ascending order for each street.

```
RIQS
ACCESS STUDENT FILE
INDEX ON SET 1
KWOC ON (3) USING STOP WORDS A, APT, APTS, AV, AVE, BLVD, CT, D, DR, E, EAST,
1, 2, B, BL, HOTEL, O, R, REAR, BLV, BUREN, GROVE, GLEN, HWY, L, LAKE, LE,
BOX,LA,
M,NEW,PAR,STREET,T,STREE,TE,MAWR,PLAIN,FT,LN,N,PK,PL,RD,S,SG,ST,TER,TERR,W,WEST.
PRINT (2).
```

Figure 11.4a. Instructions to RIQS used to produce the index of student addresses by street name.

```
AUSTIN                              BRUMMEL

        001030                              000619

        000727                              000619

AVERS                                       000619

        009354                              000619

BARTON                                      001920

        000520                              001511

        000520              BRYANT

        000520                              002712

BENNETT                                     002744

        002536              BURNHAM

BROADWAY                                    000200

        002707                              000200

        002737                              000200

BROWN                       CALLAN

        001019                              000333

        001019                              000320

        001001                              000143

        001001                              000329

        001019                              000333

        001019              CARRIAGE

        001001                              000515

        000913              CASE

        002310                              000829

        001001
```

Figure 11.4b. INDEX output showing addresses of students
living on specific streets.

It should be noted that RIQS cannot index on more than one "key," and a small user-written post-processor was necessary to put the street numbers in ascending order.[2] The stop word capability of RIQS proved useful here, enabling student residences to be indexed only on the true street name and not on the extraneous lane, parkway, road, etc. that are part of the street nomenclature of every town (Figure 11.4). Different indexing criteria were employed depending on the nature of the group being worked with. For the small number of students living outside the Evanston–Chicago area, we indexed by item four—name of the city.

The second major goal of the project was calculation of aggregate statistics indicating distributional differences in residence on the basis of several key variables such as school, class, and sex (fraternal affiliation was found to be grossly inaccurate and was not employed). For instance, we hypothesized that men were more likely to live off-campus than women, that relatively liberal Arts and Sciences students were more likely to live off-campus than their more conservative Technological Institute counterparts, and that a large percentage of off-campus students chose to live in a section of Rogers Park referred to as "the Jungle" because its rents are cheaper than in the more expensive Evanston area. The SPSSFILE capability of RIQS was used to automatically create a file that was immediately capable of being processed by SPSS (Statistical Package for the Social Sciences).

Using SPSS[3], a frequency distribution of the variables school, class and sex was calculated for each of the five geographic groups. (Figures 11.5a and 11.5b.)

```
? SPSSLINK 1
SPSS-ØNLINE
NEW VERSIØN-PRØGRAM LIBRARY WRITEUP NUCC296
USE ØVER 100 VARIABLES ØR ØVER 5 SUBFILES? N
USE A SAVE-FILE THIS RUN? Y
AUTØ-MØDE.
? 1. GET FILE;STUDENT
? 10. PRINT FØRMATS;I007S000(A)
? 15. CØDEBØØK;I007S000
? 99. FINISH
? EXECUTE
ENTERING SPSS.
 SPSSØNLINE - NØRTHWESTERN UNIVERSITY (V3.0)

 - - - CØDEBØØK - - -

 SUBFILE

 VARIABLE - I007S000    SCHØØL

 VALUE LABEL      VALUE      FREQ  REL %  ADJ %  CUM %

                  CAS        768   31.5   31.5   31.5
                  ED          84    3.4    3.4   35.0
                  GRAD       980   40.2   40.2   75.2
                  JØUR       173    7.1    7.1   82.3
                  MUS        133    5.5    5.5   87.8
                  SPCH       205    8.4    8.4   96.2
                  TECH        93    3.8    3.8  100.0
                  BLANK        0    0.0   ****  100.0

                  TØTAL     2436  100.0  100.0  100.0


 ØBSERVATIØNS: VALID -    2436      MISSING -          0
```

Figure 11.5a. Frequency counts of school variable for Evanston group.

```
 SPSSØNLINE - NØRTHWESTERN UNIVERSITY (V3.0)

 - - - CØDEBØØK - - -

 SUBFILE

 VARIABLE - I009S000    SEX

 VALUE LABEL      VALUE      FREQ  REL %  ADJ %  CUM %

                  FEMALE     841   34.5   34.5   34.5
                  MALE      1595   65.5   65.5  100.0
                  BLANK        0    0.0   ****  100.0

                  TØTAL     2436  100.0  100.0  100.0


 ØBSERVATIØNS: VALID -    2436      MISSING -          0
```

Figure 11.5b. Frequency counts for sex variable for Evanston group.

The raw Ns were then used in the preparation of the Inter-Area Parameter Table which indicates differences between the areas in terms of percentage of students living there.

TABLE 1a. School

	Educ.	Journ.	CAS	Music	Speech	Tech.	Grad.	Population
Campus	61.0	55.6	65.0	43.9	63.1	64.7	17.3	51.0
Evanston	20.7	28.5	19.6	27.7	25.0	11.9	41.9	26.0
	(84)	(173)	(768)	(133)	(205)	(93)	(980)	(2436)
Rogers Park	3.2	3.6	2.9	5.2	2.6	3.8	11.5	5.3
Chicago–Other	4.9	4.8	5.6	10.6	4.3	7.8	13.1	7.7
Illinois–Other	10.3	4.6	6.6	11.6	4.6	8.8	14.6	8.9
Non–Illinois	0.5	3.0	0.3	1.0	0.4	2.9	1.7	1.1
	100.6	100.1	100.0	100.0	100.0	99.9	100.1	100.0
N	408	608	3919	481	819	781	2339	9335

TABLE 1b. Class

	Fresh	Soph	Junior	Senior	Grad	Special	Population
Campus	83.8	75.7	56.1	40.4	17.7	8.3	51.0
Evanston	3.0	13.0	27.8	38.3	41.4	32.1	26.0
Rogers Park	0.5	1.9	3.1	6.6	11.3	4.8	5.3
Chicago–Other	5.5	4.2	5.6	6.1	13.1	19.0	7.7
Illinois–Other	6.9	4.8	6.9	7.1	14.2	34.5	8.9
Non–Illinois	0.3	0.4	0.5	1.5	2.2	1.2	1.1
	100.0	100.0	100.0	100.0	99.9	99.9	100.0
N	1892	1550	1604	1561	2664	84	9335

TABLE 1c. Sex

	Male	Female	Population
Campus	48.0	55.7	51.0
Evanston	27.7	23.4	26.0
	(1595)	(841)	(2436)
Rogers Park	5.9	4.2	5.3
Chicago–Other	8.1	7.1	7.7
Illinois–Other	9.2	8.6	8.9
Non–Illinois	1.2	0.9	1.1
	100.1	99.9	100.0
N	5768	3587	9335

All figures are percentages.
The real sum of each column equals 100%. Discrepancy due to rounding error.
The raw N's calculated by SPSS in Figures 5a and 5b are shown in parentheses.

Table 11.1. Inter–Area Parameter Tables

After obtaining the desired statistics, we realized that most of the hypotheses were not proven to be very strong; some were, in fact, refuted. For example, only 0.3 of a percentage point separates the number of CAS students living off-campus from the number of Tech students—clearly demolishing that hypothesis. Similar lack of differences can be seen for male versus female. Further examination of the data yielded other interesting results, among them the indication that few students presently lived in "the Jungle"— an area with a traditional reputation of being a student ghetto. We thus concluded that many commonly held community beliefs about the number and nature of those students living off-campus were based more perhaps on historical myth than upon present reality.

Results and Conclusions

The existence of a sizeable off-campus community, even in a medium-sized town such as Evanston, has a large impact—both in its fact and perhaps more so in its myth. Such an impact is usually exaggerated by the perceived disparity of life styles, financial resources, mores, and political beliefs between the students and other town residents. Such perceptions are often misleading and often work to the detriment of the students involved, and in a wider sense, to the detriment of the university itself. Through the Demographic Handbook, we hoped to provide a new and more productive perspective from which to view certain problems of the university community. While the theoretical nature of the work was admittedly minimal, we believe that the descriptive data obtained was well worth the effort. Our results helped to clarify or support a few myths and dispel many others. We produced hard data where before there was only conjecture and crude impression. The results are publicly available and have already been used in voter registration programs, in mobility research, and in discussion of university tax obligations. More importantly, they have been used by students in the analysis, planning and direction of their own community.

In terms of research parlance, the optimal research environment is often defined as one in which the tools used (i.e., the computer) are transparent to the user. They enable him to achieve his goal, while impinging little upon his workaday consciousness. Such, however, is seldom the case in the real world. Indeed, one soon learns that one does not transparently *use* the RIQS system. Rather, one totally experiences it—to the betterment or worse of one's individual psyche (the system suffers not). We must admit that, on the whole, our experiences were definitely on the positive side, with RIQS doing everything we expected and sometimes a few enlightening and beneficial things that we did not expect.

Information systems and computers in general are often held in disdain by social critics as being agents of centralized, oppressive power (a la 1984). In practice, they often tend to be agents of impersonal mediocrity (i.e., incorrect credit references, billing mistakes, etc.). It is our hope that they be recognized as tools, with certain inherent advantages and limitations, and that these tools be made available to those affected by decisions as well as those making them.

NOTES

1. We would like to thank Jeremy Wilson and Gabor Zsolnay of the Northwestern University Planning Department and Lorraine Borman and Donald Dillaman of the Vogelback Computing Center for their assistance and support in the preparation of "A Demographic Handbook of Northwestern."

2. Several added enhancements are scheduled to be added to the RIQS system in the near future, among them the ability to do multi-key indexes.

3. An on-line, interactive version of SPSS developed at Vogelback Computing Center was used to perform the analysis.

Chapter 12

System Performance Evaluation of Interactive Retrieval

WAYNE D. DOMINICK
Northwestern University

The Problem

An often neglected aspect of implementing on-line software is the problem of effective system monitoring and performance evaluation. This problem takes on many facets: gathering data on user/system interactions, storing and processing these data, and generating summary reports and plots which can be used to pinpoint system deficiencies and to suggest modifications and improvements to the system. The purpose of this study was to develop monitoring techniques for the RIQSONLINE information retrieval system and to provide the framework for conducting performance evaluations of that system. The methodology employed was to instrument the RIQSONLINE processor with monitoring routines designed to collect data on user on-line interactions with the system and to produce a RIQS-compatible data base of all monitored information.[1] With this approach, the RIQS system is used both to monitor itself and to process the monitored data.

By the very nature of its design objectives, a user-oriented program or system must include within its capabilities the collection and feedback to the system designers of appropriate usage statistics. A system that ignores this aspect can never become truly responsive to the continually varying needs of its user community.

If a system is designed for on-line interactive processing, an automated monitoring of user/system interactions is indispensable.[2] In such an interactive mode of access, user requests of the system are often spontaneously generated rather than prepared and well thought out in advance. Thus a user's demands of the system tend often to reflect what he expects that the system should be able to do rather than what he knows, from a detailed study of available manuals, that the system can do. System designers that neglect such monitoring may tend to overlook many valuable capabilities and implicitly suggested

216

improvements to the system that they, themselves, may not have initially recognized or deemed useful.

The required extent of such interaction monitoring is certainly dependent upon the particular system, but it should at least provide for the collection of such information as: the type of application for which the system is being used, the system capabilities most frequently utilized, the errors made by users in attempting to work within the framework of the system, the type of features users seem to expect from the system that are not provided for by the system, and user comments including bug reporting and suggested system improvements. Interaction monitoring can thus represent a viable method for accomplishing user/system interaction evaluation, including an examination of the on-line query language design: its ease of learning and ease of usage and the error diagnosis/ recovery procedures of the system.

The foregoing analysis presented only one aspect of on-line system performance monitoring, i.e., interaction monitoring for system responsiveness to the user. There is an entirely different aspect of system performance that must also be adequately monitored— the effectiveness and efficiency of the system in performing the tasks that it purports to accomplish.

In order to measure this aspect of system performance, the functioning of the system should be observed over the entire spectrum of user applications. This can be effected by first hypothesizing what the critical phases or processes in the execution of the system are, and then instrumenting the system with a monitor or log generator to record, for each execution of each such phase, appropriate data such as: the type of phase or process currently being executed, the time of occurrence or duration of that process, possibly the system resources required by that process, and whatever other factors influence or distinguish the execution of the process. At the termination of the appropriate phase or phases, indication could be entered into the log indicating the success or failure of the user's request. Since this discussion is directed toward on-line applications, the timings mentioned above should be recorded both in real time (or elapsed real time) for on-line response time analysis and in central processor (CP) and input/output (I/O) time for system efficiency analysis. Subsequent analysis of this monitored data should provide valuable insight into both the effectiveness and the execution efficiency of the system, over a wide range of user applications, indicating where the system bottlenecks, if any, are located and where further developmental effort should be directed. Additionally, the data analysis should indicate whether the originally hypothesized phases or processes were, in actuality, the critical ones or whether further additions or subdivisions of these phases should be incorporated into the monitoring facility.

The concept of system self-monitoring—instrumenting a system so as to monitor its own processing—provides an ideal approach toward effecting both user/system interaction evaluation as well as evaluation of system execution efficiency. No other system evaluation technique—simulation, benchmarking, recall-precision studies, etc.—can address both of these areas. However, since the self-monitoring facility itself requires system resources and thus causes some degradation of the system's response time and efficiency, careful controlled experiments must be performed to determine accurately the overhead associated with the data collection.Those statistics must be continually weighted against the usefulness of the monitored data to provide guidelines for reductions in or extensions to the monitor.

The above capabilities should provide a workable framework for both evaluating the system at any point in time and also for maintaining an historical data base of monitored data for evaluating the effect of additions and modifications to the system. These monitoring/evaluation processes can thus be a viable management tool for periodically assessing a system's reliability, effectiveness, efficiency and responsiveness to the user community for which it was developed.

The remainder of this chapter will examine the data collected by the monitor, the processing done on these data and the results of the study. For these analyses, the full capabilities of the RIQSONLINE system were employed, including selective retrieval, statistical processing via the link to SPSS (the Statistical Package for the Social Sciences) and graphical processing via the RIQSONLINE graphics package for data plotting.

The Data

The data base (RIQSLOG) consists of data collected from monitoring of actual user interactions with the RIQSONLINE system. Each record in the data base represents one user access of the system, from log-on to log-off. The data base record format and schema layout are shown in Figures 12.1 and 12.2, respectively, with a sample record shown in Figure 12.3.

Data items 1 through 10 are single-valued entries consisting of log-on information such as the date of access, real and central processor (CP) time on and statistics representing the data base to be searched. Additionally, since various levels of monitoring options are available to the user for data base privacy, an indication of the user-allowed monitoring level is recorded, as well as the user's name and department or affiliation, if the user allows his searches to be monitored. Data items 11 through 24 are multiple-valued entries, with the corresponding subitems of each representing the queries performed over the data base. When the user has indicated that he is done searching his data base (via a HALT or STOP type-in), he is queried for any comments about the system, which are recorded on the log file in item 25, and finally items 26 through 29 are recorded indicating the errors made during the access and log-off timings. All of the real time entries in the data base utilize the RIQS units capability for storing data in terms of hours, minutes and seconds.

In accordance with the system evaluation objectives outlined in the previous section, the above items collected by the RIQSONLINE monitor far from exhaust the totality of data available for monitoring. These items were selectively chosen as representing the most critical areas of RIQSONLINE execution processing and/or the most significant aspects of the user/system interaction processing.

As can be seen from the record format, this is a highly numerically oriented data base and thus lends itself well to the management information system capabilities of RIQS. While the existing RIQSLOG data base consists of approximately 1000 records involving over 5000 separate queries over many different data bases, this chapter will examine only a small subset of this total population. In particular, the selected subset consists of some 130 on-line sessions (data base records) containing approximately 625 individual queries against a bibliographic data base.

Research Strategy

The primary analyses performed on the data include the calculation of summary statistics over the data base including frequency counts, means, standard deviations, and correlations as well as the generation of numerous data plots illustrating the relationship between

```
RIQS
CREATE LOG FILE


RECORD DEFINITION

(1) DATE OF ACCESS
(2) REAL TIME ON
(3) C.P. TIME ON
(4) FILE NAME ACCESSED
(5) TOTAL NUMBER OF RECORDS IN FILE
(6) NUMBER OF ACTIVE RECORDS IN FILE
(7) NUMBER OF WORDS IN FILE
(8) AVERAGE NUMBER OF WORDS PER RECORD
(9) MONITOR ON OR OFF
(10) USER'S NAME AND DEPARTMENT
(11) REAL TIME OF FIRST SEARCH COMMAND REQUESTED
(12) C.P. TIME OF FIRST SEARCH COMMAND REQUESTED
(13) SEARCH TEXT
(14) NUMBER OF SEARCH TERMS
(15) REAL TIME OF SEARCHING INITIATED

(16) C.P. TIME OF SEARCHING INITIATED
(17) NUMBER OF RECORDS SCANNED
(18) REAL TIME OF SEARCHING COMPLETE
(19) C.P. TIME OF SEARCHING COMPLETE
(20) NUMBER OF PRINT REPORTS
(21) NUMBER OF WORDS IN PRINT REPORTS
(22) NUMBER OF DISPLAY REPORTS
(23) NUMBER OF WORDS IN DISPLAY REPORTS
(24) DISPLAY REPORTS LISTED OR DIVERTED
(25) COMMENTS
(26) TOTAL NUMBER OF USER ERRORS
(27) NUMBER OF ERRORS OF EACH TYPE
(28) REAL TIME OFF
(29) C.P. TIME OFF


MULTIPLE (11) THRU (24), (27)


DATA RESTRICTIONS
TYPES

INTEGER (5) THRU (8), (14),(17),(20) THRU (23),(26),(27)
DATE WITH FORMAT MM/DD/YY (1)
INTEGER WITH UNITS 1HR=60MIN, 1MIN=60SEC (2),(11),(15),(18),(28)
DECIMAL (3),(12),(16),(19),(29)
```

Figure 12.1. RIQSLOG record format.

variables under differing conditions. Several examples of the use of RIQSONLINE to perform these analyses follow.

The first example, shown in Figure 12.4, illustrates the use of the standard procedures MEAN and STDDEV by computing these statistics for the total real time and total central processor (CP) time of the RIQSONLINE accesses contained in this log data base. Real time and CP time are stored in the data base in number of seconds. The variables REALTIME and CPTIME are the input parameters to the procedures and the variables MEANR, MEANCP, STDR and STDCP are the output variables in which the results of the computations are returned. After the procedure calls have been executed, these output variables are available to the user to perform additional calculations, or merely to be displayed as this example illustrates.

The use of procedures as a means for defining a collection of statements to be treated as a unit and called into execution whenever needed is extremely useful in an environment in which the user desires to execute the same statements over different sets of records or depending upon differing combinations of conditions. An example of this application

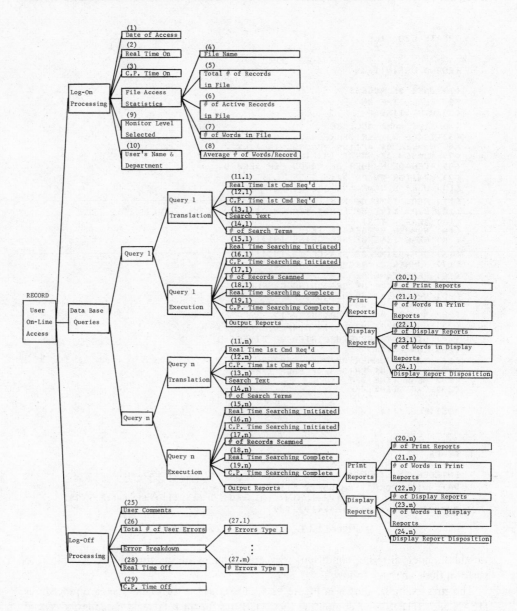

Figure 12.2. RIQSLOG record schema.

using the RIQS log file involved analyzing the relationship between the elapsed central processor time for the execution of a query and the size of the output reports generated by that query. It is essential to have a procedure to perform the desired calculations of these values, and thus be able to execute the procedure repeatedly over specified groups of data base records depending upon the date of system access, the data file that was searched, the size of the data file, etc.

```
1.  DATE ØF ACCESS
        05/25/72
2.  REAL TIME ØN
        14HR,49MIN,26SEC
3.  C.P. TIME ØN
        .181
4.  FILE NAME ACCESSED
        ASIS
5.  TØTAL NUMBER ØF RECØRDS IN FILE
        157
6.  NUMBER ØF ACTIVE RECØRDS IN FILE
        157
7.  NUMBER ØF WØRDS IN FILE
        55168
8.  AVERAGE NUMBER ØF WØRDS PER RECØRD
        351
9.  MØNITØR ØN ØR ØFF
        ØN
10. USER'S NAME AND DEPARTMENT
        WAYNE DØMINICK, CØMPUTER SCIENCE DEPT
11. REAL TIME ØF FIRST SEARCH CØMMAND REQUESTED
        SUB-1....  14HR,50MIN,07SEC
        SUB-2....  14HR,53MIN,24SEC
        SUB-3....  14HR,55MIN,47SEC
        SUB-4....  14HR,57MIN,54SEC
12. C.P. TIME ØF FIRST SEARCH CØMMAND REQUESTED
        SUB-1....  .209
        SUB-2....  1.731
        SUB-3....  29.916
        SUB-4....  33.373
13. SEARCH TEXT
        SUB-1....  BEGIN SEARCH IF # 6 GE MAY, 1968 AND # 6 LE NØV,
                   1968 THEN PUT IN SET 2 ; IF # 13 EQ ( ' LANGUAGE '
                   ØR ' LANGUAGES ' ) AND # 13 NE ( ' PRØGRAMMING '
                   ØR ' GRAPHIC ' ) THEN PUT IN SET 3 ; FØR N = 1 TØ
                   LAST IF # 15. N GE 5.00 AND # 15. N LE 5.99 THEN
                   PUT IN SET 4 ; LØØP ; END
        SUB-2....  BEFØRE SEARCH PRINT ' LISTING ØF ENTIRE - ASIS -
                   FILE ' ; BEGIN SEARCH PRINT RECØRD ; END
        SUB-3....  BEGIN SEARCH IF # 14 EQ ( ' CØMPILE ' ØR '
                   CØMPILER ' ØR ' SYNTAX ' ) THEN DISPLAY RECØRD ;
                   END
        SUB-4....  HALT
14. NUMBER ØF SEARCH TERMS
        SUB-1....  4
        SUB-2....  0
        SUB-3....  3
15. REAL TIME ØF SEARCHING INITIATED
        SUB-1....  14HR,53MIN,06SEC
        SUB-2....  14HR,55MIN,00SEC
        SUB-3....  14HR,57MIN,23SEC
16. C.P. TIME ØF SEARCHING INITIATED
        SUB-1....  .322
        SUB-2....  1.771
        SUB-3....  29.959
17. NUMBER ØF RECØRDS SCANNED
        SUB-1....  157
        SUB-2....  157
        SUB-3....  157
18. REAL TIME ØF SEARCHING CØMPLETE
        SUB-1....  14HR,53MIN,19SEC
        SUB-2....  14HR,55MIN,39SEC
        SUB-3....  14HR,57MIN,31SEC
19. C.P. TIME ØF SEARCHING CØMPLETE
        SUB-1....  1.686
        SUB-2....  29.883
        SUB-3....  33.332
20. NUMBER ØF PRINT REPØRTS
        SUB-1....  0
        SUB-2....  157
        SUB-3....  0
21. NUMBER ØF WØRDS IN PRINT REPØRTS
        SUB-1....  0
        SUB-2....  26043
        SUB-3....  0
22. NUMBER ØF DISPLAY REPØRTS
        SUB-1....  0
        SUB-2....  0
        SUB-3....  15
23. NUMBER ØF WØRDS IN DISPLAY REPØRTS
        SUB-1....  0
        SUB-2....  0
        SUB-3....  2858
24. DISPLAY REPØRTS LISTED ØR DIVERTED
        SUB-3....  DISPLY FILE DIVERTED TØ V
25. CØMMENTS
        SAMPLE RIQSLØG RECØRD
26. TØTAL NUMBER ØF USER ERRØRS
        0
28. REAL TIME ØFF
        14HR,59MIN,07SEC
29. C.P. TIME ØFF
        33.401
```

Figure 12.3.   Sample RIQSLOG record.

```
ENTER SEARCH CØMMAND ØR TYPE HALT

? BEGIN SEARCH
? LET REALTIME=(#28-#2)/60  LET CPTIME=#29-#3
? CALL MEAN(REALTIME,MEANR)
? CALL MEAN(CPTIME,MEANCP)
? CALL STDDEV(REALTIME,STDR)
? CALL STDDEV(CPTIME,STDCP)
? AFTER SEARCH
? DISPLAY ACRØSS 'REAL TIME (IN MINUTES)' / TAB 10 'MEAN=' MEANR  /
? TAB 10 'STDDEV=' STDR SKIP 2 'C.P. TIME (IN SECØNDS)' /
? TAB 10 'MEAN=' MEANCP / TAB 10 'STDDEV=' STDCP
? END

BEFØRE SEARCH

SEARCHING INITIATED

AFTER SEARCH
      REAL TIME (IN MINUTES)
              MEAN= 19.2
              STDDEV= 21.6

      C.P. TIME (IN SECØNDS)
              MEAN= 4.14
              STDDEV= 6.91
```

Figure 12.4. Statistical calculations: Means and standard deviations.

For this purpose, the following procedure was defined. The intent of the procedure is to check for existence of the data items containing CP timings and output report size and compute and return a CP duration (#19.I-#16.I) and a total report size (#21.I+#23.I) for each monitored query over which the procedure is executed. Formal parameter "I" represents the index into the multiple-valued data items containing the timings and report sizes.

```
? PROCEDURE CPWORDS (I, CP, WORDS)
? LET CP=0
? IF #16.I GT 0 AND #19.I GT 0 AND #21.I GE 0 AND #23.I GE 0 THEN
? LET CP=#19.I-#16.I, LET WORDS=#21.I+#23.I;
? ENDP
```

This procedure may now be used in conjunction with the standard procedures to calculate the mean of CP time for query execution and the mean of the size of the output reports generated, as shown in the following search.

```
? FØR I=1 TØ LAST
? CALL CPWØRDS(I,CPTIME,SIZE)
? IF CPTIME GT 0 THEN CALL MEAN(CPTIME,MEANCP) CALL MEAN(SIZE,MEANS);
? LØØP
? AFTER SEARCH
? DISPLAY ACRØSS 'MEAN ØF C.P. TIME =' TAB 25 MEANCP /
? 'MEAN ØF REPØRT SIZE =' TAB 25 MEANS
? END

SEARCHING INITIATED

AFTER SEARCH
      MEAN ØF C.P. TIME =      .903
      MEAN ØF REPØRT SIZE =   328.
```

Figure 12.5. Combined use of standard procedures and
user-defined procedures.

In order to analyze the interrelationship between variables, additional procedures can be defined to generate a data plot of two variables and the correlation between two variables.

The definition for a data plotting procedure within RIQSONLINE is as follows:

? PROCEDURE PLOTXY (X, Y) PLOT X VRS Y ENDP

The definition required for a correlation procedure may be specified as follows:

```
ENTER SEARCH COMMAND OR TYPE HALT

? PROCEDURE CORR(X,Y,R)
? SET UP N,SPXY,SX,SY,SSX,SSY
? BEGIN SEARCH
? LET N=N+1
? LET SPXY=SPXY+X*Y
? LET SX=SX+X
? LET SY=SY+Y
? LET SSX=SSX+X**2
? LET SSY=SSY+Y**2
? AFTER SEARCH
? LET R=(N*SPXY-SX*SY)/
?       (((N*SSX-SX**2)**0.5)*((N*SSY-SY**2)**0.5))
? DISPLAY 'CORRELATION = ' R
? ENDP
```

Figure 12.6. Correlation procedure definition.

These procedures, once defined, can be called into execution whenever needed. In the context of the RIQS log data base, they can be utilized to examine the relationship between the central processor time for search execution and the size of the output reports generated. The sequence of user commands in Figure 12.7 illustrates these capabilities by scanning a previously defined subset of the data base (SET 1) and generating a data plot and correlation of these variables under the criteria that report size is less than 2000 words.

```
? BEGIN SEARCH OF SET 1
? FOR I=1 TO LAST
? CALL CPWORDS(I,CPTIME,SIZE)
? IF CPTIME GT 0 AND SIZE LT 2000  THEN
? CALL CORR(CPTIME,SIZE,RESULT)  CALL PLOTXY(CPTIME,SIZE);
? LOOP
? END

SEARCHING INITIATED

AFTER SEARCH
    CORRELATION =
    .664


NO. OF RECORDS  GENERATED TO THE PLOT FILE =   100
NO. OF POINTS   GENERATED TO THE PLOT FILE =   473

DO YOU WANT THE POINTS LISTED
? DIVERT,POINTS,VOGELBACK.

POINTS      FILE DIVERTED TO V

DO YOU WANT THE PLOT GENERATED
? Y
```

Figure 12.7. Correlation and data plot generation.

The correlation was displayed after the search was executed (note that the DISPLAY command was entered as part of the definition of the procedure CORR, and thus was not required in the above search) and a file of points representing the data was generated. The resultant plot, taken from the screen of an IMLAC graphics terminal, is shown in Figure 12.8.

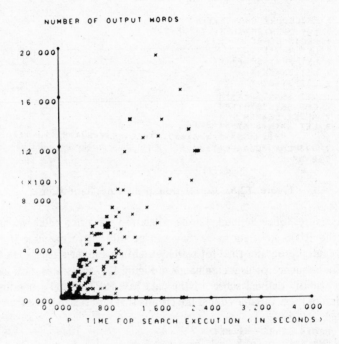

Figure 12.8. IMLAC graphics processor plot.

Figure 12.8 thus shows the relationship between central processor time for query execution and the size of the output files generated by that query. Several interesting results are revealed:

1. For this data base, only one search out of the 473 analyzed (those generating less than 2000 words of output) required more than 2.3 seconds of CP time.

2. There is a positive correlation between processing time and output file size. Additionally, if we eliminate those searches for which no reports were generated (this can occur when the query is not satisfied or when hit records are merely put into a set and not displayed or printed), then an SPSS run yields a correlation of 0.80 at the 0.001 significance level, indicating a strong positive correlation.

3. The extreme points on the plot reveal the impact of "query complexity" on search time. Table 12.1 illustrates seven of these extreme points showing a measure of their complexity composed of number of search terms or arithmetic terms, number of IF statements, and/or number of OR operators.

Search CP Time in Seconds	Query Complexity
3.019	41 Search terms 5 IF statements 24 OR operators
2.012	15 Search terms 19 IF statements
1.959	15 Search terms 20 IF statements
1.953	15 Search terms 20 IF statements
1.952	15 Search terms 18 IF statements
1.948	15 Search terms 18 IF statements
1.643	24 Arithmetic terms 1 IF statement 12 OR operators

Table 12.1. Query complexity analysis of plot extrema

These results illustrate that general trend analysis must be tempered with investigation of extrema as well.

Some very interesting data, which would have been virtually impossible to determine without on-line monitoring, was the length of time it takes a user of RIQSONLINE to enter his search commands, and a comparison of this query entry time to the time needed to process the resultant search, including output report generation. In Figure 12.9, 97 percent of the searches were executed in less than 16 real-time seconds, including report generation. This time includes both the CP time for RIQSONLINE execution plus any wait time due to the operating system. Further analysis of the 19 searches which took longer than 16 seconds indicated that 5 of them were due to large output files being generated and the rest were due to unusually long on-line storage waits.

Perhaps the most important information gained from this data, however, results from analyzing the amount of time it takes the user to enter queries into RIQSONLINE:

In 72 percent of the queries, the real time for query input was less than 3 minutes.

In 92 percent of the queries, the real time for query input was less than 6 minutes.

In 4 percent of the queries, the real time for query input was greater than 8 minutes, with a maximum of 22 minutes.

Additionally, for each of the 626 input/execute cycles monitored, the following ratio was plotted:

$$\frac{\text{real time for query input}}{\text{total real time for input and execution of that query}}$$

Almost invariably, the computed ratio was between 0.8 and 1.0 indicating that a very substantial amount of the total real time for performing a search is attributable to entering the query into the system. These analyses have proved extremely useful in pinpointing one of the major bottlenecks of the system, indicating clearly that future effort must be directed toward reducing the query input time for the RIQSONLINE user.

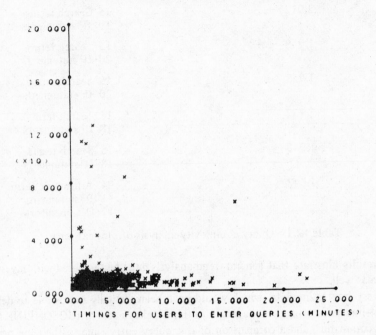

RIQSLOG - REAL TIME OF QUERY ENTRY VRS EXECUTION

TIMINGS FOR SYSTEM TO EXECUTE QUERIES (SECONDS)

TIMINGS FOR USERS TO ENTER QUERIES (MINUTES)

Figure 12.9. Query entry–query execution.

On the basis of these analyses several proposals have been made for reducing query input time, including a restructuring of the translation phase of the system to reduce the core requirement for query syntax checking and the provision for an alternate input file capability whereby canned searches could be read in their entirety from a file rather than typed in on a line-by-line basis from the on-line terminal.

The design of the RIQSLOG data base, together with the processing capabilities of RIQSONLINE have facilitated many other types of system performance evaluation analyses, too numerous to examine here in detail. Some of the additional analyses include:

The determination of the most common errors made by users and the context in which they occur.

The generation of data plots representing user learning curves.

The frequency counts of the RIQSONLINE commands and features used most often.

The effect of data base size, number of records scanned, query complexity, etc. on the time required to execute a query.

The development of a performance measure for predicting the time and cost required to execute an arbitrary query.

The determination of the impact of the monitor on the performance of RIQSONLINE.

Conclusions

This study has shown us the value of instrumenting on-line software with monitoring routines to discover deficiencies in the system and its user interface as well as to isolate the parameters critical to system performance. As a result of the analyses performed, improvements have already been made to RIQSONLINE and several areas for future work have been defined. The ease of using RIQSONLINE itself, especially the data plotting capability on the IMLAC graphics terminal, to analyze the monitored data was a major advantage in carrying out the study.

We are sufficiently encouraged by the results to date to enhance the monitor as new capabilities are added to RIQSONLINE, in order to continually facilitate determination of the effect of new features on total system performance.

CITED REFERENCES

1. Benjamin Mittman and Wayne D. Dominick, "Developing Monitoring Techniques for an On-Line Information Retrieval System," *Information Storage and Retrieval*, Vol. 9, No. 6, June, 1973, pp. 297-307.
2. Wayne D. Dominick, "The Man/Machine Interface, System Monitoring and Performance Evaluation Methodology for On-line Interactive Systems," M. S. Thesis, Computer Sciences Department, Northwestern University, Evanston, Illinois, August, 1972.

Section Three:

MEDICAL AND CLINICAL SCIENCES

The medical and clinical sciences have been faced with an almost unmanageable explosion of information. Medical and clinical data are traditionally stored in row upon row of file folders. The introduction of computer-based processing has begun to impact the medical researcher in his or her search for relevant case studies. It is now possible to store selected information from patient records, so that research can benefit from immediate and selective access to symptoms, diagnoses, treatment, patient progress, etc. In addition, related fields, such as speech research, find effective storage and retrieval capabilities of extreme importance.

The research described by Loretta Taymans in Chapter 13 involves the study of the phonological development of a small child, by observing the evolution of utterances. The sheer mass of data in this case suggested the possibility of computer-based analysis. RIQS was used to structure, store and retrieve raw data which permitted the production of useful printed indexes.

More traditional medical research applications are found in Chapters 14 and 15. Jessen and Paul first describe a cardiology information retrieval system, which was developed using RIQS, to handle thousands of cases from a major pediatric cardiology center. In Chapter 15, Levit and Dominick discuss the establishment of an important data base of skin biopsy information. Both of these applications illustrate the importance of selective retrieval to medical research.

Delivery of health care can be improved if the data processing needs of the clinical practitioners can be met in a timely and individualized manner. A prototype health care system for spinal injuries, developed at Northwestern Memorial Hospital—Wesley Pavilion in connection with the Rehabilitation Institute of Chicago, is described by Flaherty and

229

her associates in Chapter 16. The data base aspects of this system are studied by means of sample records and queries.

Finally, a health care data base, containing profile data of thousands of hospitals, is discussed by Colussi and Kosnik in Chapter 17. Data gathered by the American Hospital Association provides the basis for an interactive inquiry system to serve the needs of research workers in the health services.

Chapter 13

The Development of English Phonology Before the Age of Two: A Structural Description of Single-Word Utterances and Early-Word Combinations

LORETTA M. TAYMANS
The Catholic University of America

The Problem

This research was concerned with an investigation of phonological development in a single child. The goals of the research were to study the child's phonological system (1) by describing the phonetic and syllabic structure of her utterances and (2) by formulating rules which captured the generalities present in the phonetic data at monthly intervals. The investigation began when the child had a fairly well-developed single word vocabulary of approximately 50 to 75 utterances. Her chronological age was 16 months and 16 days at the time. A sample of her speech at this point was tape recorded in the home, utilizing verbal interaction between the parent(s) and the child as well as the investigator and child. Thereafter the child's speech was sampled monthly. This resulted in four separate files of data of increasing size and complexity.

Due to the subject's age, it was not possible to structure the tape recording sessions so that her known vocabulary would occur and be repeated a desired number of times. Consequently, it was necessary to obtain large samples of data in the hope that they would be sufficiently representative of her phonological system at the time. Because of the large number of utterances contained in each corpus and the phonetic detail present in each utterance, a computer program was sought which would permit the coding of the data in an easily recognized form and allow for detail and flexibility in retrieval.

Few studies have been done utilizing large bodies of phonetic data on single subjects or large subject samples because of the difficulty involved in data management. One such study was undertaken at the University of Texas at Austin (Williams [1]). Here, large numbers of school-age subjects were tested employing a standard test of articulation. The subject's errors were recorded in terms of the target sound expected in the word. The evaluation included information regarding the frequency of substitution and the phonetic features of the substituted sound. Each line of the data base generally included only one item of information. The description of the data base from the Williams' study, however, was most helpful in the initial organization of the data of this study.

In the research reported here, some means of representing whole utterances which could be plotted as a two-dimensional matrix in terms of phones and their phonetic features was sought. By contrast with the Williams' study, each line of the data base concerned with phonetic features would then contain multiple items. Further requirements included selective retrieval of phonetic features in relationship to each other and to other variables, as well as the indexing of vocabulary items according to a variety of conditions.

In the selection of linguistic variables and phonetic parameters, two goals were kept in mind. It was hoped that the program arrived at would allow for adequate study of the present data; but it was also desired that the program have sufficient generality that it could be readily adapted to study any kind of phonetic data in the future. The latter goal was paramount in working out the phonetic feature system to be employed. Consequently, every effort was made to include as many classes of sounds as possible and to allow for minute variations in the specifications of individual phones. To this end, the Chomsky-Halle[2] feature system was adapted. Many modifications were made in both the definition of the features and their application.

It will be seen, when the file description is presented, that each utterance generated a rather large record once all of the variables and parameters had been selected. If all of these had to be separately keypunched, the time involved and the opportunities for error would have been prohibitive. This problem was reduced tremendously by generating as much of the data by rule as was possible. The feature by phone input required the writing of a separate program so that the phone code could be automatically translated into features.[3]

The Data

The data base is divided into four files which are named Corpus 1, 2, 3, and 4, respectively. The file description for Corpus 2 is as follows: (See Figure 13.1)

The first five lines (items) represent card input. Line 1 indicates whether that item of data was derived from one of three samples and within samples whether the item was elicited during the first or second hour of taping on a given day. Line 2 represents the utterance of the child in normal English spelling. The term utterance is used here to indicate that sometimes line 2 contained two or more words which were interpreted sometimes as a single morpheme and at other times as two or more morphemes. Some utterances contained additional elements or syllables that could not be unambiguously interpreted. Additional spaces were added either before, between, or after words to indicate where these elements were.

Line 3, named Word Type, was used to indicate whether the utterance was considered spontaneous (S), imitated (I), echoed (E), or repeated (R). Next the syllabic shape (line 4) for each utterance was determined by labeling each phone in the original phonetic transcription as either a consonant (C) or a vowel (V). For example, the utterance, *Baby have it*, was coded CVCV CVCV/ to indicate that this was interpreted as a two-morpheme utterance with *have it* being considered a single morpheme since neither of these elements ever occurred separately. Line 4 was of particular importance because it was used to write rules which would generate the data on lines 6 through 9.

```
FILE HAS THE NAME CORPUS2
AND CONTAINS 1260 RECORDS


ITEM NUMBERS AND NAMES
------------------------

      1.    SAMPLE AND HOUR NUMBER
      2.    WORD
      3.    WORD TYPE
      4.    SHAPE
      5.    PHONE CODE
      6.    NUMBER OF MORPHEMES
      7.    NUMBER OF SYLLABLES
      8.    FUNCTION OF C'S
      9.    PLACEMENT OF V'S
     10.    CONSONANTAL
     11.    VOCALIC
     12.    CORONAL
     13.    ANTERIOR
     14.    HIGH
     15.    LOW
     16.    BACK
     17.    TENSE
     18.    ROUND
     19.    CONTINUANT
     20.    NASAL
     21.    LATERAL
     22.    TRILL
     23.    INSTANT RELEASE
     24.    ASPIRATION
     25.    VOICE
     26.    SYLLABIC
     27.    COMPRESSED WORD
     28.    UNCOMPRESSED WORD
```

Figure 13.1 RIQS record definition.

Line 6 was generated by stating that the number of spaces in a string of Cs and Vs on line 4 was equal to the number of morphemes plus one. The number of syllables in an utterance (line 7) was determined by considering any single V or a string of contiguous Vs as a single unit. The number of such units was then equal to the number of syllables in a string of Cs and Vs. The function of Cs (line 8) refers to the position of consonants relative to vowels. The integers 1, 2, and 3 were used to designate pre-, inter-, and post-vocalic consonants. A consonant may also precede another consonant, occur between two consonants, or follow another consonant. These Cs were labeled 4, 5, and 6, respectively, and a series of statements was written specifying their occurrence. The utterance *boxcar* serves as an example. It would appear in line 4 as CVCC CVC. Line 8 would look as follows: 1 35 1 3/. Line 9, named Placement of Vs, was necessary in order to separate single vowels (V) from diphthongs (VV) and from triphthongs (VVV) for purposes of retrieval later on.

Line 5 was used to convert the phonetic symbols to a phone code which consisted of a series of letters followed by numbers and separated by commas. The word *baby* transcribed as (bebi) became B 1, V 3, B 1, V 1/ on line 5 of the card input. (See Figure 13.2.) Items 10 through 26 represent the complete list of phonetic features used to specify each of the phones occurring in line 5. A separate program was written which specified the feature by phone input.

Line 27, entitled Compressed Word, was added so that the spaces were deleted from line 2 permitting the alphabetical indexing of whole utterances. Line 28, Uncompressed Word, was added so that the blank spaces in line 2 could be coded for later retrieval if desired. The blank spaces referred to vowel segments usually, which were not interpreted.

```
RECØRD NUMBER      1
      (1) SAMPLE AND HØUR NUMBER
      1.1
      (2) WØRD
      BABY
      (3) WØRD TYPE
      S
      (4) SHAPE
      C ,V ,C ,V ,V
      (5) PHØNE CØDE
      B 1 ,V 1 ,B 1 ,V 2 ,V 1
      (6) NUMBER ØF MØRPHEMES
      1
      (7) NUMBER ØF SYLLABLES
      2
      (8) FUNCTIØN ØF C'S
      1 ,B ,2 ,B ,B
      (9) PLACEMENT ØF V'S
      B ,1 ,B ,B ,2
      (10) CØNSØNANTAL
      + ,- ,+ ,- ,-
      (11) VØCALIC
      - ,+ ,- ,+ ,+
      (12) CØRØNAL
      - ,- ,- ,- ,-
      (13) ANTERIØR
      + 1 ,- ,+ 1 ,- ,-
      (14) HIGH
      - ,+ ,- ,+ ,+
      (15) LØW
      - ,- ,- ,- ,-
      (16) BACK
      - ,- ,- ,- ,-
      (17) TENSE
      B ,+ ,B ,- ,+
      (18) RØUND
      B ,- ,B ,- ,-
      (19) CØNTINUANT
      - ,B ,- ,B ,B
      (20) NASAL
      B ,B ,B ,B ,B
      (21) LATERAL
      B ,B ,B ,B ,B
      (22) TRILL
      - ,B ,- ,B ,B
      (23) INSTANT RELEASE
      + ,B ,+ ,B ,B
      (24) ASPIRATIØN
      + 1 ,B ,+ 1 ,B ,B
      (25) VØICE
      + ,+ ,+ ,+ ,+
      (26) SYLLABIC
      B ,B ,B ,B ,B
      (27) CØMPRESSED WØRD
      BABY
      (28) UNCØMPRESSED WØRD
      BABY
```

Figure 13.2. Printout of a record containing the word "baby."

These 28 lines constituted the input data on each utterance. Each utterance was then numbered as a separate record for input to the RIQS system. Because of the size of each record and the number of records in each RIQS file, all of the data was stored on magnetic tape.

Research Strategy

The general strategy followed was to obtain an overview of the structure of utterances in order to determine what avenues appeared most productive for further study as suggested by the data. Furthermore, it was considered important to determine how to use the RIQS system most efficiently and economically. A great deal of redundancy had been built into the original program, and so it was possible to retrieve the same information in a variety of ways.

Following the creation of the RIQS files, each file or corpus was divided into 10 sets. These sets were added to the master file for later indexing. The set descriptions for Corpus 2 are shown in Figure 13.3.

```
SET DESCRIPTIØNS
-----------------


                  NØ. ØF      CREATIØN
   ID. NØ.       ELEMENTS       DATE         DEFINITIØN

      1             291      AUG25, 1972     SAMPLE 1
      2             518      AUG25, 1972     SAMPLE 2
      3             451      AUG25, 1972     SAMPLE 3
      4             668      AUG25, 1972     TYPE S
      5             137      AUG25, 1972     TYPE I
      6               7      AUG25, 1972     TYPE E
      7             448      AUG25, 1972     TYPE R123
      8             931      AUG25, 1972     MØRPHEMES = 1
      9             317      AUG25, 1972     MØRPHEMES = 2
     10              12      AUG25, 1972     MØRPHEMES = 3
```

Figure 13.3. Descriptions of sets defined for CORPUS 2.

All indexes were done on intersections of particular sets. Each sample was first indexed in terms of the number of morphemes. Summarizing the information on terms, pointers, and average length of list, across all samples and all corpora, it could be seen that the mean length of utterances counted in morphemes showed a steady developmental trend. Both terms and pointers increased as averages decreased. This indicated that as the child's output increased so also did the number of words at her command. With an increasing vocabulary there was less likelihood that she would repeat; thus the gradual decrease in the average length of a list.

In subsequent analyses, it was imperative to know which utterances were either imitated or echoed as opposed to those which were spontaneous. Therefore, further indexing was also done as follows (1,8,4) (1,8,5) (1,8,6) (1,8,7) and so on. (See Figure 13.4)

This information was used to determine when word types should be studied separately and when they could be grouped for more in-depth analysis. In addition, this type of overview of the data suggested the direction of further analysis. For example, the number of echoed utterances, which were infrequent in the early samples, increased in Corpus 4. Imitation also showed a steady increase across the four corpora. This was an unexpected development and seemed to warrant further exploration. The KWOC index was also used extensively in other types of analyses.

Following the general plan of looking at overall structure first, SPSS files were created using morphemes, syllables, and shapes as variables. A frequency distribution and descriptive statistics were calculated for all of these variables. These kinds of sorting, counting, and descriptive operations lend great efficiency to a study of this kind and they reduce the complexity of the task of accounting for occurrences in phonological terms. Because this

```
INDEX ON INTERSECTION OF (1,8,5)
INVERT ON (27).

                                                    FILE INVERSION
                                                    --------------


        1       AOH                      189

        1       BACK                     291

        1       BEAR                     261

        1       CAKE                     255

        1       CHICAGO                  217

        1       COW                       18

        1       DADDY                    161

        1       DIAPER                    46

        1       DOG                       19

        1       DOOR                     183

        1       HAIR                      99

        1       HELICOPTER               246

        4       KANGAROO                  15    16    17    209

        1       KITTYCAT                  39

        1       LAKE                     219

        1       LIPSTICK                 212

        3       LORETTA                  159   172   175

        1       MOMMY                     95

        1       MONKEY                    37

        1       OPEN                     152

        1       SHOE                     263

        1       TOAST                    239
```

Figure 13.4. Index showing the utterance, the frequency of occurrence
in the file, and the record number containing the utterance.

is a study of a single individual, designed to look at development at specified points in time, even simple descriptive statistics do not capture the most significant generalizations adequately; consequently, they will be used sparingly in this study. Figure 13.5 illustrates the creation of a subfile through RIQS and printout of simple frequencies by SPSS in an on–line mode.

The next major area of analysis included an in–depth exploration of the consonant and vowel systems. To accomplish this task the phonetic features (lines 10 through 26 of the file description) were used. By manipulating these features, it was possible to look at consonants and vowels in a great variety of ways or to select a given feature across a particular set of data. Since both consonant and vowel systems were relatively simple at

```
? IF #7 EQ 1 SPSSFILE 1 ØF #4;END


? SPSSLINK 1

SPSSØNLINE
USE ØVER 100 VARIABLES ØR ØVER 5 SUBFILES? NØ
USE A SAVE-FILE THIS RUN?   Y
AUTØ-MØDE.
? 1. GET FILE; CØRPUS2
?10. CØDEBØØK; ALL
?99. FINISH
?EXECUTE

ENTERING SPSS.

- - - CØDEBØØK - - -


VARIABLE - SHAPE

VALUE LABEL       VALUE       FREQ   REL %  ADJ %   CUM %

                  CVCC          2      .7     .7      .7
                  CVC          62    21.1   21.1    21.8
                  CVVC        101    34.4   34.4    56.1
                  CVVV          9     3.1    3.1    59.2
                  CVVVC        10     3.4    3.4    62.6
                  CVV          79    26.9   26.9    89.5
                  CV           12     4.1    4.1    93.5
                  VC            1      .3     .3    93.9
                  VVC           4     1.4    1.4    95.2
                  VVV           1      .3     .3    95.6
                  VV           13     4.4    4.4   100.0

         TØTAL           294   100.0  100.0   100.0
```

Figure 13.5. Using the on-line RIQS/SPSS linkage to obtain
frequency counts of the variable SHAPE.

the beginning of the study, it was possible to look at large groups of phones, but as the complexity of the system increased, it was desirable to look at smaller and smaller portions of the data.

Frequently occurring vowel sounds were counted in the following manner:

```
*  *
? BEFØRE SEARCH LET V10 = 0,
? LET V11 = 0,
? LET V12 = 0,
?  BEGIN SEARCH ØF SET 1 FØR N = 1 TØ LAST
? IF #5.N EQ 'V10' AND #9.N EQ '1' LET V10 = V10 + 1;
? IF #5.N EQ 'V11' AND #9.N EQ '1' LET V11 = V11 + 1;
? IF #5.N EQ 'V12' AND #9.N EQ '1' LET V12 = V12 + 1; LØØP;
?
  AFTER SEARCH DISPLAY 'FREQUENCY CØUNTS' V10, V11, V12;END



SEARCHING INITIATED

AFTER SEARCH
   FREQUENCY CØUNTS
   3.00
   21.0
   73.0
```

Figure 13.6. Reading the phone code (item 5) and the corresponding
placement of Vs (item 9) to arrive at frequency of
vowel sounds.

Since all other vowel sounds were known to be infrequent, they were retrieved in the following manner:

```
? BEGIN SEARCH ØF SET 1
? FØR N = 1 TØ LAST IF #5.N NE ('V 1' ØR 'V 2' ØR 'V 3' ØR 'V 4'
? ØR #←'V 5' ØR 'V 6' ØR 'V 7' ØR 'V 8' ØR 'V 9' ØR  'V10' ØR
? 'V11' ØR 'V12' ØR 'V13' ØR 'V14' ØR 'V15' ØR 'V16' ØR 'V17' ØR
? 'V18' ØR 'V19' ØR 'V20') AND #9.N EQ '1' DISPLAY #5.N;LØØP;END

SEARCHING INITIATED


NØ. ØF REPØRTS ØN DISPLAY FILE =    27

DØ YØU WANT THE DISPLAY REPØRTS LISTED
? YES


  RECØRD NUMBER    33
      (5.2) PHØNE CØDE
      V50


  RECØRD NUMBER    46
      (5.4) PHØNE CØDE
      V49


  RECØRD NUMBER    47
      (5.8) PHØNE CØDE
      V49

          ·
          ·
          ·


  RECØRD NUMBER   146
      (5.4) PHØNE CØDE
      V28


  RECØRD NUMBER   155
      (5.6) PHØNE CØDE
      V50


  RECØRD NUMBER   156
      (5.4) PHØNE CØDE
      V50


  RECØRD NUMBER   160
      (5.7) PHØNE CØDE
      V49


  RECØRD NUMBER   161
      (5.7) PHØNE CØDE
      V49


  RECØRD NUMBER   266
      (5.5) PHØNE CØDE
      V49
```

Figure 13.7.   Retrieval of infrequent vowel sounds.

```
BEGIN SEARCH OF SET 2
IF (5) EQ 'V 4' THEN PUT IN SET 14.,

INDEX ON SET 14
KWOC ON (27).
PRINT (5).

BABY                    HAIR                    LORETTAGLASSES
        B 1                     F11                     R 3
        V 4                     V 4                     V 4
        B 1                     R 3                     D 3
        V 7                                             V 7
        V 1             HEAD                            V65
                                F11                     F67
BEAR                            V 4                     V 7
        F 1                     V 7
        V 4                                     MOMMY
        V12             LORETTA                         N 1
        R 2                     V14                     V12
                                R 3                     N 1
        B 2                     V 4                     V 4
        V 4                     L 1                     V11
        R 3                     V 8
                                                MOMMYGLASSES
        D 1                     V10                     N 1
        V 7                     R 3                     V12
        B 1                     V 4                     N 1
        V 4                     D 3                     V 1
        V11                     V 8                     V 5
                                                        F67
        W 1                     V20                     V 4
        V 7                     W 1                     V11
        V11                     V 4
        Y 1                     J 1             RABBIT
        V 4                     V 4                     V10
        R 2                                             R 3
                                V10                     V 5
        B 1                     V 4                     B 1
        V 4                     L 1                     V 4
        R 2                     V 8                     Q 1

CHAIR                           R 3                     R 3
        F11                     V 4                     V 5
        V 4                     V 7                     B 1
        R 3                     L 1                     V 4
                                V 8                     Q 1
DADDYCOOKIE
        D 1                     L 2                     V10
        V 4                     V20                     R 3
        D 1                     R 3                     V 5
        V 1                     V 4                     B 1
        K 2                     V 7                     V 4
        V19                     L 1                     Q 1
        C 2                     V 8
        V 7                                     TOGETHER
        V 1                     W 1                     V18
                                V 4                     Z 1
DADDYGLASSES                    D 3                     V 4
        D 1                     V20                     D 3
        V 5                     R 3                     V10
        D 1                     V 4
        V 1                     L 1
        V 8                     V 8
        F67
        V 4
```

Figure 13.8.   Listing of phone codes by vocabulary.

In further study of the vowel system, it was necessary to sort out the vocabulary that accounted for particular vowels. For this purpose each vowel was placed in a set temporarily and the KWOC index was employed. (Figure 13.8)

The following type of search was used to retrieve consonant sounds in terms of phonetic features:

```
ENTER SEARCH CØMMAND ØR TYPE HALT

? BEGIN SEARCH ØF SET 1 FØR N = 1 TØ LAST IF #8.N EQ '2'
? AND #11.N EQ '-' AND #19.N EQ '+' AND #20.N EQ '-' AND
? #13.N EQ ('+1' ØR '+2' ØR '+3')

? DISPLAY #2, #5.N;LØØP;END

SEARCHING INITIATED


NØ. ØF REPØRTS ØN DISPLAY FILE =      1

DØ YØU WANT THE DISPLAY REPØRTS LISTED
? YES


RECØRD NUMBER     151
     (2) WØRD
     ØPEN
     (5.2) PHØNE CØDE
     F 1
```

Figure 13.9. Using various phonetic features as criteria for
retrieval of consonant sounds.

This search asked for fricative consonants in an intervocalic position by place of articulation. As a preliminary search, it would indicate the number and kinds of phones present. If both were small, a hand count could easily be made. If either the number or kind of phone types was large, then the retrieval conditions were made more specific. Further exploration of the consonant system was similar to that followed for vowels in that the vocabulary which accounted for classes of sounds or phone types within classes was sorted.

A third area of interest was related to how frequently occurring words were realized phonetically. It was important to know, for example, if the word *baby* was always rendered as a CVCV and if the Cs and Vs were either identical or variable. Therefore, all utterances appearing in the alphabetical index of a sample were retrieved in the following manner: IF (2) EQ 'BABY' PRINT (3) (5). The printout included the record number, word type, and phone code for each occurrence of *baby* either as a single word or as a word combination. It was later found that the KWOC index could be used for this purpose with considerable savings in keypunching time as well as computer time.

Results and Conclusions

The basic assumption of this study was that phonological development was systematic. So the first task was to give a structural description of the data of each corpus in such a way that the progression of structure would be revealed over time. The major components of the structural description were indicated in the previous section on research strategy. To date, only the analysis of Corpus 1 has been completed. An outline of the form of the results for the first corpus will indicate how the other corpora will be handled also. When all analyses have been completed, the final discussion should deal with the pattern of development and the specific details of phonetic and phonological structure which changed over time.

In comparing one corpus with another or one sample with another, there were basically three sets of summarizing information which could be scrutinized.

1. Absolute and relative frequencies as well as other simple descriptive statistics were used to describe the variables relating to the overall structure of utterances.

2. The end result of the in-depth analysis of the phonetic data of the consonant and vowel systems was a series of rules stating how phone types were realized and distributed along with the constraints on their occurrence.

3. A final lexicon of utterances was proposed as being representative of the child's phonological system at the time of a given corpus. These utterances were presented in the phonetic form in which they were most likely to occur.

Linguistic data are inherently complex. Various components of the grammar of any language tend to interact with each other. More specifically, phonetic parameters do not exist independently of each other. As a result, examination of these kinds of data requires that the program of analysis be sufficiently flexible to allow for the retrieval of multiple variables in a variety of contexts. The RIQS system appears to have met this requirement rather well.

NOTES AND CITED REFERENCES

1. Williams, Frederick (Ed.), "Analysis of Production Errors in the Phonetic Performance of School-Age Standard-English-Speaking Children," U. S. Department of H.E.W., 1971.

2. Chomsky, Noam, and Morris Halle. *The Sound Pattern of English.* New York: Harper and Row, 1968.

3. Once the above details were worked out from a linguistic point of view, the assistance of a computer programmer was sought. I am indebted to Dr. Philip Friedman for introducing me to John Burns who was familiar with the RIQS system developed at Vogelback Computing Center. He performed the tedious task of programming the data base so that RIQS files could be created.

Chapter 14

CIRS: Cardiology Information Retrieval System

DALE C. JESSEN
Information Services, Northfield, Illinois

MILTON H. PAUL, M.D.
Northwestern University Medical School

Introduction

CIRS, a Cardiology Information Retrieval System, is a total system designed to store and selectively retrieve a large volume of cardiology patient information.

As manual patient history files began to grow in size, the need for an automatic information handling system became evident. Initiation of exploratory or short-term research projects was impractical due to costly and time consuming data gathering. Weeks or months would be spent scanning and collecting the conventional patient history records before any analysis could begin. A structured cardiology patient data file was needed containing relevant clinical information such as the date, clinical event, diagnosis, procedures, complications, physical measurements, and selected comments from each patient's medical history.

The CIRS data base information is extracted from conventional physician entries in the patient's medical record and represents both outpatient and inpatient observations and treatments for infants and children attending a major pediatric cardiology center.

The information is extracted and coded by a medical data secretary and entered in script for each patient on a single CIRS record card (Figure 14.1). This card is filed in the cardiology office as a security record and all subsequent entries are continued on the card. This card and the subsequent computer-generated summaries represent the only abstracted records routinely assembled and maintained for each patient. The medical data secretary also provides for the file management and initiates the search requests via the computing center staff.

242

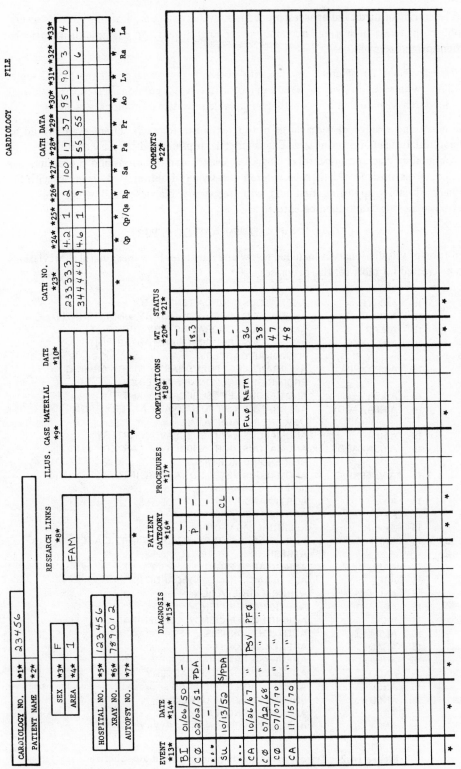

Figure 14.1. CIRS record card.

The storing of medical diagnoses, procedures, events and complications presents several problems in terms of storing large amounts of English text. An example of a particular patient diagnosis might be:

Transposition (D) of great arteries with posterior (a–v canal type) ventricular septal defect with secundum atrial septal defect with valvular pulmonary stenosis with right aortic arch with double conus with questionable subvalvular pulmonary stenosis.

The entry and storage of a diagnosis in this text form for each patient event would be impractical. Instead of entering large English text descriptions, a dictionary of abbreviations of common cardiac and noncardiac diagnoses, events, complications and procedures was created. A diagnosis would then be entered as a string of abbreviated diagnoses with the primary diagnosis appearing first and with secondary diagnoses following. Thus, the previous diagnosis would then be entered as:

TGAD VSDP ASD PSV AAR DC Q/PSB

A portion of this dictionary is included below and illustrates how meaningful abbreviations can be created for most cardiac diagnoses.

15	A/CHTE	ANOMALOUS CHORDA TENDINAE
15	A/CO	ANOMALOUS CORONARY ARTERY, UNDESIGNATED
15	A/FAR	ANOMALOUS FEMORAL ARTERY, RIGHT
15	A/LCOXPA	ANOMALOUS LEFT CORONARY ARTERY INTO PULMONARY ARTERY
15	A/LPAXRPA	ABERRANT LEFT PULMONARY ARTERY ARISING FROM RIGHT PULMONARY ARTERY
15	A/LSA	ANOMALOUS LEFT SUBCLAVIAN ARTERY
15	A/RPAXAODS	ABERRANT RIGHT PULMONARY ARTERY FROM DESCENDING AORTA
15	A/RSA	ANOMALOUS RIGHT SUBCLAVIAN ARTERY
15	A/RSAXAODS	ANOMALOUS RIGHT SUBCLAVIAN ARTERY INTO DESCENDING AORTA
15	A/VDSPXIVC	ANOMALOUS VENOUS DRAINAGE INTO SPLEEN INTO INFERIOR VENA CAVA
15	AA	AORTIC ARCH
15	AAA	AORTIC ARCH ANOMALOUS
15	AAA/R	RESIDUAL (AS VSD/R)
15	AAI	AORTIC ARCH INTERRUPTED OR AORTIC ARCH ATRESIA
15	AAR	AORTIC ARCH RIGHT
15	ABE	ACUTE BACTERIAL ENDOCARDITIS
15	AFI	ATRIAL FIBRILLATION
15	AI	AORTIC INSUFFICIENCY
15	AIC	AORTIC INSUFFICIENCY, CONGENITAL
15	ALT	ALTITUDE SICKNESS
15	ANAO	ANEURYSM AORTA
15	ANBA	ANEURYSM BRACHIAL ARTERY
15	ANCO	ANEURYSM CORONARY ARTERY
15	ANEI	ANEMIA, IRON DEFICIENCY
15	ANFO	ANEURYSM, FOSSA OVALIS
15	ANP	ANNULAR PANCREAS
15	ANPA	ANEURYSM PULMONARY ARTERY

Figure 14.2. Terms sorted by item number and alphabetized by code edition 01/30/71.

For each patient event, an entry is made containing the following information:

EVENT—e.g., birth, inpatient visit, surgery
DATE—date of event
DIAGNOSIS—diagnosis made by doctor
PROCEDURES PERFORMED—e.g., open heart surgery, septostomy, homograft
COMPLICATIONS—e.g., arrhythmia, pneumonia
AGE—number of days from birth
WEIGHT—weight in pounds at event
STATUS—e.g., excellent operative result, cardiac functional class II
COMMENTS—English text comments on the event

Other information that is very useful to the cardiology researcher is data obtained from cardiac catheterization. Since many values of blood pressure, blood oxygen content, etc. are recorded and calculated during a catheterization, only a selected representative number are actually recorded in the automated patient record. All of these values are numeric items and include such items as:

PULMONARY AND SYSTEMIC BLOOD FLOW
PULMONARY VASCULAR RESISTANCE
PEAK SYSTOLIC BLOOD PRESSURES: Aorta, Ventricles, Pulmonary Artery
MEAN BLOOD PRESSURES: Left and Right Atrium
OXYGEN SATURATIONS: Aorta or Systemic Artery

Frequently, special diagnostic tests, unusual films and teaching slides are collected on a particular patient. A record of the type of illustrative case material and the date on which it was collected is entered in the CIRS file to indicate that this additional material is available.

The RIQS record for each patient consists of 33 items, seven of which are singular and 26 of which are multiple items. Item numbers 1 through 7 consist of fixed patient information such as the hospital number, name, sex and x-ray number for each patient. Items 8 through 10 contain various research and illustrative case material references. Items 11 and 12 are not defined. Items 13 through 22 are completed for each patient event and items 23 through 33 are entered for each catheterization performed. (Figure 14.3)

The current CIRS data base was created from approximately 17,000 cardiology patient records collected at the cardiology department of The Children's Memorial Hospital. RIQS continues to be used to enter new patients, update old patient records and search the patient file.

Initial Data Entry

Each patient's record is initially entered into the CIRS file from information on the patient's CIRS record card. To simplify keypunching and editing, a program, called PREFOL, was written to preprocess the data keypunched from the data form. PREFOL scans the punched data for errors, issues diagnostics when necessary, generates a listing for proofreading, and punches RIQS format input cards. After the data has been proofread, corrected and rechecked, the data cards punched by PREFOL are used as input to the RIQS initial entry phase.

(1) Cardiology Number
(2) Patient Name
(3) Sex
(4) Area
(5) Hospital Number
(6) X-ray Number
(7) Autopsy Number
(8) Research Links
(9) Illustrative Case Material
(10) Date of Material

(13) Event
(14) Date of Event
(15) Diagnosis
(16) Patient Category
(17) Procedures Performed
(18) Complications
(19) Age
(20) Weight
(21) Status
(22) Comments

(23) Catheterization Number
(24) Qp – pulmonary blood flow
(25) Qp/Qs – pulmonary blood flow/systemic blood flow
(26) Rp – pulmonary resistance
(27) SA – saturation
(28) PA – blood pressure, pulmonary artery
(29) PR – blood pressure, right ventricle
(30) Ao – blood pressure, aorta
(31) LV – blood pressure, left ventricle
(32) RA – mean pressure, right atrium
(33) LA – mean pressure, left atrium

Figure 14.3. CIRS file item structure.

File Update

As each new patient event occurs, information concerning the type of event, date, diagnosis, procedures performed, etc. is recorded on the patient's CIRS record card. The updates to the CIRS record cards are then keypunched for input to a program called PUP, Preprocessor for the Update Phase. PUP allows the updates to be punched in a more efficient manner than if they were punched in RIQS update format directly. PUP validates the keypunched information, issues error messages and generates a printed listing of the updates for proofreading.

When updating a RIQS record, RIQS requires the specific RIQS record number of the patient record to be updated. Since this arbitrary record number assigned by RIQS at the record creation time is not available on the CIRS record card, an index—in order by cardiology number—is kept by PUP. This index, created by another program, contains the name and RIQS record number associated with each patient's cardiology number.

After the update cards have been proofread and corrected, they are then processed by PUP again, this time generating RIQS update cards. These cards are then used as direct input to the RIQS update phase.

File Searching

File searching is the most important aspect of the CIRS system since the effort of creating and maintaining the file was made to make possible the easy search for cases exhibiting the combination of characteristics currently under study.

Using the simple yet sophisticated RIQS search commands, file searches are made of the CIRS file to locate patient records meeting the precise search criteria. For example, a search to retrieve all records of patients with posterior (A–V canal type) ventricular septal defect who were born after January 1, 1965, have been catheterized, have since died and have had a postmortem examination would be as follows:

IF (13) EQ ('DEM' AND 'CA') AND (15) EQ 'VSDP'

AND (14.1) GE JANUARY 1, 1965 THEN PRINT RECORD

The compound search commands permit both simple searches such as major diagnostic categories or very selective searches such as specific case findings.

A request to retrieve the record (patient name not recalled) of a patient with coarctation of the aorta who had unsuccessful surgery complicated by massive bleeding at our center who subsequently had further surgery elsewhere would be as follows:

IF (13) EQ ('SU' AND 'SUE') AND (15) EQ ('COA')

AND (18) EQ ('HEM') THEN PRINT RECORD

Specialized Output

The output generated by RIQS of all patient records satisfying the search criteria was extremely voluminous. Since only one item was printed per line, patient records would frequently extend over three or four pages of computer printout. This form of output was unfamiliar to the physicians requesting the searches as well as being rather unwieldy.

Instead of using the RIQS search output directly, another program, called REPORT, was developed to read the entire search output file generated by RIQS and produce neat and compact output reports (Figure 14.4). These reports take the familiar form of the original CIRS record cards and four or five patient records usually fit on each page of output. Thus, the physician receives the patient history record of all patients retrieved by RIQS in a familiar form that is easily interpreted.

Other types of graphical output may be generated from the RIQS search output. The medical or surgical experience of the center for individual diagnostic categories can be presented and updated as calendar frequency plots such as illustrated here for surgical correction of patent ductus arteriosus (Figure 14.5). These can be expanded to include complication and mortality incidence.

In one case a researcher theorized that a particular cardiac defect was provoked by atmospheric pollution levels prevailing during the time period surrounding conception. A search was made of all children born with this cardiac defect retrieving their associated birthdates from 1934 to 1969 (Figure 14.6). From the birthdate the approximate date of conception was computed. A histogram was then generated that plotted the frequency of defect versus the year and month of conception. Using available pollution data another graph was derived of the relative pollution levels during the years. From the two graphs it could be shown that there was no evident relationship between the incidence of the defect and atmospheric pollution levels.

Numeric data from the cardiac catheterization studies can be plotted to rapidly explore two and three variable relationships.

```
      CARDIOLOGY INFORMATION RETRIEVAL SYSTEM-VERSION 1.0          09/02/73             15.46.53.     PAGE        3
      IF (15) EQ ≠TETP≠ THEN PRINT RECORD..

***                         04661      M          3          120164    120164               406
                                                  CATH       QP    QP/RS RP   SA   PA   PR   AO   LV   RA   LA
                                                  720102     6.2   2.6   2    86   12   160  90   90   10   9.5
      EVENTS    DATE      DIAGNOSIS                          P CAT      PROCEDURE COMP      AGE       WEIGHT     STATUS

      BI        10/06/67  -                                             -                   1         4
      CO        03/05/68  PVA VSD Q / PDA                               -                   150       12.1
      SU        03/09/68  S / TETP                                      COO                 154       -
      .  .  .   -         -                                             -                   0         -
      CO        12/18/69  S / TETP                                      -                   803       24.9
      CO        06/11/70  S / TETP                           -          -         -         9         27.5       -
      CA        05/03/72  S / TETP HYRV TS ASD TI            -          -         -         1669      -          -

      COMMENTS
      FISTULOUS COMMUNICATION WITH SINUS OF VALSALVA

        NAME                FILE       SEX        AREA       HOSPITAL   XRAY      AUTOPSY   RIQS
***                         05265      F          2          021113     104205    059030     587
      EVENTS    DATE      DIAGNOSIS                          P CAT      PROCEDURE COMP      AGE       WEIGHT     STATUS

      BI        05/16/58  -                                  -                              1
      CO        11/28/58  TRN                                P                              196
      CI        02/22/59  TGAA VSD PVA CHF ROS               -                              282
      DEM       02/22/59  TETP VSD PDA                       -                              282

        NAME                FILE       SEX        AREA       HOSPITAL   XRAY      AUTOPSY   RIQS
***                         01157      M          3                     170286               781
      ILLUS.    DATE
      CYNOCY
      EVENTS    DATE      DIAGNOSIS                          P CAT      PROCEDURE COMP      AGE       WEIGHT     STATUS

      BI        10/21/68  -                                  -                              1         -
      CO        11/12/68  TETP                               P                              22        9.4
      CO        12/17/68  - Q / FM                           -                              57        13.4
      CO        03/11/69  NSHO Q / PLCYNT                    -                              141       19.1

      COMMENTS
      CYNOCY - CYANOSIS AS INFANT - THEN NO CYANOSIS .
```

Figure 14.4. Output generated by REPORT from RIQS search output.

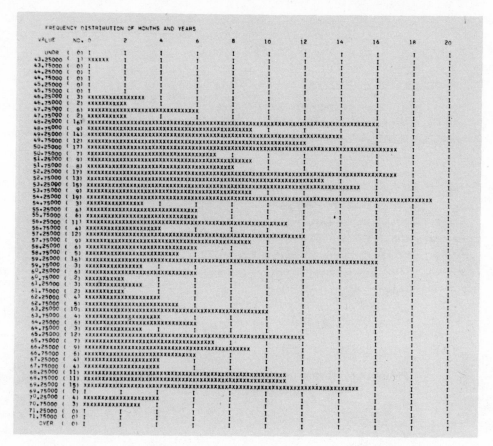

Figure 14.5. Frequency of surgical correction of patent ductus.

When the cardiology patient files were converted, for ease of filing, from an alphabetical to a numerical filing system the CIRS file simplified the conversion process. The secretarial staff was saved from having to type or write identification data on 17,000 file folders. Using the RIQS file, the patient name, cardiology number, birthdate and hospital number were printed on a self-adhesive label for easy application to the file folders. (Figure 14.7)

Besides research activity, the CIRS file has proven to be a valuable administrative tool. Periodically, after new additions and updates have been applied to the file, alphabetical listings and numerical cross references are generated. Each of the listings produced, one in order by name, the other in order by cardiology number, contains the patient's name, cardiology number, hospital number and birthdate. Since all cardiology records are kept in order by cardiology number, the two listings are an essential item in locating patient records.

The CIRS file or a derivative of it will eventually be integrated into active daily patient use when input/output facilities are established within the cardiology department.

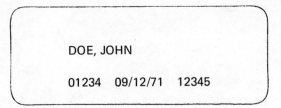

Figure 14.6. Histogram of frequency of defect versus month and year of conception.

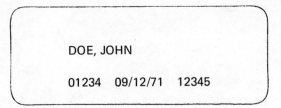

DOE, JOHN

01234   09/12/71   12345

Figure 14.7. Sample of self-adhesive label.

Results and Conclusions

The RIQS system has facilitated the establishment of a cardiology information retrieval system that encompasses abstracted clinical data from 17,000 patient records. The system provides a very useful research function by allowing rapid scanning of data for initiation of exploratory research projects obviating the need for chart retrieval and examination until more detailed data is sought. The system also functions to provide a basic administrative tool by generating patient listings, numerical cross references and patient chart labels.

Chapter 15

Selective Retrieval, Statistical and Interactive Graphical Analysis of Skin Biopsy Data

FRED LEVIT, M.D.
Northwestern University Medical School

WAYNE DOMINICK
Northwestern University

The Problem

As part of the diagnostic examination of patients with dermatologic problems, a skin biopsy is often performed. The skin biopsy procedure consists of removing a portion of skin, processing it for microscopic examination, examination of the prepared tissue by a histopathologist, and the return of a report on the examination to the original physician. During the last 20 years the number of skin biopsies being submitted to the Department of Dermatology at Northwestern University Medical School and most other institutions has been steadily increasing. The factors involved in this increase are expected to continue operating in the future and a continual increase in the number of skin biopsies performed is expected.

During 1972, over 5000 skin biopsies were processed by this department. Even if there is no further increase in the annual number of specimens processed, each decade will provide 50,000 biopsies. At the present time, there are over 50,000 specimens on hand.

Every specimen submitted is accompanied by a data sheet containing a variety of kinds of information. Items of information include such things as the name of the patient, the name of the physician, the site of the biopsy, the duration of the lesion, a clinical diagnosis, and so on. The final report includes all of the information on the original data sheet plus the histopathologist's description of the tissue, the histopathologist's diagnosis, and some information as to whether special stains were done on the tissue, or whether the slide is an unusually good example of its type and should be retained as a teaching slide.

Skin biopsy data which have been filed for a number of years are an important source of material for a wide variety of research projects. It should be possible to go throughout the entire mass of data and extract whatever information is needed. Obviously, when 100,000 report sheets must be gone through in order to obtain the desired information, manual handling of the information is simply impossible. If the information sought must be found on the basis of multiple complex criteria, then manual methods are hopeless.

Paper methods of storing the information are also unsatisfactory. Ordinarily, as the mass of data accumulates, the paper is transferred to storage areas which are less and less accessible. If it is really desirable to work with this data, it is obvious that machine methods are necessary.

The machine methods selected for handling this data must meet certain criteria. Because a portion of the data consists of an English language text description of the histologic appearance of the tissue, the data handling method must be able to read English language text and do so at a speed which makes it economical. Because some of the data involves dates and durations, the data handling method must be able to interpret and compare dates, and be able to interpret and compare durations involving periods from hours to multiples of years. Because tissues are filed by serial number, obviously the method used must be able to perform arithmetic comparisons as well. Obviously, it should be possible to intermix all these functions.

In searching a file such as a skin biopsy file, the criteria used may range from very simple, such as finding a biopsy record by its serial number, to much more complex, for example, selecting slides which resemble in their histologic characteristics diseases not actually present. This would involve searching the English language text of the histopathologic description for certain phrases which might be characteristic of a given disease and at the same time searching the histologic diagnosis to be sure that this was not the actual disease present.

For the reasons outlined above, the biopsy data was entered into an automated information storage and retrieval system, RIQS, resulting in a machine-readable data base, which can be updated and searched as desired. The following sections of this chapter will describe the content of the data base and some of the retrievals and analyses that can be performed on the data.

The Data

The BIOPSY file contains about 5000 records for each year, permanently stored on tapes. The data base record format and a sample record are shown in Figures 15.1 and 15.2, respectively. Most of the data items contain textual (alphanumeric) content such as patient name, sex, race and information relevant to the biopsy—site, clinical and histopath description and diagnosis, comments, etc. Date items are used where appropriate and patient age (7) and duration of lesion (11) are stored as numeric data with units ranging from hours through years.

For the purposes of this chapter, a subset of the full BIOPSY data base, consisting of the first 500 records, was used. Within these records the patient name (5) and doctor name (9) have been replaced by the record number to ensure data privacy.

Research Strategy

The primary uses of the RIQS system have been to obtain the selective retrieval of records from the BIOPSY file on the basis of complex search criteria. The most common analyses

```
FILE DESCRIPTION -- BIOPSY              FILE


FILE CONTAINS 3229 RECORDS


ITEM NUMBERS AND NAMES


    1.   BICPSY NO.
    2.   CLINIC NO.
    3.   DATE RECEIVED
    4.   BIOPSY DATE
    5.   NAME
    6.   SEX
    7.   AGE
    8.   RACE
    9.   DOCTOR
   10.   BIOPSY SITE
   11.   DURATION OF LESION
   12.   CLINICAL HISTORY
   13.   CLINICAL DESCRIPTION
   14.   CLINICAL DIAGNOSIS
   15.   HISTOPATH DESCRIPTION
   16.   HISTOPATH DIAGNCSIS
   17.   COMMENTS
   18.   HISTCPATHOLOGIST
   19.   SPECIAL STAINS
   20.   RECUTS
   21.   TEACHING SLIDE
   22.   PREVIOUS BIOPSY NC.


ITEM DESCRIPTIONS


    1.   SIMPLE, INTEGER
    2.   SIMPLE, ALPHANUMERIC
    3.   SIMPLE, DATE
    4.   SIMPLE, DATE
    5.   SIMPLE, ALPHANUMERIC
    6.   SIMPLE, ALPHANUMERIC
    7.   SIMPLE, DECIMAL WITH UNITS  ,  1 Y = 12.00 M  ,  1 M =  4.29 W  ,  1 W =  7.00 D  ,  1 D = 24.00 H
    8.   SIMPLE, ALPHANUMERIC
    9.   SIMPLE, ALPHANUMERIC
   10.   SIMPLE, ALPHANUMERIC
   11.   SIMPLE, DECIMAL WITH UNITS  ,  1 Y = 12.00 M  ,  1 M =  4.29 W  ,  1 W =  7.00 D  ,  1 D = 24.00 H
   12.   SIMPLE, ALPHANUMERIC
   13.   SIMPLE, ALPHANUMERIC
   14.   SIMPLE, ALPHANUMERIC
   15.   SIMPLE, ALPHANUMERIC
   16.   SIMPLE, ALPHANUMERIC
   17.   SIMPLE, ALPHANUMERIC
   18.   SIMPLE, ALPHANUMERIC
   19.   SIMPLE, ALPHANUMERIC
   20.   SIMPLE, ALPHANUMERIC
   21.   SIMPLE, ALPHANUMERIC
   22.   SIMPLE, ALPHANUMERIC
```

Figure 15.1. Biopsy file description.

involve searching for the occurrence or nonoccurrence of specific keywords or phrases in clinical or histopath description or diagnosis and generating reports consisting of the records, or specific data items within records, which satisfy the search criteria.

The first sample search generates a listing of specific data items for records which contain the phrase 'BASAL CELL CARCINOMA' in the histopath diagnosis (16) but not in the clinical diagnosis (14) and where the duration of lesion (11) is greater than forty years. The search is shown in Figure 15.3.

The second example illustrates the retrieval of all records which contain any of a series of diagnoses. Specifically, the search generates a listing of biopsy numbers (1) of all patients whose histopath description (15) contains any of the words 'LYMPHOCYTIC,' 'INFILTRATE' or 'INFILTRATION.' Figure 15.4 illustrates the search text and retrieval.

Another application may be the generation of an age distribution for a given diagnosis. The search text of Figure 15.5a generates an SPSS file of a patient's age normalized to

```
RECORD NUMBER      1
    (1) BIOPSY NO.
    172
    (3) DATE RECEIVED
    1-3-72
    (4) BIOPSY DATE
    12-30-71
    (5) NAME
    1
    (6) SEX
    F
    (7) AGE
    57Y
    (8) RACE
    W
    (9) DOCTOR
    1
    (10) BIOPSY SITE
    LEFT FRONTAL SCALP.
    (11) DURATION OF LESION
    2Y
    (12) CLINICAL HISTORY
    ASYMPTOMATIC AREA, PATIENT NOT AWARE OF CHANGE.
    (13) CLINICAL DESCRIPTION
    LARGE IRREGULAR PLAQUE WITH NODULARITY AND VARIABLE PIGMENT.
    (14) CLINICAL DIAGNOSIS
    BASAL CELL CARCINOMA.
    (15) HISTOPATH DESCRIPTION
    THE EPIDERMIS SHOWS EFFACEMENT OF THE RETE RIDGES, AND WITHIN
    THE DERMIS ONE SEES IRREGULAR MASSES OF BASALOID CELLS.  THE
    SURROUNDING STROMA IS FIBROTIC.
    (16) HISTOPATH DIAGNOSIS
    BASAL CELL CARCINOMA
    (18) HISTOPATHOLOGIST
    W. A. CARO
```

Figure 15.2.   Sample biopsy record.

years for all records in which the histopath diagnosis (16) contains the diagnosis 'BASAL CELL CARCINOMA.'

Figure 15.5b illustrates the use of the on-line version of SPSS in order to generate an age distribution from the SPSS file 1 of Figure 15.5a.

Additional analyses have been conducted over the BIOPSY file by using some of the RIQSONLINE graphics capabilities. Figures 15.6 through 15.11 are photographs taken from the screen of an IMLAC graphics terminal illustrating plot generation within RIQSONLINE and interactive plot modification and analysis, resulting in the isolation of a piece of incorrect data in the BIOPSY file.

Figure 15.6 contains the search text employed to generate a data plot of patient age (7) against the duration of lesion (11). The search was prestored on a file called BIOPSY1, which was called into execution via a BEGIN SEARCH FROM command. This capability for saving searches on files can prove very useful for canned searches which must be executed over a data base repetitively. The search only scans a previously defined subset of the data base, namely SET 1, which contains all records for which both (7)=Age and (11)=Duration of Lesion have been entered. The search normalizes these quantities to years (they are stored in the data base in hours) and then generates two subplots, the first representing males (#6 EQ 'M') and the second representing females (#6 EQ 'F').

Figure 15.7 shows the plot as generated to the graphics terminal. The data points plotted with an X represent males and those plotted with an O represent females. All axis scaling and labeling is provided internally with no user input required.

```
ENTER SEARCH COMMAND OR TYPE HALT

? BEGIN SEARCH
? IF #16 EQ 'BASAL CELL CARCINOMA' AND
?    #14 NE 'BASAL CELL CARCINOMA' AND
?    #11 GT 40 Y
? THEN DISPLAY #10 THRU #16;
? END

SEARCHING INITIATED


NO. OF REPORTS ON DISPLAY FILE =    2

DO YOU WANT THE DISPLAY REPORTS LISTED
? Y


RECORD NUMBER   102
    (10) BIOPSY SITE
    LEFT BREAST.
    (11) DURATION OF LESION
    45Y
    (13) CLINICAL DESCRIPTION
    2 CM PLAQUE, AREA OF REDNESS, SMALL ROLLED BORDER.
    (14) CLINICAL DIAGNOSIS
    SUPERFICIAL BASAL CELL EPITHELIOMA.
    (15) HISTOPATH DESCRIPTION
    THERE IS MILD HYPERKERATOSIS AND PARAKERATOSIS.  THE SURFACE
    EPIDERMIS IS OF NORMAL THICKNESS, BUT CONTINUOUS WITH THIS ONE
    SEES AN IRREGULAR PROLIFERATION OF BASALOID CELLS INTO THE UPPER
    DERMIS.  THIS PROLIFERATION IS ARRANGED IN THICK CORDS AND
    PATCHES AND CIRCUMSCRIBED SMALL AREAS OF CONNECTIVE TISSUE.  IN
    MOST AREAS THERE IS MARKED PERIPHERAL PALISADING.
    (16) HISTOPATH DIAGNOSIS
    BASAL CELL CARCINOMA


RECORD NUMBER   283
    (10) BIOPSY SITE
    GLABELLA AREA.
    (11) DURATION OF LESION
    44Y
    (13) CLINICAL DESCRIPTION
    PIGMENTED LESION.
    (14) CLINICAL DIAGNOSIS
    SEBORRHEIC KERATOSIS VS.  NEVUS.
    (15) HISTOPATH DESCRIPTION
    THE EPIDERMIS IS IRREGULAR, AND WITHIN THE DERMIS ONE SEES
    VARIABLY SIZED MASSES OF BASALOID CELLS.  IN ADDITION, THERE IS
    CONSIDERABLE PIGMENT SCATTERED THROUGHOUT THE DERMIS.  THE
    DERMIS ITSELF IS EDEMATOUS
    (16) HISTOPATH DIAGNOSIS
    PIGMENTED BASAL CELL CARCINOMA
```

Figure 15.3. First example.

Figure 15.8 illustrates the plot after several modification options have been utilized. Specifically, the plot was re-scaled to include only the points with a Y value (Duration of Lesion) of greater than or equal to 15 years and text was inserted into the plot for X and Y axis labels and for the plot title. These modifications were accomplished via light pen option selection and keyboard type-ins for labeling. The plot contains an extreme point on the Duration and Lesion axis in the lower left corner. This point is so positioned that it represents a patient whose duration of lesion is between 15 and 23 years but whose age is only eight years. The next figure examines this situation more closely.

```
ENTER SEARCH COMMAND OR TYPE HALT

? BEGIN SEARCH
? IF #15 CONTAINS ('LYMPHOCYTIC' OR 'INFILTRATE' OR 'INFILTRATION')
? THEN DISPLAY SUPPRESS #1;
? END

SEARCHING INITIATED


NO. OF REPORTS ON DISPLAY FILE =    182

DO YOU WANT THE DISPLAY REPORTS LISTED
? Y
        472
        772
       1572
       1872
       1972
       2272
       2372
       2472
       2572
       3172
       3372
       3572
       3672
       3772
       3972
       4072
        :
        :
       etc.
```

Figure 15.4.   Second example.

```
ENTER SEARCH COMMAND OR TYPE HALT

? BEGIN SEARCH
? IF #16 CONTAINS 'BASAL CELL CARCINOMA' AND #7 GT 0
? THEN LET AGE = #7 / 1 Y , SPSSFILE 1 OF AGE;
? END

SEARCHING INITIATED


SPSS SAVED FILE NUMBER 1 EXISTS ON SPSSFL1
    CATALOG IT IF YOU WISH TO RETAIN IT


   *    *    *    *    *
```

Figure 15.5a.   Third example.

In Figure 15.9, the data point mentioned above has been selected via the light pen and the exact X and Y coordinate values as well as the RIQS record number from which the point was derived have been displayed. Thus we see that the patient of record number 187 has an age of eight years, but his duration of lesion has a value of 18 years! This clearly indicates an incorrect item of data. By light penning the DISPLAY RECORD option of this figure, record number 187 will be displayed in its entirety.

```
ENTER SEARCH COMMAND OR TYPE HALT

? SPSSLINK 1
SPSS-ONLINE
NEW VERSION-PROGRAM LIBRARY WRITEUP NUCC296
USE OVER 100 VARIABLES OR OVER 5 SUBFILES? N
USE A SAVE-FILE THIS RUN? Y
AUTO-MODE.
? 10.GET FILE;D42BIOPSY
? 20.CODEBOOK;AGE
? 30.FINISH
? EXECUTE
ENTERING SPSS.
 SPSSONLINE - NORTHWESTERN UNIVERSITY (V3.0)

- - - CODEBOOK - - -

SUBFILE

VARIABLE - AGE          AGE

VALUE LABEL      VALUE      FREQ   REL %   ADJ %   CUM %

                 37.00       1      1.0     1.0     1.0
                 38.00       1      1.0     1.0     1.9
                 39.00       1      1.0     1.0     2.9
                 42.00       1      1.0     1.0     3.8
                 43.00       3      2.9     2.9     6.7
                 44.00       5      4.8     4.8    11.4
                 45.00       3      2.9     2.9    14.3
                 46.00       1      1.0     1.0    15.2
                 47.00       3      2.9     2.9    18.1
                 48.00       5      4.8     4.8    22.9
                 49.00       2      1.9     1.9    24.8
                 50.00       4      3.8     3.8    28.6
                 51.00       4      3.8     3.8    32.4
                 52.00       1      1.0     1.0    33.3
                 53.00       2      1.9     1.9    35.2
                 54.00       4      3.8     3.8    39.0
                 55.00       2      1.9     1.9    41.0
                 56.00       3      2.9     2.9    43.8
                 57.00       3      2.9     2.9    46.7
                 58.00       1      1.0     1.0    47.6
                 59.00       8      7.6     7.6    55.2
                 61.00       3      2.9     2.9    58.1
                 62.00       5      4.8     4.8    62.9
                 63.00       6      5.7     5.7    68.6
                 65.00       1      1.0     1.0    69.5
                 67.00       2      1.9     1.9    71.4
                 68.00       1      1.0     1.0    72.4
                 69.00       1      1.0     1.0    73.3
                 70.00       4      3.8     3.8    77.1
                 71.00       1      1.0     1.0    78.1
                 72.00       6      5.7     5.7    83.8
                 73.00       1      1.0     1.0    84.8
                 74.00       6      5.7     5.7    90.5
                 75.00       1      1.0     1.0    91.4
                 76.00       3      2.9     2.9    94.3
                 77.00       1      1.0     1.0    95.2
                 81.00       2      1.9     1.9    97.1
                 87.00       1      1.0     1.0    98.1
                 90.00       1      1.0     1.0    99.0
                 94.00       1      1.0     1.0   100.0
                 BLANK       0      0.0    ****   100.0

                 TOTAL     105    100.0   100.0   100.0


OBSERVATIONS: VALID -      105       MISSING -         0
```

Figure 15.5b.   Age distribution via SPSSONLINE.

```
ENTER SEARCH COMMAND OR TYPE HALT

? BEGIN SEARCH FROM BIOPSY1


  BEGIN SEARCH OF SET 1
  LET AGE = #7/1Y   LET DURATION = #11/1Y
  IF #6 EQ 'M' THEN PLOT AGE VRS DURATION;
  IF #6 EQ 'F' THEN PLOT AGE VRS DURATION;
  END

SEARCHING INITIATED




NO. OF RECORDS   GENERATED TO 1ST PLOT FILE =   205
NO. OF POINTS    GENERATED TO 1ST PLOT FILE =   205

NO. OF RECORDS   GENERATED TO 2ND PLOT FILE =   205
NO. OF POINTS    GENERATED TO 2ND PLOT FILE =   205


DO YOU WANT THE PLOT GENERATED
?
```

Figure 15.6. Search text for plot generation.

Figure 15.10 is the display of the first part of record number 187. It can be seen from this display that for this record, either item (7) or item (11) has been entered incorrectly into the data since a duration of lesion greater than a patient's age cannot be valid. After a full screen of information has been displayed, the system waits for the user to hit a function key telling the system to continue. Figure 15.11 represents the remainder of record 187.

This example illustrates the use of the RIQSONLINE graphics capabilities only within the area of extrema analysis for isolating bad data within a file. Its use for trend analysis and examining the relationships between variables or data items can be of even greater importance.

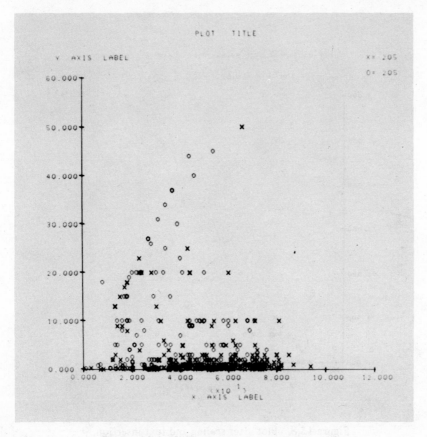

Figure 15.7. IMLAC graphics processor plot.

Conclusions

The major use for the complete BIOPSY file, which now contains over 20,000 records, has involved searches for records meeting certain histopathologic criteria. In these searches it has been possible to locate the few records out of the total file which meet the complex criteria of the search. This, together with the availability of statistical analysis of the file, has converted what was at one time a dead and almost useless mass of stored information into one which can easily be searched and manipulated. This has made easy and quick a type of dermatologic research which formerly was infrequently done because it was frustratingly tedious.

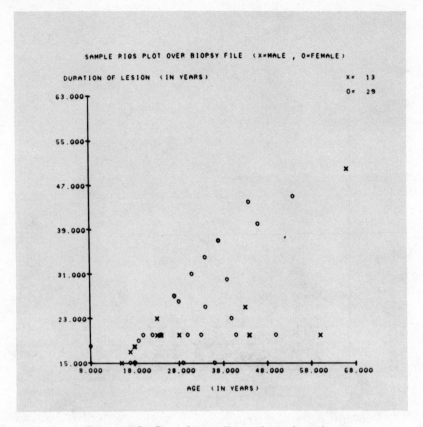

Figure 15.8. Plot after scaling and text insertion.

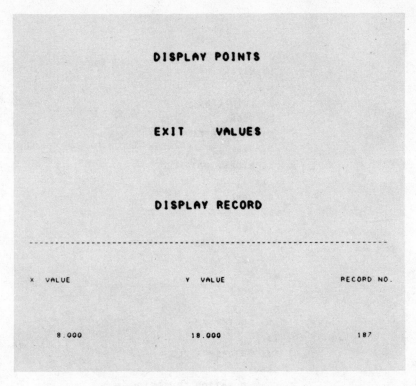

Figure 15.9. Data point VALUES option.

```
RECORD NUMBER   187
    (1) BIOPSY NO.
    18772
    (2) CLINIC NO.
    FERGUSON
    (3) DATE RECEIVED
    1-17-72
    (4) BIOPSY DATE
    1-14-72
    (5) NAME
    187
    (6) SEX
    F
    (7) AGE
    8Y
    (8) RACE
    W
    (9) DOCTOR
    187
    (10) BIOPSY SITE
    SCALP.
    (11) DURATION OF LESION
    18Y
    (12) CLINICAL HISTORY
    ENLARGING WARTY GROWTH.


    WAITING
```

Figure 15.10.   Displayed record (first part).

```
(13) CLINICAL DESCRIPTION
VERRUCOUS LESION 5 X 4 CM.
(14) CLINICAL DIAGNOSIS
WART VS.  VERRUCOUS NEVUS.
(15) HISTOPATH DESCRIPTION
THIS IS A PAPILLOMATOUS LESION WITH MARKED HYPERKERATOSIS.  THE
EPIDERMIS SHOWS SOME IRREGULAR ACANTHOSIS WITH VACUOLIZATION OF
EPIDERMAL CELLS.  THIS VACUOLIZATION CHANGES ARE CONSIDERED
ARTIFACT DUE TO FREEZING OF TISSUE.  WITHIN THE DERMIS ONE SEES
DILATATION OF THE SUPERFICIAL VESSELS AND A PATCHY INFLAMMATORY
INFILTRATE OF LYMPHOCYTES.
(16) HISTOPATH DIAGNOSIS
CONSISTENT WITH EPIDERMAL NEVUS
(17) COMMENTS
THIS LESION HAS THE HISTOPATHOLOGIC PICTURE OF A VERRUCA
VULGARIS, BUT THE LIFELONG HISTORY SUPPORTS THE DIAGNOSIS OF AN
EPIDERMAL NEVUS
(18) HISTOPATHOLOGIST
W.  A.  CARO



*  *  *  *  *


(PRESS -CR- TO RETURN TO GRAPHICS)
?  _
```

Figure 15.11.   Displayed record (second part).

Chapter 16

The Midwest Regional Spinal Cord Injury Care System[1]

KATHLEEN R. FLAHERTY
Northwestern University

THOMAS MARTIN
E.I. Du Pont de Nemours & Co.

BYRON B. HAMILTON, M.D.
Rehabilitation Institute of Chicago

GUSTAVE J. RATH
Northwestern University

The Problem

In June of 1972, the Federal Government inaugurated a series of special demonstration centers on spinal cord injury care. The purpose of the project was to establish a regional system of treatment of spinal cord injuries and to evaluate that system.

The Midwest Regional Spinal Cord Injury Care System (MRSCICS) is centered in Chicago, Illinois and represents an area consisting of all of Illinois and parts of Wisconsin, Michigan, and Indiana. Of approximately 20 million people in the area, it has been estimated that 500 new spinal cord injuries occur annually. The system of care for the region is provided through Northwestern Memorial Hospital—Wesley Pavilion, the acute care facility, and the Rehabilitation Institute of Chicago. Both are components of Northwestern University—McGaw Medical Center and have been coordinated to offer a continuous system of care to spinal cord injured individuals.

The objectives of this demonstration project directed at comprehensive care of the spinal cord injured may be summarized as follows: decreased incidence, mortality, extent and complications of the spinal cord injury; increased functional capability, vocational, educational, and significant societal placement; and decreased duration and cost of acute and rehabilitation care. The operational method of achieving these objectives is by putting together an organized system of care composed of *prevention*, rapid *evacuation*, early *acute care*, early *rehabilitation*, and long term *follow-along*.

In order to demonstrate that the spinal cord injury care system concept is (or is not) cost/effective, an information system has been developed to document how well the objectives have been achieved as well as what methods were actually used. Indicators of

264

system input and output were incorporated in a data base to be used as an evaluation instrument.

The nature of the instrument requires that information for 229 variables be gathered from medical charts, verbal communication with patients, medical and allied health staffs, and from financial records of the two system hospitals and the multitude of feeder facilities. The system currently processes approximately two hundred spinal cord injured inpatients annually (a number which will increase significantly with the opening of the new Rehabilitation Institute of Chicago in 1974 and expanding awareness of system availability in the region). During the scheduled five-year project it is anticipated that the data base will contain, at minimum, the specified prospective data attributes on 900 individuals. Retrospective data will cover patients admitted during the one year prior to system implementation, increasing the anticipated record content of the data base to 1000. An adequate basis for comparison of the outcomes of care under presystem, nonsystem, and system of care conditions will be afforded.

Thus, the data base is very large. Manual response time would be extremely long, and man hours and personnel costs correspondingly high. The frequent manipulation expected of this data coupled with high information reliability requirements seemed to indicate a computerized storage and retrieval system.

The suitability of the RIQS program for the purposes of MRSCICS seemed very appropriate from a listing of certain of its features. RIQS is capable of storing and retrieving the records of patients, updating, and searching the records. Additionally, it is capable of printing reports, and with the link with the Statistical Package for the Social Sciences of performing whatever statistical computations might be required on the data. Since RIQSONLINE makes information retrieval possible via remote terminal, interaction with the data base is possible from any point in the country and on-the-spot comparisons of data with that of the other spinal cord centers becomes simplified. Dates, numeric and free English forms for input data are all allowed as item forms without coding. This simplifies understanding and visual verification of both input and output data. Internal validity checks are built in. The password capability increases RIQS appeal for storage and retrieval of personal medical information where confidentiality is critical. The availability of knowledgeable consultation at the Vogelback Computing Center of Northwestern University and the simplicity of the language itself obviated, on limited funds, the services of experts in computer programming and contributed significantly to the consideration and eventual selection of RIQS as the language for computerization of the MRSCICS data base.

The Data

Ten records have been chosen to illustrate RIQS manipulations applied to the MRSCICS study. The patient population selected for this illustration represents a match of system patients,[2] the experimental population, with an equal number of nonsystem patients, the control population. The patients were chosen on the basis of type of injury (paraplegic[3] or quadriplegic[4]) to provide major variable control, and date of injury for randomness control.

Figure 16.1 displays the RIQS record definition of the data base in terms of item numbers and names. Figure 16.2 contains the partial contents of a patient record after file creation.

1. Patient name
2. Home address at time of accident
3. Present home address
4. Social security number
5. Number of admissions
6. Names of hospitals
7. Medical record numbers
8. Was patient in trauma system
9. Trauma registry number
10. Other files this person is included in
11. Dummy
  : :
15. Record number
16. Date of last addition to record
17. Date next action due on record
18. Action due to be taken
19. Dummy
  : :
23. Birth date
24. Place of birth — city, state, country
25. Sex
26. Race
27. Religion
28. Marital status at time of accident
29. Change in marital status
30. Date of change in marital status
31. Number of children at time of accident
32. Change in number of children
33. Date of change in number of children
34. Number of dependents at time of accident
35. Change in number of dependents
36. Date of change in number of dependents
37. Family role before accident
38. Change in family role
39. Date of change in family role
40. Type of residence before accident
41. Living with whom before accident
42. Dummy
  : :
50. Educational level at time of accident
51. Change in education level

52. Date of change in education level
53. Occupation before injury
54. Yearly income from occupation
55. Yearly income from other sources
56. Occupations after discharge
57. Date occupation started
58. Date occupation ended
59. Yearly income from occupation
60. Yearly income from other sources
61. Dummy
  : :
70. Time of injury
71. Date of injury
72. Age at time of accident
73. Place of injury — city, state
74. Distance of place of injury from residence
75. Patient conscious after accident
76. Awareness of feeling below level of injury
77. Type of accident
78. Circumstances of accident
79. Pathology of disability
80. Time arrived at emergency facility
81. Distance from scene of accident
82. Was injury worsened between accident and care
83. Initial neurological deficit
84. Initial level of neurological deficit
85. Level of bony injury
86. Initial completeness
87. Associated craniocerebral injuries
88. Other injuries
89. Paralysis or other neurological deficit
90. Time deficit first noted
91. Lower limbs motor loss
92. Upper limbs motor loss
93. Drug treatment
94. Time of treatment with drugs
95. Method of immobilization
96. Dummy
  : :

Figure 16.1. Data items.

99. Name of hospitals
100. Location of hospitals — city, state
101. Reason for admission
102. Where transferred from
103. Admission date
104. Time of admission
105. Means of transportation
106. Cost of transportation
107. Transportation handled by
108. Level of spinal cord injury at admission
109. Completeness of deficit at admission
110. Motor loss of lower limbs at admission
111. Motor loss of upper limbs at admission
112. Functional gain composite at admission
113. Urinary management at admission
114. Urine sterility at admission
115. Bladder classification at admission
116. Dummy
:   :
125. No. of days spent in emergency room
126. No. of days spent in intensive care
127. Date occurrence of decubiti noted- - 1
128. Location of decubiti- - 1
:   :
135. Date other complication noted- - 1
136. Description of other complication- - 1
:   :
151. Date of operation- - 1
152. Type of operation- - 1
:   :
157. Types of assistive devices
158. Types of behavior problems
159. Care for behavior problems
160. Units of physical therapy
161. Units of occupational therapy
162. Primary physician

163. Rehabilitation team
164. Liaison nurse
165. Dummy
:   :
174. Dummy
175. Discharge date
176. Reason for discharge
177. Type of residence discharged to
178. Living with whom after discharge
179. Level of spinal cord injury at discharge
180. Completeness of deficit at discharge
181. Motor loss in lower limbs at discharge
182. Motor loss in upper limbs at discharge
183. Functional gain composite at discharge
184. Urinary management at discharge
185. Urine sterility at discharge
186. Bladder classification at discharge
187. Dummy
:   :
195. Cost of hospitalization
196. Source of funds- - 1
197. Amount contributed- - 1
:   :
208. Dummy
:   :
215. Date of suicide attempts
216. Method of suicide attempts
217. Reason for suicide attempt
218. Result of suicide attempt
219. Dummy
220. Dates of visits to out-patient facility
221. Name of out-patient facility
222. Reason for out-patient visit
223. Cost of out-patient visit
224. Dummy
:   :
227. Date of death
228. Place of death
229. Cause of death

Figure 16.1(Continued). Data items.

```
RECORD  NUMBER      4

 15.   RECORD NUMBER
          4
 16.   DATE OF LAST ADDITION TO RECORD
          1/5/73
 17.   DATE NEXT ACTION DUE ON RECORD
          2/5/73
 18.   ACTION DUE TO BE TAKEN
          NEEDS UNITS OF THERAPY
 23.   BIRTH DATE
          4/15/54
 24.   PLACE OF BIRTH - CITY, STATE, COUNTRY
          SUB-2.... ILLINOIS
          SUB-3.... USA
 25.   SEX
          MALE
 26.   RACE
          CAUCASIAN
 27.   RELIGION
          PROTESTANT
 28.   MARITAL STATUS AT TIME OF ACCIDENT
          MARRIED
 31.   NUMBER OF CHILDREN AT TIME OF ACCIDENT
          0
 34.   NUMBER OF DEPENDENTS AT TIME OF ACCIDENT
          1
 37.   FAMILY ROLE BEFORE ACCIDENT
          BREADWINNER
 40.   TYPE OF RESIDENCE BEFORE ACCIDENT
          PRIVATE HOME ( WITH NO MODIFICATIONS )
 41.   LIVING WITH WHOM BEFORE ACCIDENT
          FAMILY
 50.   EDUCATIONAL LEVEL AT TIME OF ACCIDENT
          11
 53.   OCCUPATION BEFORE INJURY
          UNSKILLED EMPLOYEE - PICKUP TRUCK DRIVER, CONSTRUCTION LABORER
 70.   TIME OF INJURY
          15.00
 71.   DATE OF INJURY
          5/4/72
 72.   AGE AT TIME OF ACCIDENT
          18
 73.   PLACE OF INJURY - CITY, STATE
          SUB-1.... CARBONDALE
          SUB-2.... ILLINOIS
 75.   PATIENT CONSCIOUS AFTER ACCIDENT
          UNCONSCIOUS
 77.   TYPE OF ACCIDENT
          INDUSTRIAL
 78.   CIRCUMSTANCES OF ACCIDENT
          FALLING OR FLYING OBJECT
 79.   PATHOLOGY OF DISABILITY
          SUBLUXATION / DISLOCATION FRACTURE
 80.   TIME ARRIVED AT EMERGENCY FACILITY
          15.40
 83.   INITIAL NEUROLOGICAL DEFICIT
          PARAPLEGIA
 84.   INITIAL LEVEL OF NEUROLOGICAL DEFICIT
          T12
 86.   INITIAL COMPLETENESS
          COMPLETE
 88.   OTHER INJURIES
          SUB-1.... LOWER LIMBS
          SUB-2.... FACIAL
          SUB-3.... CHEST
          SUB-4.... TORSO
 91.   LOWER LIMBS MOTOR LOSS
          COMPLETE
 92.   UPPER LIMBS MOTOR LOSS
          NONE
 99.   NAME OF HOSPITALS
          SUB-1.... DOCTOR ≠ S HOSPITAL
          SUB-2.... NORTHWESTERN MEMORIAL HOSPITAL - WESELY PAVILION
          SUB-3.... REHABILITATION INSTITUTE OF CHICAGO
```

Figure 16.2. Partial printout of a patient record.

```
100.   LOCATION OF HOSPITALS - CITY,STATE
          SUB-1.... CARBONDALE, ILLINOIS
          SUB-2.... CHICAGO, ILLINOIS
          SUB-3.... CHICAGO, ILLINOIS
101.   REASON FOR ADMISSION
          SUB-1.... ADMISSION FOR INITIAL EMERGENCY CARE
          SUB-2.... DAMISSION FOR EMERGENCY CARE
          SUB-3.... ADMISSION OF CONTINUING CARE
102.   WHERE TRANSFERRED FROM
          SUB-1.... SCENE OF ACCIDENT
          SUB-2.... HOSPITAL
          SUB-3.... HOSPITAL
103.   ADMISSION DATE
          SUB-1.... 5/4/72
          SUB-2.... 5/4/72
          SUB-3.... 6/14/72
104.   TIME OF ADMISSION
          SUB-1.... 15.40
          SUB-2.... 22.30
          SUB-3.... 13.00
105.   MEANS OF TRANSPORTATION
          SUB-1.... AMBULANCE
          SUB-2.... HELICOPTER
          SUB-3.... AMBULANCE
107.   TRANSPORTATION HANDLED BY
          SUB-1.... FIRE DEPARTMENT
108.   LEVEL OF SPINAL CORD INJURY AT ADMISSION
          SUB-1.... T12
          SUB-2.... T12
          SUB-3.... T12
109.   COMPLETEMESS OF DEFICIT AT ADMISSION
          SUB-1.... COMPLETE
          SUB-2.... COMPLETE
          SUB-3.... COMPLETE
110.   MOTOR LOSS OF LOWER LIMBS AT ADMISSION
          SUB-1.... COMPLETE
          SUB-2.... COMPLETE
          SUB-3.... COMPLETE
111.   MOTOR LOSS OF UPPER LIMBS AT ADMISSION
          SUB-1.... NONE
          SUB-2.... NONE
          SUB-3.... NONE
113.   URINARY MANAGEMENT AT ADMISSION
          SUB-1.... NO COLLECTING DEVICE
          SUB-2.... INDWELLING CATHETER
          SUB-3.... INDWELLING CATHETER
114.   URINE STERILITY AT ADMISSION
          SUB-2.... STERILE
          SUB-3.... L INFECTED - PROTEUS RETTGERI
115.   BLADDER CLASSIFICATION AT ADMISSION
          SUB-1.... UPPER MOTOR NEURON
          SUB-2.... UPPER MOTOR NEURON
          SUB-3.... UPPER MOTOR NEURON
135.   DATE OTHER COMPLICATION NOTED - 1
          SUB-3.... 6/22/72
136.   DESCRIPTION OF OTHER COMPLICATION - 1
          SUB-3.... HEMATURIA
137.   DATE OTHER COMPLICATION NOTED - 2
          SUB-3.... 6/26/72
138.   DESCRIPTION OF OTHER COMPLICATION - 2
          SUB-3.... SPASTICITY
139.   DATE OTHER COMPLICATION NOTED - 3
          SUB-3.... 6/26/72
140.   DESCRIPTION OF OTHER COMPLICATION - 3
          SUB-3.... CEREBRAL INVOLVEMENT, ONTEMPORAL AREAS
```

Figure 16.2(Continued).   Partial printout of a patient record.

```
142.   DESCRIPTION OF OTHER COMPLICATION - 4
         SUB-3.... HETEROTOPIC BONE
151.   DATE OF OPERATION- 1
         SUB-2.... 5/24/72
152.   TYPE OF OPERATION - 1
         SUB-2.... ORTHOPEDIC - OPEN REDUCTION AND CASTING LEFT ANKLE
153.   DATE OF OPERATION- 2
         SUB-2.... 5/24/72
154.   TYPE OF OPERATION - 2
         SUB-2.... PULMONARY - TRACHEOSTOMY
157.   TYPES OF ASSISTIVE DEVICES
         SUB-3.... WHEELCHAIR
175.   DISCHARGE DATE
         SUB-1.... 5/4/72
         SUB-2.... 6/14/72
         SUB-3.... 8/23/72
176.   REASON FOR DISCHARGE
         SUB-1.... TRANSFER TO ANOTHR ER HOSPITAL
         SUB-2.... TRANSFER TO ANOTHER HOSPITAL
         SUB-3.... ACHIEVEMENT OF GOALS
177.   TYPE OF RESIDENCE DISCHARGED TO
         SUB-1.... HOSPITAL
         SUB-2.... HOSPITAL
         SUB-3.... PRIVATE HOME ( WITHOUT MODIFICATIONS )
178.   LIVING WITH WHOM AFTER DISCHARGE
         SUB-1.... INSTITUTIONAL SETTING
         SUB-2.... INSTITUTIONAL SETTING
         SUB-3.... FAMILY
179.   LEVEL OF SPINAL CORD INJURY AT DISCHARGE
         SUB-1.... T12
         SUB-2.... T12
         SUB-3.... T12
180.   COMPLETENESS OF DEFICIT AT DISCHARGE
         SUB-1.... COMPLETE
         SUB-2.... COMPLETE
         SUB-3.... COMPLETE
181.   MOTOR LOSS IN LOWER LIMBS AT DISCHARGE
         SUB-1.... COMPLETE
         SUB-2.... COMPLETE
         SUB-3.... COMPLETE
182.   MOTOR LOSS IN UPPER LIMBS AT DISCHARGE
         SUB-1.... NONE
         SUB-2.... NONE
         SUB-3.... NONE
184.   URINARY MANAGEMENT AT DISCHARGE
         SUB-1.... INDWELLING CATHETER
         SUB-2.... INDWELLING CATHETER
         SUB-3.... EXTERNAL CATHETER
185.   URINE STERILITY AT DISCHARGE
         SUB-2.... INFECTED - PROTEUS RETTGERI
         SUB-3.... INFECTED - PROTEUS RETTEGERI
186.   BLADDER CLASSIFICATION AT DISCHARGE
         SUB-1.... UPPER MOTOR NEURON
         SUB-2.... UPPER MOTOR NEURON
         SUB-3.... UPPER MOTOR NEURON
195.   COST OF HOSPITALIZATION
         SUB-1.... 10247
         SUB-2.... 7962
196.   SOURCE OF FUNDS - 1
         SUB-2.... WORKMAN ≠ S COMPENSATION
         SUB-3.... WORKMAN ≠ S COMPENSATION
197.   AMOUNT CONTRIBUTED - 1
         SUB-2.... 10174
         SUB-3.... 7961
198.   SOURCE OF FUNDS - 2
         SUB-2.... PATIENT
199.   AMOUNT CONTRIBUTED - 2
         SUB-2.... 72
```

Figure 16.2(Continued).   Partial printout of a patient record.

Research Strategy

The MRSCICS data base will be used to measure the impact of the system of care on the spinal cord injured in the area and achievement of system objectives. Demographic characteristics of the various patient subpopulations (presystem, nonsystem, and system) will be compiled and retrieved for reporting system input. Estimates on mortality in spinal cord injuries will be kept in the instrument together with indicators of morbidity. Morbidity measures have been specified in the areas of extent of injury and complications; subpopulations will be compared for variations. Life function as indicated by educational and vocational achievement will be monitored. Number of hospital days accrued in a given period may be tabulated with concomitant costs and differences among patient types. Data suitable for testing hypotheses in a variety of spinal cord injury research projects will be collected; these concern methods of prevention of the injury or its consequences; psycho-social attributes of trauma victims at the time of accident; and the effect of early treatment with steroids and osmotic agents.

One area in which significant impact of the system is anticipated is length of hospital stay. The system of care is expected to reduce the length of stay for spinal cord injured patients, particularly when the patient is admitted to Northwestern Memorial Hospital—Wesley Pavilion immediately post trauma. Figure 16.3 illustrates the date of injury, date of entry into MRSCICS and date of first definitive discharge on a study sample.[5] Records 2, 6, 7, 8 and 10 represent system patients; the remainder are nonsystem patients. A RIQS generated plot comparing the length of stay versus date of injury appears in Figure 16.4. The system patient is represented by an $\overline{X}$ while the X signifies the nonsystem individual. According to the graph, in all but one pair the system patient had a significantly shorter length of stay than did the nonsystem patients.[6]

In Figure 16.5 the relationship between length of stay and cost of hospitalization was sought. The search commands requested that paraplegics be indicated separately from quadriplegics. As might have been expected, costs were proportional to length of stay; the longer the hospitalization, the greater the costs incurred for spinal injuries. An additional anticipated outcome was that the more extensive injury (the quadriplegic) found in the search (indicated by $\big(/\big)$ in the plot) had both a longer stay and a higher cost than did the paraplegic. By combining these results with the data in Figure 16.4 illustrating a shorter length of stay for system patients, it may be inferred that the hospitalization costs for the system patient will be proportionally less than those for a nonsystem patient.

Figure 16.6 illustrates the function of the MRSCICS data base as a tool in drawing a demographic profile of the spinal cord injured individual. Sex, race, religion, and age were tabulated and also portrayed graphically in the histogram format. Such a description is of considerable interest to researchers in MRSCICS, other spinal injury centers, and the Department of Health, Education and Welfare. Additional work with the data base will indicate from where in the region MRSCICS patients come, what the circumstances of the accidents are, and how long it takes to get into the Spinal Cord Injury Care System.

A final illustration of an application of the data base is the construction of a computer simulation model of MRSCICS. This research endeavor acts as a check on data base adequacy and can provide the basis for a powerful system management tool. If the data base cannot provide an adequate basis for simulation, it is quite likely that some of the important data describing the system is missing from information currently collected.

```
RECØRD NUMBER      1
    (71) DATE ØF INJURY
    5/20/73
    (99) NAME ØF HØSPITALS

    ST.  LUKES HØSPITAL *REHABILITATIØN INSTITUTE ØF CHICAGØ
    (103) ADMISSIØN DATE
    5/20/73 *7/3/73
    (175) DISCHARGE DATE
    7/3/73 *8/14/73


RECØRD NJMBER      2
    (71) DATE ØF INJURY
    3/23/73
    (99) NAME ØF HØSPITALS
    CENTRAL CØMMUNITY HØSPITAL *NMH - WESLEY PAVILIØN *
    REHABILITATIØN INSTITUTE ØF CHICAGØ
    (103) ADMISSIØN DATE
    3/23/73 *3/23/73 *5/1/73
    (175) DISCHARGE DATE
    3/23/73 *5/1/73 *6/5/73


RECØRD NJMBER      3
    (71) DATE ØF INJJRY
    2/15/73
    (99) NAME ØF HØSPITALS
    ST.  JØHNS HØSPITAL *METHØDIST HØSPITAL *REHABILITATIØN
    INSTITUTE ØF CHICAGØ
    (103) ADMISSIØN DATE
    2/15/73 *2/15/73 *4/23/73
    (175) DISCHARGE DATE
    2/15/73 *4/23/73 *8/16/73


RECØRD NUMBER      4
    (71) DATE ØF INJJRY
    4/13/73
    (99) NAME ØF HØSPITALS
    CØNDELL MEMØRIAL HØSPITAL *REHABILITATIØN INSTITUTE ØF CHICAGØ

    (103) ADMISSIØN DATE
    4/13/73 *6/5/73
    (175) DISCHARGE DATE
    6/5/73 *9/11/73
```

Figure 16.3. The first underlined date in each record indicates the date of entry into MRSCICS (either facility). The second underlined date in each record indicates the date of first definitive discharge to the community.

```
RECORD NUMBER      6
     (71) DATE OF INJURY
     3/5/73
     (99) NAME OF HOSPITALS
     NORTHWEST COMMUNITY HOSPITAL *NMH - WESLEY PAVILION *

     REHABILITATION INSTITUTE OF CHICAGO
     (103) ADMISSION DATE
     3/5/73 *3/5/73 *4/10/73
     (175) DISCHARGE DATE
     3/5/73 *4/10/73 *5/22/73


RECORD NUMBER      7
     (71) DATE OF INJURY
     5/16/73
     (99) NAME OF HOSPITALS
     NMH - WESLEY PAVILION *REHABILITATION INSTITUTE OF CHICAGO
     (103) ADMISSION DATE
     5/16/73 *6/14/73
     (175) DISCHARGE DATE
     6/14/73 *8/16/73


RECORD NUMBER      8
     (71) DATE OF INJURY
     1/7/73
     (99) NAME OF HOSPITALS
     CENTRAL DU PAGE HOSPITAL *NMH - WESLEY PAVILION *REHABILITATION
     INSTITUTE OF CHICAGO
     (103) ADMISSION DATE
     1/7/73 *1/7/73 *1/21/73
     (175) DISCHARGE DATE
     1/7/73 *1/31/73 *3/8/73


RECORD NUMBER      9
     (71) DATE OF INJURY
     1/9/73
     (99) NAME OF HOSPITALS
     COMMUNITY GENERAL HOSPITAL *REHABILITATION INSTITUTE OF CHICAGO
     (103) ADMISSION DATE
     1/9/73 *2/28/73
     (175) DISCHARGE DATE
     1/9/73 *5/10/73


RECORD NUMBER      10
     (71) DATE OF INJURY
     4/11/73
     (99) NAME OF HOSPITALS
     ST. ANTHONYS HOSPITAL *NMH - WESLEY PAVILION *REHABILITATION
     INSTITUTE OF CHICAGO
     (103) ADMISSION DATE
     4/11/73 *4/11/73 *5/21/73
     (175) DISCHARGE DATE
     4/11/73 *5/21/73 *8/22/73
```

Figure 16.3. (Continued)

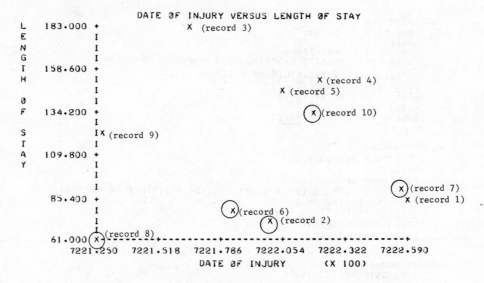

Figure 16.4. Length of stay and date of injury: system versus nonsystem. ⓧ system; X nonsystem. X

Results and Conclusions

It is premature at this time to draw conclusions of the impact of the Midwest Regional Spinal Cord Injury Care System. Federal funding and demonstration of the system is expected to run five years at which point full-scale evaluation will have been undertaken pooling data from all centers. Intended research directions have been illustrated elsewhere in this paper.

In this evaluation demonstration, the machine-readable data base is considered as a means of organizing specific information from a multitude of sources and of updating the information as indicated. With very rapid response time the records can be searched for specific attributes not only on home ground, but from any center where data comparisons might be desired. Additionally, the SPSSLINK and RIQS plotting features allow generation of statistical measures and illustrations which, in view of uncoded input and output, may be readily incorporated into the body of a report. The built-in input validity checks increase information reliability and the password feature has effectively restricted access to confidential information.

Thus during the time in which data base development has been carried out, the suitability of RIQS to this system has become increasingly more evident. The data base as illustrated here was drawn up by a group of medically oriented people with an uncertain picture of its information management requirements and with little or no understanding of computerization. The tendency within the system has been to regard the data base as the ideal repository of data on system management, patient management, research information, test outcomes, as well as the evaluation indicators.

```
? BEFØRE SEARCH
? DEFINE SET 1 AS 'RIC ADMISSIØNS WITH CØMPLETED CØSTS AND DATES'
? BEGIN SEARCH
? FØR N = 1 TØ LAST
? IF #101.N EQ 'ADMISSIØN' AND #99.N EQ 'REHABILITATIØN'
? AND (#103.N AND #175.N AND #195.N) GT 0,
? PUT IN SET 1;LØØP;END

SEARCHING INITIATED




NØ. ØF RECØRDS ADDED TØ SET  1 BY SEARCH =    7
NØ. ØF RECØRDS  IN  SET   1 AFTER SEARCH =    7


*  *  *  *  *


ENTER SEARCH CØMMAND ØR TYPE HALT

? BEGIN SEARCH ØF SET 1
? FØR N = 1 TØ LAST,
? IF #83 EQ 'PARAPLEGIA' AND #99.N EQ 'REHABILITATIØN'
? LET PCØST = #195.N, LET CØST = PCØST,
? LET PSTAY = #175.N - #103.N, LET STAY = PSTAY,
? LET N = 100,
? PLØT PSTAY VRS PCØST,
? SPSSFILE 1 ØF PCØST, PSTAY;
? IF #83 EQ 'QUADRIPLEGIA' AND #99.N EQ 'REHABILITATIØN'
? LET QCØST = #195.N, LET CØST = QCØST,
? LET QSTAY = #175.N - #103.N, LET STAY = QSTAY
? LET N = 100
? PLØT QSTAY VRS QCØST;LØØP
? SPSSFILE 2 ØF CØST, STAY;END

SEARCHING INITIATED


SPSS SAVED FILE NUMBER 1 EXISTS ØN SPSSFL1
 CATALØG IT IF YØU WISH TØ RETAIN IT


SPSS SAVED FILE NUMBER 2 EXISTS ØN SPSSFL2
 CATALØG IT IF YØU WISH TØ RETAIN IT



 TYPE IN THE DESIRED LABEL FØR THE X-AXIS

? LENGTH ØF STAY

 TYPE IN THE DESIRED LABEL FØR THE Y-AXIS

? CØST ØF STAY

 TYPE IN THE DESIRED TITLE FØR THE PLØT

? CØSTS VRS LENGTH ØF STAY FØR RIC ADMISSIØN

DØ YØU WANT THE PLØT DISPLAYED
? YES
```

Figure 16.5a. Search statements and resulting plot illustrating costs versus the length of stay for RIC admission.

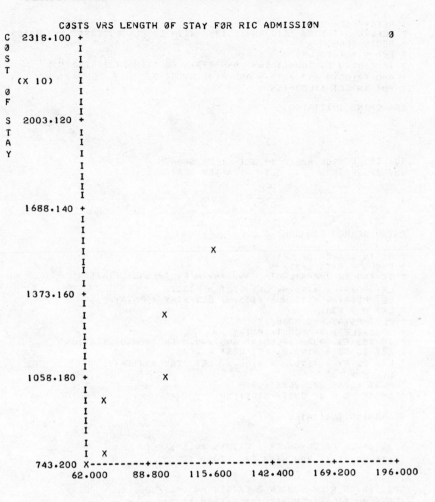

Figure 16.5b. X indicates paraplegic; ∅ indicates quadriplegic.

```
SPSSØNLINE - NØRTHWESTERN UNIVERSITY (V3.0)

DUMP ØF LABEL INFØRMATIØN..

I025S000 SEX
I026S000 RACE
I027S000 RELIGIØN
I072S000 AGE AT TIME ØF ACCIDENT

- - - CØDEBØØK - - -

SUBFILE

VARIABLE - I025S000    SEX

VALUE LABEL       VALUE     FREQ  REL %  ADJ %  CUM %

              FEMALE         1    10.0   10.0   10.0
              MALE           9    90.0   90.0  100.0
                BLANK        0     0.0   ****  100.0

                TØTAL       10   100.0  100.0  100.0
VARIABLE - I025S000 SEX

        CØDE
        I
  FEMALE  ****** (      1)
        I  10.0%
  MALE    ********************************************** (       9)
        I  90.0%
   BLANK  * (       0)
 (MISSING) I    0.0%
        I....I....I....I....I....I....I....I....I....I....I
        0    1    2    3    4    5    6    7    8    9   10
        FREQUENCY

ØBSERVATIØNS: VALID -       10    MISSING -        0




VARIABLE - I026S000    RACE

VALUE LABEL       VALUE     FREQ  REL %  ADJ %  CUM %

              CAUCASIA       8    80.0   80.0   80.0
              MEXICAN        1    10.0   10.0   90.0
              NEGRØID        1    10.0   10.0  100.0
                BLANK        0     0.0   ****  100.0

                TØTAL       10   100.0  100.0  100.0
VARIABLE - I026S000 RACE

        CØDE
        I
 CAUCASIA  ***************************************** (       8)
        I  80.0%
 MEXICAN   ****** (      1)
        I  10.0%
 NEGRØID   ****** (      1)
        I  10.0%
   BLANK   * (       0)
 (MISSING) I    0.0%
        I....I....I....I....I....I....I....I....I....I....I
        0    1    2    3    4    5    6    7    8    9   10
        FREQUENCY

ØBSERVATIØNS: VALID -       10    MISSING -        0
```

Figure 16.6. Frequency counts of demographic variables.

```
VARIABLE - I027S000   RELIGIØN

VALUE LABEL       VALUE      FREQ  REL %  ADJ %  CUM %

             CATHØLIC       3    30.0   30.0   30.0
             PRØTESTA       5    50.0   50.0   80.0
             UNKNØWN        2    20.0   20.0  100.0
                BLANK       0     0.0   ****  100.0

                TØTAL      10   100.0  100.0  100.0

VARIABLE - I027S000 RELIGIØN

        CØDE
             I
 CATHØLIC   *************** (        3)
             I  30.0%
 PRØTESTA   ************************* (       5)
             I  50.0%
 UNKNØWN    *********** (       2)
             I  20.0%
   BLANK    * (        0)
 (MISSING)   I   0.0%
             I....I....I....I....I....I....I....I....I....I....I
             0    1    2    3    4    5    6    7    8    9   10
             FREQUENCY

ØBSERVATIØNS: VALID -        10      MISSING -          0




VARIABLE - I072S000   AGE AT TIME ØF ACCIDENT

VALUE LABEL       VALUE      FREQ  REL %  ADJ %  CUM %

                   15        1    10.0   10.0   10.0
                   16        2    20.0   20.0   30.0
                   19        1    10.0   10.0   40.0
                   20        1    10.0   10.0   50.0
                   23        2    20.0   20.0   70.0
                   29        2    20.0   20.0   90.0
                   36        1    10.0   10.0  100.0
                BLANK        0     0.0   ****  100.0

                TØTAL      10   100.0  100.0  100.0

VARIABLE - I072S000 AGE AT TIME ØF ACCIDENT
        CØDE
             I
    15     ****** (        1)
             I  10.0%
    16     ********** (       2)
             I  20.0%
    19     ****** (        1)
             I  10.0%
    20     ****** (        1)
             I  10.0%
    23     ********** (       2)
             I  20.0%
    29     ********** (       2)
             I  20.0%
    36     ****** (        1)
             I  10.0%
   BLANK    * (        0)
 (MISSING)   I   0.0%
             I....I....I....I....I....I....I....I....I....I....I
             0    1    2    3    4    5    6    7    8    9   10
             FREQUENCY

ØBSERVATIØNS: VALID -        10      MISSING -          0
```

Figure 16.6. (Continued).

NOTES

1. This investigation was supported by the Department of Health, Education and Welfare, Social and Rehabilitation Service Grant No. 13P-5586 4/5-01 given to the Midwest Regional Spinal Cord Injury Care System, Northwestern University, Northwestern Memorial Hospital—Wesley Pavilion and the Rehabilitation Institute of Chicago. We gratefully acknowledge the contributions of Paul R. Meyer, Jr., M.D. and Joel S. Rosen, M.D., co-directors of the Midwest Regional Spinal Cord Injury Care System.

2. System patients are those spinal cord injured individuals admitted to Northwestern Memorial Hospital—Wesley Pavilion within 72 hours of injury; nonsystem patients enter either system hospital in greater than 72 hours after injury.

3. Paraplegic is paralyzed from the waist down.

4. Quadriplegic is paralyzed from the neck down.

5. The revised version of the MRSCICS data base will be structured to obviate this method of obtaining dates.

6. As the number of paired system = nonsystem patients increases and comparable data is accumulated from other spinal injury centers, meaningful conclusions may be drawn as to the actual impact of a system of care on the length of stay variable.

Chapter 17

The Interactive Hospital Profile Facility - An Integral Part of the Health Services Research Center's Health Care Data Base[1]

SANDRA L. COLUSSI. and KENNETH R. KOSNIK
Northwestern University

Introduction

The Health Services Research Center[2] has completed the initial phase of development for a Health Care Data Base organized specifically to meet the needs of its research staff. The Remote Information Query System developed at Northwestern was used for the portion of the project that provided for an interactive hospital profile facility. While our focus here will be on the characteristics and uses of this single facility, its function is best explained by relating it to the data base project as a whole.

Background

A variety of data pertaining to health care institutions is continually being collected and processed as part of the ongoing activities of the American Hospital Association. An Annual Survey of Hospitals has been conducted since 1945 which queries over 7000 institutions on items concerning services, manpower, utilization, and costs, and other statistics vital to a hospital's operation. On a monthly basis, the Hospital Administrative Services (HAS) Program receives detailed finance, manpower, and work load data from over 3000 participating institutions. In addition to these established programs, the American Hospital Association frequently surveys its member institutions on questions of importance to the health care field.

While the research value of these extensive data has long been recognized, those using them have been confronted with serious problems in their organization. The data processing needs of the American Hospital Association demand that only current information related

280

to a single program be organizationally grouped together, with the retention of outdated files as a purely archival activity. The researcher, on the other hand, requires the same accessibility to archived data as he does to current information, if he is to characterize the changes in health care institutions over time. He further demands some type of registry mechanism to integrate the diverse, separately maintained data that are collected for a given institution. With sporadic reporting the unwelcome companion of voluntary programs, such an indexing schema is vitally needed to address questions of data availability. Finally, even to draw together several years of data from a single source, the researcher needs some mechanism to deal with the periodic changes made to the survey instruments.

In view of these demands, the Health Services Research Center undertook the reorganization of a sizable portion of the available hospital data of the American Hospital Association, aiming toward providing researchers with a data base having the maximum possible uniformity, easy accessibility, and the desired indexing facility. The initial version of the data base would contain HAS and selected Annual Survey data for the years 1967 through 1972, with provisions for later linking to other data resources. Because of the volume of the HAS data (an estimated 36.8 million observations) and also their particularly confidential nature, the decision was made to maintain them separately from the other primary source. The selected Annual Survey data would be incorporated into a master set of hospital profiles which would also be used to characterize any additional information for the hospital that was available within the data base.

The Development of Hospital Profiles

Figure 17.1 illustrates the processing steps required to develop hospital profiles from the yearly Annual Survey files. Hospitals responding to the Annual Survey provide the American Hospital Association with financial and operating statistics, together with broad descriptive data characterizing the services provided by the institution. The yearly Annual Survey files contain not only these survey responses, but also supplementary information such as the demographic characteristics of the hospital's locale. To begin the construction of hospital profiles, it was first necessary to choose a useful subset of the total set of variables available on these files. The tapes for the years 1967 through 1972 were then separately processed to retrieve the selected variables for each institution, and transform them to a form that could be uniformly interpreted over time (Program CONVAG). The resulting yearly files were then merged to produce a single file with all yearly records for a given hospital grouped chronologically (Program MERG). These Annual Survey profiles were then supplemented with information from two additional sources:

1. *The HAS Header File*—This file was produced when organizing the HAS data for membership in the data base, and denoted the months between 1967 and 1972 in which a given institution reported to HAS.
2. *The Merged Hospital System File*—This file was produced from data obtained from a recent survey that identified institutions belonging to merged systems of hospitals.

This supplementary data was retained in a general information record appended to a hospital's set of yearly Annual Survey profiles (Program CONVAD). The end product was a file of hospital profiles concisely represented for processing speed and efficiency.

While the Hospital Profile File described above was a valuable data resource, it was apparent that the research environment could additionally be served by an automated system that would permit the characteristics of the profile records to be examined by the

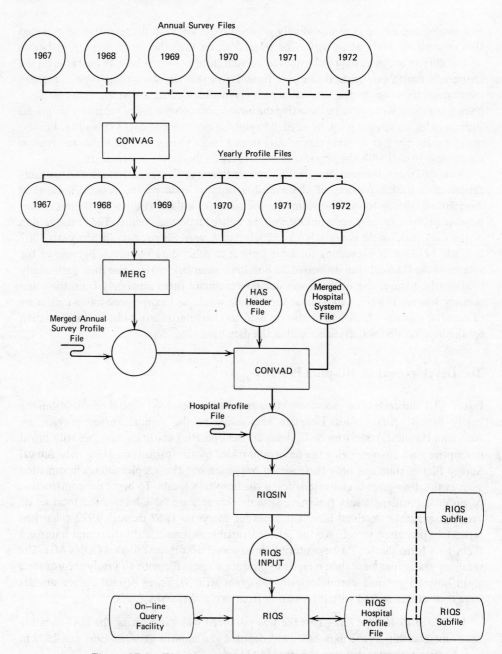

Figure 17.1. The construction of the hospital profile facility.

researcher directly without programming assistance. To provide such searching flexibility and ease, a program was written to transform the hospital profile data into a form suitable as input to the Remote Information Query System (Program RIQSIN). In addition to providing convenient interrogation facilities, the RIQS link with the Statistical Package for the Social Sciences would add another dimension to the analysis that could be performed by the researcher unassisted.

The data base design provided for the initial creation of a complete RIQS Hospital Profile File of 7990 institutions. While it was recognized that a file of that size (an estimated 4.7 million words) could not be searched interactively, the batch processing facility could be used for questions addressing the total available hospital universe. Furthermore, it was proposed that most studies would only want to address some predefined fraction of this universe, and that the GENERATE facility of RIQS could be used to efficiently create special RIQS subfiles for researchers that would be small enough to use interactively.

While the total Hospital Profile File now exists, we have temporarily postponed the creation of its RIQS counterpart of 7990 hospitals. To obtain operational subfiles for use by the research staff, we have used the program RIQSIN to perform preliminary hospital selection in addition to its usual formatting tasks. It is hoped that by delaying the creation of the entire RIQS file, researchers using these subfiles will be encouraged to supply their criticisms of the chosen record structure before its final adoption.

One such subfile of 2344 hospitals was created to assist in the selection of control hospitals for a study of merged systems of hospitals. The successful use of the RIQS Hospital Profile File for this application has been encouraging in view of the stated goals of the project. After providing a more detailed description of the RIQS record structure for the file, we will present a simplified version of the research methodology used for the selection of control groups in that study.

The RIQS Record Structure

Figures 17.2 and 17.3 provide a description of the data items of the RIQS hospital profile record, together with a sample record from a constructed subfile. Items 2 through 24 use the subitem facility to denote the year for which the data item applies, with subitems 1 through 6 corresponding to the years 1967 through 1972. Items 26 through 43 use the subitem facility to denote which of a set of possible responses are applicable. (For these items, the appropriate year was associated with the item number itself.) Finally, we note that most items are described as codes rather than their language equivalents. To provide for the easy translation of these codes, the researcher is supplied with an on-line facility for retrieving information related to their interpretation. Figures 17.4 and 17.5 illustrate this type of documentation.

Item No.	Item Name	Item Description
1	Hospital ID	A unique identification code assigned to the institution by the AHA.
2	Control Code	Code to denote the type of organization managing the hospital.
3	Service Code	Code to denote the type of service the hospital provides to the majority of admissions.
4	Length of Stay	Code to denote whether the majority of patients are admitted for less than 30 days, or more than 30 days.
5	State Code	Code to denote state.
6	County Code	Code to denote county.
7	SMSA Number	Number identifying the Standard Metropolitan Statistical Area in which the institution is located.
8	SMSA Size	Code denoting the population of the SMSA.
9	Days Covered	The number of days in the hospital's reporting period.
10	Ending Date	End of the reporting period.
11	Bed Change Code	Code to denote whether a bed change occurred during the reporting period.
12	Change Date 1	Date of first bed change.
13	Change Beds 1	Beds added or deleted in first bed change.
14	Change Date 2	Date of second bed change.
15	Change Beds 2	Beds added or deleted in second bed change.
16	Short Term Beds	Beds staffed in a unit in which the average length of stay is less than 30 days.
17	Long Term Beds	Beds staffed in a unit in which the average length of stay is greater than 30 days.
18	Total Beds	Total beds staffed for use.
19	Statistical Beds	Weighted average of beds staffed for use based on bed changes made throughout the year.
20	Response Code	Code indicating whether the hospital responded to the Annual Survey.
21	Service Index*	Index used to rank hospitals according to provided facilities.
22	Inpatient Days	Total number of patient days of care rendered to patients discharged during the reporting period.
23	Total Admissions	Total number of patient admissions during the reporting period.

*Edwards, Mary, Hon D. Miller, and Rex Schumacher, Classification of Community Hospitals by Scope of Service: Four Indexes, *Health Services Research* 7:130 Winter 1972.

Figure 17.2. Brief description of RIQS record items

Item No.	Item Name	Item Description
24	Total Costs	Total expenses incurred during the reporting period.
25	Item not used	
26	1967 Facilities & Services	Codes indicating which of a set of 55 facilities and services the hospital indicated as being present.
27	1967 Approvals	Codes indicating which of a possible 13 professional approvals the hospital had.
28	1968 Facilities & Services	See item 26.
29	1968 Approvals	See item 27.
30	1969 Facilities & Services	See item 26.
31	1969 Approvals	See item 27.
32	1970 Facilities & Services	See item 26.
33	1970 Approvals	See item 27.
34	1971 Facilities & Services	See item 26.
35	1971 Approvals	See item 27.
36	1972 Facilities & Services	See item 26.
37	1972 Approvals	See item 27.
38	1967 HAS Months	Numbers indicating the months in 1967 in which the hospital reported to HAS.
39	1968 HAS Months	See item 38.
40	1969 HAS Months	See item 38.
41	1970 HAS Months	See item 38.
42	1971 HAS Months	See item 38.
43	1972 HAS Months	See item 38.
44	HAS Response Code	Code indicating whether an institution has ever reported to HAS from 1967–1972.
45	Merge Code	Code indicating which (if any) merged system the hospital belonged to.

Figure 17.2 (Continued). Brief description of RIQS record items.

```
RECØRD NUMBER    54
    (1) HØSPITAL ID

    (2) CØNTRØL CØDE
    23 *23 *23 *23 *23 *23
    (3) SERVICE CØDE
    10 *10 *10 *10 *10 *10
    (4) LØS
    01 *01 *01 *01 *01 *01
    (5) STATE CØDE
    12 *12 *12 *12 *12 *12
    (6) CØUNTY CØDE
    19 *19 *19 *19 *19 *19
    (7) SMSA NUMBER
    00 *00 *00 *00 *00 *00
    (8) SMSA SIZE
    00 *00 *00 *00 *00 *00
    (9) DAYS CØVERED
    365 *366 *365 *365 *365 *366
    (10) END CØV MØNTH
    670900 *680900 *690900 *700930 *710930 *720930
    (11) BED CHANGE CD
    01 *02 *02 *02 *02 *02
    (12) CHANGE DATE 1
    670715 *   *   *   *
    (13) CHANGE BEDS 1
    -1 *   *   *   *   *
    (16) SHØRT TERM BEDS
       *  *27 *27 *   *
    (17) LØNG TERM BEDS
       *  *00 *00 *   *
    (18) TØTAL BEDS
    27 *27 *27 *27 *27 *27
    (19) STAT BEDS
       *27 *27 *27 *27 *27
    (20) RESPØNSE CØDE
    01 *01 *01 *01 *01 *01
    (21) SERVICE INDEX
    02 *03 *03 *04 *02 *03
    (22) INPATIENT DAYS
    7187 *7216 *7133 *7164 *6981 *6673
    (23) TØTAL ADMISSIØNS
    1042 *933 *1059 *1110 *1135 *1194
    (24) TØTAL CØSTS
           *390630 *421287 *483653 *518795 *567128
    (26) 1967 FACILITIES AND SERVICES
    01 *02 *03 *07 *08 *13
    (27) 1967 APPRØVALS
    01 *09 *10
    (28) 1968 FACILITIES AND SERVICES
    02 *03 *06 *07 *08 *13 *20
    (29) 1968 APPRØVALS
    01 *09 *10
    (30) 1969 FACILITIES AND SERVICES
    02 *08 *13 *20 *35 *36
    (31) 1969 APPRØVALS
    01 *09 *10
    (32) 1970 FACILITIES AND SERVICES
    05 *13 *20 *35 *43
    (33) 1970 APPRØVALS
    01 *09 *10
    (34) 1971 FACILITIES AND SERVICES
    08 *13 *35
    (35) 1971 APPRØVALS
    01 *09 *10
    (36) 1972 FACILITIES AND SERVICES
    05 *08 *13 *35
    (37) 1972 APPRØVALS
    01 *09 *10
    (38) 1967 HAS MØNTHS
    01 *02 *03 *04 *05 *06 *07 *08 *09 *10 *11 *12
    (39) 1968 HAS MØNTHS
    01 *02 *03 *04 *05 *06 *07 *08 *09 *10 *11 *12
    (40) 1969 HAS MØNTHS
    01 *02 *03 *04 *05 *06 *07 *08 *09 *10 *11 *12
    (41) 1970 HAS MØNTHS
    01 *02 *03 *04 *05 *06 *07 *08 *09 *10 *11 *12
    (42) 1971 HAS MØNTHS
    01 *02 *03 *04 *05 *06 *07 *08 *09 *10 *11 *12
    (43) 1972 HAS MØNTHS
    01 *02 *03 *04 *05 *06 *07 *08 *09 *10 *11 *12
    (44) HAS RESPØNSE CØDE
    01
    (45) MERGE CØDE
    00
```

Figure 17.3.   Sample RIQS record from constructed subfile
of hospital profiles.

```
SERVICE CØDES
*************

THE TABLE BELØW SHØWS THE SERVICE CØDES DEFINED FØR THE YEARS
1967 THRU 1972.  IF A CATEGØRY WAS NØT DEFINED FØR A
PARTICULAR YEAR, AN ASTERISK APPEARS IN THE CØLUMN FØR
THAT YEAR.

TYPE ØF SERVICE            CØDE NUMBER
***************            ***********
                          1967 1968 1969 1970 1971 1972
                          **** **** **** **** **** ****


GENERAL MEDICAL AND
   SURGICAL               10   10   10   10   10   10
HØSPITAL UNIT ØF AN INST.
   (PRISØN HØSP., CØLL.
    INFIRMARY, ETC.)      11   11   11   11   11   11
PSYCHIATRIC               22   22   22   22   22   22
TUBERCULØSIS              33   33   33   33   33   33
MATERNITY                 44   44   44   44   44   44
EYE, EAR, NØSE AND THRØAT 45   45   45   45   45   45
ØRTHØPEDIC                47   47   47   47   47   47
CHRØNIC AND/ØR
   CØNVALESCENT           48   48   48   48   48   48
ØTHER SPECIALTY           49   49   49   49   49   49
INSTITUTIØN FØR MENTAL
   RETARDATIØN            62   62   62   62   62   62
EPILEPSY                  72   72   72   72   *    *
ALCØHØLISM AND/ØR
   ADDICTIVE DISEASES     82   82   82   82   82   82
NARCØTIC                  *    42   42   42   42   42
GERIATRIC                 *    43   43   43   *    *
PHYSICAL REHABILITATIØN   *    46   46   46   46   46
HØSPTIAL UNIT WITHIN A
   MENTAL RETARDATIØN
   SCHØØL                 *    *    *    12   12   12

CHILDRENS INSTITUTIØNS
**********************

GENERAL MEDICAL AND
   SURGICAL               50   50   50   50   50   50
PSYCHIATRIC               52   52   52   52   52   52
TUBERCULØSIS              53   53   53   53   53   53
EYE, EAR, NØSE AND THRØAT 55   55   55   55   55   55
ØRTHØPEDIC                57   57   57   57   57   57
CHRØNIC AND/ØR
   CØNVALESCENT           58   58   58   58   58   58
ØTHER SPECIALITY          59   59   59   59   59   59
HØSPITAL UNIT ØF AN INST. 51   51   51   51   51   51
PHYSICAL REHABILITATIØN   *    56   56   56   56   56
```

Figure 17.4. On-line documentation available for the interpretation of service codes.

```
LIST ØF AHA APPRØVALS
*********************

1.  ACCREDITATIØN BY JØINT CØMMISSIØN ØN ACCREDITATIØN ØF
    HØSPITALS.
2.  CANCER PRØGRAM APPRØVED BY AMERICAN CØLLEGE ØF SURGEØNS.
3.  RESIDENCY APPRØVED BY AMERICAN MEDICAL ASSØCIATIØN.
4.  INTERNSHIP APPRØVED BY AMERICAN  MEDICAL ASSØCIATIØN.
5.  MEDICAL SCHØØL AFFILIATIØN, REPØRTED BY AMERICAN
    MEDICAL ASSØCIATIØN.
6.  HØSPITAL CØNTRØLLED PRØFESSIØNAL NURSING SCHØØL REPØRTED
    BY NATIØNAL LEAGUE FØR NURSING.
7.  HØSPITAL CØNTRØLLED PRACTICAL NURSING TRAINING PRØGRAM
    APPRØVED BY STATE ØR EQUIVALENT GØVERNMENTAL AUTHØRITY,
    REPØRTED BY NATIØNAL LEAGUE FØR NURSING.
8.  MEMBER ØF CØUNCIL ØF TEACHING HØSPITALS ØF THE ASSØCIATIØN
    ØF AMERICAN MEDICAL CØLLEGES.
9.  HØSPITAL CØNTRACTING ØR PARTICIPATING IN BLUE CRØSS PLAN,
    REPØRTED BY BLUE CRØSS ASSØCIATIØN.
10. CERTIFIED FØR PARTICIPATIØN IN THE HEALTH INSURANCE FØR
    THE AGED (MEDICARE) PRØGRAM BY THE DEPARTMENT ØF HEALTH,
    EDUCATIØN AND WELFARE.
11. ACCREDITATIØN BY AMERICAN ØSTEØPATHIC ASSØCIATIØN.
12. INTERNSHIP APPRØVED BY AMERICAN ØSTEØPATHIC ASSØCIATIØN.
13. RESIDENCY APPRØVED BY AMERICAN ØSTEØPATHIIC ASSØCIATIØN.


APPRØVALS
*********

THE TABLE BELØW SHØWS THE APPRØVALS AVAILABLE FØR THE YEARS 1967
THRU 1972.  THE APPRØVAL NUMBER APPEARS AT THE LEFT ØF THE LINE.
A 1 INDICATES THAT THE APPRØVAL WAS AVAILABLE FØR THE YEAR
UNDER CØNSIDERATIØN.  AN * INDICATES THAT THE APPRØVAL WAS
NØT AVAILABLE.


APPRØVAL NUMBER      1967   1968   1969   1970   1971   1972
***************      ****   ****   ****   ****   ****   ****

        1             1      1      1      1      1      1
        2             1      1      1      1      1      1
        3             1      1      1      1      1      1
        4             1      1      1      1      1      1
        5             1      1      1      1      1      1
        6             1      1      1      1      1      1
        7             1      *      *      *      *      *
        8             1      1      1      1      1      1
        9             1      1      1      1      1      1
       10             1      1      1      1      1      1
       11             *      1      1      1      1      1
       12             *      1      1      1      1      1
       13             *      1      1      1      1      1
```

Figure 17.5. On-line documentation for the interpretation
of approval codes.

An Application of the Hospital Profile Facility to the Selection of Control Groups

One aim of a recent Center study of merged systems of hospitals was to identify experiences of these systems that could be attributed to their merged corporate structure. For this analysis, a mechanism was needed to predict what the experiences of a system should have been had merger not taken place. The mechanism devised was a control system of independent hospitals, whose combined experience could be compared with the merged system under study. Ideally, each hospital of a study system would have an identical twin in its constructed control system. Since this type of match was impossible to obtain, an alternative approach was taken which involved constructing a control system of hypothetical hospitals. The characteristics of these surrogate twins would be determined from the average experience of a group of control hospitals that were similar to the study hospital in certain specified ways. It was in the selection of these control groups that the RIQS Hospital Profile Facility was first employed. Figure 17.6 shows how a control system related to its corresponding merged system.

Merged System of N Hospitals	Hypothetical Hospitals	Control Group Hospitals
Study Hospital 1	Hypothetical Hospital 1	Control Group 1
	(Represents average experience of Control Group 1)	Hospitals chosen for similarity to Study Hospital 1
Study Hospital 2	Hypothetical Hospital 2	Control Group 2
	(Represents average experience of Control Group 2)	Hospitals chosen for similarity to Study Hospital 2
. . .	. . .	. . .
Study Hospital N	Hypothetical Hospital N	Control Group N
	(Represents average experience of Control Group N)	Hospitals chosen for similarity to Study Hospital N

Figure 17.6.   The construction of a control system for a given merged system of hospitals.

To illustrate the selection process used, we will now consider the problem of constructing a control system for the following group of hospitals that merged in 1969.

Merged System	1969 Statistical Beds
Hospital 1	25
Hospital 2	65
Hospital 3	23
Hospital 4	140
Hospital 5	663

To establish a fundamental similarity between the study hospitals and the control hospitals, all institutions in the defined control groups would be required to have the following characteristics for the year of merger, 1969:

1. The organization managing the hospital was either nongovernmental not-for-profit, or a government hospital district or authority. (Item 2.3, the control code for 1969, had the value of either 16, 21, 22, or 23.)
2. The type of medical service supplied by the hospital was general. (Item 3.3, the service code for 1969, had a value of 10.)
3. The average length of stay for the majority of patients was less than 30 days, short term. (Item 4.3, the length of stay for 1969, had a value of 1.)
4. The hospital was not a known member of a merged system of hospitals. (Item 45. the merge code, had a value of 0.)

Figure 17.7 shows the statements used to obtain a set of hospitals (set 1) having these characteristics.

```
BEGIN SEARCH
  LET CNT=0;
  IF #2.3 GT 15 AND #2.3 LT 17 LET CNT=CNT+1;
  IF #2.3 GT 20 AND #2.3 LT 24 LET CNT=CNT+1;
  IF #3.3 GT 9 AND #3.3 LT 11 LET CNT=CNT+1;
  IF #4.3 GT 0 AND #4.3 LT 2 LET CNT=CNT+1;
  IF #45 LT 1 LET CNT=CNT+1;
  IF CNT GT 3 PUT RECORD IN SET 1;
  END

SEARCHING INITIATED




NO. OF RECORDS ADDED TO SET  1 BY SEARCH = 2143
NO. OF RECORDS  IN  SET  1 AFTER SEARCH = 2143


*   *   *   *   *
```

Figure 17.7. RIQS search used to obtain a set of hospitals similar to those in the merged system.

To perform a detailed comparison of the merged system and the control system, both Annual Survey and HAS data were required for two years prior to the merger date and also two years after merger. This requirement motivated the following data availability constraints:

1. For the years 1967 through 1972 the hospital reported data to HAS for at least nine months of each year.
2. The hospital responded to the Annual Survey for the years 1967 through 1972.

Figure 17.8 illustrates the selection of those hospitals within set 1 that met the stated data availability criteria (set 2).

```
BEGIN SEARCH ØF SET 1
  LET IHAS1=0; LET IHAS2=0; LET IHAS3=0;
  LET IHAS4=0; LET IHAS5=0; LET IHAS6=0;
  FØR I=1 TØ LAST
     IF #38.I GT 0 LET IHAS1=IHAS1+1; LØØP;
  FØR I=1 TØ LAST
     IF #39.I GT 0 LET IHAS2=IHAS2+1; LØØP;
  FØR I=1 TØ LAST
     IF #40.I GT 0 LET IHAS3=IHAS3+1; LØØP;
  FØR I=1 TØ LAST
     IF #41.I GT 0 LET IHAS4=IHAS4+1; LØØP;
  FØR I=1 TØ LAST
     IF #42.I GT 0 LET IHAS5=IHAS5+1; LØØP;
  FØR I=1 TØ LAST
     IF #43.I GT 0 LET IHAS6=IHAS6+1; LØØP;
  LET CNT=0;
     IF IHAS1 GT 8 LET CNT=CNT+1;
     IF IHAS2 GT 8 LET CNT=CNT+1;
     IF IHAS3 GT 8 LET CNT=CNT+1;
     IF IHAS4 GT 8 LET CNT=CNT+1;
     IF IHAS5 GT 8 LET CNT=CNT+1;
     IF IHAS6 GT 8 LET CNT=CNT+1;
  LET IRES=0;
  FØR I=1 TØ LAST
     IF #20.I GT 0 AND #20.I LT 2 LET IRES=IRES+1; LØØP;
  IF IRES GT 5 AND CNT GT 5 PUT RECØRD IN SET 2;
  END

SEARCHING INITIATED



NØ. ØF RECØRDS ADDED TØ SET  2 BY SEARCH =  684
NØ. ØF RECØRDS  IN  SET  2 AFTER SEARCH =  684


*  *  *  *  *
```

Figure 17.8. RIQS search used to determine the hospitals of set 1 meeting the data availability constraints.

Control groups were then selected from the hospitals of set 2. For each study hospital, a bed range was defined to identify hospitals for its control group that were of similar size.

Bed Range = 1969 statistical bed size ±20 percent

The 20 percent band was used to obtain a representative number of hospitals in each of the five control groups, while still maintaining hospitals of similar size in the groups. Figure 17.9 shows this selection process for the system under study.

```
BEGIN SEARCH ØF SET 2
  IF #19.3 GT 19 AND #19.3 LT 31 PUT RECØRD IN SET 3;
  IF #19.3 GT 51 AND #19.3 LT 79 PUT RECØRD IN SET 4;
  IF #19.3 GT 17 AND #19.3 LT 29 PUT RECØRD IN SET 5;
  IF #19.3 GT 111 AND #19.3 LT 169 PUT RECØRD IN SET 6;
  IF #19.3 GT 529 AND #19.3 LT 797 PUT RECØRD IN SET 7;
END

SEARCHING INITIATED




NØ. ØF RECØRDS ADDED TØ SET  3 BY SEARCH =   16
NØ. ØF RECØRDS  IN  SET  3 AFTER SEARCH =   16




NØ. ØF RECØRDS ADDED TØ SET  4 BY SEARCH =   68
NØ. ØF RECØRDS  IN  SET  4 AFTER SEARCH =   68




NØ. ØF RECØRDS ADDED TØ SET  5 BY SEARCH =   14
NØ. ØF RECØRDS  IN  SET  5 AFTER SEARCH =   14




NØ. ØF RECØRDS ADDED TØ SET  6 BY SEARCH =  116
NØ. ØF RECØRDS  IN  SET  6 AFTER SEARCH =  116




NØ. ØF RECØRDS ADDED TØ SET  7 BY SEARCH =   23
NØ. ØF RECØRDS  IN  SET  7 AFTER SEARCH =   23


*  *  *  *  *
```

Figure 17.9. RIQS search used to select control groups.

Profile characteristics for the hypothetical hospitals were obtained by calculating control group means for selected variables of interest. Those included patient days, total admissions, total costs, number of facilities, number of approvals, long term beds, and the service index. This computation was easily performed using the RIQS–SPSS interface, as is illustrated in Figure 17.10 for some sample means.

```
BEGIN SEARCH ØF SET 3
SPSSFILE 1 ØF
#17.1, #17.2, #17.3, #17.4, #17.5, #17.6,
#19.1, #19.2, #19.3, #19.4, #19.5, #19.6,
#21.1, #21.2, #21.3, #21.4, #21.5, #21.6,
#22.1, #22.2, #22.3, #22.4, #22.5, #22.6,
#23.1, #23.2, #23.3, #23.4, #23.5, #23.6,
#24.1, #24.2, #24.3, #24.4, #24.5, #24.6;
END
```

Create an SPSSFILE of selected variables.

```
1.00 GET FILE
1.05    ANNUAL
2.00 MISSING VALUES
2.05    I017S001 TØ I024S006(0)
3.00 CØNDESCRIPTIVE
3.05    I023S001 TØ I023S003
4.00 STATISTICS
4.05    ALL

ENTERING SPSS.
SPSSØNLINE - NØRTHWESTERN UNIVERSITY (V3.0)

- - - CØNDESCRIPTIVE - - -


VARIABLE - I023S001 TØTAL ADMISSIØNS

MEAN          973.188  STD ERR      80.703  STD DEV      322.814
VARIANCE   104208.563  KURTØSIS      -.806  SKEWNESS       -.042
RANGE        1123.000  MINIMUM     413.000  MAXIMUM     1536.000

ØBSERVATIØNS- VALID -      16    MISSING -         0


VARIABLE - I023S002 TØTAL ADMISSIØNS

MEAN          962.313  STD ERR      73.263  STD DEV      293.053
VARIANCE    85880.229  KURTØSIS      -.834  SKEWNESS        .078
RANGE        1044.000  MINIMUM     477.000  MAXIMUM     1521.000

ØBSERVATIØNS- VALID -      16    MISSING -         0


VARIABLE - I023S003 TØTAL ADMISSIØNS

MEAN          992.063  STD ERR      72.809  STD DEV      291.236
VARIANCE    84818.329  KURTØSIS      -.523  SKEWNESS        .119
RANGE        1068.000  MINIMUM     455.000  MAXIMUM     1523.000

ØBSERVATIØNS- VALID -      16    MISSING -         0
```

Figure 17.10. Compute the means and associated statistics
for selected variables.

With control groups selected that defined the characteristics of the control system, researchers could proceed to use the HAS data for the detailed comparative analysis of the study.

Conclusions

The response to the RIQS Hospital Profile Facility by the Health Services Research Center staff has been very positive. Although the initial data requests have been handled by those involved in the development of the data base, more direct involvement from staff researchers is expected as their familiarity with the facility increases. Most notably, we are pleased with the flexibility that the system offers. With the Hospital Profile File maintained in both binary and RIQS format, we can utilize the strengths of the RIQS system in terms of its high-level search language, interactive mode, and SPSS interface without demanding that it handle all potential processing problems.

NOTES

1. This project was partially supported by the National Center of Health Services Research and Development.
2. Health Services Research Center is a research organization of the Hospital Research and Educational Trust (an affiliate of the American Hospital Association) and Northwestern University.

APPENDIX

RIQS Data Structures*

RIQS External Characteristics

A RIQS file consists of records made up of numbered and named items. Items may be simple or multiple. Examples of simple items might be biopsy number, biopsy site, duration of lesion, clinical diagnosis, etc. A multiple item is a one-dimensional array of similar information such as authors, yearly dividends, courses taken, etc. During the file creation phase of RIQS, item numbers, item names, data types and data restrictions are specified. Data types include alphanumeric, alphabetic, integer, decimal and date. Integer and decimal items may be specified in any consistent set of units. For example, an item which describes a duration of time may be defined in units of years, months, weeks, days, or hours. File creation is done as a batch processing job.

The search language of RIQS consists of statements which define the search criteria and the processing to be accomplished during search. These statements include:

PRINT and DISPLAY, for batch and on-line printing of specified output.

LET, for defining variable names and assigning values to these variables. Variables may be assigned string values. They may be defined also by means of arithmetic expressions made up of terms which can be item numbers, variable names, numeric constants, dates, or unit values. The LET statement allows calculations to be performed on numeric

---

*Extracted from B. Mittman, R. Chalice, D. Dillaman, "Mixed Data Structures in a Multi-Purpose Retrieval System," *Journal of the American Society of Information Science,* March–April 1973, Vol. 24, No. 2.

items within retrieved records, thus enabling computations to be performed over the data of a file. For example:

$$\text{LET RAINFALL} = \text{RAINFALL} + (13)$$

where item (13) contains the annual rainfall in a given region under study.

PLACE and RELEASE, for placing selected records in a set and for releasing specified sets.

IF. . .THEN, for specifying search conditions and defining actions to be performed on records or items which satisfy the conditions. Search conditions may involve the relations LT (less than), LE (less than or equal), EQ (equals or contains), GE (greater than or equal), GT (greater than), and NE (not equal). Any number of conditions may be connected together using AND, OR, or NOT and parentheses nesting to any level.

Searches may be done on-line or in a batch mode. Only one data file may be searched at a time. The user may define up to 34 different sets of records during an interrogation session. The sets become part of the file until released. Any of the defined sets may be searched again without having to search the rest of the file. The data file to be interrogated resides as a disk file on the CDC 6400 system or on a back-up magnetic tape.

An illustration of an on-line, RIQS search of a biopsy research file is given in Figure A.1.* The file consists of biopsy records and two previously defined sets, one for male patients and one for females. The male file is to be searched for lesions whose duration was less than one week and for which the clinical diagnosis contained the words 'ACNE' or 'GRANULOMA'. Three such records were found and certain items were reported back to the teletype.

RIQS also provides a variety of index and update commands. The index commands provide KWIC and KWOC indexes which may utilize stopwords or keywords and offer a number of output format options.

Northwestern University
On-line Search

Do you want a description of your file
?   Yes

File has the name biopsy and contains 2214 records

Type in one or more of the following integers, separating them by commas and terminating the list by a semicolon

1.   Print item names
2.   Print item structures and types
3.   Print set descriptions
?   1, 2, 3;

Item numbers and names

1.   Biopsy no.
2.   Clinic no.

Figure A.1.   Sample search of BIOPSY file.

---

*The BIOPSY file was developed by Dr. Fred Levit of Northwestern University Medical School.

3. Date received
4. Biopsy date
5. Name
6. Sex
7. Age
8. Race
9. Doctor
10. Biopsy site
11. Duration of lesion
12. Clinical history
13. Clinical description
14. Clinical diagnosis
15. Histopath description
16. Histopath diagnosis
17. Comments
18. Histopathologist
19. Special stains
20. Recuts
21. Teaching slide
22. Previous biopsy no.

Item descriptions

1. Simple, integer
2. Simple, alphanumeric
3. Simple, date
4. Simple, date
5. Simple, alphanumeric
6. Simple, alphanumeric
7. Simple, decimal with units
    1 Y = 12.00 M, 1 M = 4.29 W, 1 W = 7.00 D,
    1 D = 24.00 H
8. Simple, alphanumeric
9. Simple, alphanumeric
10. Simple, alphanumeric

11. Simple, decimal with units
    1 Y = 12.00 M, 1 M = 4.29 W, 1 W = 7.00 D,
    1 D = 24.00 H
12. Simple, alphanumeric
13. Simple, alphanumeric
14. Simple, alphanumeric
15. Simple, alphanumeric
16. Simple, alphanumeric
17. Simple, alphanumeric
18. Simple, alphanumeric
19. Simple, alphanumeric
20. Simple, alphanumeric

Figure A.1.(Continued).

21. Simple, alphanumeric
22. Simple, alphanumeric

Set descriptions

Id. No.	No. of Elements	Creation Date	Definition
1	974	Nov 14, 1970	Males
2	1219	Nov 14, 1970	Females

Enter search command or type halt

? Begin search of set 1
? If #11 Lt 1 W and #14 Eq ('Acne' or 'Granuloma') then
? Display #1, #4, #5, #10, #11, #14, #16; end

Searching initiated

No. of reports generated to print file = 0
No. of reports generated to display file = 3

Do you want the display reports listed
? Yes

Record number 158

1. Biopsy no.
    178670
4. Biopsy date
    05/04/70
5. Name
10. Biopsy site
    Face
11. Duration of lesion
    3D
14. Clinical diagnosis
    R/O L. E. Acne
16. Histopath diagnosis
    Consistent with polymorphous light eruption

Record number 539

1. Biopsy no.
    216570
4. Biopsy date
    5/26/70
5. Name
10. Biopsy site
    Left wrist
11. Duration of lesion
    2D
14. Clinical diagnosis
    Pyogenic granuloma R/O vasculitis

Figure A.1. (Continued).

16. Histopath diagnosis
    Consistent with polymorphous light eruption

Record number 1746

1. Biopsy no.
   337370
4. Biopsy date
   8-20-70
5. Name
10. Biopsy site
    Face
11. Duration of lesion
    2D
14. Clinical diagnosis
    Acne vulgaris, R/O fungal granuloma
16. Histopath diagnosis
    Dermal inflammation, type not specified

* * * * *

Enter search command or type halt

? Halt

RIQS execution completed

Figure A.1. (Continued).

Mixed Data Structures

To satisfy the design objective of rapid retrieval, RIQS is provided with a mixture of data structures for the internal record organization. Experience with the earlier systems of TRIAL and INFOL pointed up the inefficiencies of storing text as linear strings of BCD characters. Textual searching had to be done by checking characters in sequence. RIQS, on the other hand, uses a scatter table, which stores all the unique words of a record, and a list of pointers to that table. The advantage gained is that text searches for words or phrases can be performed by simply looking up the search words in the table, using the scatter algorithm. If the words sought are not found in the table for a given record, then that record cannot possibly satisfy the search request, and the next record can be processed. Records can thus be eliminated from the search with just a few probes of the scatter table. If, however, the words being sought are in the table, additional processing is required to determine if they are in the correct items. When output is to be generated, the item pointers and scatter table pointers are traced to reconstruct the original order of the information. This process will be illustrated using the search appearing in Figure A.1.

The scatter table is the heart of the RIQS record structure. In it are stored all words, numbers and symbols appearing in the record. Unique words and symbols appear only once in the table. Numeric data appear in both BCD format for output purposes and in floating point format for computational purposes. The scatter table is made up of two sections, for strings of 1-10 characters (one CDC 6400, 60-bit computer word) and strings of 11-20 characters (two computer words). The length of the two sections varies from record to record depending upon the number of unique words, numbers, and symbols in the record. During file creation, each record's scatter table is adjusted to maintain approximately 60 percent occupancy. Collisions in the scatter table are handled by linear recovery.

In order to retain the relationship between each item and the ordered set of words and symbols which appear in each item, a linear list is maintained. For each alphanumeric item, there exists a set of 15-bit pointers to the scatter table. This sequence of pointers permits the report generator to reconstruct each item which is to be output by the system. To illustrate this process, let us trace the searching procedure and report generation procedure for the search given in Figure A.1. The internal format for record number 158 of the biopsy file is illustrated in Figure A.2.

During file creation, the scatter table, the item pointers and the scatter table pointers are generated as each item in the record is read. All numeric items (integer, decimal, dates and units) are stored in both BCD and floating point form in the scatter table and are pointed to directly from the item pointer list. As an example, item 1, Biopsy No., is stored in the scatter table in relative locations 26 (BCD-form) and 38 (floating point form). Item 1 pointers go directly to the scatter table. It should be noted that other information about each item such as the item names, the item descriptions, the units equations, etc. are stored in other tables that refer to the entire file.

Numeric information, which is defined by units equations, such as item 11, is stored both in the BCD representation of the input and the floating point number corresponding to the smallest unit defined. Thus, item 11 points to the BCD string '3D' for 3 days and to the floating point number '72' = 3D x 24H/D. The floating point representation for dates is the Julian date from January 1,0000.

Textual information is stored in the scatter table as individual words and symbols. Item pointers for alphanumeric items point to linear lists of scatter table pointers which maintain the input order of the text. For example, item 16 points to the linear list of scatter table pointers contained in words 62 and 63. These pointers (15-bits each) reconstruct the text "CONSISTENT WITH POLYMORPHOUS LIGHT ERUPTION."

During the search shown in Figure A.1, the following procedures are executed:

A.   Record retrieval from specified sets

    1.   Scan record pointers in mass storage record index.

    2.   Check bits which signify set membership.

       a.   If record is in set 1, got to 3. (The mass storage index to Record 158 contains a bit indicating its membership in set 1.)

       b.   If not, go to 1.

    3.   Read record from mass storage to core, go to B.

B.   Matching retrieval criteria to scatter table contents

    1.   Item 11 is traced directly to the floating point entry in the scatter table. This entry in compared to 168 (1W = 7x24 = 168H).

       a.   If Item 11 is less than 168, go to 2. (Item 11 for Record 158 = 72 which is less than 168.)

       b.   If not, go to A.

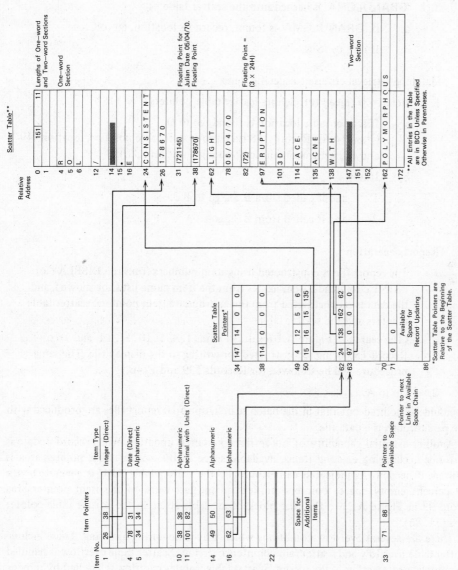

Figure A.2. Format of record no. 158 from biopsy file.

2.   'ACNE' is hashed into the scatter table.

    a.   If 'ACNE' is found, record its location, go to C.
('ACNE' is found at location 135.)

    b.   If not, go to 3.

3.   'GRANULOMA' is hashed into the scatter table.

    a.   If 'GRANULOMA' is found, record its location, go to C.

    b.   If not, to to A.

C.   Matching retrieval criteria to specific items

1.   Item 14 is traced through its scatter table pointers.

    a.   If scatter table location is found, go to D.
(Item 14 for Record 158 traces to scatter table pointers, locations 49 and 50, which contain scatter table location 135.)

    b.   If not,

        1.   and if called from B.2 ., go to B.3.

        2.   and if called from B.3., go to A.

D.   Report generation

1.   The report file is constructed using item numbers from the DISPLAY or PRINT commands, item names from the item name list (not shown), and the data is reconstructed from the appropriate item pointers, scatter table pointers and the scatter table.
(The search in Figure A.1 results in items 1, 4, 5, 10, 11, 14, and 16 of Record 158 being reconstructed for writing to the display file. The same procedure will be followed for Records 539 and 1746.)

2.   Go to A.

It should be pointed out that in the batch search, up to 10 report files are produced with one pass through the data file.

Another essential capability of any retrieval system is updating. When record update is performed, changing existing items, available space in the scatter table pointer area is utilized, if needed. As indicated earlier, initially the scatter table itself is generated with 40 percent empty space. Pointers are kept in the last word of the item pointer area (word 33 in Figure A.2) to the first block of available space in the scatter table pointer area (71, 86).

There are several overflow conditions which may arise during updating. These include scatter table overflow and scatter table pointers overflow. Scatter table overflow is handled by complete re-creation of the record. Scatter table pointer overflow is handled by moving the scatter table to provide additional pointer area. Space produced by item deletion or contraction is placed into an available space chain. Pointers to that chain appear as the first word of the previous link. In Figure A.2, word 71 contains 0, 0 indicating that no further links are on the available space chain. Scatter table pointers for a given item need not appear in consecutive locations, but may also be chained. Experience with update has shown the clear advantages of using mixed list structures in maintaining the internal record organization in RIQS.

LIST OF CONTRIBUTORS

LORRAINE BORMAN, Manager of Information Services, Vogelback Computing Center, Northwestern University.

JAMES A. BROWN, Associate Professor of Anthropology, Northwestern University.

PAUL CARTWRIGHT, Graduate Student, Department of Sociology, McGill University.

SANDRA L. COLUSSI, Ph. D. Candidate, Department of Computer Sciences, Northwestern University.

WAYNE DOMINICK, Ph. D. Candidate, Department of Computer Sciences, Northwestern University.

CHARLES F. DOUDS, Associate Professor of Management, DePaul University.

KATHLEEN R. FLAHERTY, Information System Coordinator, Midwest Regional Spinal Cord Injury Care System, and Ph. D. Candidate, Department of Industrial Engineering and Management Sciences, Northwestern University.

HAROLD GUETZKOW, Professor of Political Science and Gordon Scott Fulcher Professor of Decision-Making, Northwestern University.

BYRON B. HAMILTON, M.D., Director of Research, Rehabilitation Institute of Chicago, and Assistant Professor of Rehabilitation Medicine, Northwestern University Medical School.

RICHARD HAY, JR., Graduate Student, Department of Sociology, and Research Associate, Vogelback Computing Center, Northwestern University.

GAIL L. HOUART, Ph. D. Candidate, Department of Anthropology, Northwestern University.

KENNETH JANDA, Professor of Political Science, Northwestern University.

DALE C. JESSEN, Principal, Information Services, Northfield, Illinois.

DANIEL L. KEGAN, Director of Institutional Research and Evaluation, Hampshire College.

KENNETH KOSNIK, Ph. D. Candidate, Accounting and Information Systems, School of Management, Northwestern University.

DAVID H. LESERMAN, Systems Analyst, Bureau of Research Services, American Hospital Association.

FRED LEVIT, M.D., Associate Professor of Dermatology, Northwestern University Medical School.

THOMAS MARTIN, Industrial Engineer, E. I. DuPont de Nemours & Co.

DAVID MINTZER, Vice President for Research and Dean of Science, Northwestern University.

BENJAMIN MITTMAN, Professor of Computer Sciences and Director of the Vogelback Computing Center, Northwestern University.

ABDULLAHI MOHAMMED, Lecturer, Department of Library Science, Ahmadu Bello University, and Ph. D. Candidate, Department of History, Northwestern University.

WILLIAM NEVILLE, Graduate Student, School of Management, Northwestern University.

ROBERT D. O'KEEFE, Research Associate, Program of Research on the Management of R & D, Northwestern University.

MILTON H. PAUL, M.D., Professor of Pediatrics, Northwestern University Medical School, and Director of Cardiology, Children's Memorial Hospital.

GUSTAVE J. RATH, Director, Design and Development Center, and Professor of Industrial Engineering and Management Sciences, Northwestern University.

ALBERT H. RUBENSTEIN, Professor of Industrial Engineering and Management Sciences, Northwestern University.

DONALD STONE SADE, Scientist-in-Charge of Cayo Santiago, Caribbean Primate Research Center, University of Puerto Rico, and Associate Professor of Anthropology, Northwestern University.

LORETTA M. TAYMANS, Assistant Professor in Speech Pathology, The Catholic University of America.

SUBJECT INDEX

Italicized numbers refer to pages with figures.

305

*Page references to RIQS, RIQSONLINE, RIQSTUTOR, SPSS, and SPSSONLINE have not been included since almost every chapter refers to these systems.

AUTHOR INDEX

Italicized numbers refer to pages with figures.